Marie-Françoise Alamichel

Widows in Anglo-Saxon and Medieval Britain

PETER LANG

Oxford • Bern • Berlin • Bruxelles • Frankfurt am Main • New York • Wien

Bibliographic information published by Die Deutsche Bibliothek
Die Deutsche Bibliothek lists this publication in the Deutsche
Nationalbibliografie; detailed bibliographic data is available on
the Internet at ‹http://dnb.ddb.de›.

British Library Cataloguing-in-Publication Data: A catalogue record for
this book is available from The British Library.

Cover design: Mette Bundgaard, Peter Lang Ltd
Cover image: from the terrier of St Paul-les-Romans (14th century) at
Valence, archives départementales de la Drôme

ISBN 978-3-03911-404-7

© Peter Lang AG, International Academic Publishers, Bern 2008
Hochfeldstrasse 32, Postfach 746, CH-3000 Bern 9, Switzerland
info@peterlang.com, www.peterlang.com, www.peterlang.net

All rights reserved.
All parts of this publication are protected by copyright.
Any utilisation outside the strict limits of the copyright law, without the
permission of the publisher, is forbidden and liable to prosecution.
This applies in particular to reproductions, translations, microfilming,
and storage and processing in electronic retrieval systems.

Printed in Germany

Contents

Introduction		7
Part One	The Anglo-Saxon Period	11
Introduction to Part One		13
Chapter One	Widowhood and Remarriage	19
Chapter Two	The Legal Status of Widows	75
Chapter Three	The Economic (In)dependence of Widows	103
Part Two	The Medieval Period	147
Introduction to Part Two		149
Chapter Four	Widowhood and Remarriage	153
Chapter Five	The Socio-economic Reality of Widowhood	201
Conclusion		329
Bibliography		333
Index		349

To my friend, Eileen R. Pears

Introduction

Most medievalists writing on the theme of women begin their volumes by emphasizing the 'insignificance of women as historical subjects during the period and hence the insurmountable difficulties of recovering their lost lives'.[1] In 1990, Georges Duby and Michelle Perrot remarked in their *History of Women* that 'women were long relegated to the shadows of history', an idea which the English version of the volume dedicated to the Middle Ages reinforced with the subtitle 'Silences of the Middle Ages'.[2] In 1995, Henrietta Leyser evoked her undergraduate years and the Victorian Syllabus that 'had little place for women. Concentrating as it did on public life and constitutional developments there seemed to its framers barely an occasion to mention them'. In 2000, Noël James Menuge warned her readers: 'Cherchez la femme'. That is the problem that so frequently confronts the medievalist. Women are not notable for their visibility in historical records, even in a later medieval context. Women exercising agency or giving voice to their own will are still more rarely observed. One should be tempted to conclude that women were in a minority in medieval societies and that they played little part in those societies'.[3] The invisibility of women had two origins: the fact that medieval texts were mostly written by men and the time it took for historians (who were mainly men) to find some interest in non-military and non-political issues. Historians have now, for a long time, had a different approach to the past – probably ever since Marc Bloch who was one of the first to view history differently and to lend credibility to social history. History was then enriched through an interdisciplinary ap-

---

[1] L.A. Finke, *Women's Writing in English*, London, New York: Longman, 1999, p.2.

[2] C. Klapisch-Zuber, ed., *A History of Women in the West, II. Silences of the Middle Ages*, Cambridge: Harvard University Press, 1992, p.ix.

[3] N.J. Menuge, ed., *Medieval Women and the Law*, Woodbridge: The Boydell Press, 2000, p.ix.

proach with the use of anthropological, geographical or literary perspectives. The study of women, both by male and female historians, rapidly burgeoned and has virtually rocketed over the last three decades. There remained the silences of women in the medieval sources.

Widows, however, do not pose the same problem as other women. Contrary to young maidens, they were not a favoured subject among medieval writers – except for moralists. On the other hand, contrary to maidens and wives, they appear very often in non-literary documents such as law codes, wills, charters, court records and the like so that Barbara A. Hanawalt has even stated that 'widows were ubiquitous in medieval Europe'.[4] Overnight they found themselves women with men's duties and powers. Sweeping away traditional divisions between the sexes, they completely disrupted traditional, well-established categories. Gender studies have rightly taught us that human divisions are more cultural constructions than purely biologically-based tendencies. Apart from the great Christine de Pizan, not many widows of the Middle Ages have voiced their feelings. The primary sources at our disposal, because of their essentially administrative character, do not deal with emotions, with the state of mind of these bereaved women. They only concern the settlement of the deceased's inheritance, the transfer of ownership of his lands and other goods. They say nothing about mourning and grief. Death, admittedly, was then a familiar fact of life and was not a forbidden subject as it often is today. One should not jump to the conclusion that resignation was the norm but rather that the (few) evocations of hardship are not to be found in public records but elsewhere in romances, chronicles, Saints' Lives or visual representations. Public records, on the other hand, give many elements and details of the everyday experiences of widows. This volume, consequently, is based on both literary and more conventional historical sources. The former tell us how widows were viewed by medieval society, how they were expected to live and behave while the latter give a more objective account of their lives.

---

4   C. Dinshaw & D. Wallace, eds., *The Cambridge Companion to Medieval Women's Writing*, Cambridge University Press, 2003, p.58.

It goes without saying that widows did not make a homogeneous group in medieval society. Age, class, character, period of time, place, occupation, economic circumstances, were identity markers that made each widow different. Yet they shared certain preoccupations specific to their status: should they choose to remain single, should (or could) they have custody of their children, did they (according to their social background) feel able to manage their estates, farm the tenement or run their deceased husband's business? Because of these common issues, we have chosen to present this study both in a chronological and a thematic way by dividing it into two main parts: before and after the Conquest. Within each great period the thematic approach rules out needless repetitions while, as the book covers the whole of the Middle Ages, the division of time into Anglo-Saxon and medieval England allows for evolution and changes to be taken into account. The two parts deal with the same varied topics: the fundamental role played by the Church in the doctrine of marriage and in the gradual making of the couple the basic unit of society. The no less fundamental part it played in the dominant male discourse about widows – the obsession with the control of these experienced women's sexuality coming first. A second common theme is that of law: among women, widows had a specific legal status that gave them special rights. These rights deeply affected their lives and their relationships with their children and other relatives. This is why so much space is devoted to family structures (parents-children relations, relations between natal and marital kin-groups) and to the legal and social aspects of inheritance in both parts of this volume. The third main topic concerns the various options widowhood offered (remarriage, withdrawal from society into a monastery, lifelong widowhood, etc.) and the degree of independence widows had in their life choices. Widowhood might initially seem a limited subject. It is, in reality, a position in women's lives that brings all sorts of family, social, economic, emotional, psychological or religious considerations into play. Some may wonder why widowhood should only be studied from the female point of view: widowers, after all, did exist in the Middle Ages. Contrary to widows, however, widowers did not make up a group of their own, their legal status or social position were not modified and many of them remarried quickly.

While there are a great many books on medieval women, those on widows are not that numerous. Both *Upon my Husband's Death: Widows in the Literature and Histories of Medieval Europe* edited by Louise Mirrer (Ann Arbor, 1992) and *Widowhood in Medieval and Early Modern Europe* edited by Sandra Cavallo and Lyndan Warner (London, 1999) deal with Europe as a whole. Cindy Carlson and Angela Weisl's *Constructions of Widowhood and Virginity in the Middle Ages* (Basingstoke, 1998) treats of widows (and maidens) in French and English medieval literature mainly. *Wife and Widow in Medieval England* edited by Sue Sheridan Walker (Ann Arbor, 1993) focuses, as its title shows, on Britain but leaves aside the Early and most of the High Middle Ages. Conversely Caroline Barron and Anne Sutton's *Medieval London Widows 1300–1500* (London, 1994) is concerned with the late Middle Ages only. All five volumes are collections of essays. This book is a study that brings together documents from the 7th to the 15th century aiming at providing a thorough account of widows' place and everyday lives in medieval England. It makes extensive and direct use of primary sources – through translations for Latin or Old English writings – in order faithfully to capture and render what being a widow meant and implied in those bygone centuries.

Part One

The Anglo-Saxon Period

Introduction to Part One

Aethelburh, King Edwin's widow in 631, Seaxburh, widow of King Eorcenberht of Kent in 664, Eanflæd, King Oswiu's widow in 670, Seaxburh, of whom the *Anglo-Saxon Chonicle* specifies that when her husband (King Cenwalh) died in 672, she 'reigned one year after him',[1] Judith, the widow of two English kings in 858 and 860, Aethelflæd, Lady of the Mercians, widowed in 911, Eadgifu, third wife of King Edward the Elder widowed in 924, Emma, first married to Aethelred who died in 1016 widowed for a second time in 1035, at the death of Cnut... A long and revealing list could be established but a quick glance at a few English queens is enough to realize that widowhood was a common experience in England before the Norman Conquest – even if the loss of a husband must have been a more frequent occurrence among these aristocratic ladies who were married at a very early age and whose husbands were often engaged in feuds, wars, and military conquests. The evidence available to scholars is incomplete, only noble and royal women are visible at the time, therefore we know next to nothing about ordinary women. Because widowhood was such a common fact of life, one would expect widows to appear in rather great numbers in Old English works. In reality, Anglo-Saxon poems celebrate the deeds of warriors, sing the rigours of survival and the necessity of courage to endure. They underline the heroic values of bravery, endurance, loyalty to the lord and women are only briefly caught sight of in the great halls. These texts belong to men, were written by men, and voice their view of the world. Women, widows or not, remain silent, apart from the moving narrator of *The Wife's Lament* and the woman who fervently expresses her worries for

---

[1] G.N. Garmonsway, ed., *The Anglo-Saxon Chronicle*, London & Melbourne: Dent (Everyman's Library), 1953–1972. For the original text, J.M. Bately, ed., *The Anglo-Saxon Chronicle*, Ms A, Cambridge: D.S. Brewer, 1986. B. Thorpe, *The Anglo-Saxon Chronicle* (*Rerum Britannicarum Medii Aevi Scriptores* 23), London: Longman, 1861, 2 volumes, vol. 1: 'Original Text'.

Wulf who is away from her (*Wulf and Eadwacer*). The few heroines who play a leading part in Old English literature are strong, full of energy and fearless. *Judith* (a poem written around 930) is based upon the scriptural narrative but the writer transforms the story of Holofernes' murder by Judith into an epic of Germanic and pagan atmosphere, makes of it a patriotic song. Because of her courage and her authority over everyone, Judith has often been compared to Aethelflæd, King Alfred's daughter and Lady of Mercia, who was a formidable warrior. Cynewulf's Elene (*Elene*, 9th century) is depicted as a warlike queen, an empress at the head of troops, a powerful and inflexible woman.[2] These women, therefore, cannot be distinguished from the male heroes of Anglo-Saxon epic poems. Works of other genres, scriptural poetry, moral verse, the Elegies, etc., share the same didactic purpose, that of setting examples, of persuading, convincing, passing judgement, or warning which means that the protagonists are heroes never concerned with the mundane realities of everyday life. Cynewulf only cares about Juliana as a martyr, not as a young girl.

As a consequence, Old English literature is of little help in a study on widows. One has to turn to a different sort of documentation (chronicles, homilies, charters, wills, etc.) though, here too, the harvest is not as plentiful as one would wish. The documents are well-known and their number is not likely to increase, which implies that our knowledge of the subject must remain fragmented. There are, in particular, very few pieces where a woman's voice speaks directly to her audience. The major primary sources available were written by clerics who, by virtue of their office in the Church, did not meet women very often. It will then come as no surprise to see women kept in the background. At the same time, one is struck by the importance given to widows in Anglo-Saxon society: they are presented as a particular kind of woman enjoying a specific legal status. They were almost courted by the Church who, since patristic times, considered

---

[2] S.A.J. Bradley very rightly writes: 'the portrait of the formidable Helen places her in that quite large gallery of women, literary and historical, recognized by the Anglo-Saxons as being in virtue, intellectual strength, vision, purpose and pratical efficacy the peers or superiors of men'. S.A.J. Bradley, trans., *Anglo-Saxon Poetry*, London & Melbourne: Dent (Everyman's Library), 1982, p.165.

widows as a class apart and reserved for them a special place of honour. The writings of the Church Fathers and their taking up by Anglo-Saxon churchmen on the one hand, and the Anglo-Saxon code laws on the other, are therefore the two main bodies of written evidence that must be referred to in order to get an idea of what being a widow meant and involved at that time. For it was much more than simply losing a husband: it meant calling into question the relationships between two lineages, the subtle network of dependencies and guardianship, the balance of economic power. Code laws give an insight into the position of widows in Anglo-Saxon society. Religious treatises and homilies deal with widowhood from a moral point of view. Indeed, after the death of her husband, a widow's every action and morals came into question. Moralists, consequently, designate proper and improper behaviour, define a woman's befitting place in society and in her family that rests essentially on a sexual consideration: chastity.

It was, therefore, for different reasons that both the Church and the earliest English kings became increasingly interested in regulating marriage. The Church was concerned in promoting the ideal of a conjugal, monogamous, indissoluble union. It was a long process which was eventually backed by the secular powers whose interest it was to weaken family solidarity.[3] Marriage regulation was also a means of domination, a further reinforcement of royal authority. Thus Pre-Conquest conceptions of marriage derive from our two main sources: first, the Bible and the writings of the Latin Church Fathers; second, the customs of the Germanic tribes. This is why our first two chapters will be devoted to the influence of the early Church and to Anglo-Saxon legislation.

Chapter one, exposing first the teaching of the Church Fathers, will not immediately present flesh and blood or even fictional widows, but the way these women were apprehended and expected to conform, to pattern themselves upon an ideal which they more or less adhered to in practice yet most likely internalized as *the* model. We will, therefore, meet an idea, an abstraction, an idealized view of what widows should do and what they should be as in a sort of 'mirror of widow'.

---

[3] This support to the Church was more conspicuous on the Continent for, although lordship was always important in Anglo-Saxon England, the latter did not become a feudal state.

Because the church fathers were so influential, they moulded the thought of all medieval scholars and were considered as infallible authorities; they were quoted time and again by all Anglo-Saxon ecclesiastics. This is why we shall, in a second stage, concentrate on the writings of Anglo-Saxon clerics such as Aldhelm, Bede, or Aelfric. Some of their writings will enable us, this time, to meet flesh and blood widows but not to hear them speak directly. Real life historical people are seen through the distorting prism of these male writers' knowledge acquired from books.

In chapter two, law codes will be discussed. These documents are a totally different genre with a different aim: instead of trying to edify and of showing a way to perfection, they are concerned with compensation for actual crimes and offences. They do not guide widows as to proper behaviour but aim to remind people of the penalties incurrable should they kill or hurt others, which might include harming a widow. Anglo-Saxon law shows that widows were considered as particularly vulnerable and as requiring special protection, which explains why they are far more referred to in the codes than are wives or daughters. Therefore, it is their need of protection which makes them conspicuous.

We shall eventually focus on material where widows are no longer silent: a few wills, charters, and letters have survived in which we can see them telling their stories. These documents will bring widows to life by giving a few details about their name, age, class, occupation, or economic freedom. We shall investigate the highly-debated issue of the degree of independence widows had: could they, in particular, bequeath their possessions, including land property, as they thought best? Christine Fell[4] argues that Anglo-Saxon women enjoyed far more rights than they did after the Norman Conquest and speaks of near-complete autonomy. From an opposite viewpoint, Pauline Stafford[5] upholds that women's choices were limited and that widows

---

4   C. Fell, C. Clark & E. Williams, *Women in Anglo-Saxon England and the Impact of 1066*, London: British Museum Publications, 1984. T.J. Rivers, 'Widow's Rights in Anglo-Saxon Law', *American Journal of Legal History*, 19 (1975), pp.208–15, had defended the same view.

5   P. Stafford, *Queens, Concubines, and Dowagers, the King's Wife in the Early Middle Ages*, Athens: Georgia University Press 1983.

probably simply confirmed their husbands' dispositions. The matter is difficult to settle because the evidence is so limited and patchy. However that may be, these personal records are extremely interesting to read because we are briefly admitted into the private life of Anglo-Saxon ladies. The latter often stated arrangements for the distribution of their valuables as well as for more common household goods. We are, therefore, given an insight into the interior of an aristocratic dwelling.

Information about early medieval widows is more abundant than about other women. Yet, as Julia Crick noticed, 'the terminology of widowhood occupies a very marginal place in the documentary record. (...) Men's widowhood is never visible but women's widowhood likewise is identified only rarely'.[6] In the law codes, women are classified by social class and by marital status: maiden, wife, widow. Men are classified by rank only and it was not until the 14th century that the term *widower* was coined.[7] A great number of the above-mentioned documents were written in English and use two different terms to refer to a widow: *wid(e)we* (also spelt *widuwe* or *wuduwe*) which, etymologically, means a woman who has been separated, left solitary[8] and *laf* which, in Old English signified 'what is left over, what remains (of persons or of things)' and, consequently, also had the sense of 'relict, widow'.[9] To these terms, one must add *widewanhad* [widowhood]. No other word was used and a widow was often quite simply referred to as a 'wif' [woman], therefore not being distinguished from other women: 'gif ceorl acwyle be libbendum wife & bearne' [if a man dies leaving a wife and a child].[10] None of the other terms belonging to the semantic field of widowhood to be found today

---

6   J. Crick, 'Men, Women and Widows: Widowhood in pre-Conquest England', S. Cavallo & L. Warner, eds., *Widowhood in Medieval and Early Modern Europe*, Harlow: Pearson Education Limited (Longman), 1999.
7   William Langland uses it in *Piers Plowman*, A x 194 (*widewers & widewes*).
8   It goes back to Indo-European *widhewo-, an adjective formed on the base *widh- [to be empty, be separated], source also of English *divide*.
9   *Laf* and *læfan* [leave] are of the same word family. The prehistoric Germanic ancestor of *læfan* was *laibjan* [remain].
10 F.L. Attenborough, ed., *The Laws of the Earliest Kings*, Cambridge: University Press, 1922, Hlothhere and Eadric's laws, § 6, pp.18–19.

in the English language had appeared at the time. Some are dated, others more recent in origin and include: bereaved (12th c.), bereavement (18th c.), bereft (19th c.), relict (16th c.), viduage (19th c.), viduity (15th c.), widowed (17th c.), widowess (16th c.), widowish (16th c.), widowity (16th c.), widowly (16th c.), vowess (16th c.). Widowhood was a common experience, it probably concerned too many women to be picked out.

Although commiseration can be felt in the documents, there is no detailed description of the state of widowhood, not to mention feelings, tears, or depression. It was not until the 12th century that medieval writers took some interest in mental states, individuality, the self and the other. Being a widow, according to Anglo-Saxon texts, essentially meant belonging to a specific social category. However, *The Wife's Lament* is here to qualify such statements. Doesn't the wife say

> I sing this song about myself, full sad,
> My own distress, and tell what hardships I
> Have had to suffer since I first grew up,
> Present and past, but never more than now;
> I ever suffered grief through banishment.
> For since my lord departed from this people
> Over the sea, each dawn have I had care
> Wondering where my lord may be on land.
> (...)
> Old is this earth-cave, all I do is yearn.
> (...)
> And joyless is the place. Full often here
> The absence of my lord comes sharply to me (1–8 & 29 & 32–33).[11]

It is clear that the female narrator knows everything about distress and sorrow. We will therefore always have to keep in mind that the texts on which we base our knowledge of the Middle Ages are often highly biased, that only a small number have survived and that one can often find a text to contradict what seemed proved for good. Truth can only be multifaceted.

---

11 R. Hamer, ed., *A Choice of Anglo-Saxon Verse*, London, Boston: Faber & Faber, 1970, p.75.

Chapter One
Widowhood and Remarriage

Founding a Tradition: The Influence of the Early Church

When Saul reached Damascus, he had converted to the new sect which he had so zealously persecuted. He launched upon a missionary career that took him from the Middle East to Cyprus, Asia Minor, Greece, and eventually to Rome. St Paul wrote frequently: ten of the Epistles are ascribed to him. His letters, intended to be read to the small and young Christian communities, dealt with theology and interpreted Christianity to the world but also gave instruction in moral or even practical issues. They are inestimable firsthand sources of early Christian history. Their influence on the Christian church as a whole has been immense.

In the 7th chapter of his first Epistle to the Corinthians, St Paul expressed his view on virginity, celibacy, and marriage. It was to become the orthodox teaching on the matter and repeatedly quoted by medieval theologians and writers. The first important point is that St Paul praised marriage:

> Art thou bound to a wife? Seek not to be loosed. Art thou loosed from a wife? Seek not a wife. But if thou take a wife, thou hast not sinned. And if a virgin marry, she hath not sinned. (I Cor. 7:27–8)
>
> But if any man think that he seemeth dishonoured with regard to his virgin, for that she is above the age, and it must so be: let him do what he will. He sinneth not if she marry. (7:36)[1]

---

[1] *The Holy Bible* (translated from the Latin Vulgate. The Old Testament was first published by the English college at Douay A.D. 1609 and the New Testament was first published by the English college at Rheims A.D. 1582), New York: The C. Wildermann Company, 1916. Douay/Rheims Bible online: http://www.drbo.org/

However he saw marriage as inferior to celibacy:

> Therefore both he that giveth his virgin in marriage, doth well; and he that giveth her not, doth better. (7:38)

His reasons for preferring celibacy to the married state, were that the unmarried would care more for God, not being distracted by a wife or a husband, earthly riches and pleasure: 'And the unmarried woman and the virgin thinketh on the things of the Lord: that she may be holy both in body and in spirit. But she that is married thinketh on the things of the world: how she may please her husband' (7:34).

On one fundamental point Paul was unequivocal: he insisted that marriages could not be dissolved:

> But to them that are married, not I, but the Lord, commandeth that the wife depart not from her husband. And if she depart, that she remain unmarried or be reconciled to her husband. And let not the husband put away his wife. (7:10–11)[2]

Concerning widows, Paul was as clear: nothing stopped them from remarrying if they wished to: 'A woman is bound by the law as long as her husband liveth: but if her husband die, she is at liberty. Let her marry to whom she will: only in the Lord' (7:39). However, he once again gave personal preference to celibacy:

> But I say to the unmarried and to the widows: it is good for them if they so continue, even as I. (7:8)

St Paul was being pragmatic there. He was well aware not everyone is gifted with perfection and understood, as well as forgave, shortcomings. This is why he added: 'But if they do not contain themselves, let them marry. For it is better to marry than to burn' (7:9). Marriage, therefore, is therapeutic: it is a remedy for incontinence, the lesser of two evils, for, as Paul emphasizes: 'I speak this by indulgence, not by commandment. For I would that all men were even as myself' (7:6–7).

Yet the Christian message conflicted on many points with the social realities of the Graeco-Roman world – as it did, later on, with the

---

[2] This precept is also to be found in the Epistle to the Romans 7:2–3.

customs of most newly-evangelized countries. In the Epistle to the Galatians, Paul denounces the established order, proclaims the end of differences in nationality, culture, wealth and gender. Henceforth, men and women have become the members of a new family whose unity, cohesion and identity rest on Christ only. The only lord and superior is God who happens to be a benevolent father. Everyone will now be treated as equals:

> For you are all the children of God by faith, in Christ Jesus. For as many of you as have been baptized in Christ, have put on Christ. There is neither Jew nor Greek; there is neither bond nor free; there is neither male nor female. For you are all one in Christ Jesus. (Gal, 3:26–28)[3]

One must not overestimate Paul's liberality: he never really called slavery into question, sending back Onesimus, a fugitive slave, to his master though advising 'Masters, do to your servants that which is just and equal; knowing that you also have a master in heaven' (Col, 4:1). However, this short passage (Gal, 3:26–28) played a major role in the more positive view about women's place in the Christian church. It rings like an appeal for looking at the world with new eyes. It brushes aside former categories and distinctions for new ones: from now on mankind will be divided into those dedicating their lives to God – and observing sexual abstinence – and the laymen who do not. This is why, gradually, women were grouped into three classes that are not social classes but three stages in life: the virgins, wives, and widows. The Church Fathers know no other classification.

Patristic authors endorsed St Paul's teaching in praise of the marriage state, though not all of them with the same enthusiasm: St Jerome's often-quoted words 'I praise marriage, I praise conjugality, but because for me they produce virgins'[4] stress his reluctance. The Church Fathers all took much interest in widows. St John Chrysostom

---

[3] Yet Paul also wrote: 'let women be subject to their husbands, as to the Lord; because the husband is the head of the wife, as Christ is the head of the church.' (Eph, 5:22–23)

[4] Jerome's letter no.XXII addressed to Eustochium. F.A. Wright, ed., *Select Letters of St Jerome*, Cambridge, Mass.: Harvard University Press, Loeb Classical Library, 1963.

(347–407) in his *Homilies on First Timothy*, taking up what St Paul had written about *true* widows (I Tim, 5:3–16), painted a compassionate portrait of widows, though not devoid of clearly patronizing ulterior motives:

> For a woman may have lost her husband, and yet not be truly a widow. As in order to be a virgin, it is not enough to be a stranger to marriage, but many other things are necessary, as blamelessness and perseverance; so the loss of a husband does not constitute a widow, but patience, with chastity and separation from all men. Such widows he justly bids us honour, or rather support. For they need support, being left desolate, and having no husband to stand up for them. Their state appears to the multitude despicable and inauspicious. Therefore he wishes them to receive the greater honour from the Priest, and the more so, because they are worthy of it.[5]

St Jerome had in mind the same conception of *true* widows when he wrote in his treatise *Against Jovinianus* (book I, chapter 3) that, after the loss of their husband, women 'are placed in a position of difficulty and tribulation':[6] widowhood is defined by hardships and great trials. A question cropped up immediately: should widows be allowed to remarry?

Tertullian (c. 155–c. 220), born in a pagan family in Carthage became a Christian around 193. Among his numerous works, three of them discuss the problem of widowhood and remarriage: in the first book of *Ad uxorem*, he urges his wife to remain a widow should she outlive him, while in the second book he tolerates her remarriage with a Christian. In *De exhortatione Castitatis*, he considers second marriage as contrary to the will of God. He goes further in his third treatise, *De monogamia*, where he regards remarriage as unlawful and adulterous.[7] The issue was tackled by other early Christian writers

5   Electronic version of St John Chrysostom's *Homilies on First Timothy*, New Advent Inc., 1997. http://www.newadvent.org/fathers/230613.htm.
6   W.H. Fremantle, ed., *The Principal Works of St Jerome*, Select Library of Nicene and Post-Nicene Fathers, ser. 2, vol. VI, Edinburgh, 1892. http://www.newadvent.org/fathers/30091.htm and http://haywardfamily.org/ccel/fathers2/npnf206/npnf2069.htm.
7   Tertullian's extremist position on remarriage was only one of the controversies which led to his separation from the Catholic Church. Because of this rupture, Tertullian was less influential than St Jerome or St Augustine. Yet, his *De*

among whom St Ambrose of Milan (c. 339–397) whose treatise concerning widows (*De viduis*) shows that he was rather against marriage as a whole – though, of course, he could not go against the official line. He compares marriage to servitude:

> It is then lawful to marry, but it is more seemly to abstain, for there are bonds in marriage. Do you ask what bonds? 'The woman who is under a husband is bound by the law so long as her husband liveth; but if her husband be dead she is loosed from the law of her husband'. It is then proved that marriage is a bond by which the woman is bound and from which she is loosed. Beautiful is the grace of mutual love, but the bondage is more constant (§ 69).[8]

This is why, in St Ambrose's eyes, widowhood becomes fortunate, a proper release: 'Widowhood is, then good, which is so often praised by the judgement of the apostles, for it is a teacher of the faith and a teacher of chastity. (...) In like manner the widow, as a veteran, having served her time, though she lays aside the arms of married life, yet orders the peace of the whole house: though now freed from carrying burdens, she is yet watchful for the younger who are to be married. (...) Widowhood is not to be shunned as a penalty, but to be esteemed as a reward' (§ 84 & 85). St Jerome followed suit. He too brought marriage into disesteem in his *Adversus Jovinianum* warning against unavoidable tribulation – term he had first applied to widowhood. The reversal is striking:

> Why do we take wives whom we shall soon, be compelled to lose? (...) If the world, which comprehends all things, passes away, yea if the fashion and intercourse of the world vanishes like the clouds, amongst the other works of the world, marriage too will vanish away. For after the resurrection there will be no wedlock. But if death be the end of marriage, why do we not voluntarily embrace the inevitable? (Book I, chapter 13)

Widowhood is now seen as providential, liberating grace.

[8] *exhortatione Castitatis* (and its numerous misogynous passages) was well-known in the Middle Ages: the Wife of Bath in Chaucer's *Canterbury Tales*, for instance, mentions Tertullian line 676.
Electronic version of St Ambrose's *De Viduis*, new Advent Inc., 1997. http://www.newadvent.org/fathers/3408.htm. See also Ambrose, Bishop of Milan, *On Virginity*, D. Callam, ed., Toronto, 1980.

The disapproval, or rather the condemnation, of sexuality explains this paradoxical position. In most patristic treatises, woman is considered as distrustful and dangerous. She is presented as Satan's tool, Eve being responsible for Man's death as well as for the death of Christ who had to die on the cross to redeem mankind. Because of her, Man was banished from the garden of Eden and as a consequence sexuality became the visible sign of human fall. Generation after generation, the sin is transmitted and must be paid and atoned for. Tertullian writing for women recently converted advised: '[you should] give the impression of a mourning and repentant Eve so that, by adopting all the clothing of the penitent, you might atone more fully for what derives from Eve, namely the disgrace of the first sin, and the hatred which followed because of the fall of the human race'.[9] Ever since Adam and Eve were driven out of Eden, Man has been dominated by his instincts. Most Church Fathers agree that women are lustful, that their sexual appetite is intense, ravenous, and baneful. For St Jerome, women stand for temptation, vice, and mortal danger. He sees sex as the expression of bestiality:

> At the same time, we must take notice the Apostle's prudence. He did not say, it is good not to have a wife; but, it is good not to touch a woman: as though there were danger even in the touch; as though he who touched her, would not escape from her who 'hunteth for the precious life', 'who causeth the young man's understanding to fly away'. Can a man take fire in his bosom and his clothes not be burned? Or can one walk upon hot coals and his feet not be scorched?' (...) Joseph, because the Egyptian woman wished to touch him, fled from her hands, and, as if he had been bitten by a mad dog and feared the spreading poison, threw away the cloak which she had touched. (*Adversus Jovinianum*, Book I, chapter 7)

Rapidly, the idea of an asexual world, the only way to flawlessness and salvation, seems to have formed in Jerome's mind. A scale of perfection had been established contrasting continence with abstinence: in the 2nd century, indeed, it had occurred to an anonymous writer to apply the parable of the sower (Mat. 13:3–9 & 18–23) to the hierarchy of states of life put forward by the New testament: virginity,

---

[9] Tertullian, *De Cultu Feminarum*, in A. Blamires, ed., *Woman Defamed and Woman Defended*, Oxford: University Press, 1992, p.51.

chastity, conjugality. Origen (c. 185–c. 254) who saw Christianity as a ladder of divine ascent, had taken up this graduated system. So did St Jerome:

> Virginity is to marriage what fruit is to the tree, or grain to the straw. Although the hundred-fold, the sixty-fold, and the thirty-fold spring from one earth and from one sowing, yet there is a great difference in respect of number. The thirty-fold applies to widows, because they are placed in a position of difficulty and distress. Hence the upper finger signifies their depression, and the greater the difficulty in resisting the allurements of pleasure once experienced, the greater the reward. Moreover (give good heed, my reader), to denote a hundred, the right hand is used instead of the left: a circle is made with the same fingers which on the left hand represented widowhood, and thus the crown of virginity is expressed. (*Adversus Jovinianum*, Book I, chapter 3).

Against Jerome's antifeminism stands St Augustine (354–430) and his characteristic moderation. In several of his treatises, including *De bono viduitatis* (c. 414), he acknowledges three qualities to marriage: faithfulness, indissolubility, and the begetting of children. Fruitfulness within a Christian family is welcomed: 'Forsooth to be engaged in the getting of children, not after the fashion of dogs by promiscuous use of females, but by honest order of marriage, is not an affection such as we are to blame in a man'(§11)[10] though he immediately adds: 'yet this affection itself the Christian mind, having thoughts of heavenly things, in a more praiseworthy manner surpasses and overcomes' (§11). For in spite of Augustine's profound understanding of human shortcomings, he too believed that Adam and Eve's transgression emphasized Man's inability to control his instincts, the subjection of spirit to flesh. It was his belief that only the Holy Spirit could reverse the situation: God alone was seen as the cause of every human movement towards good. And Augustine reminds us that, though marriage is not to be despised and cannot be rejected, sexuality is a concession: the ideal couple is therefore that of Mary and Joseph – the divine intervention that enabled them to have a son underlining the close link between sexuality and sin.

The Church Fathers' insistence on virginity, as a way of life for Christian women, relies on a symbolic association between the purity

---

10   St Augustine, *De bono viduitatis*. http://www.newadvent.org/fathers/1311.htm.

of the body and the purity of the soul. The purpose of virginity is to help the soul develop the power of seeing God. Because of the Fall, the state of blessedness Adam and Eve experienced is lost for ever. Virginity, however, offers an earthly approximation to the angelic life promised after the resurrection:[11] chaste purity of body and spirit is required to 'await the Spouse of blessing',[12] to become one of Christ's bride (Ap. 14:4). St Augustine reminds his readers[13] that all Christians are members of the Church and that St Paul added: 'I joined you unto one husband a chaste virgin to present unto Christ' (II Cor. 11:2). Did not Jesus himself say: 'there are eunuchs, who were born so from their mother's womb; and there are eunuchs, who were made so by men; and there are eunuchs, who have made themselves eunuchs for the kingdom of heaven'? It ensues that the Fathers saw widowhood as a chance given to women to find the way to holiness, 'Christian chastity' might then rank with 'angelic virginity', to use Jerome's terminology.[14]

Though Jerome condemned Tertullian's extreme views about the remarriage of widows, he also expressed reluctance and discouraged women from doing so:

> Let us consider what the Apostle says: 'Be ye transformed by the renewing of your mind, that ye may prove what is good and acceptable and perfect will of god'. What he says is something like this – God indeed permits marriage, He permits second marriages, and if necessary, prefers even third marriages to fornication and adultery. But we who ought to present our bodies a living sacrifice, holy, acceptable to God, which is our reasonable service, should consider, not what God permits, but what He wishes: that we may prove what is the good and acceptable and perfect will of God. It follows that what He merely permits is neither good, nor acceptable, nor perfect.[15]

---

11 'In the resurrection of the dead they will neither marry nor be given in marriage, but will be like the angels'. What others will hereafter be in heaven, that virgins begin to be on earth. Jerome, *Adversus Jovinianum*, § 36.
12 St Ambrose, *De viduis*, § 81.
13 St Augustine, *De bono Viduitatis*, § 13.
14 St Jerome, *Adversus Jovinianum*, Book I, chapter 41.
15 Ibid., Book I, chapter 37.

St Ambrose, on the other hand, stuck to St Paul's doctrine: 'I do not forbid second marriages, only I do not advise them. (...) I do not forbid second, but do not approve of often repeated marriages'.[16] Similarly, Augustine, unambiguously, declared that a widow had a perfect right to remarry after the death of her husband:

> Men are wont to move a question concerning a third or fourth marriage, and even more numerous marriages than this. On which to make answer strictly, I dare neither to condemn any marriage, nor to take from these the shame of their great number. (...) I dare not to be more wise that it behoveth to be wise. For who am I, that I should think that that must be defined which I see that the Apostle hath not defined? For he saith, 'A woman is bound, so long as her husband liveth'. He said not, her first; or, second; or, third; or, fourth; but 'A woman' saith he, 'is bound, so long as her husband liveth; but if her husband shall be dead, she is set free; let her be married to whom she will, only in the Lord; but she shall be more blessed, if she shall have so continued'. I know not what can be added to, or taken from, this sentence, so far as relates to this matter.[17]

The situation for medieval theologians and canon lawyers, who inherited these conflicting views, was therefore complex and confusing. Whatever their own conviction, they could find support in the writings of eminent authorities. The early Church had felt the necessity of unanimity and consensus on all sorts of questions of doctrine – including widowhood. Bishops of the whole church assembled. No reliable account of the proceedings of the first council held in Nicaea in 325 has survived. However, the bishops adopted twenty canons which are extant. Canon 8 states that remarried widows and widowers should not be prohibited from receiving communion.[18] More generally speaking, the Christian Church never forbade the remarriage of

---

16 St Ambrose, *De Viduis*, § 68.
17 St Augustine, *De bone Viduitatis*, § 15.
18 J.A. Brundage in 'Widows and Remarriage: Moral Conflicts and their Resolution in Classical Canon Law', S.S. Walker, ed., *Wife & Widow in Medieval England*, Ann Arbor: University of Michigan Press, 1993, pp.17–31 points out p.18 that the Council of Laodicaea 'cautioned widows and widowers not to remarry hastily', and that the Second Council of Braga 'required those who remarried to do penance for lascivious conduct'.

widows and widowers: St Paul's teaching remained the official doctrine.

Continuing the Tradition: the Anglo-Saxon Homilists.

Together with St Paul's teaching, St Augustine's views on most subjects, including marriage and widowhood, became the accepted position of the medieval church. Aldhelm of Malmesbury (c. 639–709) and Aelfric (c. 955–c. 1010), two highly learned abbots and authors, also tackled the question of marriage versus virginity, largely basing their own texts on the treatises by Jerome, Ambrose and by Augustine: Aldhelm 'felt that he was writing in a venerable patristic tradition, and much of his discussion of virginity is traditional'.[19] Aldhelm wrote his lengthy Latin treatise on celibacy for a female audience, addressing his work to the nuns of Barking (Essex). His deposition takes up most of the arguments of the Church Fathers: virginity is defined as complete asceticism, it implies both corporeal chastity and spiritual purity (dedication). The bee is given as an example of virginity at work: 'she produces her sweet family and children, innocent of the lascivious coupling of marriage'.[20] Once more, virginity is said to be 'next kin to angelic beatitude' (§ VII) and Aldhelm mentions John the Evangelist who 'offered up to Christ – who is a passionate lover of chastity and a jealous teacher of holiness – the welcome sacrifice of virginity made with spontaneous devotion'. John was greatly rewarded since he 'was found worthy to hear the 144,000 virgins singing a new song with sweet-sounding harmonies of melody and to behold (them) with his pure eyes' (§ VII). However lawful wedlock is not to be scorned (§

---

19   M. Lapidge & M. Herren, eds., *Aldhelm, The Prose Works*, Ipswich, Cambridge: D.S. Brewer, Totowa: Rowman & Littlefield, 1979, p.52.
20   The bee as a type of virginity is a standard rhetorical concept. Aldhelm's indebtedness to St Ambrose, who used this poetic image in *De Virginibus ad Marcellinam*, is obvious. All quotations from Aldhelm's *De Virginitate* are taken from M. Lapidge & M. Herren, eds., *Aldhelm, The Prose Works*.

VIII), even though it is inferior to virginity. Aldhelm expands St Paul's recommendation 'both he that giveth his virgin in marriage doth well: and he that giveth her not doth better' (I Cor. 7:38) through a series of comparisons in which virginity always prevails over marriage: shining gold is preferable to pure silver, red-glowing jewel is superior to white marble, taffeta and silk are better than woollen threads of fibres, etc. Aldhelm's originality does not lie in the idea but in this long list of eleven detailed instances. Though Aldhelm affirms that marriage is good, he cannot resist contrasting 'angelic chastity' with 'marital wantonness' (§ XVII) and from reminding everyone that only 'earthly celibates are compelled in a wonderful manner to become heavenly citizens' (§ XVIII).

At this point, Aldhelm differs slightly from his predecessors. He explains that the Church accepts a three-fold distinction not merely of women but of the whole human race. Then, as 'virginity, chastity, and conjugality differ the one from the other in three ranks' (§ XIX), Aldhelm gives us a second series of correspondences:

> So that virginity is gold, chastity silver, conjugality bronze; that virginity is riches, chastity an average income, conjugality poverty; that virginity is freedom, chastity ransom, conjugality captivity; that virginity is the sun, chastity a lamp, conjugality darkness; that virginity is day, chastity the dawn, conjugality night; that virginity is a queen, chastity a lady, conjugality a servant; that virginity is the homeland, chastity the harbour, conjugality the sea; that virginity is the living man, chastity a man half-alive, conjugality the (lifeless) body; that virginity is the royal purple, chastity the re-dyed fabric, conjugality the (undyed) wool. (...) To these three levels of rank, therefore, into which the flourishing multitude of believers in the catholic Church is divided, the gospel parable has promised hundred-fold, sixty-fold and thirty-fold fruit according to the outlay of their merits. (§ XIX)

Throughout the treatise, Aldhelm refers to 'chastity' for the second-best category, never limiting it to widowhood. He goes into details explaining that a chaste person is someone who 'having been assigned to marital contracts, has scorned the commerce of matrimony for the sake of the heavenly kingdom' (§ XIX): the death of a spouse is nowhere mentioned.

At the time when Aldhelm was writing, marriage was still an ill-defined notion. It took the Church a long time to set up universal laws and the indissolubility of marriage was not firmly established as a dogma until about A.D. 900. The doubts, hesitations, uncertainties of the missionaries sent to evangelize England or Germany are obvious: Bede (670–735) reports the questions sent by Augustine (of Canterbury) to Pope Gregory after his arrival in Kent in 597. Among them, three concern marriage or conjugal life for 'these uncouth English people require guidance on all these matters':[21] 'Is it permissible for two brothers to marry two sisters, provided that there be no blood ties between the families?' The pope's reply is interesting for though he asserts 'This is quite permissible', all the same he prudently adds: 'There is nothing in Holy Scripture that seems to forbid it'. Augustine's second question concerns the impediments to marriage (blood and spiritual relationships) while the third one deals with maternity and sexual relations. His questions, therefore, are not about some abstruse spiritual issue but focus on practical, prosaic matters. Similarly, one finds among the Bonifatian correspondence several letters in which Boniface (c. 675–754) consults the pope about what degrees of relationship marriage may take place (letter XVIII),[22] in which he asks Bishop Pehthelm's advice about whether a godfather is allowed to marry the mother of the child (letter XXIII), wishes to obtain a copy of the questions sent by Augustine to Pope Gregory I (letter XXIV), or wonders whether a man may marry his uncle's widow (letter XLI): in the first half of the 8th century, the rules were not yet clearly laid down.

It comes then as no surprise to find many instances in Anglo-Saxon documents of what were, later on, to be considered as unlawful marriages. It seems, indeed, that among Anglo-Saxon peoples, it was not unusual for marriages to be dissolved.[23] As we shall see, formerly married women, both separated and widowed, were significantly well-represented in the monasteries. Bede relates with great enthusiasm

---

21 Bede, *A History of the English Church and People*, L. Sherley-Price, ed., Harmondsworth: Penguin Books, 1955–1968, p.77.
22 E. Emerton, ed., *The Letters of St Boniface*, New York: Columbia University Press, 1940; with a new introduction and bibliography by T.F.X. Noble, 2000.
23 Letters of admonition sent to the Frankish kings Pepin (d. 768) and Lothair II (835–869) by Pope Zacharias and Pope Nicholas I show that the habit was widespread.

how Queen Aethelthryth, though twice married, 'preserved the glory of perpetual virginity. (...) She begged the king to allow her to retire from worldly affairs and serve Christ the only true King in a convent. And having at length obtained his reluctant consent, she entered the convent of the Abbess Ebba' (IV. 19). *The Anglo-Saxon Chronicle* reports that in the year 718, 'Ingeld, brother of Ine, passed away, and their sisters were Cwenburh and Cuthburh; and that Cuthburh founded the monastic community at Wimborne. She was given in marriage to Ealdfrith, King of Northumbria, but they parted during their lifetime'.[24] Such a situation was no longer to be allowed[25] in the next centuries once ecclesiastical authorities stuck to fixed rules acknowledged by all. As St Paul had unequivocally stated 'but to them that are married, not I, but the Lord, commandeth that the wife depart not from her husband' (I Cor. 7:10), marriage eventually implied a monogamous and indissoluble relationship, combined with a full community of life. But at the time Aldhelm was writing, the institution was not clearly delimited and marriage remained a largely civil affair. This is why Pope Gregory II made this (rather unorthodox for us today) reply to Boniface in 726:

> As to your question, what a man is to do if his wife is unable, on account of disease, to fulfil her wifely duty: it would be well if he could remain in a state of continence. But, since this is a matter of great difficulty, it is better for him who cannot refrain to take a wife. He may not, however, withdraw his support from the one who was prevented by disease, provided she be not involved in any grievous fault. (letter XVIII)

This is also why newly-converted peoples sometimes adapted Christianity to their own customs. In 668, Theodore, a Greek originally

---

24 G.N. Garmonsway, ed., *The Anglo-Saxon Chronicle*, p.43.
25 Except if both spouses wished to enter a monastery. Besides, Aelfric explains several times that a couple may separate for a vow of chastity: 'separation is allowed to those who love exalted chastity more than anxious lust', *The Homilies of the Anglo-Saxon Church. The First Part, Containing the Sermones Catholici or Homilies of Aelfric. In the Original Anglo-Saxon, with an English Version*. B. Thorpe, ed. + trans., London: the Aelfric Society, 1844, vol. II, p.325.

from Tarsus, arrived in England to become archbishop of Canterbury. The penitential attributed to him contains the following decrees:

> A woman may not put away her husband, even if he is a fornicator, unless perchance, for a monastery. Basil so decided. But either [= husband or wife], according to the Greeks, may give the other permission to join a monastery, for the service of God, and [as it were] marry it, if he [or she] was in a first marriage; yet this is not canonical. But if such is not the case, [but they are] in a second marriage, this is not permitted while the husband or wife is alive.[26]

Aldhelm probably knew this ruling concerning women who left their husband in favour of the monastic life. He had studied in the famous school of Canterbury under Hadrian, head of the abbey of St Peter and St Paul, and under Theodore himself. Because English monasteries welcomed married women who wished to dedicate their lives to God, Aldhelm substituted *chastity* for *widowhood*.

Michael Lapidge, in the introduction to his translation of Aldhelm's *De Virginitate* points out that the abbot 'addresses his audience with extreme deference and refers very delicately to their marital (or virginal) status. I would suggest that much of the doctrine and structure of the *De Virginitate* is determined by this audience of noble ladies-turned-nuns, some at least of whom had rejected their worldly marriages. (...) The new feature is "chastity", the state attained by someone who has been married but who has rejected this marriage for the religious life. This newly devised category allowed Aldhelm to praise by implication those Barking nuns such as Cuthburh who had spurned their marriages'.[27] Michael Lapidge, and Stephanie Hollis after him,[28] identify this Cuthburh with the sister of the Wessex kings Ingeld and Ine mentioned in the above-quoted extract of *The Anglo-Saxon Chronicle*. We have seen that she left her husband Ealdfrith of

---

26 J.T. McNeill & H. M. Gamer, ed., *Medieval Handbooks of Penance*, New York: Columbia University, 1938, *Poenitentiale Theodori*, Book II, chapter 12, articles 6 & 8.
27 M. Lapidge & M. Herren, eds., *Aldhelm, The Prose Works*, p.52 & p.56.
28 S. Hollis, *Anglo-Saxon Women and the Church – Sharing a Common Fate*, Woodbridge: The Boydell Press, 1992.

Northumbria, whom Aldhelm knew well,[29] to join the community at Barking. Like many monasteries in England at that time, Barking was a double house governed by an abbess. In the second part of his treatise, Aldhelm gives a long catalogue of both male and female virgins. Catalogues of Old Testament heroines in the three tiers of perfection (virginity, chaste widowhood, faithful widowhood) thought to be attainable by women, are to be found in the works by St Ambrose and St Jerome. By definition, men are not concerned and therefore not mentioned. Michael Lapidge puts forward the fact that Barking was a double monastery to account for Aldhelm's inclusion of male virgins.

Yet, one may also suggest the possibility of a larger Anglo-Saxon tradition. The Second Council of Nicaea (787) forbade further foundations of double monasteries. Aelfric lived and wrote at the time of the tenth-century revival of English monasteries known as the Benedictine monastic reform. Under the leadership of Dunstan (c. 909–988), Archbishop of Canterbury, Aethelwold, Bishop of Winchester in 963, and Oswald (?–992), Bishop of Worcester and Archbishop of York, many monasteries were founded or refounded under reformed lines, that is to say a strict return to the Rule of St Benedict for communities of celibate monks who were not supposed to own personal property: a simpler, more solitary, more austere type of monastic life was restored. Aelfric's *Life of St Aethelwold* emphasizes the scale of the reform and underlines the separation between men and women:

> And thus it was brought to pass with the king's consent that monasteries were founded everywhere among the English people, partly by the counsel and action of Dunstan and partly by that of Ethelwold, some with monks and some with nuns, living according to the rule under abbots and abbesses.[30]

In spite of this, Aelfric, just like Aldhelm, applies 'the three states which bear witness of Christ: that is maidenhood, and widowhood,

---

29 He dedicated his enigmas to the king (*Epistola ad Acircium*). We can gather from the prologue to the letter that Aldhelm and Ealdfrith were godfather and godson.
30 Aelfric, *Life of St Aethelwold*, D. Whitelock, ed. + trans., *English Historical Documents*, vol. 1, c. 500–1042, no.235.

and lawful matrimony'[31] to mankind as a whole in his *Catholic Homilies*. John the Baptist serves as the example for virginity, Anna stands for all widows while Zacharias is the married man *par excellence*. Aelfric, always anxious to explain issues in ways which his audience will most readily understand, elaborates upon these three states by using the traditional references to the parable of the sower which he clarifies by adding concrete, dailylife details:

> These three states are agreeable to God, if men righteously live in them. Maidenhood is both in men and women. Those have right maidenhood who from childhood continue in chastity, and despise in themselves all lust, both of body and mind, through God's succour. Then shall they have from God a hundredfold meed in the everlasting life. Widows are those who, after the death of their consorts, live in chastity for love of God: they shall have a sixtyfold meed from God for their tribulation. Those who rightly hold their marriage vow, and at permitted times, and for procreation of children, have carnal intercourse, shall have a thirtyfold meed for their discretion.[32]

The original Old English words used by Aelfric are interesting to analyze. Though the homilist insists that 'maidenhood is both in men and women', he only has at his disposal the gender exclusive term *mægð-had* which reflects the widely shared conviction that virginity (a word that came into English around 1300) only concerns women. This is why Aelfric makes his point of view clear each time he broaches the question: 'they who continue in pure virginity, for the joy of everlasting life, bring forth fruit an hundredfold. This degree belongs chiefly to God's servants, *male and female*, those who from childhood ever chastly live in the service of God'.[33] It is also obvious that Aelfric considers that widowhood (*wudewan-had*) concerns both women and men. Because there was no such word as *widower*, he mentions 'widows' (*widewan*) but, interestingly enough, speaks of 'the death of their consorts' selecting the term *gemacan*, which can be used both for a husband or a wife, and not the words *wer, ceorl* which

---

31   *The Homilies of the Anglo-Saxon Church. The First Part, Containing the Sermones Catholici or Homilies of Aelfric. In the Original Anglo-Saxon, with an English Version.* B. Thorpe, ed. + trans., vol. I, p.361.
32   Ibid., p.149.
33   Ibid., vol. II, p.95.

he always employs when he explicitly refers to a husband, therefore a male human being.[34] One of his other homilies goes even further. Dealing once again with the parable of the sower, Aelfric refers to 'men' when mentioning widowhood:

> The other evangelist wrote, that some part of the seed which sprang up on the good land yielded fruit thirtyfold, some sixtyfold, some an hundredfold. *Augustinus Magnus sic docet*: believing laymen, who live in lawful wedlock, yield thirtyfold fruit of good works, if they keep their marriage according to the written institutes, that is, that they cohabit for the procreation of children at permitted times, and abstain from a pregnant and month-sick woman; and when they can no longer procreate, cease from cohabitation. There are, nevertheless, many more of those who will live according to their own lusts, than of those who keep this precept. This is the rule for laymen, according to the written institute; let him who breaks it make atonement as his confessor shall teach him. They who chastly, for love of God, continue in widowhood, yield fruit sixtyfold. It is very unfitting and shameful that worn-out and impotent men desire marriage, while marriage is ordained for nothing but the procreation of children. They who continue in pure virginity, for the joy of everlasting life, bring forth fruit an hundredforth. This degree belongs chiefly to God's servants, male and female, those who from childhood ever chastly live in the service of God.[35]

Aelfric's open-mindedness is all the more remarkable as he is writing in a long-established tradition which unambiguously applied to women only. The author of 13th-century *Hali Meiðhad*, which is yet another treatise on virginity, addresses a female audience and considers *meiðhad* as a way of life for Christian women exclusively: 'Listen, daughter, and behold, and incline your ear; and forget your people and your father's house'. The tract gives a gruesome picture of the pains of marriage for women, denouncing 'carnal filthiness and a

---

34 'þa com þær sum wuduwe, seo wæs Anna gehaten. Seo leofode mid hire were seofon gear' [then came a widow, who was called Anna. She had lived with her husband seven years], Ibid., vol. I, pp.146–147. 'Eal seo gelaðung, ðe stent on mædenum and on cnapum, on ceorlum and on wifum…' [all the church, which consists in maidens and in youths, in husbands and in wives…], Ibid., vol. I, pp.566–567.
35 Ibid., vol. II, pp.93–95.

husband's embrace', or the miseries of motherhood.[36] One must pay tribute to Aelfric who, though heavily drawing on the works of the Church Fathers, managed to get rid of their misogyny by including the whole of the human race – and this in spite of the lack of the appropriate vocabulary. Aelfric's texts are amazingly modern.

The treatises we have been going through all present an idealized view of what women should do. Widows are expected to conform to an ideal of chastity, modesty and patience for proper behaviour on earth ensures a place in heaven among the redeemed. These sources, therefore, are above all normative: they define a model, an aim, an ideal totally divorced from real life.

Putting the Church's Precepts into Practice

Canon Law versus Germanic Customs

The Anglo-Saxon Chronicle ('edited' for the first time in 891) as well as Bede's *Ecclesiastical History of the English People* (completed in 731) enable us to catch a glimpse of a few Anglo-Saxon women, and among them a certain number of widows. As already made clear, the ladies mentioned by Bede are all of royal blood – queens or princesses[37] – or are abbesses who had become nuns at a very early age or after the death of their husband. One does not expect to find in Bede's *History* many stories about women or marriage/remarriage: Bede was a monk and a priest, he was in favour of the celibacy and chastity of clerics in major orders. His sources and informants, all mentioned in his preface, were ecclesiastics who shared this point of view: Albinus

---

36 B. Millett & J. Wogan-Browne, eds., *Medieval English Prose for Women, Selections from the Katherine Group and Ancrene Wisse*, Oxford: Clarendon Press, 1990–1992, p.3.

37 The term 'princess' only came into the English language in the fourteenth century. For very long, it was not an official title of the nobility. The daughters of Anglo-Saxon kings are simply referred to by their names.

(† 732), Abbot of the monastery of St Peter and St Paul in Canterbury, Nothelm († 736), who became Archbishop of Canterbury in 735, Cyneberht, bishop of the kingdom of Lindsey at the time Bede was writing, Daniel, made bishop of Winchester in 705 and who corresponded with Boniface, the monks of Lastingham[38] and those of Lindisfarne. All these men were devoted to Roman christianity and stood up for it. And yet the institution of marriage holds an important place in Bede's book. The evangelization of the Anglo-Saxons was recent, it dated back to Saint Augustine's mission to Kent in 597, for the south of England and, for the north, to the arrival of Irish monks on the island of Iona in 563. The Church was confronted by Germanic customs which contradicted its teaching.

The Anglo-Saxon Chronicle specifies that to wed the widow of one's father (of course this implies a second wife) was a widespread habit among pagan Germanic kings: the object of this practice was to provide the dynasties with greater continuity and to limit rivalries between families:

> 616: In this year Aethelberht, king of Kent, passed away; he reigned fifty-six years. After him his son Eadbald succeeded to the kingdom, who abandoned christianity and followed heathen custom, having his father's widow to wife.[39]

Bede provides us with more details and explains why it was prohibited to marry one's step-mother. Aethelberht was the first king of Kent to become a convert to Christianity following Augustine's mission in 597. Augustine had brought with him the sexual restrictions imposed by the Latin Church Fathers. The Gospels report the words uttered by Adam under divine inspiration (*Genesis*, chapter 2:24): 'Have ye not read, that he who made man from the beginning, Made them male and female? And he said: 'For this cause shall a man leave father and mother, and shall cleave to his wife, and they two shall be in one

---

38 A monastery near Whitby referred to in Bede's *History*, III 23.
39 Moses' law was also concerned with ensuring descendants to the deceased: 'Teacher, Moses laid it down for us that if there are brothers, and one dies leaving a wife but no child, then the next should marry the widow and provide an heir for his brother' (Luke, 20:28), *The Revised English Bible*, Oxford University Press, Cambridge University Press, 1989.

flesh. Therefore now they are not two, but one flesh. What therefore God hath joined together, let no man put asunder' (Matthew, 19:4–6). Saint Paul is horrified when referring to a case of immorality, an outrage against decency taking place among the Christian community of Corinth:

> It is absolutely heard that there is fornication among you and such fornication as the like is not among the heathens: that one should have his father's wife. And you are puffed up and have not rather mourned: that he might be taken away from among you that hath done this thing. I indeed, absent in body but present in spirit, have already judged, as though I were present, him that hath so done. In the name of our Lord Jesus Christ, you being gathered together and my spirit, with the power of our Lord Jesus: to deliver such a one to Satan for the destruction of the flesh, that the spirit may be saved in the day of our Lord Jesus Christ. (I, Cor. 5:1–5)

We have already mentioned that Bede reproduced the questions sent to Pope Gregory I by Augustine. Amidst the nine questions, the fifth one concerns marriage: 'Is it lawful for a man to marry his step-mother or sister-in-law?' The pope replied:

> To wed one's step-mother is a grave sin, for the Law says: 'Thou shalt not uncover the nakedness of thy father'.[40] Now the son cannot uncover the nakedness of his father; but since it says, *'They shall be one flesh'*, whosoever presumes to wed his step-mother, who has one flesh with his father, thereby commits this offence. (*Hist. Eccl.* I, 27)

In other words, the Church likened such marriages to incest which explains Bede's strong reaction: 'The death of Aethelberht and the accession of his son Eadbald proved to be a severe setback to the growth of the young Church; for not only did he refuse to accept the Faith of Christ, but he was also guilty of such fornication as the Apostle Paul mentions as being unheard of even among the heathen, in that he took his father's wife as his own. His immorality was an

---

[40] 'No man may approach a blood relation for intercourse. I am the Lord. You must not bring shame on your father by intercourse with your mother: she is your mother; do not bring shame on her. You must not have intercourse with a wife of your father: that is to bring shame upon your father...' (*Leviticus*, 18:6–8)

incentive to those who, either out of fear or favour to the king his father, had submitted to the discipline of faith and chastity, to revert to their former uncleanness. However, this apostate king did not escape the scourge of God's punishment; for he was subject to frequent fits of insanity and possessed by an evil spirit' (*Hist. Eccl.* II, 5). Eadbald was eventually compelled to repudiate his step-mother, and first wife,[41] after his conversion to christianity:

> He renounced his idolatry, gave up his unlawful wife, accepted the Christian Faith, and was baptized, henceforward promoting the welfare of the Church with every means at his disposal. (*Hist. Eccl.* II, 6)

Eadbald was forced to abide by the new rules but the Church had much difficulty forbidding marriages of this kind. As Pope Gregory had written to Augustine, 'there are many among the English who, while they were still heathen, are said to have contracted these unlawful marriages' (*Hist. Eccl.* I, 27).

Less than a century later, one of Augustine's successors to the archbishopric of Canterbury was Theodore of Tarsus. According to Bede, he summoned the first general council of the English church in 673 at Hertford and asked the assembled bishops to pay particular attention to ten canons laid down by the fathers in ancient times. All but one of these canons concern administration and discipline within the church. Chapter ten deals with divorce which is rejected: marriage is indissoluble, 'no man may leave his lawful wife except, as the gospel provides, for fornication' (*Hist. Eccl.* IV, 5). Nothing is said about widowhood. The penitential attributed to Theodore is a collection of his rulings made by his disciples; it is presented as answers made by the archbishop to a certain Eoda, not as a direct work. It shows that Theodore had still to deal a lot with heathen practices. It also attaches much importance to moral offences and to family relationships: marriage, divorce, and remarriage are points often alluded to. Here too, Theodore makes a certain number of concessions, permitting remarriage to penitent adulteresses, to those separated by captivity, or to men rejected by their wives after five years. He was

---

41   According to a later tradition Eadbald's second wife was a Christian princess of the Franks called Ymma.

clearly grappling with reality. Book II, chapter 12, article 10 treats of widowers and widows:

> When his wife is dead, a man may take another wife after a month. If her husband is dead, the woman may take another husband after a year.

The difference between one month and twelve months shows that a double standard was applied. Yet, as this period of twelve months for women is also to be found in several Anglo-Saxon law codes, one can gather that the main reason for such a clause was not morality but simply to be certain of the paternity of a child born after the death of the husband. Moreover, the penitential limits to two the number of marriages a woman may lawfully contract.

Theodore's penitential became very influential in England as well as on the continent. Together with Gregory the Great's replies to Augustine or the Council of Hertford, it shows that the church was trying to impose its view on all aspects of society. As already noted, the process was a particularly long one. A century and a half after Aethelberht's reign, Aethelbald (King Alfred's brother) succeeded his father Aethelwulf to the throne in 858. The same year he married his step-mother Judith, the daughter of the Frankish king Charles the Bald. King Alfred's tutor and biographer, the Welsh Asser, proclaims his indignation in his *Life of King Alfred*:

> Once King Aethelwulf was dead, Aethelbald, his son, against God's prohibition and Christian dignity, and also contrary to the practice of all pagans, took over his father's marriage-bed and married Judith, daughter of Charles [the Bald], king of the Franks, incurring great disgrace from all who heard of it; and he controlled the government of the kingdom of the West Saxons for two and a half lawless years after his father. (§ 17)[42]

Judith had an eventful life. King Aethelwulf, accompanied by his son Alfred (who was then only six years old), went to Rome in 855–6. Hincmar (c. 806–882), Archbishop of Rheims, kept annals known as *Annals of St Bertin* (*Annales Bertiniani*) from 861 to his death in 882. Thanks to his book we know that on their way to Rome, Aethelwulf

---

42   S. Keynes & M. Lapidge, eds., *Alfred the Great, Asser's Life of King Alfred and Other Contemporary Sources*, Harmondsworth: Penguin Books, 1983, p.73.

and Alfred went through the kingdom of Charles the Bald, that they were received at the Frankish court and 'escorted right to the boundary of the realm with all the courtesies due to a king'.[43] Aethelwulf was a widower: his first wife, Osburh, had died recently. On his way back from Rome 'Aethelwulf, king of the Western English, was betrothed to King Charles's daughter Judith. On 1 October, in the palace of Verberie, he received her in marriage'.[44] The marriage was a political one: the king of the West Franks was the most obvious ally against the enemy threatening from the north.[45] Judith was then fifteen years old. King Aethelwulf lived two years after he returned from Rome and Judith was a widow at the age of seventeen. She did not wait the recommended twelve months to remarry and wedded her late husband's son, Aethelbald, who died two years later in 860. Judith was a widow for the second time. She was only nineteen. She returned to her father and 'was being kept at Senlis under his protection and royal and episcopal guardianship, with all the honour due to a queen, until such time as, if she could not remain chaste, she might marry in the way the apostle said, that is suitably and legally'.[46] Apparently she could not 'remain chaste' long for, in 862, she was abducted by Baldwin Iron-Arm, the administrator of the *pagus Flandrensis* (the region around Bruges) who saw in Judith a good means of social advancement. According to Hincmar's *Annals of St Bertin*, Charles the Bald was furious, he summoned the great laymen and clerics of his kingdom and asked the bishops to excommunicate the two guilty ones. As the couple had found refuge at the court of Lothair II[47] (c. 835–869), he invited the king of Lotharingia to hand them over to him. After the intercession of Pope Nicholas I (858–867), he eventually acknowledged his daughter's marriage which was publicly celebrated:

---

43   J.L. Nelson, ed., *The Annals of St-Bertin*, Manchester: University Press, 1991, p.80.
44   Ibid., p.83.
45   In 856, Charles the Bald had to face a Norman attack of unprecedented strength. The raiders took control of the lower Seine valley.
46   J.L. Nelson, ed., *The Annals of St-Bertin*, p.97.
47   Lothair had some very serious problems with the church because of his own matrimonial life. Hincmar strongly criticized the king in his *De divortio Lotharii regis* (860).

in 863, 'Charles held a synod in the palace of Verberie on 25 October. In reponse to an appeal from the pope, he received his daughter Judith back into his good graces'.[48] Baldwin achieved his aim for he gained lands and high offices; Charles the Bald established him as Count of Flanders with control over a number of coastal territories between the North sea and the Scheldt. Judith and Baldwin's son, Baldwin II, married Alfred the Great's daughter Aelfthryth.[49]

In addition to this first break with past practices, there was also the question of degrees of relationship. St Boniface was born in England, near Exeter, in about 673. When he was about thirty years old, he was ordained priest. In 718 he went to Rome and was received by pope Gregory II who dispatched him to Germany. From 719 till his death in 754, Boniface was a missionary in Hesse and Thuringia, then over the whole of Germany and Neustria. He baptized thousands of people, founded churches and monasteries – calling nuns and monks from England – and organized the Frankish church. He often wrote to the popes in Rome or to English bishops for guidance. One of his recurrent concerns was to be given a precise answer concerning prohibited degrees of marriage. In a letter dated November 22nd 726, Pope Gregory II gave Boniface his instructions:

> You ask first within what degrees of relationship marriage may take place. We reply: strictly speaking, in so far as the parties know themselves to be related they ought not to be joined together. But since moderation is better than strictness of discipline, especially toward so uncivilized a people, they may contract marriage after the fourth degree.[50]

Pope Gregory III went back over the matter in 732, stating:

---

48 J.L. Nelson, ed., *The Annals of St-Bertin*, p.110.
49 In the prologue to his chronicle, Aethelweard alludes to this union when telling his cousin Matilda that 'Aelfred sent his daughter Aelfthryth to the land of Germany to marry Baldwin, who had by her two sons, Aethelwulf and Earnwulf, and also two daughters, Ealhswith and Eormenthryth. From Aelfthryth, as a matter of fact, Count Earnwulf, who is your neighbour, is descended'. A. Campbell, ed., *The Chronicle of Aethelweard*, London: Nelson's Medieval Texts, 1962, p.2.
50 E. Emerton, ed., *The Letters of St Boniface*, no.XVIII, p.31.

> We decree, that [in contracting marriage] every one shall observe the rules of relationship even to the seventh degree.
>
> In so far as you are able, prevent a man who has lost his wife from marrying again in the future more than once.[51]

Knowing now where to stand, Boniface was in great doubt about what a man he knew maintained:

> I have further to seek the advice of your Paternity[52] in regard to a certain perplexing and scandalous report which has come to us recently and has greatly disturbed us, filling with confusion the priests of our churches. A certain layman of high station came to us recently and said that Gregory of sainted memory, pontiff of the Apostolic See, had granted him permission to marry the widow of his uncle. She had formerly been the wife of her own cousin but had left him during his lifetime. She is known to be related in the third degree to the man who now desires her and who declares that permission was granted him. (...)
>
> The aforesaid man declares that he has a license from the Apostolic See for such a marriage as this! But we do not believe this to be true; for a synod of the church of the Saxons beyond the sea, in which I was born and reared, namely the synod of London, convoked and directed by disciples of St Gregory, the archbishops – Augustine, Laurentius, Justus, and Miletus – declared such a marriage union, on the authority of Holy Scripture, to be heinous crime, an incestuous and horrible offense, and a damnable sin.[53]

Pope Zacharias' reply was unequivocal:

> As to the man who wishes to marry his uncle's widow (...) and has spread abroad the story that our predecessor of blessed memory granted him license to take her in this scandalous marriage – God forbid that our predecessor should have ordered such a thing! The Apostolic See never orders anything contrary to the prescriptions of the fathers or of the canons. Cease not, beloved brother, to warn them, exhort them, and urge upon them to refrain from such an abominable union lest they perish eternally. Let them remember that they are redeemed by the blood of Christ and not deliver themselves of their own will into the power of the devil by this incestuous marriage.[54]

---

51   Ibid., no.XX, p.35.
52   Boniface is writing to Pope Zacharias (742).
53   E. Emerton, ed., *The Letters of St Boniface*, no.XL, p.59.
54   Ibid., no.XLI, p.64.

This letter, which reinforced Boniface's firm belief, probably put the evangelist's mind at ease. But another case was to puzzle and worry him for longer. It concerns another man wishing to marry another widow. Consanguinity was a clear impediment to marriage; on the other hand, it is obvious that Boniface had never heard or read that spiritual relationships could prevent a marriage from taking place. In very moving letters, he confesses 'a sin which [he has] committed by granting to a certain man the right to marry':

> The priests throughout Gaul and Frankland maintain that for them a man who takes to wife a widow, to whose child he has acted as godfather, is guilty of a very serious crime. As to the nature of this sin, if it is a sin, I was entirely ignorant.[55]

Boniface seems sincerely sorry, almost distressed. He regrets granting the man the right to marry: he committed an unwitting sin and the husband and wife are now an easy prey for 'the devil by this incestuous marriage'. What perturbs greatly Boniface is to know whether the priests in Gaul and Frankland are right or wrong because '[he has] never seen it mentioned by the fathers, in the ancient canons, nor in the decrees of popes, nor by the Apostles in their catalogue of sins'.[56] This is why he sent a letter to Bishop Pehthelm of Whithorn in Scotland and another one to Archbishop Nothelm of Canterbury in 735. He obviously could not understand the reason for such a prohibition: 'I cannot possibly understand how, on the one hand, spiritual relationship in the case of matrimonial intercourse can be so great a sin, while, on the other hand, it is well established that by holy baptism we all become sons and daughters, brothers and sisters of Christ and the Church'.[57] Unfortunately the replies of the two English authorities are lost. However it is well known that spiritual affinity nullified marriages in the Middle Ages.

---

55   Ibid., no.XXIII, p.39.
56   Ibid., no.XXIII, p.40.
57   Ibid., no.XXIV, p.41.

The Part played by Queens

Concerning the degree of independence and of influence women may have had, one must be well aware that the sources we are referring to, mainly Bede's *Ecclesiastical History* or *The Anglo-Saxon Chronicle*, can be used to affirm anything and everything, As they give information in dribs and drabs, leaving whole chapters of history unclear, it is very easy to overestimate minor details. Scholars who wish to emphasize the respected position of women in Anglo-Saxon society or, conversely, who want to stress their lack of rights and power, will both find passages to support their opinion. One must therefore be extremely cautious for it is difficult to draw conclusions. It seems, however, that the balance of evidences through the centuries was not in women's favour.

Bede underlines the fact that when Augustine landed in Kent, the king's wife, Queen Bertha, was already a Christian. This, of course, made Aethelberht's conversion to Christianity easier. As Bede was writing the history of how Christianity came to the English people, he attached much importance, and gave much place, to women who played a role in spreading the Christian faith around them: in his eyes, a Christian wife had to convert her heathen husband. This is why he dwells upon the life of Aethelburh, Aethelberht and Bertha's daughter, and her efforts to convince her husband King Edwin (II, 9–11 & II, 20) or that of Eanflæd who persuaded her husband King Oswiu (641–670) to found the monastery of Gilling to make reparation for the shameful murder of his co-king Oswine in 651 (III, 14 & 24).[58] This is also why he vehemently condemns the wife of King Rædwald († before 627) for she 'and certain perverse advisers persuaded him to apostatize from the true Faith. So his last state was worse than the first: for, like the ancient Samaritans, he tried to serve both Christ and the ancient gods, and he had in the same temple an altar for the holy sacrifice of Christ side by side with an altar on which victims were offered to devils' (*Hist. Eccl.* II, 15).[59]

---

58 Both accounts are alluded to in *The Anglo-Saxon Chronicle*.
59 The treasure-laden burial ship found under a grave mound at Sutton Hoo (Suffolk) was probably Rædwald's. It contained many pagan funeral goods, a

Bede was not interested in the political influence of queens. He mentions in passing that the Northumbrian queen Bebbe gave her name to the royal city Bamburgh (*Hist. Eccl.* III, 6 & III, 16). According to Nennius' *Historia Brittonum*, Bebbe was the first wife of King Aethelfrith (592–616), the second one being Acha, the mother of St Oswald. Nothing beyond her name is known of Bebbe. He also refers, for a second time, to Rædwald's wife – still without giving her name. The lady seems to have had a strong personality and to have been particularly convincing for, when her husband was about to surrender Edwin, who had taken refuge at his court,

> she dissuaded him, saying that it was unworthy in a great king to sell his best friend in the hour of need for gold, and worse still to sacrifice his royal honour, the most valuable of all possessions, for love of money. In brief, the king did as she advised, and not only refused to surrender the exiled prince to the envoys of his enemy but assisted him to recover his kingdom. (*Hist. Eccl.* II, 12)

For a better historical picture of the role of queens, one must turn to archaeology or consult chronicles. Coins[60] have been found struck in the name, and with the portrait, of Cynethryth, wife of Offa, King of the Mercians (757–96). Cynethryth is the only English queen consort to have issued coins in her own name. For all that, *The Anglo-Saxon Chronicle* does not even hint at her: young Eadburh is referred to, in all the manuscripts, as 'the daughter of King Offa' (789) and nothing is said of the mother – whether she was Cynethryth or not. Old English chronicles overwhelmingly refer to men: the tenth-century *Chronicle of Aethelweard* mentions 12 women versus 231 men (0.05%) and *The Anglo-Saxon Chronicle* 45 versus 1092 (0.04%)![61] In spite of that, the political influence of queens, even when widows, is visible at times. However their power appears more conspicuously

---

hanging bowl which carried fittings of Celtic workmanship as well as bowls and spoons (which are inscribed 'Saulos' and 'Paulos' and may have been baptismal gifts) of Byzantine production. Rædwald's syncretism never ended.

60   The 1991 exhibition 'The Making of England. Anglo-Saxon Art and Culture AD 600–900' organised jointly by the British Library and British Museum displayed one of these coins (found at Eastbourne, Sussex). See the catalogue of the exhibition edited by Leslie Webster and Janet Backhouse, p.249.

61   Only identifiable (= named) women and men have been taken into account.

in the 7th and 8th centuries than in later centuries. In those remote times, women already signed royal charters as witnesses. The early history of the monastery of Peterborough is particularly interesting in this respect. In 656, King Wulfhere of Mercia, after taking 'the advice of his brothers, Aethelred and Merwala, and the advice of his sisters, Cyneburh and Cyneswith',[62] decided to have the monastery completed. On the day of the consecration of the monastery, the king bestowed on it gifts of land and liberties. The charter was put in writing and the king declared:

> I ask you, brother Aethelred, and my sisters Cyneburh and Cyneswith, for your souls' salvation, to be witnesses and to write it with your finger.[63]

The two sisters' signatures (a cross, as for all the other witnesses) come in seventh position, just after those of several kings but before that of the Archbishop of Canterbury, and those of all the bishops and ealdormen. Nineteen years later, in 675, King Aethelred confirmed his brother's charter and the document was signed by many witnesses including the king's wife, 'Osthryth, Aethelred's queen'. When, in 963, King Edgar had the monastery rebuilt (it had been destroyed by the Danes), only men signed the new document: King Edgar, Archbishop Dunstan of Canterbury, Archbishop Oswald of York, bishops, abbots, ealdormen 'and many other prominent men'.[64] To be honest, one must remember that King Edgar was not married at the time: he wedded Aelfthryth two years later in 965.

The Anglo-Saxon Chronicle stresses the military role of certain queens. In 722, Aethelburh, Ine's wife, 'destroyed Taunton, which Ine had built'.[65] The most remarkable female warrior was, indisputably, King Alfred's daughter, Aethelflæd, who fought against the Danes by

---

62 G.N. Garmonsway, ed., *The Anglo-Saxon Chronicle*, London, Melbourne: Dent, 1953 [new edition 1972], 656, p.29.
63 Ibid.
64 Ibid., 675, p.37
65 Ibid., 722, p.43. After the conquest, Earl Ralph of Norfolk and Suffolk plotted against King William. The rebellion was a failure and the Earl fled by boat. 'His wife remained behind in the castle, which she held until [the inhabitants of the country] made terms with her, whereupon she left England with all her followers who wished to accompany her' (1076, p.211).

her husband's side and went on as a widow for many years till 918, when she died 'twelve days before midsummer at Tamworth, and in the eighth year of her rule over Mercia, as its rightful lord'.[66] Only a masculine term is available to refer to institutionalized power: no other word exists therefore Aethelflæd, though known as 'the Lady of the Mercians', becomes a 'lord'[67] where social structure is concerned. Society does not completely reject women from power and authority but vocabulary shows that this must remain an exception. Aethelflæd was not the only widow to be in power. In 672, King Cenwalh of Wessex died and 'Seaxburh, his queen, reigned one year after him'.[68] The question which must be considered is: did these women impose themselves because of their very strong personality or did their status as widows impose them? The first hypothesis is likely to be the right one because there were any number of kings' widows throughout these centuries and only a very few of them seem to have played a role on the political scene. The fact that these women were widows probably did not impose them on their people but more likely justified, legitimized their rule. These women, however, did not succeed in handing down their power to their daughters: King Aethelred evoked the strictly masculine system of succession to the throne when he enjoined his 'successors, be they [his] sons, be they [his] brothers, or kings that shall succeed [him], that [his] benefaction may stand'[69] and in 919, 'the daughter of Aethelred, lord of the Mercians, was deprived

66   Ibid., 918, p.105.
67   Before her husband's death, Aethelflæd shared power with her husband. This is why 'bishop Werfrith and the community at Worcester give and grant by charter to Aethelred and Aethelflæd, their lords, the messuage within the town wall.' In A.J. Robertson, ed. + trans., *Anglo-Saxon Charters*, Cambridge University Press, 1939, p.37. Several women in *Domesday Book* are called *homo*. F.E. Harmer mentions 'Aelueua (= Aelfgifu) homo Aschil' [*Domesday Book*, i, 212], 'Godid (= Godgyth) homo Asgari' [*Domesday Book*, i, 137, 137b, 139b, 140), 'Wluuen (= Wulfwynn) homo regis E'. [*Domesday Book*, i, 150b]. Similarly, between 1058 and 1066, King Edward gave leave to 'Tole min mann Urkes lafe' [(his) man Tole, Urk's widow], to bequeath her land and possessions to the monastery at Abbotsbury'. See F.E. Harmer, ed. + trans., *Anglo-Saxon Writs*, Manchester University Press, 1952, p.121.
68   G.N. Garsmonsway, ed., *The Anglo-Saxon Chronicle*, 672, p.35.
69   Ibid., 656, p.31.

of all authority in Mercia: she was taken to Wessex three weeks before Christmas. Her name was Aelfwynn'.[70] She was therefore put out of action eighteen months after her mother's death.

After the 9th century, the queens (of Wessex) remain in the background of all sources; they are rarely mentioned. Asser tells us that even at the time of Alfred's father, King Aethelwulf had:

> ordered that Judith, the daughter of King Charles whom he had received from her father, should sit beside him on the royal throne until the end of his life, though this was contrary to the (wrongful) custom of that people. For the West Saxons did not allow the queen to sit beside the king, nor indeed did they allow her to be called 'queen', but rather king's wife.[71]

The Anglo-Saxon Chronicle and 8th-century charters confirm Asser's account: we occasionally meet in the witness lists of charters, women who are referred to as *regina*. In the *Chronicle*, we are told about Aethelburh, Ine's *cwen*, or about *cwen* Frithugyth travelling to Rome. But when we reach the 9th-century, and Wessex, we find no references to the kings' wives – let alone their widows. There is no allusion to King Alfred's wife in his charters, only her death is recorded in the *Chronicle* (904). Here too, we have to turn to Asser to obtain a few (very few) elements and none concerns any political involvement on the part of the queen:

> In the year of the Lord's Incarnation 868 (the twentieth of King Alfred's life), the same much-esteemed King Alfred, at that time accorded the status of 'heir apparent', was betrothed to and married a wife from Mercia, of noble family, namely the daughter of Aethelred (who was known as Mucil), ealdorman of the Gaini. The woman's mother was called Eadburh, from the royal stock of the king of the Mercians. I often saw her myself with my very own eyes for several years before her death. She was a notable woman who remained for many years after the death of her husband a chaste widow, until her death.[72]

Asser stresses the fact that Alfred's marriage reinforced the political alliance between Mercia and Wessex. He does not even give the name

---

70   Ibid., 919, p.105.
71   S. Keynes & M. Lapidge, eds., *Alfred the Great, Asser's Life of King Alfred and Other Contemporary Sources*, § 13, p.71.
72   Ibid., § 29, p.77.

of the bride (Ealhswith), only speaking of 'a wife from Mercia'! He insists on the right, that is to say, useful and noble pedigree of the young woman and, more interestingly for us, refers to Ealhswith's mother's last years when he used to meet her often. Asser, who was Bishop of Sherborne, appreciated her because she conformed to the Church's model of the patient, temperate and chaste widow.

The documents, consequently, support the view that the West Saxon queens were kept in the background. It is true that, from the 9th century onwards, the *Anglo-Saxon Chronicle* becomes mostly concerned with the movements and attacks of the Vikings and the resistance of the English. Apart from Aethelflæd, women have no place, play no part in these military activities and therefore are not made mention of. It is only after the second half of the 10th century that things seem to have improved: queens reappear in charters and other documents though still called 'the king's wife'. In the documents edited and translated by A.J. Robertson,[73] one finds an agreement made between the Bishop of Wells and the Abbot of Abingdon in 958 with King Eadwig's permission. 'Aelfgifu þæs cininges wif & Aeþelgifu þæs cyninges wifes modur' [Aelfgifu, the king's wife and Aethelgifu the king's wife's mother][74] come first in the list of witnesses. When Eadwig's successor, King Edgar, confirmed 'the freedom of Taunton for the episcopal see of the Holy Trinity and St Peter and St Paul at Winchester' Bishop Aethelwulf thanked the royal couple by giving gold and silver to the king and 'Aelfþryde his gebeddan' [Aelfthryth, his wife] was offered '50 mancuses of gold, in return for her help in his just mission'. Aelfthryth signed this renewal of freedom 'Ego Aelfþryþ regina' in the twentieth position after the king, the archbishops, the bishops, and the abbots but before all the other laymen. In his will, Ealdorman Aelfheah gave the same Aelfthryth ('ðæs cyninges wifæ' [the king's wife]) his estate at Shirburn. The queen happens to be cited first in the witness list.[75]

---

73   A.J. Robertson, ed., *Anglo-Saxon Charters*, pp.58–59.
74   Ibid., pp.58–59.
75   D. Whitelock, ed., *Anglo-Saxon Wills*, Cambridge University Press, 1930, pp. 22–25.

Then comes to the forefront an outstanding woman, Emma (Aelfgifu) who first married King Aethelred (1002) and then King Cnut (1016). The consort of the king of Wessex (and afterwards of England) was often called 'Lady': King Edward's third wife is 'the Lady Eadgifu' in the will of Brihtric and his wife Aelfswith. Though in her will, Mantat the anchorite greets 'Cnut cing & Emma hlæfdie' [King Cnut and Lady Emma], Emma became known as '*seo* hlæfdige' [*the* Lady]. In *The Anglo-Saxon Chronicle*, the term is used as soon as she is introduced: '1002: In the same spring the Lady, Richard's daughter, came hither to this country'. Remarkably enough she kept this title even after her second husband's death. Several charters have been kept in which she appears positioned immediately after the king ('the witnesses of this are King Edward and the Lady Aelfgifu'):[76] she was a particularly influential and ambitious woman, queen and widow. *The Anglo-Saxon Chronicle* also went on calling her 'the Lady' till her death in 1052. The manuscripts, however, vary slightly; the Worcester Chronicle records that:

> In this year on 6 March passed away Aelfgifu, the Lady: she was the widow of King Aethelred and King Cnut.

The Peterborough chronicle connects her to her sons. She is 'Aelfgifu Emma, the mother of King Edward and of King Harthacnut'; the Abingdon chronicle gives the wrong date but more details and the title 'Lady-dowager' is used for the first time:

> In this same year on 14 March passed away the Lady-dowager, the mother of King Edward and of Harthacnut: she is called Emma. Her body lies in the Old Minster beside King Cnut.

Edith was the last pre-Conquest queen and the first whose consecration[77] is recorded in *The Anglo-Saxon Chronicle*: in 1051, after

---

76   A.J. Robertson, ed., *Anglo-Saxon Charters*, no.CI, pp.188–189. See also D. Whitelock, ed., *Anglo-Saxon Wills*, no.XXX, pp.78–79.

77   King Henry I's wife, Matilda, is the second queen whose consecration is reported: 'At Martinmas she was given to him in marriage at Westminster with great ceremony, and archbishop Anselm wedded her to him and afterwards consecrated her queen'.

Earl Godwine tried to bully King Edward and gathered an army against him, Edward refused to yield to the Earl's demands, and eventually sent the Godwine family into exile. 'The king forsook the Lady [Godwine's daughter], who had been consecrated his queen, and had her deprived of all that she owned in land, and in gold, and in silver, and of everything, and committed her to his sister [the abbess] at Wherwell'. Edith held a less visible place at court than her mother-in-law, the Lady. However, she regularly signed royal diplomas such as, for instance, arrangements made between Bishop Wulfwig and an Earl Leofric and his wife Godgifu and 'this was done with King Edward's full consent and with his cognisance and that of "Eadgyđe his gebeddan" [his wife Edith]'.[78] The queen is mentioned before the archbishops, bishops, abbots, earls, etc. In another charter she is called 'Lady Edith' and is positioned just after her husband.[79] After 1066, Edith joined the convent at Wilton (near Salisbury). At her death, William the Conqueror was careful to pay her a large tribute: her funeral was part of his concern to prove his right to the English throne by stressing the continuity in the royal line:

> 1075: Edith, the Lady-dowager, passed away at Winchester, seven days before Christmas, and the king had her body brought to Westminster with great ceremony, and buried her beside King Edward, her lord.

This brief survey of the status of the Anglo-Saxon queens raises more questions than it answers about these women's precise position. Our knowledge is slight and rests upon a small number of documents that never depict a queen in details, never describe what these women looked like (physically speaking), never give us an illuminating insight into their psychologies. Yet, one can assert that, throughout Anglo-Saxon history, a great lady could take part in public affairs. It seems it was mostly a question of character. Concerning widows, the harvest is even poorer. Basing our judgement on the example of two widowed queens, we have seen that the early Anglo-Saxons did not seem to have anything against a woman's government. But, on the whole, widowhood was far more a reason for retirement. And if the

---

78   A.J. Robertson, ed., *Anglo-Saxon Charters*, no.CXV, pp.213–215.
79   Ibid., no.CXVII, pp.217–219.

Lady Aelfgifu remained in power beside her son Edward, she had to disappear from the political scene once the king married Edith in 1045: the Lady could play a role but the Lady-dowager could not. The obvious place of retirement for a widow was a monastery. We are better documented on monastic women[80] and the foundation of Anglo-Saxon monasteries and it has long been noted that widows were numerous to take the veil.

Widows as Abbesses

We have seen that Bede mentions several instances of Christian princesses who, when married to pagan kings succeeded in converting their husbands and their peoples to Christianity. During the same period, monasteries were founded in England and conventual life appealed to a great number of princesses and queens. Many royal widows became abbesses. Monasteries were not founded as retreats from the world but as a means of spreading the Christian faith to all parts of the various kingdoms, of establishing centres of educational, political and social significance. They were places of learning and provided the essential pastoral care for the rural population in their vicinity. The aristocratic spread of Christianity is very pronounced in Bede's *Historia Ecclesiastica* and monasteries are presented as beacons of both royal and divine power. They were, indeed, places where the family traditions of their founders were preserved by choosing, as successive abbots or abbesses, descendants of the founder. Members of the founding family or other benefactors were usually buried in the monastery and the community took part in their salvation by praying and singing masses on their anniversaries. One must not be surprised, consequently, to find so many widows of royal descent among the foundresses and rulers of Anglo-Saxon monasteries.

---

80 See S. Hollis, *Anglo-Saxon Women and the Church – Sharing a Common Fate*, Woodbridge: the Boydell Press, 1992; L. Eckenstein, *Women under Monasticism: Chapters on Saint-lore and Convent Life between A.D. 500 and A.D. 1500*, New York: Russell and Russell, 1963.

The best-known episode concerns the foundation of the monastery of Ely in 673 with Aethelthryth (one of the daughters of Anna [† 654], king of the East Angles) as first abbess. Monasteries for women only appeared in England in the mid-7th century. Before, the English princesses went to monasteries in Gaul such as Faremoutiers, Chelles, Les Andelys 'for their education, or to be betrothed to their heavenly Bridegroom'.[81] Aethelthryth's half-sister, Sæthryth, and her sister, Aethelburh, became abbesses of Faremoutiers-en-Brie (Seine-et-Marne). Another sister, Wihtburh († 743), founded the monastery of East Dereham. The two remaining sisters were married: Seaxburh to Eorcenberht of Kent and, in about 652, Aethelthryth to Tondberht 'a prince of the South Gyrwas; but he died shortly after the wedding' (*Hist. Eccl.* IV 19). Aethelthryth was not a widow for long as, probably in 660, 'she was given to King Ecgfrith' who was her junior by about ten years.[82] Bede is one of our main sources as regards the life of Aethelthryth. She commanded his enthusiasm and he even appended a hymn in 54 lines celebrating her virginity (IV, 20). Indeed, 'though she lived with [Ecgfrith] for twelve years, she preserved the glory of perpetual virginity'.

At the Northumbrian court, Aethelthryth is said to have conceived a great admiration for the prelate Wilfrid, Bishop of York. 'The pious King Ecgfrith and Queen Aethelthryth were both obedient to Bishop Wilfrid in everything, and their reign was marked by fruitful years of peace and joy at home and victory over their enemies' so does Eddius Stephanus tell us in his *Life of Wilfrid*[83] and he also specifies that the queen gave Wilfrid a huge property at Hexham: 'At Hexham he built a church to the glory of God and the honour of St

---

81   Bede, *The Ecclesiastical History of the English People*, L. Sherley-Price, ed., III 8, p.154.
82   Aethelthryth was born around 636. Bede tells us that Ecgfrith died in 685 'on 20 May, in the fortieth year of his age and the fifteenth of his reign' (*Hist. Eccl.* IV, 26). He was therefore born in 645.
83   J.F. Webb & D.H. Farmer, eds., *The Age of Bede*, Harmondsworth: Penguin Books, 1965–1988. Eddius Stephanus: *Life of Wilfrid*, chapter 19, pp.125–126.

Andrew on land given by the saintly Queen Aethelthryth'.[84] But then Eddius Stephanus adds:

> While Ecgfrith was on good terms with the bishop, as many will tell you, he enlarged his kingdom by many victories; but when they [the king and the queen] quarrelled and the queen separated from him to give herself to God, the king's triumphs ceased, and that within his own lifetime.

Here Bede is more revealing than Eddius:

> Bishop Wilfrid said that Ecgfrith promised to give estates and much wealth to him if he could persuade the queen to consummate the marriage, knowing that there was no man for whom she had a higher regard. (...) For a long time Aethelthryth begged the king to allow her to retire from worldly affairs and serve Christ the only true King in a convent'. (*Hist. Eccl.* IV, 19)

In the same way as contemporaries of Bede questioned Aethelthryth's virginity ('certain people doubted it' *Hist. Eccl.* IV, 19), several historians have challenged the historical reliability of Bede's account. Stephanie Hollis[85] was the first to cast doubts on the veracity of the 'official' version. She argues that the marriage being childless 'Ecgfrith's reluctance to part with Aetheltryth is likely to have been seriously overstated' and that 'puzzling, too, is the prospect of a woman intent on maintaining perpetual virginity who contracted not one, but two marriages'. In accordance with what we underlined when dealing with 'canon law versus Germanic customs', she sees Aethelthryth as 'the representative emblem of the formerly married women who accounted for a significant number of female religious in the conversion period, a phenomenon made possible only by customary freedom of separation and the tenuousness of the ecclesiastical conception of marriage as an indissolubly binding union in which women were in the power of their husbands'. It is obvious that Bede was not in favour

---

84 Ibid., chapter 22, p.128. W. Bright, *Chapters of Early English Church History*, Oxford: Clarendon Press, 1878, p.235 & M. Roper, 'Wilfrid's Landholdings in Northumbria', D.P. Kirby, ed., *St Wilfrid at Hexham*, Newcastle, 1974, pp.72–73 & 169–71 argue that Aethelthryth had received the expensive property at Hexham from her husband.

85 S. Hollis, *Anglo-Saxon Women and the Church – Sharing a Common Fate*, pp.65–74.

of formerly married monastic women therefore 'in celebrating the perpetual virginity of a married woman who left her husband to found a monastery, Bede gives a mythic, idealizing form of expression to the preponderance of widows and formerly married women among the founders of female monasticism'. Christine Fell[86] distinguishes between Bede the historian describing Aethelthryth's secular life and Bede the hagiographer likening Aethelthryth to the virgin martyrs of the early church. Pauline Stafford[87] believes Aethelthryth's supposed virginity and her religious vocation were used as excuses by Ecgfrith in order to divorce a sterile wife. Pauline Thompson[88] takes the opposing view of these papers and argues that Bede may, after all, have said the truth and that the queen may have taken upon herself 'the challenge to translate the centrally important principles of sanctity – courage, suffering, and above all, virginity – out of a *literary* ideal (one drawn primarily from the Saints' Lives of the Roman tradition) into a lived one, a challenge which must have required not only profound conviction but considerable personal authority and political savvy'. I personally am inclined to favour Stephanie Hollis' hypothesis because Bede's disapproval of married women and widows entering monastic life is detectable through his glorification of dedicated virgins who 'deserve special mention' (*Hist Eccl.* III, 8). Bede gives as model Aethelburh, Aethelthryth's sister, who 'lived in a life of great self-denial, also preserving the glory of perpetual virginity which is well pleasing to God' (III, 8), or 'a nun named Begu who for thirty or more years had been dedicated to the Lord in virginity' (IV, 23) and emphasizes the fact that living in a monastery implies observing 'strictly the virtues of justice, devotion, and chastity' (IV, 23).

However that may be, Wilfrid supported the principle that a wife could leave her husband in order to retire to a religious settlement. We

---

86 C.E. Fell, 'Saint Aeðelþryð: a Historical Hagiographical Dichotomy Revisited', *Nottingham Medieval Studies* 38, (1994), pp.19–34.

87 P. Stafford, *Queens, Concubines and Dowagers: the King's Wife in the Early Middle Ages*, Athens: University of Georgia Press, 1983.

88 P. Thompson, 'St Aethelthryth: the Making of History from Hagiography', M.J. Toswell & E.M. Tyler, ed., *Studies in English Language and Literature, 'Doubt Wisely', Papers in honour of E.G. Stanley*, London & New York: Routledge, 1996, pp.475–492.

remember that in 673 Theodore, Archbishop of Canterbury, summoned a council of bishops at Hertford. Though Bede reports that 'Wilfrid, bishop of the Northumbrian race, was represented by his proctors' (*Eccl. Hist.* IV, 5), it goes without saying that Wilfrid must have known Theodore's position about marriage. As we have already seen, the council decided that 'if anyone puts away his own wife who is joined to him by lawful matrimony, he may not take another if he wishes to be a true Christian'. We have also seen that Theodore's Penitential allowed husband and wife to part if one of them wanted to join a monastery, though adding that it was not canonical. Yet in the case of 'a second marriage, this is not permitted while the husband or wife is alive'. In spite of such rulings, Aethelthryth left her husband:

> When at length and with difficulty she gained his [the king's] permission, she entered the monastery of the Abbess Aebbe, Ecgfrith's aunt, which is situated in a place called Coldingham, receiving the veil and habit of nun from Bishop Wilfrid. (*Eccl. Hist.* IV, 19)

The story does not end here and we learn that Aethelthryth spent a year's novitiate at Coldingham and then 'was herself appointed abbess in the district called Ely, where she built a monastery' (*Eccl. Hist.* IV, 19). *The Anglo-Saxon Chronicle* helps us to date the event:

> 673: In this year King Egbert, king of Kent, passed away. The same year there was a synod at Hertford, and St Aethelthryth founded the monastery at Ely.

Bede specifies that Aethelthryth 'wished to have her monastery here because, as has also been said, she sprang from the race of the East Angles'. The compiler of the twelfth-century *Liber Eliensis* explains that the former queen gave the whole Isle of Ely to the foundation and adds that it was a territory which she had received as a dower from her first husband.[89]

---

89   E.O. Blake, ed., *Liber Eliensis*, London, Offices of the Royal Historical Society, Camden Third Series, vol. no.XCII, 1962, I, 4.
The *Liber Eliensis* is not a reliable historical document even though the compiler seems to have drawn on an Old English life of St Aethelthryth. In his introduction, E.O. Blake mentions a 'Book of the Miracles of St Aethelthryth' written by Aelfhelm, a clerk at Ely in the mid-tenth century. In the same

King Ecgfrith remarried and the new queen, Iurminburh, was bitterly hostile to Wilfrid: 'She used all her eloquence to describe to Ecgfrith all St Wilfrid's temporal glories, listing his possessions, the number of his monasteries, the vastness of the buildings, his countless followers arrayed and armed like a king's retinue'.[90] In 677 Theodore divided Wilfrid's diocese into three sees and Wilfrid appealed to Rome. When Wilfrid came back from Rome, King Ecgfrith refused to obey Pope Agatho's injunctions. After years of conflict and exile, a compromise was reached at the synod of the River Nidd in 705 during which Abbess Aelffled bore testimony that King Ealdfrith (King Ecgfrith's and her own half-brother) had wished on his death bed for a reconciliation. Wilfrid was restored to the bishopric of the church at Hexham. Bede reports that Wilfrid 'on a certain occasion went to the monastery of nuns in a place called Wetadun (Watton), over which Abbess Hereburh was at that time presiding' (*Hist. Eccl.* V, 3). We then discover that Hereburh is one of these numerous widows who retired to monasteries for we are told that:

> 'After we had arrived', he said, 'and had been joyfully received by them all, the abbess told us that one of the nuns, who was her own daughter, was afflicted by a grievous illness'.

King Ecgfrith had been slain in a battle against the Picts in 685. Though Eddius Stephanus had underlined Iurminburh's dislike of Wilfrid, he was honest enough to note that once a widow, 'after the king was killed, she changed from a she-wolf into a lamb of God indeed, a perfect abbess and mother of her community'.[91] At that time Aethethryth had been dead for six years. She had been succeeded in the office of abbess by her sister Seaxburh, widow of King Eorcenberht of Kent who had 'put down all heathen practices in his realm,

century, Aelfric told the story of Aethelthryth in his *Lives of Saints*. The account in the *Old English Martyrology* and Aelfric's version are derived from Bede's narrative. At least two *Vitae* of the saint were composed (by Gregory of Ely) in the twelfth century in prose or in verse.
90   J.F. Webb & D.H. Farmer, eds., *The Age of Bede*. Eddius Stephanus, *Life of Wilfrid*, chapter 24.
91   Ibid., chapter 24.

and was the first of the English kings to enforce the observance of Lent'[92] and had died in 664. Seaxburh had founded and been the abbess of Minster-in-Sheppey. In 695, she had her sister's body exhumed; it was found incorrupt (an obvious sign of saintliness) and put in a rich coffin of white marble which was interred in the church. From that moment onwards, the sick could be cured by coming to Ely. Other female saints were to be connected to St Aethelthryth, all of them belonging to her close family: first Seaxburh, then Seaxburh's daughter Eormenhild, the widow of King Wulfhere of Mercia († 675) who became a nun and eventually the abbess of her mother's monastery at Sheppey before being the third abbess of Ely. She was the mother of St Werburh of Chester.

The story of the foundation of the monastery at Ely is well-known thanks to Bede's account, however partial it may be. Yet the same conclusions could be drawn from any monastery for they all played the same important religious, political and economic role. Many women, and among them a large proportion of widows, entered religious houses. Why did these widows join these communities? Did they all join as willingly as Aethelthryth? What sort of life did they lead once they had taken the veil? The number of Anglo-Saxon queens who founded and ruled monasteries is so great that one might as well use Bede's account as a starting point for a more general analysis.

The monastery of Ely was a family business: the first three abbesses were very close kinswomen. Similarly in the monastery of Whitby, Aelfflæd and her mother, Queen Eanflæd, ruled conjointly after abbess Hilda's death in 680. Among the letters written to Boniface asking for his advice, one finds that of abbess Eangyth and her only daughter Heaburg which alludes to their distress and heavy responsibilities. One cannot exclude the fact that some women may have felt great and genuine enthusiasm for a new form of spirituality, that they may have been attracted to the peace of ascetic life in a particularly restless world dominated by war, feuds and plots of all sorts. One cannot, therefore, put aside true religious vocations. Yet there were other reasons for the great number of nuns. As already briefly

---

92   G.N. Garmonsway, ed., *The Anglo-Saxon Chronicle*, 640, p.27.

mentioned, the foundation of a monastery was often a good means for rich families of the aristocracy to assert their power, to strengthen their prestige, to control territories. Women were major pawns in power strategies set up by the aristocracy: they were used as tokens of peace and alliance between families, and for their potential for handing down nobility. Nuns were allotted a specific task which was to pray for the salvation of the whole family and to keep the memory of the dead alive. As a matter of fact, women played a key role in the shaping of a family identity and were expected to pass this consciousness on to their children. The most revealing example is not to be found in an English document but in the manual of instruction the Frankish noblewoman Dhuoda wrote for her son William in the years 841–3:

> Pray for your father's relatives, who have bequeathed him their possessions by lawful inheritance. You will find who they were, and their names, written down in chapters toward the end of this little book. Although the Scripture says, 'A stranger luxuriates in another's goods,' it is not strangers who possess this legacy. As I said earlier, it is in the charge of your lord and father, Bernard.
>
> To the extent that these former owners have left their property in legacy, pray for them. And pray that you, as one of the living, may enjoy the property during a long and happy lifetime. For I think that if you conduct yourself towards God with worthy submission, the loving One will for this reason raise up these fragile honors for your benefit.
>
> If through the clemency of almighty God, your father decides in advance that you shall receive a portion of these estates, pray then with all your strength for the increasing heavenly recompense to the souls of those who once owned all these. Circumstances now do not allow your father to do so, since he has many urgent duties. But you, insofar as you have the strength and the opportunity, pray for their souls.[93]

Nuns and abbesses were the principal instruments of the noble families in their pursuit of the sacred through their donations to churches, their foundations of monasteries, their entering monasteries and their concern for the memory of the dead in the name of the whole family. They were considered as contributing, through their prayers, to the temporal success of their living kinsmen and to the redemption of

---

[93] M. Thiébaux, ed., *Dhuoda, Handbook for her Warrior Son, Liber Manualis*, Cambridge: University Press, 1998, book 8, § 14, p.205.

the deceased. Widows would pray for the members of the various families they were related to. The motivations of the founders or donators are often clearly stated when a charter or a will has survived. They all lay emphasis on the idea that the living must do their utmost to help the dead of their close family be delivered from the power of sin. In the time of King Edmund, Ealdorman Aelfgar, required his daughter Aethleflæd to 'grant the estate at Ditton after her death to whatever holy foundation seems to her most advisable, for the sake of our ancestors' souls'. The family was particularly linked to the community at Stoke. This is why he granted his daughter several estates, 'on condition that she does the best she can for the community at Stoke for the sake of my soul and of our ancestors' souls' and directly 'the estate at Greenstead to Stoke for my soul and for Aethelweard's and for Wiswith's'. About 1002, Aelfgar's younger daughter, Aelfflæd, being the last of the line granted all promised estates to Stoke begging the king:

> And I humbly pray you, Sire, for God's sake and for the sake of my lord's soul and for the sake of my sister's soul, that you will protect the holy foundation at Stoke in which my ancestors lie buried, and the property which they gave to it as an immune right of God for ever: which property I grant exactly as my ancestors had granted it, that is the estate at Stoke to the holy foundation with everything that belongs to the village there, and the wood at Hatfield which my sister and my ancestors gave.

Around 806, Earl Oswulf and his wife Beornthryth granted an estate to the congregation of Christchurch at Canterbury stating in details what they hoped obtaining in exchange:

> I Oswulf, earl by God's grace, and Beornthryth my wife, give to Almighty God and to the holy congregation at Christ Church, Canterbury, the estate at Stanstead, amounting to twenty ploughlands, in the hope, and for the reward, of the eternal and future life, and for the salvation of our own souls and those of our children. And with great humility we pray that we may be in the fellowship of those who are God's servants there, and of those who have been lords there, and of those who have given their lands to the church; and that our anniversary may

be celebrated every year with religious offices, and also with the distribution of alms, as theirs are.[94]

The whole system rested thus upon the concept of gift and counter-gift familiar to the Anglo-Saxons: kings, queens and noble men or women gave the lands monasteries needed and hoped to receive eternal life in return. Bede relates that when Oethelwald (King Oswald's son) gave Cedd, Bishop of the East Saxons, a grant of land on which to build a monastery, 'he firmly believed that the daily prayers of those who served God there would greatly help him' (*Hist. Eccl.* III, 23). From our royal abbesses, the church required less that they should serve as martyrs than they should continue their royal patronage in the very tangible form of land grants for abbeys.

The great aristocrats were attributed special charisma: a saint could only come from a noble family. Aethelthryth, Saexburh, and Eormenhild were all queens. Bede sings Aethlthryth's high birth in his hymn: 'Of royal blood she sprang, but nobler far / God's service found than pride of royal blood' (*Hist. Eccl.* IV, 20). Three men who became Boniface's assistants in Germany sent a letter to Abbess Cuniburg in 739 addressing her as 'their beloved lady, most devoted to Christ, eminent for the nobility of her royal blood'.[95] In his *De Virginitate*, Aldhelm made a catalogue of female virgins insisting on their nobility. Eugenia is 'sought in marriage by a suitor born of a noble family', Agnes' suitor is a prefect's son, Demetrias is 'born from the stock of a noble family'.[96] When St Agatha questioned by Quintianus introduces herself in Aelfric's *Festival of St Agatha*, she says:

'I am from a nobly-born family, as all my family can bear witness for me'. Then said the judge: 'Why do you behave yourself with low habits as if you were a maid-servant?' Agatha answered: 'I am God's hand-maiden, and for a man to be Christ's servant is a great nobility'.

---

94   F.E. Harmer, ed., *Select English Documents of the 9th & 10th centuries*, no.I, p.39.
95   E. Emerton, ed., *The Letters of St Boniface*, no.XXXIX, p.55.
96   Aldhelm, *The Prose Works*, M. Lapidge & M. Herren, eds., p.110, p.112 & p.116.

The nobility of saints was a hagiographical topos both for men and women: it served to heighten the degree of their renunciation. Besides, sainthood could not derive from secular life. When, in Saints' Lives, a few words are told about the married life of a woman, it is only to emphasize the lady's qualities before renouncing the world. Aethelthryth, though married twice, 'preserved the glory of perfect virginity'. Hild 'spent her first thirty-three years very nobly in the secular habit' (*Hist. Eccl.* IV, 23). In spite of their qualities and virtues, it is from their monastic foundation and their position as abbesses that their sanctity ensues: secular female saintliness simply did not exist.[97] As S. Ridyard has argued, the model for Anglo-Saxon royal saints 'distinguishes sharply between the legends and cults of the royal ladies, both virgins and widows, and those of the martyred kings... The royal ladies attained sanctity within the religious life'.[98] Therefore women were presented with a single representational system which created an order for their world and which certainly influenced their way of thinking and behaviour: the ideal hagiographical model of the *sponsa Christi*, for virgins, and of the handmaiden of Christ for formerly married women. The Scriptures, the patristic works, and Saints' Lives all set forth the same values, shaped the same identity and social role for women. It is difficult to assess the impact of literature on life and on someone's psyche. However, it is striking to see that only one role was attributed, and quoted as an example, to women. One can easily imagine that this ideal model was incorporated by certain women as a conscious, or subconscious, guiding principle. Yet, as Saints' Lives show, young ladies of high birth were often forced to marry and could only dedicate their lives to God after the death of their husband. This may have been another of the reasons for the great number of widows in Anglo-Saxon monasteries.

---

[97] In Francia, a few clerics wrote manuals for laymen such as Alcuin († 804) with his *Liber de Virtutibus et Vitiis* (Book of Virtues and Vices) for Earl Guy. Book two of the *De institutione laicali* (818–21) by Jonas, Bishop of Orleans, is a real treatise of conjugal spirituality.

[98] S.J. Ridyard, *The Royal Saints of Anglo-Saxon England: A study of West Saxon and East Anglian Cults*, Cambridge: University Press, 1988, p.240.

Very few Saints' Lives of the 7th or 8th centuries have survived in England. They mostly concern the early stages of the history of the English Church and therefore male evangelists.[99] Several Latin *Vitae* written in the 7th century in the Frankish kingdom deal with female saints. *The Life of St Gertrude of Nivelles* was composed around 670. One evening her father, Pepin of Landen († 640) who was mayor of the palace, invited King Dagobert to a lavish reception. The son of the Duke of Austrasia was there too and asked the king and Gertrude's parents to promise the young girl in marriage to him:

> On grounds of earthly ambition and mutual friendship, the king decided to grant the young man his request and persuaded the father of the young girl to have her, together with her mother, come up to him without their knowing the reason why. In the course of the dinner, the king asked her if she would take for husband this extremely wealthy young man, all dressed in silk. But she, beside herself, turned him away, uttering the following oath: 'I want no husband on earth, neither him nor another, I only want Christ, my Lord'.[100]

Several elements in this story are typical of hagiographical works: an aristocratic circle, a forced marriage, the wish to devote one's life to God at all costs, the young girl's strength of character (or extraordinary power divinely given to her) which enables her to challenge her father and the king, and eventually... to win. *The Life of St Salaberge of Laon*[101] written at the end of the 7th century shows that other saints had to obey their parents and to marry before being able, once widows, to enter a monastery. St Salaberge († c. 670) became abbess of Laon after being married twice against her will; first by her parents to a certain Richram who died two months after the wedding; then by King Dagobert who gave her to one of his councillors. They had five children, all of whom Salaberge consecrated to God.

---

99 St Cuthbert, St Wilfrid, St Guthlac, Pope St Gregory, and English missionaries on the Continent: St Boniface, St Willibrord.
100 B. Krusch & W. Levison, eds., *Scriptores rerum merowingicarum* II in B. Krusch, ed., *Monumenta Germaniae Historica*, Hanover & Leipzig, 1937–1951, § 1, pp.454–455. My translation.
101 G.H. Pertz, ed., *Scriptores* (V) in B. Krusch, ed., *Monumenta Germaniae Historica*, Hanover, 1884.

Apart from the *Old English Martyrology*, which gathers life notes of about 200 saints,[102] and which was probably compiled during King Alfred's reign, one must wait for the 10th century[103] and the reform movement to find many texts commemorating early English saints. The cult of Aethelthryth was promoted by Aethelwold, Bishop of Winchester, who 'filled the monastery with monks observing a rule, and appointed a superior over them'[104] after the place had long been neglected because of the Viking raids. King Edgar's charter to Ely (970) gives more details:

> Now as the result of the frequent admonitions of Bishop Aethelwold, I have in mind to endow, with the help of God, the monastery at Ely with its own freedom and special honour, and afterwards with possessions for the sustenance of those whom we place there for the service of God, and who shall continually dwell there. The foundation was consecrated in days of old in honour of the holy Peter, chief of the apostles, and it was embellished by the miracles of God himself which frequently took place at the tomb of Etheldreda, the holy maiden, who lies there uncorrupted until this day in a pure white tomb made of marble. Of her we read how she passed her life here and how she served God by her excellent mode of life, and of her death, and how she was taken up unblemished from her tomb, as Bede, the teacher of the English, has written in his books.[105]

---

102 Most of the female saints are early Christian martyrs who die either because they rebuff suitors or because they refuse to worship pagan idols. Four of them are Anglo-Saxon saints: Pega, 'St Gutlac the hermit's sister', Etheldreda (= Aethelthryth), Ethelburga ('she founded the nunnery in Britain that is called Barking, and in her days divine miracles came to pass in the same minster'), and Hilda. In each case, the hagiographer simply synthesized what can be read in Bede's *Historia*. G. Herzfeld, ed. + trans., *An Old English Martyrology*, London: Kegan Paul, trench, Trübner & Co., Early English Text Society no. 116, 1900.

103 Aelfric's account of Aethelthryth's life merely repeats Bede. Yet Aelfric appended the story of a couple who, after having three children, took a vow of chastity. Aelfric focuses his narrative on the husband: masculine chastity is therefore presented as a counterpoint to Aethelthryth's own continence. See W.W. Skeat, ed., *Aelfric's Lives of Saints*, London: Trübner & Co, Early English Text Society no.76, 82, 84, 114, 1881–1900, reprinted as 2 vols., 1966, part II p.441.

104 A.J. Robertson, ed., *Anglo-Saxon Charters*, p.101.

105 Ibid.

Moreover, a clerk of Ely called Aelfhelm wrote a (now lost) *Book of the Miracles of St Aethelthryth* around 970. The number of Saints' Lives increased tremendously in the 11th and 12th centuries and many concern our Anglo-Saxon abbesses.

Whatever the century when the Lives of these female saints were composed, they have certain elements in common. The sources present the postulants, the nuns and the abbesses as particularly well-versed in divine studies and religious writings. Great monasteries, indeed, were places of culture and knowledge[106] and intellectual fulfilment may also have to be taken into account in the appeal of monasteries to women. The *Liber manualis* proves that Dhuoda was extremely familiar with the Bible, especially with the Book of Psalms.[107] Noble young girls had a religious upbringing and felt at home in monasteries where they could go deeper into texts and concepts already known to them. Aldhelm hints at the numerous subjects studied at Barking which included the Scriptures, exegetical commentaries, historical chronicles, grammar and prosody:

> Your remarkable mental disposition – unless I'm mistaken – roaming widely through the flowering fields of scripture, traverses (them) with thirsty curiosity, now energetically plumbing the divine oracles of the ancient prophets foretell-

---

106 But not all monasteries. Bede disapproved of the practice which had spread for monasteries to be under the rule of the founder's kin. In his eyes many wealthy laymen founded monasteries for wrong reasons and declared themselves abbots or abbesses though being totally incompetent in spiritual matters: 'Also with equal shamelessness they obtain places where their wives may construct monasteries, in which with the same stupidity they, although laywomen, permit themselves the role of spiritual guides to the handmaids of Christ. (...) almost everyone of the leading nobles has bought himself a monastery of this kind during his time in office and has involved his wife in the same wicked offence'. Bede goes on saying that these laymen lack the training needed to teach monastic life and applies them 'that curse in the Gospel: 'If the blind lead the blind, both will fall into the pit'. Bede, *Letter to Egbert*, J. McClure & R. Collins, eds., Oxford: University Press, 1994.

107 M. Thiébaux, specifies that Dhuoda also borrowed from the *Etymologies* and *Synonyms* of Isidore of Seville, the grammarian Donatus, the Benedictine Rule, popular prayer-books, Gregory the Great's *Moralia in Job*, Augustine's *Tractates on the Gospel of John*, and computing manuals M. Thiébaux, ed., *Dhuoda, Handbook for her Warrior Son, Liber Manualis*, p.10.

ing long in advance the advent of the Saviour with certain affirmations; (...) now exploring widely the fourtold text of the evangelical story, expounded through the mystical commentaries of the catholic fathers and laid open spiritually to the very core and divided up by the rules of the fourfold ecclesiastical tradition according to *historia, allegoria, tropologia,* and *anagoge*; now, duly rummaging through the old stories of the historians and the entries of the chroniclers, who by their writing have delivered to lasting memory the chance vicissitudes of times gone by; now, sagaciously inquiring into the rules of the grammarians and the teachings of experts on spelling and the rules of metrics (as they are) measured out into accents (and) times, fitted into poetic feet, broken up into cola and commata – that is, into pentimemeres and eptimemeres – and, indeed, divided individually into a hundred kinds of metre.[108]

Rudolf of Fulda insists on Leoba's great knowledge. When she was old enough, she was sent to the monastery of Wimborne where 'she was entrusted to the aforesaid mother Tette to be educated in divine studies. (...) The girl grew up and was taught with such care by the abbess and all the nuns that she had no interests other than the monastery and the pursuit of sacred knowledge'.[109] Bede presents Abbess Hild as a woman of culture whose opinion was highly valued: 'So great was her prudence that not only ordinary people but also kings and princes sometimes sought and received her counsel when in difficulties. She compelled those under her direction to devote (...) much time to the study of the holy Scripture' (*Hist Eccl.* IV, 23). Bede mentions that five men who had studied in Hild's monastery were promoted to the episcopate.

This leads us to a key reason for the lure of monasteries: abbesses were influential and respected women. During the 7th and 8th centuries they could exercise their power over both nuns and monks for most Anglo-Saxon monasteries were double-houses at that time. Double houses were an importation from Gaul, the English peculiarity being that the superior was always an abbess. According to *The Penitential of Theodore,* 'it is not permissible for men to have monastic women, nor women, men'; yet because of the numerous double monasteries, 'we shall not overthrow that which is the custom in this region'.[110] Bede

---

108 Aldhelm, *The Prose Works*, M. Lapidge & M. Herren, eds., pp.61–62.
109 C. Talbot, ed., *The Anglo-Saxon Missionaries in Germany*, 1954, p.212.
110 J.T. Mc Neill & H.M. Gamer, eds., *Medieval Handbooks of Penance*, 'The Penitential of Theodore', Book II, chapter 6.

mentions many of these double-houses among which Bardney, Barking, Coldingham, Ely, Hartlepool and Whitby. H. Leyser writes that 'throughout the country there may well have been as many as fifty. In every known case the first abbess was of royal birth'.[111] Rich and noble families had everything under control: military power was reserved for the fathers and sons while the female members of the family strengthened ties between families, when married, or held positions of influence as abbesses, when consecrated virgins or widows. It was essential for these aristocratic families to be at the heart of powerful networks of relations and each member was allotted a very precise role. Widows who became abbesses were thus allowed power and authority.

The relations between the sexes in these double monasteries varied considerably. Rudolf of Fulda wrote a *Life of Leoba* shortly before the translation of the saint's remains in 837 or 838. He made a description of Wimborne and its stout walls which is generally accepted as historically reliable:

> Here two monasteries were of old founded by kings, surrounded with high and stout walls, and supplied with a sufficiency of income by a reasonable provision: one a monastery of clerics, and the other of women. From the beginning of their foundation, each of them was regulated by that rule of conduct, that neither of them was entered by the opposite sex. For a woman was never permitted to enter the congregation of men, or any man the house of nuns, except priests only, who used to enter the churches solely to perform the office of mass. Truly, any woman who renounced the world and wished to be associated with their community, entered it never to go out again, unless a good reason or matter of great expediency sent her out by the advice [of the abbess]. Moreover, the mother of the congregation herself, when she had need to make arrangements or give orders about any outside affairs for the profit of the monastery, spoke through the window, and from there decided whatever expediency required to be arranged or commanded.[112]

We have already met the first abbess of the monastery of Wimborne. She was Cuthburh († 725), a sister of King Ine of Wessex, of whom

---

111 H. Leyser, *Medieval Women. A Social History of Women in England 450–1500*, p.24. Leyser is referring to Roberta Gilchrist's estimate.
112 D. Whitelock, ed., *English Historical Documents*, no.159, p.782.

The Anglo-Saxon Chronicle says that she had been married to Ealdfrith, king of Northumbria, 'but they parted during their lifetime'. Rudolf of Fulda mentions that 'after some abbesses and spiritual mothers, there was preferred a religious virgin, Tette by name'. Abbess Tette, who was Leoba's teacher maintained strict discipline. Discipline was apparently lacking at Coldingham where, according to Bede, the monastery burnt down through divine vengeance because of the dissolute life of the nuns and monks; Bede relates that an Irishman had a vision in which a stranger told him: 'all of [those there], men and women alike, are sunk in slothful slumbers or else they remain awake for the purposes of sin. And the cells that were built for praying and for reading have become haunts of feasting, drinking, gossip, and other delights' (*Hist. Eccl.* IV, 25). Bede, however, prefers to dwell on the example of Hild, first abbess of Whitby, never stopping singing her praise (*Hist. Eccl.* IV, 23). Moreover when, in 739, three companions of St Boniface felt rather depressed, they did not write to an abbot but to abbess Cuniburg asking her prayers for help. They insisted on the reverence and great admiration they had for her stating that 'if any one of us should happen to visit Britain we should not prefer the obedience and government of any man to subjection under your good-will; for we place the greatest confidence of our hearts in you'.[113] It is clear that the power and authority of abbesses were not questioned, that their positions of influence were accepted – even by contemporary monks and clerics.

For rich widows, therefore, joining monasteries and becoming abbesses could mean both recognition and respect. They were acknowledged by society at large as having the necessary qualities, the competence to face the day-to-day problems encountered when running the houses. The position, indeed, involved many responsibilities. Abbess Eangyth, one of the women writing to St Boniface in the early 8th century, found the task rather heavy:

> Then there is added the difficulty of our internal administration, the disputes over diverse sources of discord which the enemy of all good sows abroad, in-

---

113 E. Emerton, ed., *The Letters of St Boniface*, no.XXXIX, pp.55–56.

fecting the hearts of all men with bitter malice but especially monks and their orders, knowing, as he does, that 'mighty men shall be mightily tormented'.

We are further oppressed by poverty and lack of temporal goods, by the meagerness of the produce of our fields and the exactions of the king based upon the accusation of those who envy us; as a certain wise man says: 'Witchcraft and envy darken many good things'. So also our obligations to the king and queen, to the bishop, the prefect, the barons and counts.[114]

Eangyth reminds us here that an abbess was a spiritual guide but also a business woman, a property administrator and a bursar, a personnel manager and a conciliator, as well as a public relations officer! In another letter, it is Boniface himself who lists the various positions and functions the monks of the monatery of Fritzlar will hold after the death of their abbot. The duties include being in charge of the canonical hours and the office of the Church, instructing the children, ruling the servants, being in charge of the kitchen, building the cells, etc.[115] A monastery was society in miniature, yet probably more orderly. Eangyth also adds to her troubles the loss of friends and relatives ('we have neither son nor brother, father nor uncle, only one daughter, whom death has robbed of all her dear ones, excepting one sister, a very aged mother, and a son of a brother') for nuns often remained very close to their family. Abbesses welcomed and brought up some of their nieces and young kinswomen, opened the doors of the monastery to men and family friends.[116] Bede relates in his *Life of St Cuthbert* that Abbess Aelfflæd who 'had charge of a great company of nuns and looked after them with motherly love (...) had a deep affection for Cuthbert. (...) She sent to Cuthbert begging him in God's name to come and talk over some important matter. He took a boat and sailed with his brethren to the appointed meeting place'.[117] On another occasion, Aelfflæd 'asked him to come to see her at one of the estates belonging to her monastery in order to converse with her and consecrate a church'.[118] Cuthbert is also asked by another abbess, Aebbe, to 'come and exhort the community. So kind a request could

114   Ibid., no.VI, p.15.
115   Ibid,. no.XXX, p.45.
116   We have seen this would not have been allowed at Wimborne.
117   J.F. Webb & D.H. Farmer, eds., *The Age of Bede*, pp.72–73.
118   Ibid., p.85.

not be refused. He came and stayed a few days, showing them the way of righteousness in deed as well as word'.[119]

All these reasons account for the attractiveness of monasteries. Young and rich ladies refusing to marry is a topos of hagiographical sources. One may wonder if this refusal did not have something to do with the situation of the wife which may not have appealed to girls betrothed at a very early age and married at fourteen or fifteen. Furthermore, it is not certain that families were strongly opposed to these young girls becoming nuns, for the religious life was a way of setting up daughters whom one did not wish to, or could not, marry off. As far as widows were concerned, they were probably pressured to remarry or take the veil according to the interests of the family. It is likely that the remarriage of noble widows was condemned because it jeopardized the handing down of the family inheritance. One must not, therefore, underestimate the number of women who were forced to enter monasteries. The cases of Queen Judith or Queen Edith show that royal widows who did not have a son lost their position at court after the death of their husband. Judith went back to her father's court and Edith retired to the monastery of Wilton. Moreover our documentation concerns ladies of very high birth who were fortunate enough to become abbesses and who, consequently, could enjoy some autonomy – though limited by their obligations and gradually by the supervision of the bishop. Ordinary nuns would get away from the guardianship of their fathers, or some other male relative, but only to find themselves put under the authority of the abbess; there was no place for personal freedom. Admittedly, personal freedom is a modern revendication; medieval people, both men and women, only conceived life in terms of groups and communities. However for high-born widows who had the choice, becoming an abbess may have been a real means of having a certain degree of freedom.

After the 8th century the situation changed for the worse. Many of the monasteries in the North which had grown to prosperity with the rising power of Northumbria, fell into decline with the decadence of that kingdom. Viking raids, which began in the late 8th century became very severe by the middle of the 9th and in the 870s the king-

---

119 Ibid., p.55.

doms of Mercia, East Anglia and Northumbria collapsed. A large number of the early monasteries were then destroyed or deserted. It was only in the 10th century that the monastic reform movement began with King Edgar (943–75) patronizing Dunstan's projects:

> 963: In the year after he was consecrated [Dunstan] established many monasteries, and drove out the secular clergy from the cathedral because they would not observe any monastic rule, and replaced them with monks. He established two abbeys, one of monks and the other of nuns, both at Winchester. Then he came to King Edgar and asked him to give him all the monasteries which the heathen had destroyed, because he wished to restore them: and the king cheerfully granted it. The bishop went first to Ely, where St Aethelthryth is buried, and had the monastery built, giving it to one of his monks whose name was Byrhtnoth; he consecrated him abbot and peopled it with monks to serve God, where formerly there had been nuns. He bought many villages from the king and richly endowed it.[120]

About 970, Edgar summoned bishops, abbots and abbesses to a synodal council to be held in Winchester. The reformers and monks gathered there agreed to standardize the structure of daily behaviour and worship throughout England. The agreement was put in writing by Aethelwold and is known as the *Regularis Concordia*.[121] Though in the foreword to 'the monastic agreement of the monks and nuns of the English nation', we are reminded that the reform concerns both houses of men and women, that King Edgar 'saw to it wisely that his Queen, Aelfthrith, should be the protectress and fearless guardian of the communities of nuns', that the archbishop added these further instructions: 'that no monk, nor indeed any man whatever his rank, should dare to enter and frequent the places set apart for nuns; and that those who have spiritual authority over nuns should use their powers not as worldly tyrants but in the interests of good discipline', that 'the election of abbots and abbesses should be carried out with the consent and advice of the King and according to the teaching of the Holy Rule',[122] nuns and abbesses are never alluded to in the code that was

---

120 G.N. Garmonsway, ed., *The Anglo-Saxon Chronicle*, p.115.
121 T. Symons, ed., *Regularis concordia anglicae nationis monachorum sanctimonialiumque*, London, 1953.
122 In order to avoid the overlordship of laymen over monasteries.

agreed upon. The text refers to 'brethren, the prior, the abbot, the father, the deacon, monks', explains that '*he* shall do..., *he* shall recite': women have totally disappeared. Aelfric refers to the text of the agreement in his Preface to the Letter to the Monks of Eynsham making it clear that, in his eyes, it concerned monks only: 'Therefore I present in writing these few things from the book of customs which St Aethelwold, Bishop of Winchester, with fellow bishops and abbots in the time of Edgar, the most blessed king of England, collected from all sides and established for the monks to observe, because until now the little book just mentioned has been unknown to your brotherhood'.[123] Participation in the work of reform is here clearly confined to men.

Double religious houses were therefore elements of the past, abbesses now only supervising nuns – but nunneries never played major historical or political roles. Their function as centres of education for young ladies increased: Wilton, for instance, vied with Shaftesbury in the 10th century as a home for the well-connected women of Wessex. Besides, many monasteries that formerly welcomed women were now reserved for men. Councils and synods reflected the increase in prestige and authority of male ecclesiastics, bishops and abbots being henceforward prominent in society. Moreover, one should not embellish reality: Bede's *Ecclesiastical History* and most other documents are only concerned with high-born ladies. The conditions, the everyday lives of ordinary widows had obviously nothing to do with those of queens or kings' daughters and, in their overwhelming majority, Anglo-Saxon women probably had no religious vocation. They had no time, no money, and no leisure to put all their energy into the preservation of 'perfect virginity'. More down-to-earth considerations preoccupied them: food, safety, sickness, accommodation, taxes – in a word, survival. Law codes enlighten us about Anglo-Saxon society and several of the laws relate to the position of widows. We will now focus on these documents whilst keeping in mind that they most likely reveal more about society as it should have been than as it actually was.[124]

---

123 J. Wilcox, ed., *Aelfric's Prefaces*, Durham Medieval Texts, no.9, 1994, p.133.
124 P. Wormald, *Legal Culture in the Early Medieval West. Law as Text, Image and Experience*, London: The Hambledon Press, 1999.

Chapter Two
The Legal Status of Widows

The Question of Guardianship

When Bede reports King Aethelberht's death (II, 5), he pays tribute to the sovereign who 'had accepted the faith' twenty-one years earlier and then mentions 'a code of laws after the Roman manner' as the king's main achievement:

> They are written in English and are still kept and observed by the people. Among these he set down first of all what restitution must be made by anyone who steals anything belonging to the church or the bishop or any other clergy; these laws were designed to give protection to those whose coming and whose teaching he had welcomed.

The codes of laws of the various peoples of the early western Middle Ages are precious documentation on social life at that time. The 'barbaric laws' were largely the product of Roman influence and were written in Latin between the end of the 5th and the 8th century.[1] In most cases, they were put in writing by order of the kings and can be considered as 'laws of peace', the kings presenting themselves as answerable to their people for order and security. The distinctive feature of the Anglo-Saxon laws is that they were written in Old English and not in Latin. But, as Bede points out, they were also a royal initiative: they were imposed on the inhabitants by public authority. King Aethelberht's code was the earliest, then followed the laws of the Kentish kings Hlothhere (673–685), Eadric (685–686) and Wihtred (694–725) and those of Ine of Wessex (688–728), Alfred (871–899), Edward the Elder (899–924), Aethelstan (924–939), Edmund (939–

---

[1] See the series *Leges* of the *Monumenta Germaniae* (now available in 1 CD-ROM, Brepols, 2000).

946), Edgar (959–975), Aethelred (978–1016), and Cnut (1016–1035). Kings, therefore, were clearly in charge of justice. The lawyers gave much importance to criminal law, a great number of clauses being mere lists of fines. Private law is less dealt with, but is of great interest to us because it concerns people's – and widows' in particular – everyday life: property and possessions, marriage, family, succession, etc. Great importance is also lent to the question of social classes, positions and ranks. Among women, widows have a special status, they are in a class of their own: this is what makes them more conspicuous.

Much emphasis is laid on widows as particularly vulnerable beings. The famous Frankish capitulary *Admonitio generalis* (802) enjoins judges to resist corruption, flattery or betrayal and to defend widows, orphans and the Church. All medieval sources insist on the fact that widows need protection,[2] that they are defenceless or ill-equipped to defend themselves. Writers often use the cliché of saints and good kings eager to help widows and to put them under their protection. These ready-made formulas show that widows were associated with wards and beggars; powerlessness and poverty were considered to be their common lot. The sources also reveal that the kings were supposed to remedy the situation. St Boniface sent a letter of admonition to King Aethelbald of Mercia in 746 about his 'atrocious crimes committed in convents with holy nuns'. Before reaching the subject, he was prudent enough to flatter the king for his good deeds:

> We have heard that you are very liberal in almsgiving, and congratulate you thereon. (...) We have heard also that you repress robbery and wrongdoing, perjury, and rapine with a strong hand, that you are famed as a defender of widows and of the poor, and that you have established peace within your kingdom.

---

[2] At a council held in Gaul about 475, the following decree was promulgated: 'Young widows who are frail in body shall be supported at the expense of the church whose widows they are'. Quoted by E. Amt, ed., *Women's Lives in Medieval Europe, a Sourcebook*, New York, London: Routledge, 1993, no.60, p.219.

Aelfric portrays Saint Edmund, King of East-Anglia from 855 to 869, as 'bountiful to the poor and to widows even like a father / And with benignity [he] guided his people / Ever to righteousness, and controlled the violent, / And lived happily in the true faith'.[3] The first line is revealing here of the status of irresponsible minor applied to a woman on her own: she regresses, is seen again as a dependent child needing a father. Aelfric distinguishes the same moral qualities and religious duties when presenting Abbot Aethelwold, Bishop of Winchester (963): 'He was terrible as a lion to the disobedient or undisciplined, but gentler than a dove to the gentle and humble. He was a father of the monks and nuns, a comforter of widows and a restorer of the poor, a defender of churches, a corrector of those going astray'.[4] In the biography of Cnut commissioned by Queen Emma, the *Encomium Emmae Reginae*, the king is presented as the ideal ruler who:

> became a friend and intimate of churchmen, to such a degree that he seemed to bishops to be a brother bishop for his maintenance of perfect religion, to monks also not a secular but a monk for the temperance of his life of most humble devotion. He diligently defended wards and widows, he supported orphans and strangers, he suppressed unjust laws and those who applied them, he exalted and cherished justice and equity.[5]

In *Vercelli Homily X* (10th century), it is not just the king who is to go to widows' aid but so must all good Christians: 'We were often reminded about obedience to our Lord, that we should perform his will and hold his command, and be generous with proper possessions and generous to the needy, and the helper of widows and comforters of orphans, and comforter of the poor and consoler of those who weep. And if we begin and sustain this work, then we will be God's darlings in heaven'.[6] Once again, widows are classified as destitute,

---

3   W.W. Skeat, ed., *Aelfric's Lives of Saints*, p.314.
4   D. Whitelock, ed., *English Historical Documents*, n°235, p.909.
5   A. Campbell, ed., *Encomium Emmae Reginae*, London: (RHS) Camden Society, 3rd series, lxxii, 1949, p.37.
6   *Vercelli Homily X* in E. Treharne, ed., *Old and Middle English, an Anthology*, Oxford: Blackwell Publishers, 2000, p.103. See also D.G. Scragg, ed., *The Vercelli Homilies and Related Texts*, London: Oxford University Press, Early English Text Society, o.s. 300, 1992.

pitiful and feeble creatures. Wulfstan reminded his fellow countrymen of these rules and concerns in his *Sermo Lupi ad Anglos* (c. 1014), lamenting the decline of Christian morals among the English in a fervent appeal to repentance. The Viking attacks were divine retribution for their numerous sins. Indeed:

> God's laws have dwindled for too long among this nation in each province. And public laws have declined all too greatly, and sanctuaries are too widely unprotected, and the houses of God are entirely despoiled of ancient rights and stripped of all that is decent inside. And widows are unjustly forced to marry, and too many are impoverished and greatly shamed. And poor men are sorely deceived and cruelly enslaved and, entirely innocent, are widely sold out of this land into the power of strangers. And children in the cradle are enslaved for minor theft widely throughout this nation because of cruel injustice. And the rights of freemen are taken away and the rights of a slave curtailed and the rights to alms are curtailed. And it can all be said most briefly that God's laws are hated and his teachings despised.[7]

Wulfstan performed particularly well two of the functions of an 11th-century bishop: preaching/sermon writing and the making of laws. He was, indeed, much interested in questions of government and the organisation of society. This is why he wrote several legal works and drew up Aethelred's laws and those of his successor, Cnut. The above extract taken from his *Sermo ad Anglos* is typical of his straightforward, rhythmical, and energetic style. There is a sense of urgency in the hammering out of the enumeration of very contemporary miseries that echo his concerns as lawmaker: God's anger is the result of people's constant breaching of divine and secular laws. The only remedy is therefore 'to bow to justice (...), to love God and follow the laws of God'.[8] In his eyes, and in medieval mentality at large, to obey the law was essential to see order, stability, and justice re-established, which included free choice of remarriage and respecting the property of widows. It is interesting to notice that Wulfstan's mention of the ill-treatment of widows comes first, just after the defilement of churches. His special care for widows is also visible in Cnut's code-law, which

---

[7] Wulfstan's *Sermo Lupi ad Anglos* in E. Treharne, ed., *Old and Middle English, an Anthology*, p.229.
[8] Ibid., p.233

he drafted, for it contains many clauses protecting widows from close relatives.

Old English law codes emphasize the idea that widows are a vulnerable class. It is obvious that their protection was given much thought. Anglo-Saxon women were all dependent on a male relative: daughters were 'protected' by their fathers, wives by their husbands. This is why one finds the following article in Aethelberht's laws:

> 82. If a man forcibly carries off a maiden, [he shall pay] 50 shillings *to her owner*, and afterwards buy from the owner his consent.[9]

Alfred's laws define the extent of the powers of the (male) head of a household; he is the guardian of his daughters, wife, (unmarried) sisters, and (widowed) mother:

> 42.§ 7. A man may fight, without becoming liable to vendetta, if he finds another [man] with his wedded wife, within closed doors, or under the same blanket; or [if he finds another man] with his legitimate daughter [or sister]; or with his mother, if she has been given in lawful wedlock to his father.

Throughout the Middle Ages, life was always considered as a series of ties, a network of bonds resting on obedience or solidarity: only communities were conceivable. People on their own, consequently, were highly suspect which means that men were united or constrained by bonds as much as were women. Everyone was to have a lord and those without one were outside the basic social structures – a painful, even terrifying experience. The law codes evoke these numerous ties, mentioning men of 'all classes, both commoners and nobles (...) who plot against the life of [their] lord' (Alfred, 4 § 2), the compensation lords are entitled to claim in case one of their men is killed (Ine, 70), slaves who have killed someone and who must be handed over by their owners 'to the dead man's lord and kinsmen' (Ine, 74), men who 'move away without permission of their lord' (Ine, 39), etc. Lords need not always have been men: kinship language had its limits and the words 'lord' and 'man' could be used for both genders:

---

9   F.L. Attenborough, ed., *The Laws of the Earliest English Kings*, p.15.

23. If anyone slays a foreigner, the king shall have two-thirds of his wergeld, and his son or relatives one-third.

§ 1. If he has no relatives, the king shall have one-half and the magnate shall have the other.

§ 2. If, however, the person [under whose protection he has been], is an abbot or an abbess, he [or she] shall share [the wergeld] with the king in the same proportion [as the magnate does].

We have already met Boniface's three assistants who wished they were in England and, should they visit Britain, wrote to abbess Cuniburg that they 'should not prefer the obedience and government of any man to subjection under [her] good-will; for [they] placed the greatest confidence of [their] hearts in [her]'.[10] *Domesday Book* contains many references to abbesses as lords: 'the church of St Mary of Shaftesbury holds Beechingstoke, and Turstin holds it of the abbess',[11] 'the church of St Mary of Wilton holds North Newnton (...). Of the land of the villans the abbess gave to a knight 3 1/2 hides and half a virgate of land. He has there 2 ploughs, and his villans 1 plough. Of the same land Aelfric the huntsman held of the abbess 1 hide and 1 1/2 virgates of land, on the condition that after his death it should return to the church because it was [part] of the demesne farm'.[12] It goes without saying that, before the Conquest, these lands already belonged to these convents.

Widowhood harmed the whole system: to which male kin-group, natal or marital, should widows be linked? Which lineage should prevail? What degree of autonomy could widows be granted? Who would have authority over the children? Indeed, at the death of the husband, the relations built up between the two families were called into question and a new social position was to be assigned to the surviving wife. This position was difficult to define for a widow combined the weakness of a woman without support and the power of a wife endowed with experience. The laws will help us to see what rules were agreed on. The early law codes show that widows were all under the

---

10   E. Emerton, ed., *The Letters of St Boniface*, no.XXXIX, p.55.
11   A. Williams & G.H. Martin, ed. + trans., *Domesday Book, A Complete Translation*, Alecto Historical Editions, 1992, London: Penguin Books, 2002, p.170.
12   Ibid., p.171.

protection (*mund*) of a male guardian. Aethelberht's laws distinguish four classes of widows for women are both grouped maritally (maiden, wife, widow) and according to their social rank. Let us list the clauses concerning fines for breach of legal protection to be found in the various codes:

A. *Kentish laws*

Aethelberht's Laws (565–616)

Breach of protection	Amount of money to be paid	Beneficiary
King's *mundbyrd*	50 shillings	
Nobleman's *mundbyrd*	12 shillings	
Ceorl's *mundbyrd*	6 shillings	
Mund of a widow:		
– Of the best class	50 shillings	
– Of the 2nd class	20 shillings	
– Of the 3rd class	12 shillings	
– Of the 4th class	6 shillings	

The price is doubled in the case of a widow not belonging to the man who has taken her.

Hlothhere and Eadric's Laws (673–685)

Breach of protection	Amount of money to be paid	Beneficiary
Breach of the peace		
– in someone's house	1 shilling	the house-owner
	+ 12 shillings	the king
– if blood is shed	house-owner's *mundbyrd*	the house-owner
	50 shillings	the king

Wihtred's Laws (695)

Breach of protection	Amount of money to be paid	Beneficiary
King's *mundbyrd*	50 shillings	
Mundbyrd of the Church	50 shillings	

B. Laws of Wessex

Alfred's laws (871–899)

Breach of protection	Amount of money to be paid	Beneficiary
King's protection	compensation	injured person
	+ 5 pounds of pure silver pennies	the king
Archbishop's protection (or guardianship)	+ 3 pounds of pure silver pennies	the archbishop
Bishop's protection (or guardianship)	+ 2 pounds of pure silver pennies	the bishop
Ealdorman's protection (or guardianship)	+ 2 pounds of pure silver pennies	the ealdorman
Breach of the peace		
Disturbing a meeting in the presence of an ealdorman	wergeld + fine + 120 shillings	the ealdorman
Disturbing a meeting in the presence of a subordinate to an ealdorman	wergeld + fine + 30 shillings	the subordinate
Fighting in the house of a ceorl	6 shillings	the ceorl
Fighting in the house of a man whose wergeld is 600 shillings	18 shillings	the house-owner
Fighting in the house of a man whose wergeld is 1200 shillings	36 shillings	the house-owner

Aethelred's laws (1008)

21. 'Every widow who conducts herself rightly is to be under the protection of God and the king'.

Cnut's laws (1016–1035)

Breach of protection	Amount of money to be paid	Beneficiary
King's protection	5 pounds	
Archbishop's/aetheling's protection	3 pounds	
Bishop's/ealdorman's protection	2 pounds	

The term *mund* could be used to designate either 'protection, guardianship, right of asylum' or the person in charge of this protection therefore a 'guardian, protector'. *Mundbyrd* was the fine imposed on those who breached legal protection. Protection could be applied to places or to people; this is why we find fines inflicted for breach of the peace of householders or of places of worship. In such cases the private authority of the owner or of the cleric had been negated. Protecting a person meant seeing to the defence of his/her interests. In his will, dating back to 835, reeve Abba specifies that:

> If, however it is not my lot to have a child, then I desire that my wife shall have [the land I received from my lords] as long as she is willing to keep it without marrying again. And my brother Alchhere is to give her his support and to see that she has profits from the land.[13]

It is clear that Abba wanted his brother to be an adviser, a support, someone his wife would be able to rely on and who would help her to manage her estate. Such a responsibility implied devoting much energy and time and this is why Abba provided his brother with a compensation to make up for his own loss of earning and to incite him to

---

13 F.E. Harmer, ed., *Select English Documents of the 9th and 10th centuries*, no.II, p.41.

work for her: 'and he is to be given half a ploughland at Chillenden for his possession and use, in order that he may the more zealously attend to and look after her needs; and with the land are to be given him four oxen, two cows, fifty sheep, and a horn'. Under King Aethelred's reign, a certain Wulfric granted

> His poor daughter the estate at Elford and that at Oakley. (...) And she shall not possess it on such terms that she can forfeit it for any reason, but she is to have the use of it as long as she can deserve it, and afterwards it is to go to the monastery at Burton because it was my godfather's gift. And I desire that Aelfhelm may be protector of her and of the land.[14]

It is difficult to know what handicap Wulfric's 'poor daughter' suffered from; whatever it may have been, her father judged it necessary to ask his brother, the Ealdorman Aelfhelm, to supervise what she was doing. It is interesting to note that in these two wills, the protectors are there to advise, to manage the estates in the women's best interests but the women clearly remain the owners. However, one can easily imagine that protecting a person was often understood as exercising power over him/her. *Mund* included the paternal or marital power that placed women under the authority of a man from a financial, material and legal point of view and Aethelberht's laws explicitly mention 'if a man takes a widow who does not belong to him' (article 76, 'unagne' = not one's own) implying that widows must all *belong* to a man.

Aethelberht's laws list four classes of widows: those belonging to the nobility and three socially inferior classes – probably the widows of freemen/ceorls, those of freedmen and those of slaves.[15] Though the fines are graded in accordance with the social standing of the widows, it must be noted that all of them are recognized as having the right to protection and to compensation. Besides, the above table shows that the amount of money to be paid was sizeable: women in the Anglo-Saxon laws are always valued at a high price probably because their ability to give birth was highly prized. The monetary compensation to be paid for violation of the *mund* of a widow of the

---

14 D. Whitelock, ed., *Anglo-Saxon Wills*, no.XVII, pp.47–49.
15 A.R. Bridbury, ed., *The English Economy from Bede to the Reformation*, Woodbridge: the Boydell Press, 1992, pp.56–85.

nobility (50 shillings) is equivalent to the amount to be paid for the violation of the king's own protection or that of the Church. The penalty incurred for breach of the mund of a nobleman is 12 shillings – almost five times less! A ceorl's *mund* is assessed 6 shillings while a third class widow's *mund* reaches 12 shillings, exactly twice the sum. One cannot make similar comparisons when turning to Alfred's laws because widows are not discussed in this code. One can only notice that the penalties have been revised upwards.

As the table shows, it is not clear to whom the compensation was paid. Aethelberht, and later kings, obviously assumed that the answer was self-evident. If one considers clauses dealing with people depending on others, one gets a few details. In Wihtred's law code one is told that an emancipated slave will have 'his freedom publicly recognized' but 'the emancipator shall have his heritage ['ierfe'] and his wergeld, and the guardianship of his household ['munde þare hina'] wherever he [the freed man] may be' (clause 8): therefore it is clear that the freed man is not the guardian of his own family but that his former master is. If anything happens to the widow of that man, the master will therefore receive the fixed compensations. One of Alfred's laws specifies:

> If anyone takes a nun from a nunnery without the permission of the king or bishop, he shall pay 120 shillings, half to the king, and half to the bishop and to the lord of the church, under whose charge the nun is. (clause 8)

Which means that the protectors (king, bishop, abbess) were compensated for the loss of the nun but that the poor woman apparently received nothing and was, to our twenty-first century eyes, unfairly treated. The laws reflect a different mentality that did not consider people as individuals but as members of groups, elements of bound sets. People thought that a powerless creature such as a nun or a slave could not survive without a guardian who was legally responsible for his/her affairs. In such a system, the victim was not always taken into account and received no compensation because what had to be secured, first and foremost, were the social ties between people, ties which implied responsibilities as well as rights. In the case of the nun, the money went, not to the woman, but to the king, bishop and abbess because their protection had been flouted. The upholding of the law, of rules on which society as a whole rested, was considered more important than one individual for it guaranteed peace and stability. The poor nun's lot may even have been worse. Indeed:

> § 1. If she lives longer than he who abducted her, she shall inherit nothing of his property.
> § 2. If she bears a child, it shall inherit no more of the property than its mother.
> § 3. If her child is slain, the share of the wergeld due to the mother's kindred shall be paid to the king, but the father's kindred shall be paid the share due to them.

The nun, though clearly the one to feel sorry for, was denied any right because her (forced) union with her abductor could not – by definition – be considered as licit. Consequently, the situation in which she found herself was at complete variance with marriage, and therefore succession, law. The lawyers' main concern was with property and the right of heirs. About 120 years later things had not changed. A clause in Cnut's laws made clear that a widow who remarried within 12 months was to forfeit the possessions she had obtained through her first marriage, 'and even if she was married by force, she is to forfeit those possessions': the rights of her first husband's relatives came first, the fact that she was not responsible for the situation was not taken into account. One can deduce from these cases that, if a widow fell victim to a crime, her *mund* was paid, not to her, but most likely to her guardian.[16]

King Aethelberht died in 616. The term *mund* in connection to widows appears again nearly 400 hundred years later in Aethelred's code of 1008: 'Every widow who conducts herself rightly is to be under the protection of God and the king.' In fact most documents, charters and wills that have survived and that allude to the question of the guardianship of women show that the Church had already been offering its protection for centuries. We have met Abba and Wulfric

---

16 T.J. Rivers notes that 'payment for any injustice to [a wife] was paid to her kindred, since obligations to the kindred were not broken upon marriage.' 'Widows' rights in Anglo-Saxon Law', *American Journal of Legal History*, 19 (1975), p.208.

who both asked one of their brothers to look after their widow or daughter but the references to the *mund* of the Church are far more numerous. In 804, Aethelric gave his mother, Abbess Ceolburh,[17] a land at Westminster and at Stoke:

> That she may have it for her life and afterwards give it to the church at Worcester; that on this account she may while she lives have there protection and defence against the claims of the Berkeley people. (...) And if she does not get protection in the city of Worcester, she is afterwards first to seek it from the archbishop in Kent, and if she does not get it there, she is to be free with her deeds and estates to choose protection where it shall please her.[18]

Quite obviously, Aethelric feared the community of Berkeley might want to take hold of his mother's inherited land. His bequest of the estate to the church at Worcester appears as a bargain: in exchange of this grant of property, his mother's protection must be ensured. In 860, Badanoth Beotting decided to become a monk

> At the foundation at Christchurch, and to place [his] children there, and entrust [his] wife and children to the lord and to the community and to the foundation after [his] death, for security and protection and guardianship in the things which they require.[19]

A married woman was under the *mund* of her husband so here the husband had to find a substitute for himself. The abbot and the community were to exercise his prerogatives after his death which included *frid* (peace, security), *mundbyrd* (protection, patronage, guardianship), and *hlaforddom* (domination, authority, the fact of having a lord). In her will (about 970), Aelfgifu required a different sort of help. Among the numerous estates she shared out, she granted one to Bishop Aethelwold and prayed him to 'always intercede for [her] mother and for [her]'.[20] Two men placed their widows under the protection of bishops: Ecgferth, in 968, 'unequivocally committed both the estate and the title-deeds, with the cognisance of the king, to Archbishop

---

17 Her death is recorded in the *Anglo-Saxon Chronicle* (807).
18 D. Whitelock, ed., *English Historical Documents*, no.81, p.513.
19 A.J. Robertson, ed., *Anglo-Saxon Charters*, no.VI, p.11.
20 D. Whitelock, ed., *Anglo-Saxon Wills*, no.VIII, p.21.

Dunstan, in order that he might act as guardian to his widow and child'[21] and Aethelric, at the end of the 10th century, gave Bishop Aelfstan woods and open lands praying him to 'protect [his] widow and the things which [he] left her'.[22] Protection was therefore something you had to pay for. Similarly after listing the articles he left to his lord as *heriot* (two horses, two swords, four shields, four spears, ten mares and ten colts), Wulfgeat of Donington prayed 'his lord for the love of God that he [would] be a friend to his wife and daughter':[23] protection was never a free service.

A question that immediately comes to mind is what sorts of risks did widows run? Why were they in such desperate need of protection?

Threats to Widows' Rights

Threats against their Property

Those most likely to cheat a widow were certainly her in-laws for several disputes concerning the ownership of land or the custody of children are recorded in the documents available. Concerning children, rules were established very early. In case of the death of the husband, Hlothhere and Eadric's laws stipulated that:

> 6. If a man dies leaving a wife and a child, it is right, that the child should accompany the mother; and one of his father's relatives who is willing to act, shall be given him as his guardian to take care of his property, until he is ten years old.

Though the children were given a guardian, the mother's maternal rights and the child's need of his mother were asserted. In order to bring up her children, the widow was to receive financial assistance.

---

21 A.J. Robertson, ed., *Anglo-Saxon Charters*, no.XLIV, p.93.
22 D. Whitelock, ed., *Anglo-Saxon Wills*, no.XVI, p.43.
23 Ibid., no.XIX, p.55.

Aethelberht's laws specified that 'if she bears a living child, she shall have half the goods left by her husband, if he dies first' while Ine's:

> 38. If a husband has a child by his wife and the husband dies, the mother shall have her child and rear it, and [every year] 6 shillings shall be given for its maintenance – a cow in summer and an ox in winter; the relatives shall keep the family home until the child reaches maturity.[24]

As Christine Fell pointed out,[25] the word used for 'child' in all the codes is *bearn* which is not a gendered word and can therefore be used both for a girl or a boy. A widow left with a little girl had the same rights as one left with a little boy.

Though widows were given the custody of their children,[26] close relatives often came into conflict with them. We have already met Queen Aethelburh who, after the death of her husband, went back to Kent with her daughter Eanflæd, her son Uscfrea and her stepson Yffi; yet 'fearing Kings Eadbald and Oswald, afterwards sent these children to Gaul to be brought up by King Dagobert, who was her friend'.[27] P. Stafford mentions 'Godgifu, widow of Earl Leofric [who] had lost lands to her grandsons Edwin and Morcar before 1066.'[28] Guibert de Nogent was born into a noble French family in the 1060s and his father died when he was six months old. In his autobiography he recalls that 'his kinsmen [were] eager for [his] father's fiefs and possessions and strove to take them by the exclusion of [his] mother, they fixed a day for advancing their claims. The day came and the nobles were in council prepared to act in despite of all justice. [His] mother,

---

24 This clause has been much debated by historians. F.L. Attenborough explains a cow was given in summer or an ox in winter according to the season in which the husband died. The six shillings were derived from the late husband's estate. T.J. Rivers believes a cow was milked and an ox harnessed to furnish the family's subsistence at the yearly value of six shillings.
25 C. Fell, C. Clark & E. Williams, *Women in Anglo-Saxon England and the Impact of 1066*, Bloomington: Indiana University Press, 1984.
26 The very existence of the laws shows that it was not self-evident.
27 Bede, *Ecclesiastical History*, II, 20.
28 P. Stafford, *Unification and Conquest*, London, New York, Melbourne, Auckland: Edward Arnold, 1989, p.176.

being assured of their greedy intentions, had retired to the church.'[29] His mother's nephew, wishing to take over some of his uncle's property suggested he might rear the children:

> 'Since, mistress,' said he, 'you have sufficient youth and beauty, it is meet that you should marry, that your life in the world may be more pleasant; and the children of my uncle should be placed under my care to be trustily brought up by me, his possessions finally coming into my hands, as is right they should.'

Documents in English emphasizing tensions between a widow and her husband's kindred are numerous. The law's main concern went to the heirs not to the surviving spouse. A widow with no living child was not entitled to inherit from her late husband: we remember Queen Judith who was sent back to her father's court after being Aethelwulf's as well as Aethelbald's wife but both marriages had been childless. This is why Aethelberht's laws distinguish between a widow who bears a child and one who does not:

> 78. If she bears a living child, she shall have half the goods left by her husband, if he dies first.
> 81. If she does not bear a child, [her] father's relatives shall have her goods, and the 'morning-gift'.

In other words, a childless widow was supposed to go home and find herself under her father's protection again. Cnut's laws reasserted the widow's right to inherit from her late husband. Indeed, even if the husband had had no time to make a valid will, 'the property is to be very justly divided among the wife, the children and the close kinsmen, each in the proportion which belongs to him' (clause 70.1). According to a late (probably between 975 and 1030) text 'concerning the betrothal of a woman', the widow could even be entitled to the whole of her husband's goods:

> 3. Then afterwards the bridegroom is to announce what he grants her in return for her acceptance of his suit, and what he grants her if she should live longer than he.

29 E. Amt, ed., *Women's Lives in Medieval Europe, a Sourcebook*, no.33. See C.C. Swinton Bland, ed., *The Autobiography of Guibert of Nogent, Abbot of Nogent-sous-Coucy*, London, New York, 1925.

4. If it is thus contracted, then it is right that she should be entitled to half the goods – and to all, if they have a child together – unless she marries again.[30]

Wulfstan in his *Institutes of Polity* stresses the fact that reeves themselves were often eager to cheat vulnerable people such as 'the blameless poor and the flock they should guard (...). They give rise to unjust laws in all sorts of ways to the injury of the poor, and rob widows over and again'.[31] Several wills prove that husbands were well aware of the difficulties that might arise, should their wives remain on their own. Thurketel, for instance, made clear in his will that '[his] wife portion is to be ever uncontested, for her to hold or to give where she pleases'.[32] Relations could be extremely strained in case of a second marriage: sometimes the husband's children had much difficulty in accepting their stepmother should inherit from their own father. In a charter in which King Ethelred granted confiscated estates to his mother, one can read that by court order:

> These are the crimes by which Wulfbold ruined himself with his lord, namely first, when his father died, he went to his stepmother's estate and took everything that he could find there, inside and out, small and great. Then the king sent to him and commanded him to give up what he had seized, but he paid no attention and his wergeld was assigned to the king.

Wulfbold was called to order four times but refused to comply so when 'the great meeting was held at London, the king's councillors assigned the whole of Wulfbold's property to the king, and himself likewise to be disposed of as the king desired, either to remain alive or to be condemned to death. And he had made no amends for all this up to the crime of his death. And after he was dead, over and above all this, his widow along with her son went and slew Eadmær the king's thegn, Wulfbold's uncle's son, and his fifteen companions on the estate at Bourne which Wulfbald had held by robbery despite the king'.[33]

A way of getting rid of a widow or, at least, of seizing her possessions, was to see her remarry rapidly or enter a monastery. In his

---

30 D. Whitelock, ed., *English Historical Documents*, no.50, p.467.
31 M. Swanton, ed., *Anglo-Saxon Prose*, p.130.
32 D. Whitelock, ed., *Anglo-Saxon Wills*, no.XXV, p.71.
33 A.J. Robertson, ed., *Anglo-Saxon Charters*, no.LXIII, pp.129–131.

Sermo Lupi ad Anglos, Wulfstan deplored the fact that widows were wrongfully and hastily forced to take a husband – which meant for these women losing all property inherited from their deceased husband for 'each widow is to remain unmarried for twelve months' (Aethelred, 21.1), 'if she chooses a husband within the year's space, she is then to forfeit the morning-gift and all the possessions which she had through her former husband; and the nearest kinsmen are to succeed to the lands and to the possession which she had before' (Cnut, 73a). This is why when Wulfstan drafted Cnut's law code, he remembered to specify that:

> 73.3 A widow is never to be consecrated [as a nun] too hastily.
> 73.4 And neither a widow nor a maiden is ever to be forced to marry a man whom she herself dislikes.

The reasons for forbidding widows from remarrying too rapidly were multiple. According to T.J. Rivers, 'if widows married or entered the convent within the first year of their husband's death, the king lost the heriot tax, a principal source of revenue.'[34] A more down-to-earth explanation is that the rule aimed at knowing for sure, who was the father of a child born after the death of the husband. Religion and canon law were also of paramount importance. We saw in chapter one that the Church considered that widows and widowers had a perfect right to remarry though, at the same time, the Christian authorities discouraged such a practice and advised them to follow the example of Anna:[35] to fast and pray. *The Penitential of Theodore* explicitly asked widows to wait a full year before taking a new husband: 'When his wife is dead, a man may take another wife after a month. If her husband is dead, the woman may take another husband after a year'.[36] At the end of his life, Wulfstan summed up the Church's stance on that issue – from the point of view of the widower:

---

34 T.J. Rivers, 'Widows' Rights in Anglo-Saxon Law', *American Journal of Legal History*, 19 (1975), p.211.
35 Luke, 2:36–37.
36 J.T. McNeill & H.M. Gamer, *Medieval Handbooks of Penance*, Book II, clause 10.

It is a proper life, that a bachelor should remain in his bachelor state until he lawfully take a maiden in marriage, and afterwards have her and no other for as long as she should live. If then her death came about, then it is most proper that he thenceforth remain a widower. By permission of the Apostle, however, a layman may at need marry a second time. But the canons forbid to it the blessings which are appointed for a first marriage. And in addition a penance is appointed for such men to perform.[37] And where a man marries again, the priest is forbidden to attend the marriage ceremony in the way he did before, or to give the blessing which pertains to a first marriage.[38] By that it may be known that is not altogether right that a man take a wife or a woman take a husband more than once. And it is certainly too much should it happen a third time, and completely wrong should it happen more often.[39]

Wulfstan places himself on the moral plane and, like all theologians dealing with marriage law, was at odds with the social realities, for remarriage was common. The fact that the Church did not have a clear-cut position, accepting remarriage while, at the same time, discouraging it, rendered its approach difficult to grasp and the rule, because of its very vagueness, was not respected.

What was clearly stated, on the other hand, was the full year of mourning before widows (but not widowers) could remarry. As a matter of fact, both religious and secular laws echo some (not overtly expressed) concern with widows' sexuality for these women were dangerously left unattached after the decease of their lawful husband. Would widows, to take up St Paul's words, contain themselves, have self-control or would they immediately burn with desire? The secular codes reveal that the lawyers were extremely concerned with safeguarding ladies' honour. In fact, women are usually only discussed as such where sexual crimes are concerned: assault, rape, abduction. One may legitimately wonder whether the lawyers did not take, perhaps unconsciously, female sexual appetite for granted. However that may

[37] The Second Council of Braga (572) imposed on those who remarried to do penance for lascivious conduct.
[38] Priests who celebrated remarriages forfeited their chances of ecclesiastical advancement. See J.A. Brundage, 'Widows and Remarriage: Moral Conflicts and their Resolution in Classical Canon Law', S.S. Walker, ed., *Wife and Widow in Medieval England*, Ann Arbor: University of Michigan Press, 1993.
[39] Wulfstan, *The Institutes of Polity* in M. Swanton, ed., *Anglo-Saxon Prose*, p. 136.

have been, this constant connection between sexuality and women reveals that it was felt necessary to govern the female body. Besides, it is undeniable that as adult single women, widows were ill equipped against threats, both against their property as we have just seen, but also against their persons. Indeed, apart from being cheated, from seeing their rights infringed upon, sexual crimes were other sources of danger to widows' well-being. It is rather difficult, however, to know if the numerous articles dealing with women's reputations and safety mirror the violent reality of the 'Dark Ages' or if they betray the husbands' and fathers' desire to keep a tight rein on their wives and daughters. For, as we shall see, the documents mentioning the assault of a lady are not in very great number. When one comes to widows, they are almost non-existent.

Threats against their Persons: Sexual Crimes

Here too, let us first list the clauses of the various codes:

A. Kentish laws

Aethelberht's Laws (565–616)

Sexual offence	Amount of money to be paid	Beneficiary
Rape		
Of a maiden belonging to the king	50 shillings	
Of a grinding slave belonging to the king	25 shillings	
Of a slave of the 3rd class belonging to the king	12 shillings	
Of the wife of a freeman by another freeman	his/her wergeld + second wife	the husband
Of the wife of a servant	twofold compensation	
Of a nobleman's serving maid	12 shillings	

Of a ceorl's serving maid	6 shillings	
Of a ceorl's 2nd class slave	50 sceattas	
Of a ceorl's 3rd class slave	30 sceattas	
Abduction		
Of a maiden	50 shillings	her owner
Of a betrothed maiden	50 shillings	her owner
	20 shillings	bridegroom
If the maiden is brought back	35 shillings	her owner
	15 shillings	the king

Wihtred's Laws (695)

Sexual offence	Amount of money to be paid	Beneficiary
Nobleman living in illicit union	100 shillings	his lord
Ceorl living in illicit union	50 shillings	

B. Laws of Wessex

Alfred's Laws (871–899)

Sexual offence	Amount of money to be paid	Beneficiary
Rape		
Wife of a man whose wergeld is 1200 shillings	120 shillings	the husband
Wife of a man whose wergeld is 600 shillings	100 shillings	the husband
A young ceorlish woman	60 shillings	herself?
Wife of a ceorl	40 shillings	the husband
Slave of a ceorl	5 shillings + fine of 60 shillings	the ceorl
Girl who is under age	same compensation as for an adult	

Assault		
Seizing a young ceorlish woman by the breast	5 shillings	herself
Throwing down a young ceorlish woman	10 shillings	
'The sum will be doubled in the case of a nun'		
'To a woman of higher birth, the compensation shall increase according to the wergeld'		
Sexual relations before marriage		
A young betrothed ceorlish woman	cattle worth 60 shillings	the surety [of the marriage]
A young betrothed woman whose wergeld is 600 shillings	100 shillings	the surety [of the marriage]
A young betrothed woman whose wergeld is 1200 shillings	120 shillings	the surety [of the marriage]
Abduction		
Of a nun	120 shillings	1/2 to the king 1/2 to the bishop and the 'lord' of the church (= abbess)

Cnut's Laws (1016–1035)

Sexual offence	Amount of money to be paid	Beneficiary
Abduction		
Of a maiden	wergeld	
Of a widow	wergeld	
Adultery		
Of a wife	seizure of her possessions	husband

The most striking element is the almost total absence of references concerning widows. Once again only hypotheses, and no absolute certainty, can be put forward to account for such a situation. If widows were physically, sexually assaulted, the attacker had to pay the fixed *mundbyrd*. In other words the fines made provision for by the law for the *mund* of widows applied to all sorts of ill-treatments and, in all likelihood, essentially to cases of abduction and sexual crimes. Therefore the lawyers probably considered that no more needed to be said about widows. Besides, one immediately notices that, when the articles of the above table mention to whom the compensation was to be paid, mainly husbands or the (male) owners of the women are referred to. It has often been noted that, from Alfred to Cnut, laws were no longer mere schedules of compensation, that crime came to be seen as an injury to the victim but also to society at large: compensation was therefore also to be paid to the king and his officials. Yet there is no such thing here: a sexual offence was a strictly private matter, only the husband or the father were directly concerned. Women seem to have been considered as goods. The great majority of the articles are about unmarried girls: once sexually assaulted their market value dropped, for it was then more difficult to find them a husband – especially if they had the misfortune to become pregnant. As a consequence, their father sustained a financial loss. For married women, husbands had been robbed of one of their possessions and had then a wife of lower quality. The laws show no concern for the woman who suffered in her flesh, only the man who has been despoiled is taken into consideration. One may therefore wonder if the lack of reference to widows may not be explained by the fact that, by definition, no sexual partner was supposed to be wounded in his honour. Moreover, everybody knew widows were not virgins so there was no drop in quality and no deceit. One can only compare the sums to be paid at the time of Aethelberht because the other codes do not give any schedules for the attack of widows. Apart from the fact that widows of the best class (= of the nobility) are valued at the same price as a maiden belonging to the king, the other widows are assessed at a lower price than the young girls mentioned. The compensation to be paid for a widow of the second class is 20 shillings while that for a grinding slave (belonging to the king) is 25 shillings. The servant of a *ceorl* is estimated 6 shillings, which is what is to be paid for the *mund* of a widow of the fourth (= slave) class. Evidently, virginity prevailed over social rank.

There are not many accounts of women being abducted, assaulted, or raped. In Saints' Lives, the young girls are saved by divine intervention and die before men achieve their end. Romances are full of girls being raped but they did not appear before the 13th century. Epics are not concerned with female characters. Chronicles and historical documents deal with more general and political events that have national or dynastic consequences. Moreover, the rape of a widow had no economic repercussion, it led to no land contestation. All these reasons explain why these sexual crimes went largely unrecorded. Only in the case of nuns did chroniclers devote some lines to the assault in order to condemn it from a moral point of view. In 745, Boniface urged King Aethelbald of Mercia to take a lawful wife and put an end to a life debauchery. His indignation was all the greater as:

> Our informants say that these atrocious crimes are committed in convents with holy nuns and virgins dedicated to God, and this, beyond all doubt, doubles the offense (...) for their bodies which are consecrated to Him by our own vows and by the words of the priest are said by Holy Scripture to be temples of God, wherefore those who violate them are shown to be sons of perdition according to the Apostle.[40]

The very few cases of abduction mentioned in *The Anglo-Saxon Chronicle* also feature mainly nuns: in 899, for instance, Aethelwold, first cousin of King Edward the Elder, abducted a lady 'without the king's consent and in defiance of the command of the bishops, because she had taken the vows of a nun'. In 1046, Swein, the eldest son of Earl Godwine, marched into Wales. On the way back, 'he had the abbess of Leominster fetched to him, and kept as long as he pleased and then let her go home'. The only widow mentioned in the *Chronicle* is Siferth's widow who was brought to Malmesbury by order of the king. The story, however, had a happy ending because 'after a short time, prince Edmund came and abducted the woman against the king's will, and made her his wife.' (1015)

---

40   E. Emerton, ed., *The Letters of St Boniface*, no.LVII, p.104.

Sometimes, however, there was no happy but, conversely, a tragic ending when the women were killed.

Murders

In the event of a person's violent death, a compensation known as the *wergeld/wergild* (= man payment) was to be paid to the victim's kindred.[41] Before the 10th century an individual's actions were considered as acts of his kinship group which means that the wergeld was paid collectively by the slayer's kin. King Alfred's laws specify that 'if a man who has no paternal relatives fights and kills a man, his maternal relatives, if he has any, shall pay one-third of the wergeld and his associates shall pay one-third. In default of payment of the [remaining] third, he shall be held personally responsible' (article 30). The *wergeld* of a woman was usually equal to that of a man of the same class:

Aethelberht's Laws (565–616)

Wergeld	Amount of money to be paid	Beneficiary
Ordinary wergeld	100 shillings	
If on the king's premises	100 shillings + 50 shillings	the king
Lieges summoned by the king	double wergeld + 50 shillings	the king
A freedman of the best class	80 shillings	
A freedman of the 2nd class	60 shillings	
A freedman of the 3rd class	40 shillings	
Servant of a ceorl	6 shillings	

---

41 The wergeld served to calculate compensation for all sorts of injuries, not only for death.

Hlothhere and Eadric's Laws (673–685)

Wergeld	Amount of money to be paid	Beneficiary
Nobleman	300 shillings	
Freeman	100 shillings	

Ine's Laws (694)

Wergeld	Amount of money to be paid	Beneficiary
Member of the king's household	1200 shillings	relatives
	+ 120 shillings	the lord
Nobleman	600 shillings	relatives
	+ 80 shillings	the lord
Ceorl	200 shillings	relatives
	+ 30 shillings	the lord
King's godson	wergeld	relatives
	wergeld	the king
Bishop's godson	wergeld	relatives
	1/2 wergeld	bishop
Godson/godfather of another	same compensation as to the dead man's lord	godfather/godson
Foreigner	?	2/3 to the king 1/3 to his son (or relatives)
Welshman holding 5 hides of land	600 shillings	
Welsh horseman in the king's service	200 shillings	
Welsh taxpayer / holding 1 hide of land	120 shillings	
Welshman holding 1/2 a hide of land	80 shillings	
Welshman holding no land	60 shillings	
An illegitimate & disowned child		the king + his lord (not the father)

Alfred's laws (871–899)

Wergeld	Amount of money to be paid	Beneficiary
Pregnant woman	full wergeld for the woman + 1/2 wergeld (of the father's kin) for the child + fine (60 or 120 shillings)	

Apart from this last clause, women do not appear in this table. Their wergelds are to be looked for in the previous lists which focused on matters directly linked to their sex, social position, and family life. The table, however, is a good means of comparison, a way of opposing men's and women's wergelds. One immediately notices that men's wergeld was no higher than women's. The highest wergeld, that of members of the king's household, reached 1200 shillings. The same amount was mentioned in Alfred's laws concerning 'a young betrothed woman whose wergeld is 1200 shillings'. The wergeld of the next class (noblemen) reached 600 shillings and the same figure is to be found in relation to 'a young betrothed woman whose wergeld is 600 shillings'. There was no discrimination between the sexes, only people's status in society determined their wergeld. In comparison, on the Continent most barbarian laws attributed a much higher wergeld to women who could have children than that of men of the same class. According to the Salic Law (c. 507–511) a killer was required to pay 200 solidi for a free Frank, which was the amount of the compensation for a woman who could no longer have children or for a girl too young to have a child. 'But if anyone kills a freewoman after she has begun to nurse, let him be held liable for 600 denarii' (41.16) and 'if anyone strikes a pregnant freewoman in the stomach or kidneys (...) and the foetus is killed and is aborted, let him be held liable for 600 solidi (104, 4–5). But if the woman was killed due to this, let him be liable for 900 solidi (104, 6). But if the child that was aborted was a girl, let him compensate 2400 solidi (104, 8)':[42] emphasis was clearly put on procreation and mother-

---

42 E. Amt, ed., *Women's Lives in Medieval Europe, a Sourcebook*, no.10, p.44.

hood. Contrary to Anglo-Saxon laws, where a person's wergeld did not seem to vary according to age, a young Frankish widow's wergeld was consequently much higher than that of a widow over 40 years of age. Moreover Germanic bodies of law reflect the importance attributed at the time to a person's ethnic origin: a Roman's wergeld was twice less than that of a Frank. One notices a similar rule in Ine's laws about the Welsh. Unfortunately nothing is said about Welsh women.

The law codes are rather cryptic. They do not give us a sharply outlined picture free from ambiguity – far from it! The legal status of widows appears full of conflicting elements. The only clear point is that widows formed a class of their own. They were supposed to decide for themselves and make life choices: they could remain single or remarry after a year if they wanted. They were not to be forced to marry a man they disliked. They were not to be consigned to monasteries. In spite of these rules, surviving lawsuits show that they were easily cheated upon. Moreover, the very fact that the kings needed to repeat that widows were to choose freely their new husband proves that it was probably not often the case! Widows were also seen as a particularly vulnerable class that needed to be protected by a male relative or by the Church. Yet, in both cases, the role of the protectors could be limited to that of an adviser: the widow was presented as the one who directed her affairs as she saw fit. She became head of the family, being the guardian of her children who were under age (that is to say under 10 at the time of King Aethelberht, and under 12 starting with King Alfred). She also came into part of her husband's property, inheriting in the same way as her children and other close relatives. And yet, widows were often considered as living in destitution: under King Aethelstan, the authorities of London levied a new tax 'and everyone shall pay his shilling who has property which is worth thirty pence, except poor widows who have no land and no one to work for them'.[43] It seems now necessary to try and assess their economic situation: what degree of independence did widows have? Did they hold, and bequeath land in their own name? What was their access to movable wealth? Were their choices and wishes respected? Let us now turn to documents in which they can be heard, in which we meet them – at last.

43   F.L. Attenborough, ed., *The Laws of the Earliest English Kings*, p.159.

Chapter Three
The Economic (In)dependence of Widows

Widows as Landholders

Anglo-Saxon law codes underscore the fact that widows needed to be protected. Charters and wills show that husbands saw to it that their widows should be well provided for – distrusting the greed of the outliving male relatives. Besides, a system of property arrangement existed to ensure good relationships between families. Tacitus had already described marriage agreements among the Germans in the first century of our era:

> Their marriage code, however, is strict, and no feature of their morality deserves higher praise. (...) The dowry is brought by husband to wife, not by wife to husband. Parents and kinsmen attend and approve the gifts – not gifts chosen to please a woman's fancy or gaily deck a young bride, but oxen, a horse with its bridle, or a shield, spear, and sword. In consideration of such gifts a man gets his wife, and she in her turn brings a present of arms to her husband. This interchange of gifts typifies for them the most sacred bond of union, sanctified by mystic rites under the favour of the presiding deities of wedlock.[1]

Tacitus' account is tendentious, it emphasizes the Germans' virtues in order to highlight the degeneracy of the Roman Empire. Yet it is also an invaluable source concerning the customs of the remote ancestors of the Anglo-Saxons. The above-extract is interesting because it mentions an 'interchange of gifts': economic co-operation was therefore the rule. It also shows that Tacitus was surprised that the dowry should be brought by the bridegroom and not by the bride.

---

[1] Tacitus, *The Agricola and the Germania*, H. Mattingly & S.A. Handford, ed., Harmondsworth: Penguin books, 1948–1970, p.116.

In pre-Conquest England, marriage – especially among the high class – was a business deal between two families. Aethelberht's laws stated that if a man had an affair with a married woman, 'he shall pay [the husband] his wergeld, and procure a second wife with his own money, and bring her to the other man's home' (art. 31). Article 31 of Ine's laws warned that 'if anyone buys a wife and the marriage does not take place, he [the bride's guardian] shall return the bridal price and pay [the bridegroom] as much again, and he shall compensate the trustees of the marriage according to the amount he is entitled to for infraction of his surety'. Though L.A. Finke, after C. Fell, reminds her readers that 'the word *agan* (own) could be understood to refer to the responsibilities of any person – man or woman – in charge of a community',[2] the numerous other monetary references are without ambiguity. Besides, L.A. Finke herself goes on, saying that 'marriage in Anglo-Saxon England was primarily a financial arrangement rather than a union for mutual affection and love'.[3] A marriage agreement dating back to the reign of King Cnut gives us the details of the transaction settled between a certain Brihtric and his daughter's suitor, called Godwine:

> Here is declared in this document the agreement which Godwine made with Brihtric when he wooed his daughter. In the first place he gave her a pound's weight of gold, to induce her to accept his suit, and he granted her the estate at Street with all that belongs to it, and 150 acres at Burmarsh and in addition 30 oxen and 20 cows and 10 horses and 10 slaves.[4]

It must be underlined that this agreement is a unilateral commitment: only the suitor specifies the lands and other possessions he intends to give his wife-to-be. The daughter, whose name is not given, seems to be at liberty to accept or reject the proposal, yet as the father is the one who carries on the negotiations, one may wonder if the girl really had room for manoeuvre. Either way 'the maiden was brought from

---

2   L.A. Finke, *Women's Writing in English*, London, New York: Longman, 1999, p.24.
3   Ibid., p.24.
4   A.J. Robertson, ed., *Anglo-Saxon Charters*, Cambridge: University Press, 1956, p.151.

Brightling' and the deal was concluded, 'whichever of them lives the longer shall succeed to all the property both in land and everything which I have given them'. Though it is not easy to know who the 'I' talking here is, one can note that widowhood is considered from the moment of engagement and the question of inheritance sorted out before the wedding ceremony has even taken place: husbands and wives were all potential widowers and widows. Similarly, the tenth-century text 'concerning the betrothal of a woman' distinguishes what the bridegroom grants the woman 'for her acceptance of his suit' and what he grants her 'if she should live longer than he.'[5]

Documents, therefore, show that marriage and widowhood were indissociable in medieval mentality and reality. They also show that the idea that widows should be provided for was constant.

An Anglo-Saxon wife was given by her husband a *morgengifu*, that is to say a gift on the morning after the consummation of the marriage. In Aelfric's *Glossary*, *morgengifu* corresponds to the latin *dos*. The gift could be in the form of money, movables, or in land. The *morgengifu* was the wife's personal property to be used, sold and bequeathed as she wished. It aimed at ensuring her financial security should she outlive her husband. Conversely, if she died first and was childless, her property – which consequently included the *morgengifu* – reverted to her own relatives. As our documentation mainly concerns noble ladies, the morning-gifts that we see mentioned are essentially estates, land being the only real source of power at the time. Morgengifts are alluded to in certain Anglo-Saxon wills. Wynflæd, a lay-abbess of the 10th century granted several estates to her son Eadmær including 'the estate at Faccombe, which was her marriage-gift, for his lifetime, and then after his death, if Aethelflæd survive him, she is to succeed to the estate at Faccombe, and after her death it is to revert to Eadwold's possession'.[6] Wynflæd, therefore, settles the terms of her succession over two generations, Aethelflæd being her daughter and Eadwold her grandson. In his will, Aelfhelm reminded people what he had given 'to [his] wife as a marriage-gift, namely,

---

5   D. Whitelock, ed., *English Historical Documents*, no.50, p.467.
6   D. Whitelock, ed., *Anglo-Saxon Wills*, no.III, p.11.

Baddow and Burstead and Stratford and the three hides at Enhale'.[7] Aelfflæd, the widow of Brihtnoth (the hero of the Old English poem *The Battle of Maldon*), granted her morning-gift, an estate at Rettendon, to the monastery of Ely. At the end of the 9th century, a lawsuit involved Aethelm Higa with Helmstan about an estate of five hides at Fonthill. Helmstan claimed the estate as his own:

> His claim to the possession of it being that Aetheldryth had made it over to Oswulf for a fair price, and that Aetheldryth had told Oswulf that it was fully in her power to sell it to him, because it had been her morning-gift when she first came to Athulf...[8]

Husbands also provided for their wives a dower – a portion of their estate – to keep them in their widowhood. The Anglo-Saxon kings tackled the question of the share of the widows' inheritance several times. King Ine's laws stated that a wife had in her possession a third of the household property (article 57). Aethelberht's laws specified that a widow with a living child would have half the goods left by the husband (article 78). *Domesday Book* gives the same percentages, depending on the county considered. In Nottinghamshire, for instance, the rule was that 'if a thegn having sake and soke forfeits his land, the king and earl between them have half his land and resources, and his lawful wife with his legitimate heirs, if there are any, have the other half'.[9] Dowers, therefore, varied considerably according to the wealth of the husband, from a few acres to huge estates.

The dower could be defined at the time of marriage or specified in a will. In his will, for instance, the ealdorman Aethelmær explained: 'all that I grant to my wife, whether estates or goods, I grant according to the terms which we settled by a compact between us'.[10] Aethelwold 'bequeathed the ten hides at Manningford to his wife for as long as her

---

7   Ibid., no.XIII, p.31.
8   F.E. Harmer, ed., *Select English Documents of the 9th and 10th-centuries*, no.XVIII, p.61.
9   A. Williams & G.H. Martin, eds., *Domesday Book*, fol. 280V, p.758. A *thegn* was 'a man of noble status as opposed to a peasant (*ceorl*), having a wergeld of 1,200s. *Sake and soke* 'used to denote the judicial and dominical rights associated with the possession of land' (pp.1431–1436 of the glossary).
10 D. Whitelock, ed., *Anglo-Saxon Wills*, no.X, p.27.

life shall last, and after her death to the New Minster for the souls of both of us'.[11] The dower differed from the morning-gift insofar as the husband had a say regarding to whom the dower was to pass after his wife's death. The widow, therefore, was the sole owner of the morning-gift and, as in the case of Aetheldryth, it was 'fully in her power to sell it', whereas the dower was a life usufruct, a temporary holding. This is why Aethelric makes it clear that what he grants to his wife is 'for her lifetime; and after her death the estate at Bocking is to go to the community at Christchurch, for our souls and for that of my father who obtained it'.[12] Similarly, Wulfgeat explains that 'he grants to his wife the estates at Kilsall and Evenlode and Roden for as long as her life lasts, and after her death the land is to revert to my kindred, those who are nearest'.[13] It was not in a will but before marrying Archbishop Wulfstan's sister (the name of the lady is not given) that Wulfric stated that:

> He promised her the estates at Orleton and Ribbesford for her lifetime, and promised her that he would obtain the estate at Knightwick for her for three lives from the community at Winchcombe.

To this dower, Wulfric added a morning-gift:

> He gave her the estate at Alton to grant and bestow upon whomsoever she pleased during her lifetime or at her death, as she preferred.[14]

A dower could not be given away, it remained within the family: the rights of the heirs were consequently taken into account. However, some husbands were particularly distrustful and only bestowed lifetime property or various movables on their wives if the latter did not remarry: 'I, Earl Aelfred, give these estates, after my time, to Werburg and to Alhthryth, the child of us both, with livestock and with produce and with everything pertaining thereto; and I give them two thousand swine with the estates if she remains unmarried in accordance with

---

11 Ibid., no.XII, p.31.
12 Ibid., no.XVI (1), p.43.
13 Ibid., no.XIX, p.55.
14 A.J. Robertson, ed., *Anglo-Saxon Charters*, no.LXXVI, p.149.

our verbal agreements'.[15] In the 9th century as well, Abba, a reeve, made the following arrangements:

> In the first place, with regard to the land which I have, and God gave me, and I received from my lords, it is my desire that if God will give me a child, he shall have the land after me. (...) If, however, it is my lot not to have a child, then I desire that my wife shall have it as long as she is willing to keep it without marrying again. (...) If, however, my wife is not willing to remain unwedded, and prefers to contract another marriage, then my kinsmen are to take the land and to give her own property to her.[16]

It has often been noted that husbands were particularly generous with their wives, always bequeathing them large parts of their property. According to Pauline Stafford, one must not lose sight of the fact that dowers could not be forfeited, 'widow's lands were declared to be exempt, with the result in some cases of actually strengthening widows' claims. Widows' dower was ever more carefully specified, one motive, I would suggest, behind the series of tenth- and eleventh-century English wills'.[17] *Domesday Book* confirms P. Stafford's suggestion: in Oxfordshire, the rule was that 'if anyone kills any man within his own court or house, his body and all his substance are in the king's power, except his wife's dower if he received her with a dowry'.[18] Consequently, a dower was a good way of being sure that a certain number of estates remained within the family. On the other hand, children and other heirs may have felt such arrangements were to their detriment.

Dowers were portions of a deceased husband's estate which the widow could use and enjoy but, as Abba's will proves, it was not a woman's 'own property'. Her 'own property' included the morning-

---

15   F.E. Harmer, ed., *Select English Documents of the 9th and 10th-centuries*, no.X, p.47.
16   *Ibid.*, no.II, pp.40–41.
17   P. Stafford, 'Women in Domesday', *Reading Medieval Studies*, vol.XV, 1989, p.88. In her book, *Unification and Conquest*, London: Edward Arnold, 1989, P. Stafford went back to the same idea: 'Widows' land was part of the old family provisions which nobles successfully exempted from royal forfeiture. Whether or not this encouraged larger dowers, it contributed to the increasing desire carefully to specify what widows were to get', p. 176.
18   A. Williams & G.H. Martin, eds., *Domesday Book*, fol. 154V, p.425.

gift but also her dowry – the money or property she had brought to the husband – and personal bequests. Daughters, indeed, came into their parents' property though many testators did, in fact, favour male heirs over female heirs. Wills show that fathers and mothers usually left land to every member of the family. In the 9th century, Lufu, a religious woman – she calls herself 'the humble handmaid of God' – made an annual gift of 'sixty ambers of malt, one hundred and fifty loaves, fifty white loaves, one hundred and twenty alm-loaves, a bullock, a pig, four sheep, and two weys of lard and cheese' to the community at Christ Church from 'the inheritance which God has given me (...) [her] inheritance at Mongeham'.[19] In 961, Eadgifu, King Edward the Elder's third wife, 'informed the archbishop and the community at Christ Church how her estate at Cooling came [into her hands]. The fact is that her father left her the estate and the title-deed having lawfully come into possession of them, as an inheritance from his ancestors'.[20] About 950, Wynflæd favoured her daughter Aethelflæd bequeathing her large estates, jewels and many objects. She did not, however, forget her son Eadmær, her grandson Eadwold and her granddaughter Eadgifu.

When a daughter got married, her family provided her with a dowry. In reality the daughter did not dispose of this marriage portion as she wished for her father, or some other male protector,[21] dealt directly with the husband and the latter became their subtenant. In *Domesday Book*, one can read that:

> In Streatley Pirot holds of Nigel d'Aubigny 4 hides and the third part of 1 hide as 1 manor. (...) Pirot holds 3 hides of this land as his wife's marriage portion, and 1 hide and a third part of 1 hide he holds in fee of Nigel d'Aubigny. (fol. 214V)

---

19   F.E. Harmer, ed., *Select English Documents of the 9th and 10th-centuries*, no.IV, p.43. By the time of *Domesday Book*, the estate of Mongeham was held by the abbot of St Augustine's (fol. 12).
20   Ibid., no.XXIII, p.66.
21   *Domesday Book* mentions the case of Ansfrid de Cormeilles who obtained several estates in Gloucestershire from Walter de Lacy 'when he married his niece.' (fol. 170).

In Suffolk, 'Edmund the Priest, commended to St Aethelthryth, held Brandeston TRE[22] and the land of Brandeston and Clopton which he received with his wife, he gave up to the church with his wife's consent by an agreement whereby he could not sell or give [it] away from the church'. (fol. 431V). Although Edmund held these lands, they were clearly his wife's property since he needed her permission to grant it 'to the church': dowries were held by the husband but passed to the widow at his death. This is why Thurketel of Palgrave explains:

> And to my wife Leofwyn I grant Shimpling, all the purchased estate and the other which I received when I married her.[23]

In addition to inherited land, women could increase their wealth by buying or selling property. When King Aethelbald died, his widow Judith 'sold up the possessions which she had acquired in the kingdom of the English, then returned to her father'.[24] Godric of Bourne bought the estate at Offham (Kent) and the transaction was as follows: 'he gave his sister Eadgifu a mark of gold and 13 pounds [of silver] and 63 pence to complete the purchase, so that he might have the right of giving and granting it during his lifetime and at his death to whomsoever he preferred. This purchase has been completed at Wye before the whole shire'.[25] A common practice was holding estates under leases for several (usually three) lives. Several agreements between religious communities and individuals have survived. They show that these leases were an appreciable source of income for the Church. In 966, Oswald, the bishop of Worcester granted three hides

> To a certain woman whose name is Aelfhild, for the love of God and the relationship between us, with everything belonging to it, for her lifetime, and after her death to two heirs, and after their death to the holy foundation at Worcester for the use of the bishop. And it shall be free from every burden,

---

22 *Tempore Regis Edwardi* ('in the time of King Edward').
23 D. Whitelock, ed., *Anglo-Saxon Wills*, no.XXIV, p.69.
24 J.L. Nelson, ed., *The Annals of St-Bertin*, p.97.
25 A.J. Robertson, ed., *Anglo-Saxon Charters*, no.CIII, p.193.

except military service and the construction of walls and bridges and carrying service for the church.[26]

Earlier, one of Oswald's predecessors had obtained the permission of the community at Worcester to lease to his kinswoman Cyneswith:

> three of the five hides of land at Elmstone. (...) She shall have the right of cutting timber in the wood which the peasants enjoy; and likewise [he] let to her separately the peasants' copse. (...) And Cyneswith shall not leave it to anyone, while the lease runs, except one of her children – whichever she pleases – if they survive. If they do not survive, she shall leave it to whichever of her kinsmen is willing to earn it from her.[27]

These documents show that women were not excluded from financial transactions and played an important role in the transfer of property.

A Major Role in the Conveyance of Property

Anglo-Saxon families were not extended kin groups but already of the nuclear type, that is to say a married man and woman with their offspring. What defined a family was the marriage bond rather than descent. In charters and wills the vocabulary to refer to relatives rapidly becomes imprecise: in documents in Latin, *avus* is either a grandfather or any ancestor, *nepos* can be used to designate both a nephew or a grandson, *avunculus* is both a paternal and a maternal uncle; *cognati, parentes, generi, propinqui* are general terms for relatives. In *Vita Aedwardi Regis* (*The Life of King Edward*), Edward when a young boy 'was carried to his kinsmen [*auos suos*] in Francia, so that with them he could spend his childhood'.[28] In fact these kinsmen were none other than his own mother's brothers, Duke Richard II of Normandy, Robert Archbishop of Rouen, as well as Godfrey and

---

26 Ibid., no.XLII, p.87.
27 Ibid., no.XVI, p.29–31.
28 F. Barlow, ed., *Vita Aedwardi Regis/The Life of King Edward*, London: T. Nelson & Sons, 1962, p.8.

William, therefore very close relations. We find the same vagueness in the *Encomium Emmae Reginae* about the same protagonists:

> Queen Emma remained alone in the kingdom, sorrowing for the bitter death of her lord and alarmed at the absence of her sons. For one of them, namely Hörthaknutr, whom his father had made king of the Danes, was in his own kingdom, and two others were residing with their relative [*cum propinquo suo*] Robert, for they had been brought to Normandy to be brought up.[29]

Old English texts are characterized by the same lack of precision. *Nefa* can be used to refer to a nephew, a grandson or a stepson while *nift/ nefene* designates either a niece, a granddaughter or a stepdaughter. Those who wished to avoid ambiguity used descriptive compounds such as *broþordohtor* for 'niece' and *broþorsunu* for 'nephew'. *Adum* is found in Old English texts meaning 'son-in-law' but also 'father-in-law'. A 'sister-in-law' is simply a *broþorwif*. In her will Aelfflæd grants an estate to her *hlauordæs medder* ('lord's mother' = mother-in-law).[30] *Geswiria* meant a 'sister's son' or a 'cousin' while *sweor* could be used for a cousin as well as for a father-in-law. Several general terms are often encountered in Old English texts: the most common ones are *mæg* that is to say a male relative, a kinsman and *mage* a female relative, a kinswoman. A *mæg* could be a cousin or a descendant but also closer kin. Aethelflæd granted 'the estate at Waldingfield to [her] kinswoman [*mira magan*] Crawe after [her] death'. Crawe was not her sister. Aethelflæd's father mentions his two daughters in his will – namely Aethelflæd and Aelfflæd.[31] And Aethelflæd bequeathes numerous estates to Aelfflæd calling her each time 'my sister'. Besides, Aelfflæd mentions Crawe in her own will and, in her turn, calls her 'my kinswoman' [*miræ magan*]. Crawe was probably a cousin of the two ladies. In several other wills, however, the word is to be found clearly referring to a brother or a sister. Leofgifu, for instance, mentions that she leaves 'to [her] brother-in-

---

29 A. Campbell, ed., *Encomium Emmae Reginae*, pp.38–39.
30 D. Whitelock, ed., *Anglo-Saxon Wills*, no.XV, p.39.
31 In fact Aelfflæd is not named. She is always referred to as his 'other daughter' or his 'younger daughter'. Similarly, in Aethelflæd's will, Aelfflæd is only 'my sister'. Fortunately enough, Aelfflæd's own will has survived.

law Godwine, and [her] kinswoman [*mire meygan*], the three hides at Warley'. Wulfric calls his brother Aelfhelm his 'kinsman' [*minan mæge*]. Other general terms include *gecynd* or *cuþa*.

The sources available, be they laws, wills, charters, Saints' Lives, chronicles, homilies, etc., converge to make of the conjugal family the basic family organization, which accounts for the vagueness of the terms referring to relations beyond it. Hagiographical sources often mention the parents of the saints either, with the early martyrs, to emphasize their wickedness because of their wish to remain pagan or, with later saints, to stress their benevolence. Leoba's parents, for example, are praised for being so zealous in religion. St Wilfrid's mother is most pious. St Guthlac's parents are noble and prosperous. Grandparents play no role and are not even mentioned. They are also quasi absent from historical documents. Very few of them appear in wills. Aethelstan the Aetheling, the son of King Aethelred by his first wife Aelfgifu, wishes everyone to remember that:

> All those things which I have granted to God, to God's church and God's servants, are done for the soul of my dear father King Ethelred and for mine, and for the soul of Aelfthryth[32] my grandmother, who brought me up, and for the souls of all those who shall give me their help with these benefactions.[33]

Among the 39 wills edited by D. Whitelock in 1930, only two testators mention living grandchildren. Wynflæd bequeathes estates, slaves, jewels and many objects to her granddaughter Eadgifu and her grandson Eadwold. Wulfgeat refers to three different generations: he grants estates to his wife, his two daughters and his grandson. In the majority of cases, however, diplomatic documents, wills and settlements, only concern parents and children. As shows the table p.121, husbands always favoured their wives with lifetime land gifts. Then came their children who were well-provided for. In the 9th century, Earl Aelfred stated: 'those persons to whom I am most anxious to grant my property and bookland, [are] my wife Werburg and the child

---

32   Edgar the Peaceful's third wife.
33   D. Whitelock, ed., *Anglo-Saxon Wills*, no.XX, p.63.

of us both'.[34] Brothers and sisters, nephews and nieces come up when the testator/testatrix has no immediate heir. In such case, however, bequests to the Church was a common rule.

The table p.121 is revealing though not totally reliable. Out of the 39 wills edited by D. Whitelock 26 have been selected.[35] For each of these 26 wills, the various legatees have been listed. Religious communities and wives distinctly head the list. Furthermore, it must be taken into account that Aelfgar was a widower and that it seems most likely that two other testators, Wulfric and Ketel were widowers as well: they could not, consequently, leave anything to their wives. None of the 9 testatrixes grant anything to a potential husband. Mantat the anchorite, by definition, lived alone in seclusion. Among the 8 remaining women, 4 (Aethelflæd, Aelfflæd, Leofgifu, Wulfgyth) were unmistakably widows and it is most likely that Wynflæd and Wulfwaru were widows too. There remains the case of Aelfgifu who is obviously of royal descent. She grants estates to 'God's church' for the soul of her royal lord who was alive at the time. Aelgifu has been associated to Aethelred's first wife or to Eadwig's wife about whom the *Anglo-Saxon Chronicle* (958) reports that Archbishop Oda dissolved the marriage on grounds of consanguinity. Aelfgifu's will contains several bequests to the king, who may therefore have been her husband, but they constitute what was known as *heriot*. Men's wills all mention the payment of *heriot* to the king or to their lord. It was a service consisting of weapons and horses restored to the lord on the death of the vassal. In Cnut's laws, 'heriots are to be determined as befits the rank: an earl's as belongs thereto, namely eight horses, four saddled and

---

34 F.E. Harmer, ed., *Select English Documents of the 9th and 10th-centuries*, no.X, p.47.
35 Those of Aelfgar, Wynflæd, Aelfgifu, Aelfheah, Aethelmær, Brihtric and Aelfswith, Aethelwold, Aelfhelm, Aethelflæd, Aelfflæd, Aethelric, Wulfric, Wulfgeat, Wulfwaru, Mantat, Thurketel of Palgrave, Thurketel Heyng, Wulfsige, Aelfric Modercope, Leofgifu, Thurstan, Wulfgyth, Edwin, Ketel, Siflæd, Ulf and Madselin. The wills of clergymen, that of the Aetheling Aethelstan, and single bequests have been excluded: our study is about family bonds and only wills mentioning multiple beneficiaries are of some interest. Ecclecsiastics bequeathe most of their property to the Church. The Aetheling has been rejected because he was single. On the other hand, all women's wills have been selected.

four unsaddled, and four helmets and four coats of mail and eight spears and as many shields and four swords and 200 mancuses of gold'. It fell to the widow to pay the tax: 'and each widow is to pay the heriot within 12 months, without fine, unless it is convenient to her to do so sooner'. On the other hand there is no mention of *heriot* for women. Yet, by the middle of the tenth-century, ecclesiastics and women started making bequests to their lords who, in exchange, were expected to enforce their followers' arrangements. This is probably why Aelfgifu had it specified:

> And I grant to my royal lord the estates at Wing, Linslade, Haversham, Hatfield, Masworth and Gussage; and two armlets, each of a hundred and twenty mancuses, and a drinking-cup and six horses and as many shields and spears.[36]

Apart from Aelfgifu, only Aethelflæd (another king's wife), her sister Aelfflæd and Wulfgyth felt obliged to pay this tax. The three of them were widows and Aelfflæd voices her fear of seeing her will violated and her need of protection:

> First I grant to my lord after my death the eight estates, namely Dovercourt, Beaumont, Alresford, Stanway, Barton, Lexden, Elmset and Buxhall; and two armlets of two pounds in weight, and two drinking-cups and a silver vessel. And I humbly pray you, Sire, for god's sake and for the sake of my lord's soul and for the sake of my sister's soul, that you will protect the holy foundation at Stoke in which my ancestors lie buried.[37]

Wulfgyth lived later than the other three, in the first part of the eleventh-century. She refers to the payment of the tax as a well-established rule, using the term *heriot,* but without giving any detail, as if what the tax consisted of had been set once for all. Therefore she only states: 'first to my lord his due heriot'.[38]

The table shows that daughters were slightly favoured in our selection of wills both by fathers and mothers. Of course, one cannot exclude the fact that some of the couples may simply have had more daughters than sons. Aelfgar, for instance, had two daughters and no

36   D. Whitelock, ed., *Anglo-Saxon Wills*, no.VIII, p.21.
37   Ibid., no.XV, p.39.
38   Ibid., no.XXXII, p.85.

son at all. Moreover, wills only concerned bookland, that is to say privileged land tenures held by charters or deeds (*boc* = document, charter, book). Bookland was therefore acquired land and was alienable and heritable. Opposed to bookland was folkland which was inalienable outside the owner's kindred and subject to all customary and fiscal burdens. This is why Earl Aelfred left three hides of bookland to his illegitimate son and added 'and if the king will grant him the folkland as well as the bookland, then let him have it and enjoy it; if that may not be, then she [the earl's daughter, Alhthryth] is to give him whichever she pleases, either the estate at Horsley or that at Longfield'.[39] This passage is a good illustration of the fact that, in the long-term interests of the families, folkland was preferably (and perhaps even only) held by a male representative of the paternal line – which might explain why parents were careful to transmit some of their bookland estates to their daughters. Another weakness of the table, however, is that it does not distinguish between a son with extensive bequests and a poorly provided-for daughter. It simply proves that female heirs were not exceptional. Many of the legatees are no longer identifiable today because nothing but their name is given and no family tie is mentioned. Therefore these people (relatives, clerics, protectors, servants?) are grouped together as 'unidentified legatees'. Lastly, servants are very often mentioned in these tenth and eleventh-century wills. The bequests consist in movables, money or a few acres of land.

---

39   F.E. Harmer, ed., *Select English Documents of the 9th and 10th-centuries*, no.X, p.48.

To whom did testators/testatrixes bequeath their property?

	Wills by Women (9 women are concerned)	Wills by men (15 men are concerned)	Wills by husband & wife (2 couples are concerned)
Religious houses	9	15	2
Archbishops & bishops	2	6	2
Abbots	3	3	1
Priests	3	3	
Heriot to king or lord	4	13	1
Members of the royal family	2	1	1
Husband			
Wife		10	
Daughter	4	5	
Son	3	4	
Grandson	1	1 (+1 'if any')	
Granddaughter	1	(1 'if any')	
'Kinswoman'	3	1	1
Sister	2	(1 agreement with sisters)	
'Kinsman'	2	2	1
Brother	2	5	1
Niece		1	
Nephew	1	4	
Nephew's children		1	
Mother		1	1
Mother-in-law	1		
Sister-in-law	1		
Brother-in-law	2		
Son-in-law		2	

Goddaughter		1	
Reeve/Steward	2	1	
Servant	5	6	1
Unidentified legatee	2	9	2

This table confirms the well-known fact that husbands favoured their wives. Out of 12 (since 3 were, in all likelihood, widowers) 10 husbands grant the largest part of their legacy to their wives. This figure emphasizes the importance, already pronounced at the time, of the conjugal couple. Concern, beyond death, for the deceased partner is obvious in all wills. Widowers and widows all grant estates to the Church for the sake of the souls of their dead wives or husbands: Aethelflæd, for instance, bequeathed 'the estate at Ham to Christchurch at Canterbury for King Edmund's soul and for her soul', Leofgifu granted several estates 'to Christ and his saints for the redemption of [her] lord's soul and [hers]', Wulffgyth gave an estate to Christchurch 'for [her] soul and [her] lord Aelfwine's and for the souls of all [her] children'. Widowers acted similarly: Ketel 'grants Stisted to Christchurch after [his] time, for the sake of [his] father's soul and for Sæflæd's', Aelfgar asked his daughter 'to be the more zealous for the welfare of [his] soul and of her mother's soul and of her brother's soul'. Though women's wills are among the very few Anglo-Saxon documents where a woman's voice speaks directly to her audience, no feelings, nothing about their frame of mind show. These pieces of writing are conventional, factual. One must keep in mind that the Anglo-Saxon will was an oral act made in front of an audience. Most wills were never recorded in writing. Sometimes a scribe was asked to put the words in writing – before or after the ceremony: the testator/testatrix was not the author of his/her written will.[40] Besides, people made their wills long before their deaths in order to protect their own rights. All this explains why wills are often

---

40   See M.M. Sheehan, *The Will in Medieval England*, Toronto: Pontifical Institute of Medieval Studies, Studies and Texts VI, 1963. See also K.A. Lowe, 'The Nature and Effect of the Anglo-Saxon Vernacular Will', *Legal History*, 19 (1988), pp.23–61.

very formal, impersonal statements. In two Old English poems, *Wulf & Eadwacer* and *The Wife's Lament*, the two female narrators fervently express their distress, the pain of waiting and of mourning. They are tormented by anxiety and longing:

> (...)   Full often here
> The absence of my lord comes sharply to me.
> Dear lovers in this world lie in their beds,
> While I alone at crack of dawn must walk
> Under the oak-tree round this earthy cave,
> Where I must stay the length of summer days,
> Where I may weep my banishment and all
> My many hardships, for I never can
> Contrive to set at rest my careworn heart,
> Nor all the longing that this life has brought me.
> (*The Wife's Lament* ll. 32–41)[41]

Unfortunately, both poems are rather cryptic and numerous interpretations have been given. It is therefore difficult to know for sure what the poet intended. Such is not the case of the two eleventh-century Latin eulogies commissioned by Queen Emma and Queen Edith: both texts are highly partial accounts of the queens' lives and actions. The *Encomium Emmae Reginae* was written in 1041–1042 when Emma was able to return to England because her son 'King Harthacnut came to Sandwich, seven days before midsummer, and he was at once received by both English and Danes' (*Anglo-Saxon Chronicle*, 1040). In 1041, 'came Edward, his brother on his mother's side, from abroad; he was the son of King Aethelred, and had long been an exile from his country, but was nevertheless sworn in as [future] king' (*Anglo-Saxon Chronicle*, 1041). It seems that Emma had encouraged her two sons, Edward and Alfred, to return to England in 1036 which resulted in the blinding and murder of Alfred. The Encomiast (probably a monk from the abbey of Saint-Bertin in Saint-Omer [Flanders]) totally clears her of suspicion by rewriting history and distorting reality: the whole text is a masterly justification of Queen Emma's actions. She is described as the ideal wife, mother and widow. The author manages to pass over Emma's first marriage to King Aethelred in silence, Edward and

---

41   R. Hamer, ed., *Anglo-Saxon Verse*, London: Faber & Faber, 1970, p.75.

Alfred becoming Cnut and Emma's 'other legitimate sons' (§ 18). When Cnut dies, Emma is presented as the model of a distressed widow:

> The Lady Emma, his queen mourned together with the natives, poor and rich lamented together, the bishops and clerics wept with the monks and nuns; but let the rejoicing in the kingdom of heaven be as great as was the mourning in the world!
> (...)
> When Cnut was dead and honourably buried in the monastery built at Winchester in honour of St Peter, the lady, Queen Emma, remained alone in the kingdom, sorrowing for the bitter death of her lord and alarmed at the absence of her sons.[42]

Queen Edith also had facts manipulated to her advantage when she commissioned the *Vita Eadwardi Regis* (1065–1067). Book one lavishes praise on her family, the house of Godwin. Book two justifies her childless union to King Edward by modelling it on hagiographic chaste marriage: Edith is depicted as chaste and modest; Edward is a spiritual model of sanctity. He is presented as the one who wished to lead a life of chastity within marriage. And when Edward is at death's door, the scene verges on melodrama:

> Then he addressed his last words to the queen who was sitting at his feet, in this wise, 'May God be gracious to this my wife for the zealous solicitude of her service. For she has served me devotedly, and has always stood close by my side like a beloved daughter. And so from the forgiving God may she obtain the reward of eternal happiness'. And stretching forth his hand to his governor, her brother, Harold, he said, 'I commend this woman and all the kingdom to your protection'. (...) Now and then he also comforted the queen, who ceased not from lamenting, to ease her natural grief.[43]

Anglo-Saxon widows seen expressing grief after the death of their husbands are thus limited to these two queens who wanted to leave a particular flattering image of themselves. It is therefore difficult to allow for genuine sorrow in productions that always show Emma and

---

42   A. Campbell, ed., *Encomium Emmae Reginae*, p.39.
43   F. Barlow, ed., *Vita Aedwardi Regis/The Life of King Edward*, pp.79–80.

Edith in a good light. Ostensibly mourning one's husband was also part of the role they had given themselves.

The table also confirms the fact that, in the long run, paternal kinsmen were favoured. Simon Keynes and Michael Lapidge mention that in one of Burgred of Mercia's charters dated 869, the king went as far as restricting the scope of alienation of bookland to a male representative of the paternal line.[44] Other kings only recommended it. Alfred's laws stipulates that 'a man who holds land by title-deed, shall not be allowed to give it out of his kindred, if there is documentary or [other] evidence that the power to do so is forbidden him by the man who first acquired it, or by those who gave it to him' (§ 41).[45] In his own will, King Alfred did not give any land out of his kindred, he granted estates to all his children, boys or girls, but left to his elder son a lion's share. He also made gifts to his nephews, all brothers' sons.[46] He then added:

> And I desire that the persons to whom I have bequeathed my bookland should not dispose of it outside my kindred after their lifetime, but I desire that after their lifetime it should pass to my nearest of kin, unless any of them have children; then I prefer that it should pass to the child in the male line as long as any is worthy of it. My grandfather had bequeathed his land on the spear side and not on the spindle side.

Ealdorman Aelfred's will was drawn up at the same time (between 871 and 889). The Earl of Surrey bequeathed all his property to his daughter Alhthryth then gave strict instructions which precluded her from freely transmitting her inheritance:

> And if she have a child, the child is to succeed to these estates after her; if she have no child, then the next of kin descended from her direct paternal ancestry

---

44 S. Keynes, & M. Lapidge, eds., *Alfred the Great, Asser's Life of King Alfred and Other Contemporary Sources*, note 24, p.309.

45 F.L. Attenborough, ed., *The Laws of the Earliest English Kings,* p.83.

46 In 873, his only sister, Aethelswith, took refuge – together with her husband King Burgred of Mercia – in Italy. She died in Pavia in 888. According to S. Keynes and M. Lapidge, Alfred's will 'was drawn up sometime between 872 and 888, and there are signs that it belongs to the 880s rather than the 870s', *Alfred the Great, Asser's Life of King Alfred and Other Contemporary Sources*, p.173.

is to have the land and the stock. And whosoever among my kinsmen on my father's side shall chance to have the power and the inclination to acquire the other estates, he is to buy these estates from her at half their value.[47]

In our own selection of wills, Wulfgeat granted several estates to his wife, specifying: 'and after her death the land is to revert to my kindred, those who are nearest'.[48] Aelfheah wanted his wife

> To possess the estate at Batcombe for her time and after her death it is to pass into the possession of our son Aelfweard if he is still alive. If he is not, my brothers are to succeed to it for as long as they live, and after their death it is to go to Glastonbury for the sake of our father and of our mother and of us all.[49]

In our 26 wills, men make bequests in greater numbers to their brothers and nephews than do women. Yet, as most of these women were widows, one can assume that paternal brothers and nephews had already been given their share at the husband's death. In spite of that, male claims are nonetheless visible in women's wills. Aelfgifu, who obviously had no children, left estates to her sister and her two brothers 'in common for their lifetime, and after their death to the Old Minster for my royal lord and for me'.[50] Leofgifu had a direct heir since her will mentions her daughter Aelfflæd to whom she granted the estate at Haughley. Nevertheless, she felt obliged to bequeath to 'Aethelric [her] brother's son the estate at Stonham and at Waldingfield and at Lithtletic'.[51] The description of these estates in *Domesday Book* allows us to realize that the daughter's estate was a large one ('8 carucates of land') while those given to the nephew were much smaller. In a single bequest to the community of Winchester, a certain Ceolwin granted 'the estate of 15 hides at Alton, which her lord [had] left her and which [had been] made over to him as his own property with the cognisance of King Alfred' having made sure that 'the community [had] promised her to arrange that Wulfstan, her brother's son,

---

47   F.E. Harmer, ed., *Select English Documents of the 9th and 10th-centuries*, no.X, p.47.
48   D. Whitelock, ed., *Anglo-Saxon Wills*, no.XIX, p.55.
49   Ibid., no.IX, p.25.
50   Ibid., no.VIII, p.21.
51   Ibid., no.XXIX, p.77.

[should] have a hide of rent-free as long as he [lived]'.[52] Therefore, though we had underlined the fact that parents were careful not to treat their daughters less fairly, it is obvious that their long-term concern was to consolidate the paternal line.

The last confirmation that can be derived from the table is the fact that relations beyond nephews and nieces were not taken into consideration: they were obviously not regarded as kinsmen close enough. When delivering his will, Abba went over all his possible heirs: he first mentions his wife and potential child, then his two brothers, his brothers' sons, his sisters' sons and stops there: 'and if it come to pass that my family dies out so utterly that there be none of them able to hold land, then let the community at Christ Church and their lord take it, and procure by means of it benefits for my soul'.[53] In our selection, Aelfgifu reverted her land to her siblings and insisted that after their death it went to the Old Minster in Winchester. Apart from her sister and brothers, no other relative is mentioned. If one excludes religious communities, Wulfwaru only made bequests to her children and servants. Leofgifu's remotest relations to be found in her will are a nephew, her sister and brother-in-law. Wulfgyth bequeathed all she owned to her two sons and two daughters and the only other individuals alluded to are Earl Godwine and Earl Harold.

As we have seen, married women (at least in the aristocracy) benefited from property inherited from their parents but also received as dower from their husband. During their married life, however, they enjoyed very little of their lands. Once widows, things changed and they obtained what they had been promised. In theory, they could now dispose of their personal property as they saw fit. At their death, their children came into their property since, just like men, they passed on a large part of what they owned on to the following generation. Widows transmitted possessions coming from two lines – their own and that of their husbands – while men's bequests derived from their family or from acquest. Widows, therefore, played a major role in the conveyance of property from one family to another. We remember that a

---

52   A.J. Robertson, ed., *Anglo-Saxon Charters*, no.XVII, pp.31–33.
53   F.E. Harmer, ed., *Select English Documents of the 9th and 10th-centuries*, no.II, p.42.

clause in Aethelberht's laws (6–7th centuries) stated that a widow with children was entitled to keep half the goods left by the husband while a childless widow only kept her *morgengifu*. Cnut's laws (11th century) reaffirmed that a dead man's property should be divided between his widow, his children, and his closest kinsmen.[54] This means that, in the case of remarriage, the woman could hand down possessions coming from her first husband to children of her second marriage. Ceolwin granted an estate of 15 hides at Alton 'which her lord left her' to the community at Winchester. However, one discovers that 'the community [had] promised her to arrange that Wulfstan, her brother's son, [should] have a hide of rent-free land as long as he [lived]',[55] which means that a nephew, on her own side, took advantage of land that, in reality, originally belonged to her husband. Widows also played a leading part in the transfer of property from families to religious communities. Their wills show that their real property and their movables were always shared out among their children and several churches. Moreover, their parents, as well as their husbands, often granted them estates for their lifetime which, after their death, were to be bequeathed to monasteries; Aelfgar gave his daughter Aethelflæd an estate at Ditton and added: 'and it is my wish that Aethelflæd shall grant the estate at Ditton after her death to whatever holy foundation seems to her most advisable'.[56] Aethelric granted all he left to his wife but 'after her death the estate at Bocking is to go to the community at Christchurch, for [their] souls and for that of [his] father who obtained it'.[57] A thegn named Alfred granted 'the estate at Stoneham after [his] death to [his] wife for her lifetime, and after her death to the New Minster at Winchester'.[58] Bede and Eddius Stephanus both stressed the fact that Aethelthryth granted the whole of her wealth and property to the Church which enabled Wilfrid to have a monastery built at Hexham:

---

54 Aethelberht's laws, § 78 & 81. Cnut's laws, § 70.1.
55 A.J. Robertson, ed., *Anglo-Saxon Charters*, no.XVII, pp.31–33.
56 D. Whitelock, ed., *Anglo-Saxon Wills*, no.II, p.7.
57 Ibid., no.XVI, p.43.
58 A.J. Robertson, ed., *Anglo-Saxon Charters*, no.XXVII, p.55.

> He built a church to the glory of God and the honour of St Andrew on land given by the saintly Queen Aethilthryth. My poor mind is quite at a loss for words to describe it – the great depth of the foundations, the crypts of beautifully dressed stone, the vast structure supported by columns of various styles and with numerous side-aisles, the walls of remarkable height and length, the many winding passages and spiral staircases leading up and down.[59]

It is now clear that widows were landholders in their own right at a time when land was the only source of power. Yet, if these women sometimes give the impression of acting in total independence, the conveyance of property usually fell within family strategies, which leads us to question how much room to manoeuvre they really had.

The Degree of Independence of Widows

Among the 26 wills selected above, we shall now only consider those of widows (six in number) and widowers (only three) and focus our attention on the content of the wills. It goes without saying that it is difficult to generalize with such a small number of documents and that one must, therefore, be very careful not to jump to conclusions. The three men's wills refer only to estates and to the heriot – consisting of war-gear, horses and gold – paid to their lord. The only personal detail is to be found in Wulfric's will: 'I grant to my goddaughter, the daughter of Morcar and Ealdgyth, the estate at Stretton and the brooch which was her grandmother's'.[60] Among the widows, three of them show more concern for details of home life: Wynflæd, Wulfwaru, and Wulfgyth. The wills of the other three are similar to men's wills: they only mention estates which they distribute among a large group of beneficiaries and the heriot they have to pay to the king. In fact Aethelflæd, Aelfflæd, and Leofgifu seem to have been particularly close to the royal court: Aethelflæd was King Edmund's second wife; Aelfflæd was Aethelflæd's sister and the wife of Brihtnoth who, as

---

59 D.H. Farmer, ed., *The Age of Bede*, p.128.
60 D. Whitelock, ed., *Anglo-Saxon Wills*, no.XVII, p.51.

ealdorman of Essex, exercised authority directly under the king. Leofgifu's will is addressed to the queen to whom she grants an estate. One may wonder if these three women, when widows, did not live at court – which would account for the small interest they took in domestic details. On the other hand, the other three were obviously living in their own residences, administering their estates with the help of reeves and stewards, managing themselves many domestic concerns such as the supervision of large numbers of servants. They mention their main homes: Wynflæd granted her daughter 'the homestead if the king grant it to her' while Wulfwaru bequeathed half an estate to her elder son and half to her younger daughter specifying that they were 'to share the principal residence between them as evenly as they [could], so that each of them [should] have a just portion of it'. Cnut's laws stipulate that a woman was to 'look after the keys of the following: namely her store-room, her chest and her coffer'(§ 76. 1a.) and that 'no wife can forbid her husband to place inside his cottage what he pleases' (76. 1b.) clearly showing that domesticity was a female prerogative. Wives and widows were in charge of women's traditional sphere of activity – the house. Saints' Lives always depict women as good housewives. When Cuthbert cures the wife of a sheriff, 'the woman, loosed from the chains of the devil, jumped up as though woken from a deep sleep, rushed out in gratitude to the saint, and caught hold of his bridle. (...) She asked them to dismount and come in to bless the house, and waited on him with her most devoted attention'.[61] Similarly, when Cuthbert cures the wife of a bodyguard of the king:

> As soon as the water touched her an astonishing thing happened: she was immediately restored to full health both of body and mind. (...) Then, rising from her bed, [she] ministered to those who had ministered to her, the patient tending to the physicians. What a pleasant sight to see that of all the members of so noble a household the lady of the house herself was the first to offer a drink to her guest.[62]

---

61 D.H. Farmer, ed., *The Age of Bede*, p.62.
62 Ibid., p.81.

In our selection of wills, Wynflæd, Wulfwaru, and Wulfgyth appear to have been particularly attached to the objects they used in their daily lives and anxious to hand them down to their children or grandchildren. Only valuables are mentioned: chests, cups, bed-clothing, tapestries were the most highly prized objects. Even books, though costly at the time, are relegated as 'small things' and seem to have been added as an afterthought in Wynflæd's will. Gifts of freedom to slaves are to be found in most Anglo-Saxon wills. Here too the three widows living on their lands give the impression of much closer relationships with ordinary people. Wulfwaru granted 'a band of twenty mancuses of gold' to four of her servants, who are mentioned by name. She also gave a 'good chest well decorated' to her household women. Wynflæd seems to have known personally a great number of her slaves: about forty of them, all referred to by name, were freed. Others, less fortunate, were bequeathed to her grandchildren. The same three widows endowed the religious houses where they wanted to be buried with liturgical objects of value such as gold crucifixes or dossals and not only with land: once again, they appear to have been concerned with practical realities.

The Content of Widows' and Widowers' Wills

- Estates: *Wynflæd, Aethelflæd, Aelfflæd, Wulfwaru, Leofgifu, Wulfgyth. Aelfgar, Wulfric, Ketel.* Usually with 'men, produce, stock, and profits'.
- Money: *Wynflæd* (mancuses of gold). *Wulfwaru* (30 mancuses of gold). *Leofgifu* (2 marks of gold to the king). *Wulfgyth* (1/2 pound). *Wulfric* (200 hundred mancuses of gold, part of his heriot. 10 mancuses of gold to the two archbishops, 5 mancuses of gold to every bishop, 1 pound to every monastic order, 5 mancuses of gold to every abbess and every abbot).
- Jewels: *Wynflæd* (1 engraved bracelet, 1 brooch, 1 old filagree brooch). *Aethelflæd* (4 armlets, part of her heriot). *Aelfflæd* (2 armlets of 2 pounds in weight, part of her heriot), *Wulfwaru* (1 armlet of 60 mancuses of gold, 1 band of thirty mancuses of gold, 1 band of twenty mancuses of gold, 2 brooches, a woman's

attire). *Aelfgar* (2 armlets of 50 mancuses of gold, part of his heriot). *Wulfric* (1 brooch to his goddaughter).

- House: *Wynflæd* (homestead for her daughter). *Wulfwaru* (The principal residence to be shared between her elder son and her younger daughter).
- Furniture: *Wynflæd* (4 chests, 2 large chests, a clothes' chest, a little spinning box, 2 old chests). *Wulfwaru* (1 good chest well decorated).
- Bed-clothing: *Wynflæd* (1 set of bed-clothing for one bed, bed-curtain). *Wulfwaru* (1 set of bed-clothing with tapestry and curtain, 1 other set of bed-clothes).
- Clothes: *Wynflæd* (gowns, tunics, cloaks, holy veil and nun's vestments, headbands, cap). *Aethelflæd* (4 robes, part of her heriot. *Wulfwaru* (1 set of mass-vestments). *Wulfwaru* (all the women's clothing for her younger daughter). *Wulfgyth* (1 woollen gown).
- Cups: *Wynflæd* (2 silver cups, 1 buffalo-horn, 1 cup with a lid, ornamented cups, 1 gold-adorned wooden cup, 2 wooden cups ornamented with dots) *Aethelflæd* (4 cups, part of her heriot) *Aelfflæd* (2 drinking-cups, part of her heriot). *Wulfwaru* (2 cups of four pounds, 6 cups of good value).
- Bowls: *Aethelflæd* (4 bowls, part of her heriot). *Wulfwaru* (1 bowl of 2,5 pounds).
- Vessels: *Aelfflæd* (1 silver vessel, part of her heriot).
- Tapestries: *Wynflæd* (1 long hall-tapestry, 1 short one, 2 seat coverings, 2 other tapestries). *Wulfwaru* (2 hall-tapestries, 1 tapestry for a chamber, 1 table-cover).
- Tent: *Wynflæd* (1 red tent).
- Books: *Wynflæd*.
- Servants: *Wynflæd* (2 freed women to serve her daughter and granddaughter).
- Slaves: *Wynflæd* (Bondmen for her son and for her grandson and granddaughter).
- Religious objects: *Wynflæd* (offering-cloths, cross). *Wulfwaru* (2 gold crucifixes, 1 dossal). *Wulfgyth* (1 little gold crucifix, 1 seat-cover for Christ's altar at Christchurch, 1 dossal).

- Weapons: *Aelfgar* (2 swords with sheaths, 3 shields, 3 spears, part of his heriot). *Wulfric* (2 silver-hilted swords + unspecified arms, part of his heriot). *Ketel* (a helmet, a coat of mail, a sword, a spear, part of his heriot).
- Horses: *Wynflæd* (1 + tame and untamed horses), *Aethelflæd* (4, part of her heriot). *Aelfgar* (3 stallions, part of his heriot). *Wulfric* (2 saddled horses, 2 unsaddled horses, part of his heriot). *Wulfric* (100 wild horses, 16 tame geldings). *Ketel* (a horse with harness, part of his heriot).
- Cattle: *Wynflæd* (mentions 6 oxen, 4 cows, 4 calves). *Wulfric* (his livestock to the monastery at Burton).

As these people belonged to the upper class, very large sums and estates in great number are mentioned. Thanks to *Domesday Book*, one can have an insight into what the estates mentioned in the wills consisted of. They included farmland as well as meadows, woodland, pasture, mills, churches, horses and cattle. They varied considerably in size and worth. Wulfwaru held estates of moderate size. In her will, she seemed to favour her two sons, granting them three estates each but her elder daughter received the estate at Winford (Somerset) which was far larger than Wulfwaru's other lands. The daughter was not cheated:

> The bishop holds Winford. Alweald held it TRE and it paid geld for 10 hides. There is land for 22 ploughs. Of this Roger holds 4 hides, Fulcran 5 hides, Kolsveinn 1 hide. In demesne they have 5 ploughs and there are 7 slaves; and 19 villans and 12 bordars with 14 ploughs. There is a mill rendering 40d, and 20 acres of meadow, pasture 2 furlongs long and 1 furlong broad, and woodland 1 league long and 2 furlongs broad. The whole was worth £9.55; now 20s more.[63]

As former queen, Aethelflæd held huge estates such as that of Lambourn (Berkshire). It had been bequeathed by King Alfred to his own wife. Aethelflæd returned it to the crown. *Domesday Book* shows it was a substantial estate:

---

63   A. Williams & G.H. Martin, eds., *Domesday Book. A Complete Translation*, p.238.

> The king holds Lambourn in demesne. King Edward held it. There are 20 hides. There is land for 42 ploughs. In demesne are 4 ploughs; and 44 villans and 60 bordars with 25 ploughs. There are 6 slaves, and a church with 1 hide belonging to it, and 2 mills rendering 20s, and woodland for 10 pigs. TRE it was worth £49; and afterwards £34; now £44.[64]

Not only did Aethelflæd possess large estates but she also possessed a lot of them. The list of lands that belonged to her is impressive: 22 estates are mentioned in her will (plus 22 hides distributed among her priests, reeves, and servants). We are lucky to have a precise description of Wulfgyth's estates because she lived just before the Conquest. The first estate mentioned in her will is Stisted (Essex) which she granted to Christchurch (Canterbury). *Domesday Book* enables us to discover that in 1086, the estate was listed as a land of Holy Trinity (Canterbury):

> Holy Trinity held Stisted as a manor and as half a hide. [There were] then 4 ploughs in demesne; now 3. The men [had] then 5 ploughs; now 6. [There were] then 8 villans; now 13. [There were] then 11 bordars; now 25. [There were] then 6 slaves: now 4. [There is] woodland for 800 pigs [and there are] 27 acres of meadow and 1 mill and 3 horses, 40 head of cattle, 120 sheep, 77 pigs. It was then worth £10; now 15.[65]

Wulfgyth had required that half the men of Stisted should be freed after the death of her sons Aelfketel and Ketel. This may partly explain why there were 6 slaves in 1066 and 4 in 1086. Wulfgyth bequeathed three estates in Norfolk to her two sons: Walsingham, Carleton, and Harling. The three of them are mentioned in *Domesday Book*. In Harling, 'Ulfkil, a free man' held 4 carucates of land while 'Ketil, a free man, held 2 carucates for a manor' in King Edward's time. In 1066, Carleton was held by Godric, a free man of Ketel's, while Walsingham was held by Ketel himself:

> Walsingham [in East Carleton] Warin holds, where Ketil, a thegn of Stigand's,[66] held TRE for 1 1/2 carucates. [There have] always [been] 2 villans and 3 slaves. And [there are] 2 ploughs in demesne and half a plough belonging

---

64   Ibid., p.139.
65   Ibid., p.974.
66   Stigand was Archbishop of Canterbury.

to the men. [There are] 4 acres of meadow. [There is] woodland for 12 pigs. Then [there were] 4 horses. Then [there were] 4 heads of cattle. Then [there were] 35 pigs; now 20. Then [there were] 25 sheep; now 60. [There are] 2 hives of bees. And [there were] 13 free men in soke of the fold and commendation only TRE, 30 acres. Then [there was] 1 plough; afterwards [and] now half [a plough]. [There are] 2 acres of meadow. [There is] 1 church, 60 acres; [it is] in the value of the manor.[67]

As there was a close connection between status and landed wealth in Anglo-Saxon England, the wills that have survived coupled with the 1086 survey, show us, once more, that the widows we are dealing with belonged to the upper classes. Their wealth was considerable and not representative of the rest of the population, not to mention the rest of widows usually considered as particularly destitute.

The fact that widows were able to make wills has often been interpreted as a proof of their independence. It is true that they exercised their right to divisions of property, that they imposed their conditions and choices: Wynflæd insists that the estate at Ebbesborne she bequeaths to her daughter will be 'as a perpetual inheritance to dispose as she pleases'. Thurketel had asked that his 'wife's portion [should] be for ever uncontested, for her to hold or to give where she pleases'. The testatrixes often used vocabulary (ready-made formulas?) that emphasized their free will: 'I desire...it is my wish...she is to have...he is to keep it'. Widows are seen defending their rights: *Domesday Book* echoes the quarrel between Hugh de Beauchamp and Azelina, the widow of Ralph Taillebois:

> In Henlow Widrus holds 1 hide and 3 virgates of Azelina. (...) Hugh de Beauchamp claims this land against Azelina saying that she has it unjustly and that it was never [part of] her dower.[68]

Widows even dishinherited some of their children. A famous lawsuit in King Cnut's time featured a certain Edwin who 'brought a charge against his own mother for a piece of land namely Wellington and Cradley'. However,

---

67   A. Williams & G.H. Martin, eds., *Domesday Book. A Complete Translation*, p.1164.
68   Ibid., p.586.

> The mother said she had no land which belonged to him at all, and she became extremely angry with her son, and called to her her kinswoman, Leofflæd, the wife of Thurkil the White, and spoke thus to her in front of them: 'Here sits my kinswoman Leofflæd, to whom I grant after my death my land and my gold, and my clothing and my raiment, and everything that I possess'. And she then said to the thegns: 'Act well like thegns, and announce my message to the meeting before all the good men, and inform them to whom I have granted my land and all my possessions, and to my own son never a thing'.[69]

Thanks to Pauline Stafford, we now read this document with a critical eye and see 'strong male interests at work'.[70] The mother was not in court. Thurkil the White went to see her and reported her evidence – which happened to be in favour of his own wife! *Domesday Book* shows us that in 1086, 'the same Hugh holds Wellington' but that in 1066 'Thorkil White held it'. Cradley now belonged to the canons of Hereford. As the court had been presided over by the bishop of Hereford, the inheritance quarrel had benefited both Thurkil and the clergy of Hereford.

This is why Pauline Stafford questioned the long-defended view of Anglo-Saxon women's near-complete autonomy:[71] 'there must be a strong suspicion that these women are often doing little more than implementing arrangements made by husbands and fathers'.[72] Some of our widows do recall and confirm their husbands', or fathers', prescriptions: Aelfflæd grants to Ely,'where [her] lord's body lies buried, the three estates which we both promised to God and his saints'. Aethelflæd abides by the terms of her father's will though she never refers to Aelfgar. Had Aelfgar's will not survived, then no one would have realized that Aethelflæd was not freely sharing out her inheritance. She did, however, alter a few of her father's recommendations:

---

69 D. Whitelock, ed., *English Historical Documents*, no.135, p.603.
70 P. Coss, *The Lady in Medieval England, 1000–1500*, Stroud: Sutton Publishing, 2000, p.16.
71 See D.M. Stenton, *The English Women in History*, London: Allen & Unwin, 1957 or C. Fell, C. Clark & E. Williams, *Women in Anglo-Saxon England and the Impact of 1066*.
72 P. Stafford, *Unification and Conquest*, p.175. See also P. Stafford, 'Women and the Norman Conquest', *Transactions of the Royal Historical Society*, Ser. 6, vol. 4 (1994), pp.221–249.

Aelfgar had granted her, and her potential child, the estate at Lavenham, 'and if she has no child, the estate is to go to Stoke[73] for our ancestors' souls'. Though Aethelflæd had no child, she bequeathed the estate to her sister and her brother-in-law first asking them to revert it, at their death, to Stoke. This modification was clearly emphasized in her will by the use of one of the above-listed formulas: 'And it is my wish that Lavenham should go to Stoke after the ealdorman's death and my sister's'. As the following table shows, she made several life grants to her sister and brother-in-law asking them, in a second stage, to conform to Aelfgar's will – which Aelfflæd scrupulously did apart for one life grant to her mother-in-law (modified arrangements are in italics):[74]

Estate mentioned in Aelfgar's will	Aelfgar's beneficiaries	Aethelflæd's will	Aelfflæd's will
Cockfield	1. Aethelflæd 2. St Edmund's	1. *Brihtnoth & Aelfflæd* 2. St Edmund's	1. St Edmund's
Ditton	1. Aethelflæd 2. Holy Foundation of Aethelflæd's choice	1. Ely	1. Ely
Lavenham	1. Aethelflæd 2. Aethelflæd's child (if any) 3. Stoke	1. *Brihtnoth & Aelfflæd* 2. Stoke	1. Stoke
Baythorn	1. Aethelflæd 2. Aelfflæd 3. Daughter's child 4. St Mary's at Barking		1. Barking

73   Stoke by Nayland (Suffolk).
74   In the table, the estates granted as heriot are not included.

Eleigh	1. Aelfflæd 2. Brihtnoth 3. Their children (if any) 4. Aethelflæd 5. Christchurch at Canterbury		1. Christchurch
Colne	1. Aelfflæd 2. Her child (if any) 3. Brihtnoth 4. Stoke		1. Stoke
Tey	1. Aelfflæd 2. Her child (if any) 3. Brihtnoth 4. Stoke		1. Stoke
Peldon	1. Aethelflæd 2. Stoke	1. *Brihtnoth & Aelfflæd* 2. Stoke	1 Stoke
Mersea	1. Aethelflæd 2. Stoke	1. *Brihtnoth & Aelfflæd* 2. Stoke	1. Stoke
Greenstead	1. Aethelflæd 2. Stoke	1. *Brihtnoth & Aelfflæd* 2. Stoke	1. Stoke
Heybridge	1. Aelfwold		
Totham	1. Brihtnoth & Aelfflæd 2. Aethelflæd 3. Mersea		1. Stoke
Ashfield	1. Stoke		
Rushbrooke	1. Aelfgar's mother 2. Winehelm		

Estates not mentioned in Aelfgar's will	Aethelflæd's will	Aelfflæd's will
Damerham	1. Glastonbury	
Ham	1. Christchurch at Canterbury	
Woodham	1. Brihtnoth & Aelfflæd 2. St Mary's at Barking	1. *Aelfthryth* 2. Barking
Hadham	1. Brihtnoth & Aelfflæd 2. St Paul's in London	1. St Paul's
Chelsworth	1. Brihtnoth & Aelfflæd 2. St Edmund's	1. St Edmund's
Fingringhoe	1. Brihtnoth & Aelfflæd 2. St Peter's at Mersea	1. Mersea
Polstead	1. Brihtnoth & Aelfflæd 2. Stoke	1. Stoke
Withermarsh	1. Stoke	1. Stoke
Stratford	1. Brihtnoth & Aelfflæd 2. Stoke	1. Stoke
Balsdon	1. Brihtnoth & Aelfflæd 2. Stoke	1. Stoke
Elmsett	1. Brihtnoth & Aelfflæd 2. Edmund	
Thorpe	1. Hadleigh	
Ten hides at Wickford	1. 'My kinsman Sibriht'	
Four hides at Hadham	1. 'My reeve Ecgwine'	
Two hides in Donyland	1. 'My servant Brihtwold'	
Two hides in Donyland	1. 'My priest Aethelmær'	
Two hides in Donyland	1. 'My kinsman Aelfgeat'	
Waldingfield	1. 'My kinswoman Crawe'	1. Crawe 2. St Gregory's at Sudbury

Estates only mentioned in Aelfflæd's will	
Freston ('an estate my ancestors bequeathed to Stoke')	1. Stoke
Wiston ('an estate my ancestors bequeathed to Stoke')	1. Stoke
Heybridge ('an estate my ancestors bequeathed for the use of the community at St Paul's minster')	1. St Paul's
Nedging	1. Crawe 2. St Edmund's
Rettendon ('Aelfflæd's marriage gift')	1. Ely
Soham ('just as my lord granted it')	1. Ely
Cheveley ('1 hide which my sister obtained')	1. Ely
Lawling	1. Aethelmær
Liston	1. Aethelmær

Contrary to her elder sister, Aelfflæd emphasizes many times the fact that she is conforming to others' wills, mentioning her father, husband, and sister: 'as my ancestors granted...which my sister and my ancestors gave...which my ancestors bequeathed... just as my ancestors have granted them...everything that my lord and my sister granted...according to the agreement my sister made about it...just as my lord and my sister have granted it'. Aelfflæd was very much constrained by other people's earlier bequests. None of the other widows in our selection explicitly mention that they are thus conforming to other people's arrangements, which, of course, does not mean they were not. In fact, the 26 wills we are analysing show one clear permanent feature: female legatees are often granted estates for their lifetime only and the subsequent beneficiary is then specified. Wulfric, for example, bequeathes two estates to his 'poor daughter' but leaves her no choice: after her death, the land is to go to the monastery at Burton. Aethelwold gives the estate of Manningford to his wife for her life and afterwards, it is promised to the New Minster in Winchester. Aethelmær grants Tidworth to his wife, 'and after her death it is to go at her funeral to the place where I shall be buried, for the souls of both of us'. Aelfheah gives the usufruct of his estate at Batcombe to his wife and makes it clear that their son is to succeed to it. If the boy happened to be dead, the estate would then pass to his brothers and, after their deaths, to Glastonbury.

Conversely male legatees tend to obtain the freehold of the estates: they are less often told to whom they have to grant the lands after their death. This does not mean that their room for manoeuvre was not limited: we have already seen that, as King Alfred stipulated (Alfred's Laws, § 41), a person who had bookland was not expected to dispose of it outside his kindred. Injunctions made by those who acquired the land in the first place were to be observed. It is interesting to note that men could be bound by their ancestors' decisions. King Alfred, for instance, reminds 'the persons who have those lands' they 'should observe the directions which stand in [his] father's will, to the best of their ability'.[75] Ketel's will survives, together with that of his mother (one of our widows), Wulfgyth. One discovers that Ketel abides by the terms of his mother's will in the same way as Aelfflæd had observed her father's arrangements: Wulfgyth granted the estate at Stisted to Christchurch 'on condition that my sons Aelfketel and Ketel may have the use of the estate for their lifetime'. Ketel did have the usufruct of the estate and, in his turn, granted 'Stisted to Christchurch after [his] time, for the sake of my father's soul and for Sæflæd's'. His agreement with his uncle Edwin implies that, if he and another uncle outlive Edwin, they shall 'succeed to the estate at Thorpe, on condition that after the death of both of us, the estate at Melton shall go to St Benedict's at Holme and the estate at Thorpe to Bury St Edmund's'. Yet this concerns just three estates (out of the 15 mentioned in the will) compared to Aelfflæd who is told to whom she must grant 26 estates out of 29! Aelfhelm left two estates to his son Aelfgar but they were not his to dispose of freely: he was to bequeath them to a holy foundation after his death 'for the souls of both of us'. Wulfric granted to 'his servant Wulfgar the estate at Balterley just as his father acquired it for him'. This shows that what was considered of utmost importance at the time were words which committed both the speaker and the hearers. Wills were an oral act that aimed at controlling part of the future. What Ketel, as well as Aelfflæd, were doing was respecting, showing the natural and expected consideration to words uttered in public: these words were seen as

75   S. Keynes & M. Lapidge, eds., *Alfred the Great, Asser's Life of King Alfred and Other Contemporary Sources*, pp.177–178.

legally binding agreements. One must take medieval mentality into account to realize the strength words had at the time: social relationships rested on oaths, promises, words of honour.

Widows, as already suggested, were free to grant their marriage gift as they wished; to this *morgengifu* a few personal estates might be added. As Victoria Thompson has argued and and as the above table shows, the two estates of Lawling and Litton Alfflæd mentions last in her will seem to have been freely disposed of and Brihtnoth's widow gave them to two men in exchange for their friendship and protection. These lands are not to be found in the wills of her father or her sister and may, consequently, have been Aelfflæd's personal property 'free from the constraints imposed by obligation to family members, living or dead. (...) In these two clauses, Aelfflæd is using what freedom she has to construct or consolidate new relationships in order to preserve the identity of her family, even after its death and burial'.[76] Similarly, her sister Aethelflæd shared out several hides to kinsmen and servants and granted the estate at Waldingfield, for her lifetime, to her kinswoman Crawe. Therefore, the two sisters were able to bequeath some of their lands freely but that amounted to a very small percentage of the property they enjoyed in their widowhood.

There remains to assess whether the testatrixes' wishes were respected or not. *Domesday Book* shows that the great religious communities usually made sure they obtained what they had been promised. In the second half of the 9th century/early 10th century, Aethelflæd and Aelfflæd's grants to Bury St Edmunds, Ely, Glastonbury, Christchurch (Holy Trinity) at Canterbury were strictly observed. In the first half of the 11th century, Wulfgyth's bequest to Christchurch was also respected. Siflæd, before leaving for abroad, granted to St Edmund's her estate in Marlingford. *Domesday Book* confirms the grant: 'Marlingford St Edmund held TRE'.[77] In accordance with Mantat the Anchorite's desire, her estate of Twywell (Northamptonshire) was entrusted to the abbey of Thorney. Yet, even

---

76 V. Thompson, 'Women, Power and Protection in Tenth- and Eleventh-Century England', N.J. Menuge, ed., *Medieval Women and the Law*, pp.15–16.
77 A. Williams & G.H. Martin, eds., *Domesday Book. A Complete Translation*, p.1127.

these great monasteries could be wronged. Leofgifu had bequeathed the estates of Hintlesham and Gestingthorp to Bury St Edmunds. In 1086, the former was held by the king and Count Alan while the latter was in the hands of Richard, son of Count Gilbert, and Earl Aelfgar. Aelfgifu's estate at Mongewell had been granted to the Old Minster in Winchester.[78] It had become part of the fief of Earl William and was held by Roger de Lacy in 1086. Monasteries of lesser importance were even more easily cheated. Wulfwaru had wished to grant her estate of Freshford to the church of St Peter of Bath: in 1086, it was listed as belonging to the bishop of Coutances. By 1066, the numerous estates left by Aethelflæd and Aelfflæd to their family religious foundation in Stoke were scattered and in the hands of various private landholders. Stoke itself was held by Robert, the father of Swein of Wessex who himself owned it in 1086. The two of them were also in possession of Withermarsh, Polstead, Stratford, and Freston. Robert fitzWymarc held Mersea in 1066 'as a manor and as 6 hides'.[79] In 1086, Swein of Wessex had added it, as well as Peldon and Totham, to his property. Tey was held by 'one free man, now Count Eustace [holds it]';[80] the same Count Eustace held Donyland, Colne 'which Aelfric Bigga held as 1 virgate and 10 acres TRE (...) This Aelfric held this land freely, but Engelric had it after the king came and the Hundred does not know how'.[81] In 1066, Greenstead was held by a certain Godric, 'a free man',[82] and by Richard, 'son of Count Gilbert', in 1086. As for Lavenham, 'Wulfwine, a thegn of King Edward's held [it] as a manor with 6 carucates of land'[83] before the Conquest while Aubrey de Vere owned it in 1086. In the same time,

---

78 'In the 960s, Bishop Ethelwold reformed Old Minster, introducing Benedictine monks in place of secular canons. The monastery, which was later known as St Swithun's Priory, survived for the next 600 years. Its church was also a cathedral. In 1070 the Saxon bishop Stigand was replaced by a Norman, Walkelin, who was charged with replacing Old Minster by an even larger cathedral.' J. Crook, *Winchester Cathedral*, Andover: Pitkin, 1998, p.2.
79 A. Williams & G.H. Martin, eds., *Domesday Book. A Complete Translation.*
80 Ibid., p.991.
81 Ibid., p.991.
82 Ibid., p.1048.
83 Ibid., p.1280.

> Alwig held Lavenham under St Edmund with the soke TRE as a manor with 2 carucates of land which he could not sell without the abbot's permission. Now Frodo holds it from King William and claims it for his fief saying that it was delivered to him.[84]

The traditional threats found at the end of most wills were, consequently, of no effect though Aelfgar, Aethelflæd and Aelfflæd's father, had warned:

> And if anyone alter [my will], may he have to account for it with God and the holy saints to whom I have bequeathed my property, so that he who shall alter this will may never repent it except in the torment of hell, unless I myself alter it before my death.

Thurstan's will is particularly interesting to analyse because it shows that, in spite of some tensions between certain widows and their husbands' kindred usually due to disputes over the ownership of land (see chapter two), other widows did come into their full inheritance. Thurstan's wife, Aethelgyth, became a particularly wealthy widow. *Domesday Book* proves that she held all the estates her husband had bequeathed to her: Wimbish (8 hides, valued at £12), Shouldham (4 ploughs, valued at £7), Pentlow (4 hides and 3 virgates, valued at £10), Ashdon (2 hides, valued at £6), Henham (13 1/2 hides less 10 acres, valued at £12), as well as the estate of Dunmow (4 1/2 hides, valued at £ 8) though Thurstan had granted it to Merewine, his wife and their children. Thurstan had also specified that he granted to his wife everything which he had in Norfolk. Here too, *Domesday Book* reveals that this was observed: her Norfolk estates included Fincham (1 carucate, 50s.), Barton (2 carucates, 2 ploughs, 20s.), Wiggenhall (2 carucates, £6), Boughton (1 carucate, 10s.), Bradenham (2 ploughs in demesne, £6), Merton (3 carucates, 1 virgate), Wilby (1 carucate, 40s.). Crimplesham (2 carucates, £8) Yaxham (4 acres of woodland, 1 acre of meadow, 12d.): in all, 'Aethelgyth's property amounted to some 60 hides, valued at £120 (...) her Norfolk property was concentrated in Clackclose Hundred where there were about 165 men under her commendation and soke. She also held six manors in Essex,

---

84   Ibid., p.1235.

and two in Suffolk'.[85] In 1086, however, she had lost everything: her lands had all passed to the Norman conquerors and no protector had been able to defend her rights.

In 1086, Englishmen held slightly more than a twentieth of the total landed wealth as tenants-in-chief of the king. Many of the Anglo-Saxons forfeited their estates by opposing William. *The Anglo-Saxon Chronicle* reports that in 1067, 'Eadric "the Wild" and the Welsh rose in rebellion and attacked the garrison of the [Norman] castle at Hereford, and inflicted severe losses upon them. (...) The king marched to Devonshire, and besieged the borough of Exeter for eighteen days'. In 1068,

> King William gave Earl Robert the earldom of Northumberland, but the inhabitants opposed and slew him and nine hundred of his men. Prince Edgar came to York with all the Northumbrians, and the citizens came to terms with him. King William marched from the south with all his levies and ravaged the borough, slaying many hundreds, and the prince returned to Scotland.[86]

Subsequent revolts took place in 1070, 1071, 1072, and 1075. Other Anglo-Saxon landowners went into exile, mostly in Scotland and Denmark, and another large number of them were reduced to living on a small part of their former estate as subtenants. Intermarriage was another means of taking over English lands: Robert d'Oilly married the daughter of Vigot of Wallingford and obtained her father's estates such as that of Letcombe Bassett in Berkshire which 'Vigot held of King Edward'.[87] Geoffrey de la Querche married thegn Leofwine's daughter and acquired numerous estates in Warwickshire, 'all the above-mentioned lands Leofwine held, and could go where he would'.[88] King William was exercising rights of wardship over heiresses. *The Anglo-Saxon Chronicle* mentions that in 1075 he 'gave the daughter of William fitzOsbern in marriage to Earl Ralph: this same Ralph was a Breton on his mother's side, and Ralph his father was

---

85   P. Coss, *The Lady in Medieval England, 1000–1500*, p.17.
86   G.N. Garmonsway, ed., *The Anglo-Saxon Chronicle*, pp.200–202.
87   A. Williams & G.H. Martin, eds., *Domesday Book. A Complete Translation*, p.154.
88   Ibid., p.668.

English, and was born in Norfolk. The king gave his [Ralph's] son the earldom of Norfolk and Suffolk'.[89] Judith, King William's niece, married Earl Waltheof who was arrested in 1075 and beheaded in 1076. She kept her husband's property and 'Countess Judith' was one of the great female tenants-in-chief of the king: in the hundred of Witchley Wapentake (Northamptonshire), for instance, she held 7 estates of the king, 'Earl Waltheof held all this land, and it was worth as much as it is worth now'.[90]

And what about widows? The example of Aethelgyth shows that some of them lost their lands in the same way as men. Some widows chose exile such as 'Gytha, mother of Harold, [who] went to the Isle of Flatholme and the wives of many good men accompanied her; she remained there for some time, and went thence oversea to St Omer'. (*Anglo-Saxon Chronicle*, 1067). The well-known letter by Archbishop Lanfranc to the bishop of Rochester indicates that many unprotected women found refuge in nunneries:

> Concerning the nuns about whom you wrote to me, dearest father, I give you this reply. Nuns who have made profession that they will keep a rule or who, although not yet professed, have been presented at the altar are to be enjoined, exhorted and obliged to keep the rule in the manner of their life. But those who have been neither professed nor presented at the altar are to be sent away at once without change of status, until their desire to remain in religion is examined more carefully. As to those who as you tell me fled to a monastery not for love of the religious life but for fear of the French, if they can prove that this was so by the unambiguous witness of nuns better than they, let them be granted unrestricted leave to depart. This is the king's policy and our own.[91]

One also discovers, thanks to *Domesday Book*, that King William imposed husbands on some widows:

> The same William holds Guiting Power. King Edward held it and he leased it to Alwine his sheriff, so that he should have it for his lifetime. But it was not a gift, as the shire bears witness. On the death of Alwine, King William gave his

---

89   Ibid., p.210.
90   Ibid., p.619.
91   Quoted by H. Leyser, *Medieval Women, a Social History of Women in England 450–1500*, p.72.

wife and land to a certain young man, Richard. Now William, the successor of Richard, holds this land thus.[92]

Pauline Stafford has argued that widows who held lands, largely the widows of royal officials, were 'often grouped together at the end of the shire survey like so many royal assets'.[93] She added that 'before and after 1066 the king was exercising rights of wardship over at least some noble widows. (...) Noble women were already living in an environment in which royal power and royal lordship played significant roles, as true for the time of King Edward as for that of King William'. However the two examples that she gives concern lords – Bishop Wulfstan of Worcester and Queen Edith – choosing husbands for heiresses, not for widows. In all Anglo-Saxon documents, girls of the high aristocracy are systematically 'given' in marriage by their father or a male relative: Bede tells us that Edwin 'sent an embassy of nobles to her brother Eadbald, then king of the Kentish folk, to request her hand in marriage' (*Hist. Eccl.* II.9) or that (see chapter 1) Aethelthryth was first married to Tondberht 'but he died shortly after the wedding, and she was given to King Ecgfrith' (*Hist. Eccl.* IV, 19).[94] Asser relates that Judith 'was given as queen – by paternal consent – to Aethelwulf, king of the West Saxons' also that Aethelflæd 'was joined in marriage to Aethelred, ealdorman of the Mercians'.[95] *The Anglo-Saxon Chronicle* paints a similar picture with King Aethelwulf who 'gave his daughter in marriage to King Burhred' (853), King Athelstan who 'gave his sister in marriage oversea to the son of the king of the Old Saxons' (924), and Prince Edgar who 'gave his consent' to his sister's marriage to King Malcolm of Scotland (1067). Because marriage was not only a bond between two individuals but also between two families, because marriage connections between the propertied were so significant for their political and economic

---

92   A. Williams & G.H. Martin, eds., *Domesday Book. A Complete Translation*, p.461.
93   P. Stafford, 'Women in Domesday', p.80.
94   Bede, *A History of the English Church and People*, L. Sherley-Price, ed., p.115 & p.238.
95   S. Keynes, & M. Lapidge, eds., *Alfred the Great, Asser's Life of King Alfred and Other Contemporary Sources*, p.87 & p.90.

situations, the brides (and one can assume often the bridegrooms as well) did not really have a say in the matter. They were under the protection of their *mund* (in most cases their father, brother or uncle) who was responsible for the negotiations and who gave their consent. All our examples show that the young ladies, or even widows in the case of Aethelthryth, depended on a close male relative and not on the king or on another lord. Pauline Stafford's mention of Queen Edith and Bishop Wulfstan choosing husbands for heiresses is a hint at a practice that obviously existed but there is no conclusive evidence that it was widespread or that it was not a new attitude imported from Normandy. The documentation at the disposal of historians never presents an Anglo-Saxon king imposing a husband on a heiress or on a widow outside his own kindred – but the documentation is limited and patchy. Conversely, documents proving that Norman kings (and lords) aimed at controlling the marriages of heiresses, as well as of male heirs who were under age and of widows, are plentiful. Therefore, though one should probably not consider 1066 as a sudden break introducing radically new social habits, one cannot either maintain that the Conquest was not accompanied by transformations in cultural, and social life. Concerning Anglo-Saxon widows, one can say that almost nothing allows us to think that the king, or another lord, was in a position to dictate to them who they should marry while it is clear that, after 1066, a feudal lord had a recognized right to control the remarriage of his tenants-in-chiefs' widows. Yet, this statement too must be qualified because, as we shall see, control over marriage by post-Conquest lords could, in some cases, be reduced to a fine, a sort of 'marriage tax'. Nevertheless, that the Conquest speeded up a process already on its way under King Edward is probably right.

Studying widows in Anglo-Saxon England does not lead to some conclusive and accurate picture of these women's lives. One must be content with impressions, contradictions, suppositions. One catches, at times, glimpses of truth – yet always partial, fragmented truth since, to start with, we know next to nothing about widows of ordinary, low classes. Both the Church and the law protected widows from forced remarriage. On the other hand family influence cannot be ignored though it is difficult to document and assess. We have seen that widows of the aristocracy were landholders in their own right, that they were not excluded from financial transactions, that they played a major role in the conveyance of property. Yet, at the same time, their vulnerability is emphasized time and again, wills show that male heirs were favoured and that widows often implemented arrangements made by husbands and fathers. The percentage of the lands they held which could be bequeathed freely was small. Compared to wives, legally speaking, widows were at their most effectual: they had the custody of their children, they enjoyed one third to one half of their husbands' patrimony, they could sue and defend themselves at court. Yet, one should not reason with a 21st-century mentality, with our constant concern with gender equality, our emphasis on individualism and coming into one's own. The danger would be to play down the distress and helplessness of these women, to lose sight of the fact that widowhood could not possibly have been a liberating experience in a world based on community life, that regarded dependence as normality, in which, therefore, the social nexus was tightly conceived. Being a woman on one's own was a disadvantage. Rather than 'a gateway to opportunity in a gender-biased and patriarchal world',[96] widowhood meant instability, precarity, hardship and isolation. Because of the lack of visibility of poor Anglo-Saxon widows, we have only considered the cases of a few highly privileged women. In spite of that, their husbands' wills betray obvious fear of seeing them dispossessed and impoverished: they all leave them the greater part of their property in order to help them be free from financial worries. Aelfflæd clearly fears her new independence and grants estates to two powerful men asking them, during her life, to be true friends and protectors. One can argue that Aelfflæd internalized the values of her patriarchal world, but one should not be blind to her appeal for basic security: there was, evidently, a gap between what the law stated and what people did. To be free, or independent, were unknown notions to people of that time and to use them is being anachronistic. Lastly, one should not believe that women were, by definition, oppressed beings

---

[96] J.T. Rosenthal, 'Fifteenth-Century Widows and Widowhood: Bereavement, Reintegration, and Life Choices', S.S. Walker, ed., *Wife and Widow in Medieval England*, p.33. As the title of the paper shows, J.T. Rosenthal was not studying Anglo-Saxon widows.

dominated by unloving husbands: most surviving men's wills prove the contrary. So does the following very moving episode Bede reports in his *Ecclesiastical History,* giving us a rare instance of conjugal affection:

> There was a man, the father of a family, who lived a religious life together with his household in a district of Northumbria which is called Incuneningum (Cunningham). He was stricken down by an illness which grew worse from day to day until he reached his end and died in the early hours of the night. But at dawn he came to life again and suddenly sat up, so that all who were sitting mourning round his corpse were terrified beyond measure and fled, except his wife, who loved him dearly and remained with him, though trembling with fear. The man comforted her, saying, 'Do not be afraid, for I have indeed risen from death which held me in its bonds, and I have been permitted to live again amongst mankind; nevertheless after this I must not live as I used to, but in a very different way'.

The man decided to enter the monastery at Melrose, 'he thereupon divided everything he possessed into three parts; he gave one part to his wife, another to his sons, and the third part he reserved for himself but immediatedly distributed it to the poor' (*Hist. Eccl.* V, 12). What interests Bede is the man's vision of Hell and Heaven and he relates it in length. The above domestic details are all the more precious as they are given in passing. One should notice that the wife gets an inheritance share equal to that of her sons. However, what is certainly the most striking is the power of love that makes the wife, 'though trembling with fear' stay by her risen husband because she 'loved him dearly'.

Part Two

The Medieval Period

Introduction to Part Two

After the Conquest, the Church (backed up by the new royal power) went on promoting the ideal of marriage as a conjugal, monogamous and indissoluble union. Marriage was eventually included among the sacraments. Chapter four will deal with these centuries when the institution of matrimony received an (almost) final definition by the canon lawyers. Concerning widows the main question was to know whether second and subsequent marriages were as fully sacramental as first ones. We shall see that the answer was no. Moralists, consequently, went on advocating celibacy and chastity insisting on the proper, that is to say austere, behaviour widows were expected to conform with. It is of course difficult to know whether the gap between the model put forward by these moralists and practices in real life was a mere furrow or a chasm! Moreover, it must not be forgotten that women had most likely internalized such an ideal as the only valuable model. Christine de Pizan, though a clear feminist, adhered to the moralists' view making hers the same conservative pieces of advice.

In the previous part of this book, we have come to the conclusion that husbands gradually got into the habit of bequeathing the greatest part of their goods to their wives and no longer to their brothers, uncles, or even sons. At the same time legal and customary practices aimed at providing widows with what they needed to support themselves and maintain their under-age children. After the Conquest, the pattern strengthened admitting of very few exceptions: the medieval family-unit included the conjugal couple and the unmarried children or one of the two parents and his/her children. Most medieval testaments emphasize the fundamental bond between husband and wife, the constant concern of the testator for the well-being of his surviving spouse. In such documents, widows always come first and it seemed quite natural that they should become the new head of the family: they were usually responsible for the liquidation of the succession, it fell to them to manage the family's affairs and properties, to look after the children and see to their financial and economic interests, their education and social welfare. In the country, they often went on tilling the lands of the deceased while in towns some of them carried on the trade of their late husbands. Widows had been rid of any type of protector or legal gardian (the Anglo-Saxon *mund*): in theory they were able to lead their lives and run their possessions in all independence. Was it really the case? After listing the duties ('the cost of death') and rights ('widows' material resources') of newly bereaved women in medieval society, chapter five deals with the various life options widows could choose focusing successively on gentlewomen, urban and peasant women. In actual fact, women did not enjoy the same degree of independence and the best off were not always those that come first to mind! Analysis of the socio-economic reality of widowhood in chapter five centres mainly on East-Anglia though including many excursions into the city of London. East-Anglia is a particularly well-documented region that has the advantage of comprehending both country manors, small and large cities. The numerous primary sources at our disposal include court rolls, charters, custumals, *Post Mortem* Inquisitions, wills and testaments, etc. The 1303–1399 court rolls of Walsham le Willows (Suffolk)[1] have provided us with most of our examples for peasant widows supplemented with wills from the register 'Baldwyne' edited by Peter Northeast.[2] The register was also useful for more well-off, though still relatively modest, families. The *Ipswich Recognizance Rolls 1294–1327* edited by G.H. Martin[3] were another particularly valuable tool together with several other documents shedding light on the condition of widows in Maldon, King's Lynn, or Norwich.

Frustratingly enough most questions, however, remain without a straight and definitive answer: did widows wish to remain single? If they did, was their choice respected? Could women living on their

1   R. Lock, ed., *The Court Rolls of Walsham le Willows*, Woodbridge: The Boydell Press, Suffolk Records Society, vol. 1 (1303–1350), 1998, vol. 2 (1351–1399), 2002.
2   P. Northeast, ed., *Wills of the Archdeaconry of Sudbury 1439–1474*, Woodbridge: The Boydell Press, Suffolk Records Society, vol. XLIV, 2001.
3   G.H. Martin, ed., *The Ipswich Recognizance Rolls 1294–1327. A Calendar*, Suffolk Records Society, 1973.

own really manage? Why did so many widows remarry? In other words: were widows free? Once again the answer is multi-faceted depending on the age, the social background, family environment and perhaps mainly on the personal character of each woman. Unfortunately psychology has rarely left traces in written documents: one is left with blanks that only suppositions or imagination can fill in.

Chapter Four
Widowhood and Remarriage

Medieval Canon Law

Marriage as a Sacrament

Though we have seen in part one that the Church Fathers, followed by early theologians, tackled the question of marriage, it remained an ill-defined notion for many centuries. Marriage was long considered a purely domestic and secular matter, a financial agreement between two families, the carnal union of a man and a woman that theologians could simply not regard as sacred. From the 12th century onwards, romance poets turned their attention to the individual, attaching value to emotions and an inner life. Minstrels sang of personalised feeling, love and desire. This illustrated a novel idea: that relations between men and women might be governed by some passion mutually experienced and confessed. Marriage was also the model in mystical works overflowing with love for Christ: indeed, the essential image for union with God, surprising as it may seem, became marital sexual love. In the most beautiful religious texts of the Middle Ages, the Church or the human soul are presented as the brides of Christ.[1]

At the same time, the canonical doctrine on marriage reached maturity, the ecclesiastical authorities eventually defining the exact constituents of a marriage. Admittedly, marriage had taken on a religious dimension before the 12th century. The earliest known instance of a blessing by a priest during a wedding ceremony is the 950 ritual

---

[1] See Richard Rolle (*'Luf is a byrnand yernyng in God, with a wonderfull delyte and ykerness (...) Lufe es a lyf copuland togedyr the lufnd and the lufed (...) luf mase us one with God'* [*Fire of Love*]), the 1400 poem with Latin refrain *Quia amore langueo* in which Christ invites the soul to respond to his love, *Pearl*, section 7 of *Ancrene Riwle*, etc.

of Durham.[2] In April 1076, a council at Winchester ruled that 'no one should give his daughter or other relative to anyone without priestly blessing, otherwise it will not be considered a legitimate marriage but the union of fornicators'.[3] The two main goals of the Church were to establish public acknowledgement and its own ecclesiastical supervision of marriage. At the 1102 council held in London presided by Anselm, Archbishop of Canterbury, the following ordinance was decreed:

> That marriage vows between a man and a woman plighted secretly and without witnesses are to be held void, if disputed by either party.[4]

As a matter of fact, the right place for the priestly blessing was at the church door (*in facie ecclesiae*) as the 1175 or 1200 Synods of Westminster asserted:

> No-one may be joined in matrimony except publicly in front of the church and in the presence of a priest. And if it is done otherwise, let them not be admitted anywhere in church without special permission of the bishop.[5]

Doesn't Alison, Chaucer's Wife of Bath, pride herself on being (rightly) a wife of experience since, as she says:

> Housbondes at chirche dore I have had five. (The Wife of Bath's Prologue, line 6)[6]

---

2 A. Corrêa, ed., *The Durham Collectar*, Woodbridge: Boydell Press, 1992. See also J. Brown, ed., contributions by F. Wormald, A.S.C. Ross, and E.G. Stanley, *The Durham Ritual; A Southern English Collectar of the 10th century with Northumbrian Additions; Durham Cathedral Library A.IV.19*, Copenhagen: Rosenkilde & Bagger, 1969.
3 D. Whitelock, M. Brett & C.N.L. Brooke, eds., *Councils & Synods: 1. A.D. 871–1204 with other Documents Relating to the English Church*, Oxford: Clarendon Press, 1981, ii p.620.
4 G. Bosanquet, *Eadmer's History of Recent Events in England*, London: Cresset Press, 1964, p.150.
5 D. Whitelock, M. Brett & C.N.L. Brooke, eds., *Councils & Synods*, p.1067.
6 All quotations from Chaucer's works are taken from L.D. Benson, ed., *The Riverside Chaucer*, Oxford University Press, 1988.

Conversely, the 12th-century chronicler La3amon is horrified when he mentions that the British king Vortigern:

> (...) he imakede heo to quene
> al after þan la3en þe stoden an hædene dæ3en
> nes þer nan Cristindom þer þe king þat maide nom
> ne preost ne na biscop ne nauere ihandled Godes boc
> als an hedene wune he heo wedde & brohte heo to his bedde. (7178–7182)[7]

It was also at the council of Westminster held in 1200 that the requirement of the publication of banns was decided (*No marriage should be contracted without a public announcement in church on three occasions*).[8] The practice seems to have originated in France in the 12th century and was made compulsory throughout Christendom at the Fourth Lateran Council of 1215. Henceforth the names of the two people contemplating marriage were to be publicly announced (in the vernacular) in the parish church by the priest on three consecutive Sundays. Marriage was now clearly defined as a public religious act, subject to ecclesiastical control. The aim of this new practice was both to prevent clandestine marriages and to discover impediments to a proposed union:

> Following in the footsteps of our predecessors, we altogether forbid clandestine marriages and we forbid any priest to presume to be present at such a marriage. Extending the special custom of certain regions to other regions generally, we decree that when marriages are to be contracted they shall be publicly announced in the churches by priests, with a suitable time being fixed beforehand within which whoever wishes and is able to may adduce a lawful impediment. The priests themselves shall also investigate whether there is any impediment. When there appears a credible reason why the marriage should not be con-

---

[7] G.L. Brook & R.F. Leslie, ed., *La3amon: Brut*, Oxford University Press, EETS vols. 250 & 277, 1963–1978.
Rosamund Allen in *Lawman's Brut*, London: J.M. Dent, 1992, p.186 provides the following translation: '(...) He made her his queen, / All according to the laws they had in heathen days; / There was no Christian rite where the king took that maid, / No priest and no bishop nor was God's book taken in their hands, / But in the heathen ritual he wedded her and he brought her to his bed.'

[8] D. Whitelock, M. Brett & C.N.L. Brooke, eds., *Councils & Synods*, p.1067.

tracted, the contract shall be expressly forbidden until there has been established from clear documents what ought to be done in the matter.[9]

The most common type of impediment was consanguinity which covered biological kin, kin by marriage and spiritual kin such as godparents and their relatives (the last two cases being referred to as *affinity* rather than consanguinity). The Church rules banned marriages to the seventh degree; consequently the Council of London (1102) reaffirmed:

> That relations to the seventh generation are not to be joined in marriage or, if they have been so joined, are not to remain together; and if anyone is aware of such incest and does not declare it he must know that he himself is an accomplice in this crime.[10]

The first Lateran Council, held in 1123, also condemned unions between blood relatives as incestuous establishing a parallel between canon and secular laws:

> We prohibit unions between blood relatives, because both the divine and secular laws prohibit them. For, the divine laws not only cast out those doing this and their progeny but also call them accursed; the secular laws call such people disreputable and deprive them of inheritance. We, therefore, following our fathers, mark them with infamy and judge them to be infamous. (Canon 33)[11]

A letter written by Lanfranc during the Council of London of 1075 is of particular interest to our study of widowhood for the archbishop stated unambiguously that the relatives of a man's dead wife were also considered as that man's blood kin:

---

9   N. P. Tanner, ed., *Decrees of the Ecumenical Councils*, London: Sheed & Ward, 1990. The book includes the documents in the original text as well as English translations. http://www.geocities.com/Heartland/Valley/8920/churchcouncils/Ecum09.htm
10 G. Bosanquet, *Eadmer's History of Recent Events in England*, p.150.
11 http://www.geocities.com/Heartland/Valley/8920/churchcouncils/Ecum09.htm#canons

vi. Following the decrees of Gregory the Great and Gregory the Lesser, no one shall take a wife from his own or his deceased wife's kindred nor a kinsman's widow, as far as the seventh degree of kinship on either side.[12]

The eleventh canon of the Synod of Westminster held in 1200 took up the same idea yet extending the ban to both spouses:

> Let not a man contract marriage with any blood relation of his former wife, similarly a woman with the blood relative of her former husband.

The rules of consanguinity were eventually modified at the Fourth Lateran Council of 1215, the Church authorities recognizing that they were too restrictive; they prevented too many unions beetween aristocratic families (and probably meant a headache for anyone wanting to find an approved partner!). From then on marriage was prohibited to the fourth degree only:

> It should not be judged reprehensible if human decrees are sometimes changed according to changing circumstances, especially when urgent necessity or evident advantage demands it, since God himself changed in the New Testament some of the things which he had commanded in the Old Testament. Since the prohibitions against contracting marriage in the second and third degree of affinity, and against uniting the offspring of a second marriage with the kindred of the first husband, often lead to difficulty and sometimes endanger souls, we therefore, in order that when the prohibition ceases the effect may also cease, revoke with the approval of this sacred council the constitutions published on this subject and we decree, by this present constitution, that henceforth contracting parties connected in these ways may freely be joined together. Moreover the prohibition against marriage shall not in future go beyond the fourth degree of consanguinity and of affinity, since the prohibition cannot now generally be observed to further degrees without grave harm. The number four agrees well with the prohibition concerning bodily union about which the Apostle says, that the husband does not rule over his body, but the wife does; and the wife does not rule over her body, but the husband does; for there are four humours in the body, which is composed of the four elements. Although the prohibition of marriage is now restricted to the fourth degree, we wish the prohibition to be perpetual, notwithstanding earlier decrees on this subject issued either by others or by us. If any persons dare to marry contrary to this prohibition, they shall not be protected by length of years, since the passage of

---

12   H. Clover and M. Gibson, eds., *The Letters of Lanfranc, Archbishop of Canterbury*, Oxford: Clarendon Press, 1978, letter 11.

time does not diminish sin but increases it, and the longer that faults hold the unfortunate soul in bondage the graver they are. (Canon 50)

Prohibition of marriage to the fourth degree, though not perpetual, was to remain the rule throughout the Middle Ages. John Gower, writing his *Confessio Amantis* between 1386 and 1390, alluded to it in his Book VIII in order to emphasize moral progress in the history of mankind:

> For evere kepten thilke usance
> Most comunly, til Crist was bore.
> Bot afterward it was forbore
> Amonges ous that ben baptized;
> For of the lawe canonized
> The Pope hath bede to the men,
> That non schal wedden of his ken
> Ne the seconde ne the thridde. (140–147)[13]

Why didn't the Church allow unlimited choice of marriage partner? In the eyes of the theologians and the Ecclesiastical authorities of the time, celibacy and asceticism were the only valued model. Even blessed by God, marriage was still somewhat suspicious since sexual reproduction was one of the effects of Adam's fault. Consequently, strict rules were necessary to avoid the stain of sin,[14] incest being considered as one of the worst evils.[15] The consequences for people

---

13 G.C. Macaulay, ed., *The English Works of John Gower*, Vol. II., 1901 [reprinted 1978].

14 Harry Rothwell's English historical documents include statutes of a diocesan synod of 1262 that remind people that 'the sacrament of matrimony was ordained to check the concupiscence which we have contracted from the infected stock of our first parents'. H. Rothwell, ed., *English Historical Documents 1189–1327*, London: Eyre & Spottiswoode, 1975, p.694.

15 Gerald of Wales was shocked to see that the Welsh would not accept the degrees prohibited by canon law: 'Incest is extremely common among the Welsh, both in the lower classes and the better educated people. "There is no fear of God before their eyes", and they have no hesitation or shame in marrying women related to them in the fourth or fifth degree, and even third cousins. Their usual excuse for abusing the ordinances of the Church in this way is their wish to put an end to some family quarrel or other. (...) Another reason given for their marrying women of their own family is their great respect for noble

found guilty of consanguinity could be terrible: their union was declared unlawful, their children illegitimate (which could leave an aristocratic family with no heir). Furthermore, Clement V, in the Council of Vienne (1311), decreed that any one who knowingly contracted marriage within the forbidden degrees should by the fact incur excommunication. Many people married in ignorance of their being related. Once they discovered the fact, they could apply to the Pope for permission to remain in the marriage. They were usually granted this when it had been done in good faith, whereas those who had been dishonest were punished. Let us take examples concerning the remarriage of widowers or widows.

In 1198, mandate was given to 'the bishop of Lincoln and the dean of Huntingdon to examine and report on the validity of the second marriage of G., an Englishman, who had previously married a woman who was godmother to his illegitimate child'.[16] Unfortunately one does not know to what conclusion the papal court eventually came. In 1235, the earl of Cornwall and Poitou was probably relieved to learn that the Pope had decided he could 'lay aside all doubt and lawfully remain in matrimony with the Countess of Gloucester, whom he had married years ago, although he had lately been told that her former husband was connected with him in the fourth degree'. Another very similar papal letter stated that in 1374 'dispensation [was] granted to Richard de Bykyrton and Joan de Rotheman to solemnize their marriage for they were in ignorance that Christiana de Halyborton, Richard's former wife, was related to Joan in the fourth degree of kindred'. In 1260, dispensation was granted to 'Maurice, son of Maurice Gerold, of the diocese of Cloyne, to remain in the marriage contracted with Matilda, to whom, when seven years old, his brother David, since deceased, had been espoused'. On the other hand, perpetual widowhood (or rather continence, to put things back in their

---

descent, which means so much to them. They are most unwilling to marry anyone of another family, who, in their arrogance, they think may be their inferior in descent and blood' in L. Thorpe, ed., *The Journey through Wales and The Description of Wales*, Harmondsworth: Penguin Books, pp.262–263.

16 W.H. Bliss, ed., *Calendar of Entries in the Papal Registers relating to Great Britain and Ireland: Papal Letters*, Vol. 1, 1198–1304, London: HMSO, 1893, p.3.

historical context) was imposed as penance in 1390 onto William de Hypsconys and Matilda Swyninton who had married 'in a certain private chapel, and without banns, knowing that they were related on both sides in the third degree of kindred'. Thanks to the petition of King Richard, they were absolved from the sentence of excommunication but were 'to be separated for a time, and were then to be dispensed to remarry, past and future offspring being declared legitimate. Whichever of the two survived the other should remain perpetually unwed.'

Apart from the fact that marriage was a public act that required witnesses, one has not yet defined what constituted a legally valid, therefore binding, marriage. The Church agreed on a definition in the second half of the 12th century. In 1140, the Italian canonist Gratian made a huge synthesis of church law known as the *Concordia discordantium canonum* or *Decretum* divided into three parts and which includes an extensive discussion of marriage in part two (cases 27–36).[17] Gratian threw himself into the reading of an impressively large collection of Biblical, Patristic, and synodial sources. He first quoted those who stated, like Isidore, John Chrysostom, Ambrose, or Pope Nicholas (among others) that 'for the union of a man and woman, their consent by itself is sufficient, according to law'. He then went on with the opposite opinion defended in particular by Augustine and several popes, who upheld that 'there is no doubt that a woman who has not experienced the nuptial mystery has not entered marriage' and who underlined the fact that incapacity for intercourse 'freed the wife to take another husband.' So that Gratian came to the conclusion that 'where there is no consent of both parties there is no marriage' (2, 32, 2, 16) and that sexual intercourse was the second necessary ingredient: 'marriage, which is begun by agreement, is completed by intercourse.' For the great theologian Peter Lombard (c. 1095–1160), the exchange

---

17 E. Friedberg & E.L. Richter, eds., *Corpus Juris Canonici*, Leipzig: B. Tauchnitz, 1879–1881 [new edition Union (N.J.): The Lawbook Exchange, 2000]. All quotations are taken from the following English translation: A. Thompson & J. Gorley, *The treatise on Laws (Decretum DD. 1–20) with the Ordinary Gloss*, Washington D.C.: Catholic University of America Press, 1993. http://faculty.cua.edu/pennington/Canon%20Law/marriagelaw.htm

of words of consent, expressed in the present tense, was sufficient (*Sentences*, Book IV, distinction 28, chapter 1). It was during the pontificate of Pope Alexander III (1159–81) that the marriage doctrine was eventually finalized: either words of consent in the present tense were required or words of consent in the future tense (betrothal) followed by sexual intercourse. The definition was firmly established in a series of decretals which the Pope issued in the 1160s and which were incorporated in Book 4 of the *Decretals of Gregory IX* (1234):

> Marriage is truly contracted through the lawful consent of a man and a woman. But the Church requires words in the present tense that express consent.
> Betrothal for a future date becomes matrimony through subsequent carnal intercourse.
> Betrothals for a future date are dissolved if the betrothed themselves dissolve them, even, if they were sealed by oath.[18]

When in the Middle English romance *King Horn*, young Rymenhild sets her heart on Horn she knows exactly what sort of commitment she is asking when she orders him:

> Thu schalt thi trewthe plighte
> On myn hond her righte,
> Me to spuse holde
> And ich the lord to wolde (305–308)[19]

Such is also the case of Belisante, another particularly determined Middle English heroine, who woos and eventually traps young Amis:

> Than answerd that bird bright,
> And swore, 'Bi Jhesu, ful of might,
> Thou scapest nought so oway!
> Thi treuthe anon thou schalt me plight,
> Astow art trewe, gentil knight,
> Thous schalt hold that day'.
> He graunted hir hir wil tho,
> And plight hem trewthes bothe to,

18 E. Friedberg & E.L. Richter, eds., *Corpus Juris Canonici*. http://faculty.cua.edu/pennington/Canon%20Law/marriagelaw.htm
19 J. Fellows, ed., *Of Love and Chivalry, An Anthology of Middle English Romance*, London: J.M. Dent & Sons, 1993, *King Horn*, pp.1–41.

> And seththen kist tho tvai.
> Into hir chaumber sche went ogain;
> Than was sche so glad and fain,
> Hir joie scha couthe no man sai. (661–672)

A week later, resolute to achieve her aim, Belisante reminds Amis of his promise. The young knight '(...) in his armes he hir nam, / And kist that miri may. / And so thai plaid, in word and dede / That he wan hir maidenhede' (764–767):[20] betrothal has now become matrimony.

The place given to consent implied that the priest played no direct role: marriage was made by the partners themselves; it had God for its author and was now seen as a grace-giving sacrament. Therefore, although the Fourth Lateran Council of 1215 required the blessing of a priest, it was unnecessary for the validity of the marriage.[21] The 1274 Second Council of Lyons was the first officially to classify marriage among the other sacraments:

> The same Holy Roman Church also holds and teaches that there are seven sacraments of the Church: one is baptism, which has been mentioned above; another is the sacrament of confirmation which bishops confer by the laying on of hands while they anoint the reborn; then penance, the Eucharist, the sacrament of order, matrimony and extreme unction which, according to the doctrine of the Blessed James, [James 5:14–15] is administered to the sick.[22]

The two good wives in Robert Mannyng of Brunne's *Handling Synne* (1303–1317) know the theory well when they explain: 'We þenke so moche on oure wedlak, / For hyt was yn þe olde testament. / And yn þe newe hyt ys sacrament.' (1978–1980)[23]

---

20   Ibid., *Amis & Amiloun*, p.92 & p.95.
21   The presence of a priest was made compulsory only after the Council of Trent in 1563.
22   J. Neusner & J. Dupuis, eds., *The Christian Faith in the Doctrinal Documents of the Catholic Church, New York: Alba House*, 1982, no.28, p.19. http://www.fordham.edu/halsall/source/1438sacraments.html
23   Robert Mannyng of Brunne, *Handlyng Synne*, I. Sullens, ed., Binghamton (N.Y.): Center for Medieval and Early Renaissance Studies, State University of New York, 1983.

Second and Subsequent Marriages

As we have seen, canon law reached maturity in the 12th century with Gratian's fundamental textbook. The Italian scholar went over the question of remarriage trying to find clarity in the ambiguous ecclesiastical status of widows. Gratian recorded the abhorrence John Chrysostom had of remarriage ('one who takes a second wife is convicted of fornication') and St Jerome's words explaining that 'second marriages are conceded to eliminate the danger of fornication' (case 31, question I, part 2, c. 9 & 10). Yet, Gratian did not side with these negative views, commenting on Jerome's statement, 'he says this to exhort widows to continence, not to condemn second or subsequent marriages' (case 31, question I, part 3, c. 11). He stuck to the accepted position of the medieval Church which was, according to St Paul's own words, that nothing stopped widows from remarrying (I Cor. 7:40) though adding: 'What the Apostle said of every widow applies also to once-married people, "she will be more blessed, if she remains as she is"' (case 31, question I, part 3, c. 13).

Gratian's chapters about widowhood are a good illustration of what the Church feared about widows and widowers and wished to see absolutely avoided. It dreaded three main sins: incest, adultery, and polygamy. As we have already mentioned, the rules about consanguinity prevented the surviving spouse from marrying a blood relative of the deceased within three generations for husband and wife 'are clearly of one flesh, and thus their blood relationships are understood to be common to both, as it is written [Gen.2:24] "the two shall be one flesh"'. The rules were strict and appear excessive to our modern eyes especially when one reads that Gregory ordered that 'if a man has betrothed a wife or given her a pledge, and her death prevents him from taking her to wife, it is unlawful for him to take anyone consanguineous to her in marriage. If this has happened, let them by all means be separated' (case 27, question II, part 1, c. 14). Gratian adopts the recommendation made by Pascal II 'writing to Bishop Reginus, describing a third kind of affinity, where union is not prohibited beyond the second degree. He says: "Further, the impediment of public propriety itself objects that it is beyond canonical authority for the spouses of two cousins to marry, one after the other, the same man, although they are married at different times"' (case 35, question II, c. 21–22). Gratian also quotes the early authorities (Pope Hyginus, Pope Innocent) who considered that 'if a woman passes to a second marriage and has offspring from it, they can in no way associate in marriage with her first husband's relatives' (Case 35, question X, c. 4 & c. 5).

Canon law imposed penalties on people convicted of adultery. Penance lasted between three and seven years during which the penitent was not to enter a church, was refused communion, was supposed to fast several days a week, could only travel on foot and was not allowed to carry arms. Penitential pilgrimages could also be required. Those who refused to submit were excommunicated. Gratian (case 31, question I, part 1, c. 1) and Gregory IX, in his *Decretals*, first remind their readers of Pope Leo's ordinance stating that 'no one may take in marriage a woman he has polluted by adultery'. Gratian goes on by referring to 'Augustine [who] testifies to the contrary, writing to Valerius, in *On Marriage and Concupiscence,* [I, x]' (case 31, question I, part 1, c. 1). In fact, several elements were to be taken into account: had the partners been aware of committing adultery? If not, remarriage was allowed because there had been no conscious, deliberate transgression:

> If someone takes a second wife in ignorance that the first is alive, he may lawfully remain with the second when the first has died, after they renew consent. (Gregory IX, *Decretals*, book 4, title VII, c. 7)

Those who had committed adultery with full knowledge of the facts were allowed to marry after doing penance: Gratian makes it clear that 'it must be understood that he can take her in marriage after penance has been completed if he survives the husband, but only if he did nothing to bring about husband's death and gave no pledge to the adulteress while her husband was alive' (case 31, question I, part 1, c. 3) mentioning, a few lines further down, that the Council of Elvira (c. 72) had ordained that 'if a widow committed adultery and then took the man as husband, we decree that she may be readmitted to Communion, after she has completed five years legal penance' (case 31, question I, part 1, c. 7). In order to prevent lovers from killing a husband or a wife in order to be able to marry, the council of Trebur (895) had decreed that the murder of the deceased spouse would lead to perpetual penance without any hope of marriage. Giving pledge was a solemn engagement representing a binding union as irrevocable as marriage. Consequently, giving pledge to one's mistress implied having two wives at the same time. Now polygamy was an intolerable crime,[24] it directly negated the plan of God which had been revealed from the beginning with Adam and Eve: conjugal communion required the equal personal dignity of husband and wife. The two spouses gave themselves with a love that was total and which, therefore, could only be unique and exclusive. The pagans were all the more detestable as they unhesitatingly married several women at the same time. In the middle-English romance *Sir Isumbras*, the hero is horrified when a heathen king offers to buy his wife:

> He seyde, 'Wylt thou thy wyfe sell me?
> I wyll yefe for here golden ad fe,
>   And ryche robes sevenne;
> She shall be crowned qwene of my lond,
> And every man bowe to her hond,
>   Shall no man bysette here steven.'
>
> The knyghte answered and seyde, 'Nay,
> My wyfe I wyll not selle away,
>   But thou me for here wyll sloo.
> I wedded her with Goddes laye
> To kepe here to my endynge daye,
>   For wele or for woo.' (277–285)[25]

---

24   Council of Lyons (1274): 'As regards matrimony, [the Holy Roman Church] holds that neither is a man allowed to have several wives at the same time nor a woman several husbands. But, when a legitimate marriage is dissolved by the death of one of the spouses, she declares that a second and afterwards a third wedding are successively licit, if no other canonical impediment goes against it for any reason.' J. Neusner & J. Dupuis, eds., *The Christian Faith in the Doctrinal Documents of the Catholic Church*, no.28, p.19.

25   M. Mills, ed., *Six Middle English Romances*, London: J.M. Dent & Sons, Everyman's Library, 1973, *Sir Isumbras*, pp.125–147.

In order to prevent what it considered as polygamy, the Church had very strict rules: Gratian mentions that 'one who has promised future nuptials to an adulteress while her husband is alive cannot have her in marriage after he dies' (case 31, question I, part 1, c. 4). Gregory IX reaffirmed the principle stating that 'if a man, while a first wife whom he has not known is alive, knowingly contracts with a second and knows her, he may not have the second, even after the first dies' (book 4, title VII, c. 2). The Church admitted separation in case of adultery, yet even in this case 'he who knowingly marries a second while his wife is alive, even if separated for fault, is to be separated from the second after the first dies. But he can contract with another woman' (Gregory IX, *Decretals*, book 4, title VII, c. 4). Canon lawyers also considered a last scenario: that of people who could sincerely believe they were widows or widowers. Yet, the rule was unequivocal: the death of the spouse had to be indubitable. Gregory IX left no room for doubt basing himself on a letter sent by Pope Clement III (1187–1191)[26] to the Bishop of Saragossa which went as follows:

> You have asked before us what should be done by you concerning certain women in your diocese whose husbands were absent because of captivity or pilgrimage. They waited more than seven years and could not discover whether they were alive or dead, although they had tried diligently to find out. Then, because of their youth or weakness of the flesh, they could not be continent and sought to unite with others in matrimony.
>
> Since the Apostle says [1 Cor. 7:39], 'The wife is bound to her husband as long as her husband is alive,' we reply thus to your question: No matter how many years this condition persists, they cannot pass canonically to another marriage so long as their husbands are alive. Nor may you permit them by the Church's authority to contract until they are certain that their husbands are dead. (Book 4, title I, c. 19)

On the same subject, Gratian had quoted a letter from Pope Leo the Great (440–461) to Nicetas, Bishop of Aquileia, which described a dramatic and highly moving situation:

> But, if some women love their second husbands so much that they insist on staying with them, instead of returning to their lawful union, it is right to

---

26   Therefore at the time of the *Reconquista* and of the third crusade.

threaten them with deprivation of ecclesiastical Communion. For they are choosing, not something excusable, but further association in crime. In their incontinence, they now commit a crime that they could have rightly expiated by merely desisting. (Case 34, question I, part 1, c. 1, § 2)

Even when there was no reason for prohibiting a second marriage, there remained reservations. One clear sign of reluctance was the debate on whether subsequent marriages were as fully sacramental as first ones. Gratian did not tackle the issue simply mentioning canons[27] of the Council of Neo-Caesarea (315):

> In general, men and women are prohibited from contracting multiple marriages. Hence priests ought not be present at the celebration of second marriages, as read in the Council of Neo-Caesarea. (Case 31, question 1, part 2, c. 7)
> (...)
> A priest should not be present at the celebration of second marriages, especially because he must impose penance for a second marriages. What priest would consent to such marriages for the sake of dinner? (Case 31, question 1, part 2, c. 8)

Pope Alexander III (1159–81) was more explicit and clearly indicated in one of his decretals that there was to be no priestly blessing for remarriages. His almost immediate successor, Urban III (1185–1187), went as far as establishing that priests who blessed second marriages were to be punished. Both decretals were incorporated in Gregory IX's collection of canon law under the heading 'Second marriages are not blessed, and those blessing them are to be punished':

> (Alexander III)
> Immediately send that chaplain to Apostolic See, without appeal, and accompanied by a testimonial letter, whom you suspended from office and benefice because he had blessed a second marriage.
> If one of two spouses has previously been blessed, the couple is not to be blessed. (Book 4, title XXI, c. 1)

---

27 Canons 3 and 7. http://www.catholicfirst.com/thefaith/churchfathers/volume37/ecouncil3707.cfm

(Urban III to the Bishop of Biscaglia)
Men or women who enter second marriages should not be blessed by the priest, because they have been blessed once, and the blessing should not be repeated. (Book 4, title XXI, c. 3)

As James A. Brundage noted, one problem that underlay both decretals,

> Centered around the problematic relationship between the nuptial blessing and the sacrament of marriage. If marriage was a sacrament, as many believed it was, then was a priestly blessing required to impart it? (...) Moreover, a requirement that marriages be blessed by a priest contradicted other papal pronouncements, including several of Alexander III himself. Beyond that, and even more fundamental, if the nuptial blessing could be received only once, it would then follow that second and subsequent marriages were not sacramental marriages, as some commentators on the *Decretum* in fact maintained.[28]

Thirteenth-century canonists or theologians did not settle the question. Saint Bonaventure (1221–1274) in his *Commentaria in Quatuor Libros Sententiarum* (*Commentary on the Sentences of Peter Lombard*) classified second marriages as sacramentally incomplete.[29] Thomas Aquinas also tackled the same part of Peter Lombard's text (book 4, distinction 42, article 3, question 2) and summarised the French theologian's reasoning:

> A second marriage is not a sacrament. For he who repeats a sacrament injures the sacrament.
> In every sacrament some kind of blessing is given. But no blessing is given in a second marriage.
> The signification of marriage is not preserved in a second marriage, because there is not a union of only one woman with only one man, as in the case of Christ and the Church. Therefore it is not a sacrament.
> One sacrament is not an impediment to receiving another. But a second marriage is an impediment to receiving orders. Therefore it is not a sacrament.

---

28 J. A. Brundage, 'Widows and Remarriage: Moral Conflicts and their Resolution in Classical Canon Law', S.S. Walker, ed., *Wife and Widow in Medieval England*, p.21.

29 *Opera Omnia S. Bonaventurae*, Ad Claras Aquas, 1882–1902, 10 vols. http://www.franciscan-archives.org/bonaventura/sent.html

On the contrary,
Marital intercourse is excused from sin in a second marriage even as in a first marriage. Now marital intercourse is excused by the marriage goods which are fidelity, offspring, and sacrament. Therefore a second marriage is a sacrament.

Further, irregularity is not contracted through a second and non-sacramental union, such as fornication. Yet irregularity is contracted through a second marriage. Therefore it is a sacramental union.

I answer that,
Wherever we find the essentials of a sacrament, there is a true sacrament. Wherefore, since in a second marriage we find all the essentials of the sacrament of marriage (namely the due matter – which results from the parties having the conditions prescribed by law – and the due form, which is the expression of the inward consent by words of the present), it is clear that a second marriage is a sacrament even as a first.

Thomas Aquinas went on with his own comment upon Peter Lombard's sentences:

Reply to Objection 1: This is true of a sacrament which causes an everlasting effect: for then, if the sacrament be repeated, it is implied that the first was not effective, and thus an injury is done to the first, as is clear in all those sacraments which imprint a character. But those sacraments which have not an everlasting effect can be repeated without injury to the sacrament, as in the case of Penance. And, since the marriage tie ceases with death, no injury is done to the sacrament if a woman marry again after her husband's death.

Reply to Objection 2: Although the second marriage, considered in itself, is a perfect sacrament, yet if we consider it in relation to the first marriage, it is somewhat a defective sacrament, because it has not its full signification, since there is not a union of only one woman with only one man as in the marriage of Christ with the Church. And on account of this defect the blessing is omitted in a second marriage. This, however, refers to the case when it is a second marriage on the part of both man and woman, or on the part of the woman only. For if a virgin marry a man who has had another wife, the marriage is blessed nevertheless. Because the signification is preserved to a certain extent even in relation to the former marriage, since though Christ has but one Church for His spouse, there are many persons espoused to Him in the one Church. But the soul cannot be espoused to another besides Christ, else it commits fornication with the devil. Nor is there a spiritual marriage. For this reason when a woman marries a second time the marriage is not blessed on account of the defect in the sacrament.

Reply to Objection 3: The perfect signification is found in a second marriage considered in itself, not however if it be considered in relation to the previous marriage, and it is thus that it is a defective sacrament.

Reply to Objection 4: A second marriage in so far as there is a defect in the sacrament, but not as a sacrament, is an impediment to the sacrament of Order.[30]

It must be underlined that this was Aquinas's personal view and that it remained foreign to the canons. There was, in fact, to be no nuptial blessing at all for second marriages of any sort, therefore even if a 'virgin marr[ied] a man who had had another wife'.[31] English ecclesiastical statutes of the thirteenth century reminded priests they were forbidden to bless what the Church called 'bigamists':

> For priests should be aware that they do not dare to bless, under canonical penalties, bigamists, male or female, crossing towards second vows, because it is not becoming for a second marriage to be blessed. (Second statutes of Exeter, 7)

> Likewise, a man or a woman passing into bigamy should not be blessed by a priest, because since they have been blessed on another occasion, it is not fitting for their blessing to be repeated. (Second statutes of Durham)[32]

The wedding ceremony itself was roughly the same for a first or a second marriage. Prior to the 12th century, the role of the priest was limited to the blessing of the couple. From the 12th century onwards, the nuptial ceremony was required to take place, as we have seen, at the door of the church. The priest was present to ensure that there

---

30 Thomas Aquinas, *The Summa Theologica*, trans. by Fathers of the English Dominican Province, New York: Benziger Bros, 1947, supplement, question 63. http://www.stjamescatholic.org/summa/index.html
31 To be honest, though, one must report that the third statutes of Worcester contained the following warning: 'Chaplains shall see, moreover, that they do not bestow from now on a solemn blessing on women who remarry, just as they shall have wished to avoid canonical penalties.'
32 F.M. Powicke & C.R. Cheney, eds., *Councils and Synods with other Documents relating to the English Church, AD 1205–1313*, Oxford: Clarendon Press, 1964. Quoted in C. McCarthy, *Marriage in Medieval England*, Woodbridge: the Boydell Press, 2004, p.144.

were no known impediments to the marriage and that the couple exchanged mutual consent. One of the earliest marriage rituals, to be found in the Bury St Edmunds missal, shows that the ceremony began with the 'blessing of the ring at the door of the church.'[33] It was followed by the spoken consent of the two partners: 'the priest should publicly interrogate the persons contracting if they mutually consent to each other and whether force or fear applied to extract their consent; then, there being no impediment, they should tell each other in the vernacular that they mutually accept each other in this way: I accept, or I receive you as mine, and: I you as mine, by these or by similar words the contract of marriage is to be signified.'[34] According to the Bury St Edmunds missal, the groom was then required to announce what he gave his bride as dowry. The father would therefore take his daughter by the right hand and give her to the groom as legitimate wife. If the bride was a maid, her hand was gloved, if she was a widow her hand was naked. The bridegroom would then recite the following formula:

> With this ring I thee wed,
> This gold and silver I thee give,
> With my body I thee worship
> And with this dowry I thee endow[35]

It must be noted that in this early ritual, the woman is given and does not give herself while the groom is the only one to express his commitment. After the vows were spoken, the wedding party entered the church for mass. For a first marriage, the blessing of the priest took place after Holy Communion, a veil being often spread over the

---

33 M. Searle & K.W. Stevenson, eds., *Documents of the Marriage Ceremony*, Collegeville (Minn.): Liturgical Press., 1992, p.149.
34 2 Salisbury 23, F.M. Powicke and C.R. Cheney, *Councils and Synods with other Documents relating to the English Church, AD 1205–1313*, I, p.376.
    The first appearance of the Latin text of consent is to be found in the English service book Magdalen Pontifical and consists of the question 'N, do you want this woman?' (K.W. Stevenson, *Nuptial Blessing: a Study of Christian Marriage Rites*, Oxford University Press, 1983, p.70).
35 M. Searle & K.W. Stevenson, eds., *Documents of the Marriage Ceremony*, p.151.

couple. This is the part of the ceremony which was supposed to be left out in cases of second and subsequent marriages. Yet it seems that many ignored the prohibition. As James A. Brundage noted, 'the commissions given to papal legates and nuncios regularly included the power to dispense clerics from the irregularity contracted by giving the nuptial blessing at second marriages'.[36]

Contrary to secular law, which imposed a full year of mourning upon widows before they could remarry, canon law stated that re-marriage could take place as soon as the widow wished. Gregory IX clearly indicated there was no rule for mourning:

> To the Bishop of Exeter.
> On the question of whether a woman can, without degradation, marry within the mourning period defined by law, we reply *to Your Solicitude*: The Apostle says, 'If her husband dies, she is set free from the husband by law,' and, 'Let her marry whom she please, only in the Lord'. By the Apostle's permission and authority the degradation is voided. (Book 4, title XXI, c. 4)

And again:

> Innocent III to Lady P.
> According to the Apostle, when her husband has died his wife is freed from him by law and has complete liberty to marry whom she wishes, but only in the Lord. So she is not to suffer legal degradation when she marries, even if it is within the time of mourning after the death of her husband, that is, within one year. She avails herself of the power which the Apostle has granted her, even though secular laws on this have not deigned to conform to the sacred canons.
> Since you plan to pass to second vows, knowing that it is better to marry than to burn, we commend your intention in the Lord. By the authority of this present letter, we expressly prohibit anyone from imputing degradation to you or the one you marry, because the Apostle has granted you complete liberty of marrying, but only in the Lord. (Book 4, title XXI, c. 5)

The example of Chaucer's Wife of Bath shows that (at least in literature) the full year of mourning was not always observed. Beautiful Alison's fifth husband is there on the funeral day of the fourth

---

[36] J.A. Brundage, 'Widows and Remarriage: Moral Conflicts and their Resolution in Classical Canon Law', S.S. Walker, ed., *Wife and Widow in Medieval England*, p.23.

spouse and '(...) at the monthes ende, / This joly clerk, Jankyn, that was so hende, / Hath wedded me with greet solempnytee' (The Wife of Bath's Prologue, 627–629). Alison is particularly well aware of Biblical and patristic texts dealing with the issue of marriage. In a comical and falsely confidential tone, she takes up the points made by St Jerome in his *Epistola adversus Jovinianum* – points which she may have learnt through her fifth husband who was particularly fond of anti-feminist writings (669–680). She is well acquainted with St Paul's teaching pointing out:

> Wher can ye seye, in any manere age,
> That hye God defended mariage
> Be expres word? I pary yow, telleth me.
> Or where comanded he virginitee?
> I woot as wel as ye, it is no drede,
> Th'apostel, whan he speketh of maydenhede,
> He seyde that precept therof hadde he noon.
> But conseillyng is no comandement.
> (...)
> The dart is set up for virginitee;
> Cacche whoso may, who renneth best lat see.
> But this wor is nat taken of every wight,
> But ther as God lust gave it of his myght. (59–67 & 75–78)

Chaucer is using here the well-known antifeminist tradition and the belief, deriving from the Church Fathers, that 'abstinence from sex was the most effective technique with which to achieve clarity of soul'.[37] We have seen that the Fathers' idea that virginity prevailed over marriage was also the stance defended by Aldhelm of Malmesbury or Aelfric in Anglo-Saxon England. It was, in fact, the position of the Church throughout the Middle Ages: preachers, moralists but also poets constantly tried to put widows back to... the right track!

---

37 P. Brown, *The Body and Society: Men, Women, and Sexual Renunciation in Early Christianity*, New York: Columbia University Press, 1988, p.78.

The Ideal of Celibacy

The Three Estates of Women

The Church encouraged chaste widowhood. St Paul's first Epistle to Timothy gave details about what was expected of widows:

> Honour widows that are widows indeed. But if any widow have children or grandchildren, let her learn first to govern her own house and to make a return of duty to her parents; for this is acceptable before God. But she that is a widow indeed, and desolate, let her trust in God and continue in supplications and prayers night and day. For she that liveth in pleasures is dead while she is living. And this give in charge, that they may be blameless. (I, Tim. 5:3–7)

Medieval clerics and moralists went on using the same parables and images as those met in the Anglo-Saxon period. Heading the list was the traditional three-fold distinction of women based on St Matthew's parable of the sower. 13th-century *Hali Meiðhad* ('Holy Virginity') commends virginity as a way of life for Christian women, virgins having the privilege of being God's brides:

> 'Syon' wes sumhwile icleopet þe hehe tur of Ierusalem; ant 'Syon' seið ase muchel on Englische ledene ase 'heh sihðe'. Ant bitacneð þis tur þe hehnesse of meiðhad, þe bihald as of heh alle widewen under hire ant weddede baðe. For þeos, ase flesches þrealles, beoð i worldes þeowdom, ant wunieð lahe on eorðe; ant meiden stont þurh heh lif i þe tur of Ierusalem.[38]

Further down, the author of this epistle on virginity reminds his audience of the rewards associated to the three states: 'of þes þreo hat – meiðhad ant widewehad, ant wedlac is þe þridde – þu maht bi þe

---

[38] B. Millett & J. Wogan-Browne, eds., *Medieval English Prose for Women, Selections from the Katherine Group and Ancrene Wisse*, pp.3–4. The editors provide the following translation: '"Zion" was once the name of the high tower of Jerusalem; and "Zion" corresponds to "high vision" in English. And this tower signifies the high state of virginity, which as if from a height sees all widows below it, and married women too. For these, as slaves of the flesh, are in the servitude of the world, and live low on earth; and the virgin stands through her exalted life in the tower of Jerusalem.'

degrez of hare blisse icnawen hwuch ant bi hu muchel þe an passeð þe oþre. For wedlac haueð hire frut þrittifald in heouene; widehad, sixtifald; meiðhad wið hundretfald ouergeað baþe.'[39] Lives of Saints, sermons, treatises of moral theology have all conveyed, repeated, developed this traditional classification which limits women to archetypes. As Leo Carruthers explains: 'In most kinds of medieval literature, women are seen principally in their sexual roles and defined in sexual terms. Whether as virgins, wives, or widows, women are seen by men, even by presumably chaste men such as preachers, in the light of that which makes them most different from men. They are therefore defined as being either presexual, sexually active or postsexual.'[40] In most religious or literary texts, women are thus classified, are not characterized by distinctive marks or qualities, not rendered individual. Once they are categorized as virgin, wife or widow, no more seems worth telling about them. This is why medieval texts rarely refer to a particular widow or wife but usually mention widows and wives as a whole. Athelwold is introduced in *Havelok the Dane* (written between 1295 and 1310) as a king beloved by all, by 'knict, bondeman, and thayn / wydues, maydnes, prestes and clerkes' (32–33).[41] Among the Katherine group (early thirteenth century), the legend of *Seinte Margarete* begins with an appeal to

> Alle þe earen ant herunge habbeð, widewen wið þa iweddede, ant te meidnes nomeliche lusten swiðe ȝeornliche hu ha schulen luuien þe liuiende Lauerd ant libben i meiðhad, þet him his mihte leouest, swa þet ha moten, þurh þet eadie meiden þe we munneð todei wið meiðhades menske, þet seli meidnes song singen wið þis meiden ant wið þet heouenliche hird echeliche in heouene.[42]

---

39   Ibid., p.20. 'Of these three states – virginity and widowhood, and marriage is the third – you can tell by the degrees of their bliss which one is superior to the others, and by how much. For marriage has its reward thirtyfold in heaven; widowhood, sixtyfold; virginity, with a hudredfold, surpasses both.'
40   L. Carruthers, 'No Womman of no clerk is preysed', Juliette Dor, ed., *A Wyf ther was*, Liege: L3, 1992, p.51.
41   G.V. Smithers, ed., *Havelok*, Oxford: Clarendon Press, 1987.
42   B. Millett & J. Wogan-Browne, eds., *Medieval English Prose for Women, Selections from the Katherine Group and Ancrene Wisse*, p.44. 'All those who have ears to hear, widows with the married, and maidens above all should

A late Middle English lyric, warning against inconsiderate and too precipitate marriage uses the same three categories devoting one stanza to each type of women. Widows wishing to remarry are presented as hypocrites looking for a husband under false pretences: once they have emptied their husband's purse, they show him the door!

> Man, bewar of thin wowynge
> For weddyng is the longe wo.
>
> Loke er thin herte be set;
> Lok thou wowe er thou be knet;
> And if thou se thou mow do bet,
> Knet up the heltre and let her goo.
>
> Wyvys be bothe stowte and bolde,
> Her husbondes aghens hem durn not holde;
> And if he do, his herte is colde,
> Howsoevere the game go.
>
> Wedowis be wol fals, iwys,
> For they cun bothe halse and kys
> Til onys purs pikyd is,
> And they seyn, 'Go, boy, goo!'
>
> Of madenys I wil seyn but lytil,
> For they be bothe fals and fekyl,
> And under the tayle they ben ful tekyl;
> A twenty devel name, let hem goo![43]

Chaucer mentions in his prologue to *The Legend of Good Women* (c. 1386) that he is going to tell the lives of virtuous ladies in order to be forgiven for only writing about women's wickedness in *Troilus and*

---

[43] attend most earnestly to how they should love the living Lord, and live in virginity, the virtue dearest to him, so that they may, through that holy maiden we commemorate today with the honour due to virgins, sing that blessed virgins' song together with this maiden and with the heavenly host eternally in heaven.'
E. Salisbury, ed., *The Trials and Joys of Marriage*, Kalamazoo, Michigan: Medieval Institute Publications, 2002. http://www.lib.rochester.edu/camelot/teams/sltxt.htm

Criseyde. The God of Love, who criticizes him, reminds him that he possesses St Jerome's treatise that gives the example of many true and good women – once again divided into the three traditional groups:

> How clene maydenes and how trewe wyves
> How stedefaste widewes durynge alle here lyves,
> Telleth Jerome, and that nat of a fewe,
> But, I dar seyn, an hundred on a rewe,
> That it is pite for to rede, and routhe,
> The wo that they endure for here trouthe. (282–287)[44]

This hierarchic division between virgins, widows, and wives inspired theologians and writers who made it poetical through several series of images. Jerome himself had compared the first ones to lilies, the second ones to violets and had alluded to the roses of martyrs in his letter to widow Furia.[45] Let us also remember the set of metaphors put forward by Aldhelm in the seventh century. The author of *Hali Meiðhad* preferred gems:

> Ne tele þu nawt edelich, al beo þu meiden, to widewen ne to iweddede. For alswa as a charbucle is betere þen a iacinct i þe euene of hare cunde, ant þah is betere a briht iacinct þen a charbucle won, alswa passed meiden, onont te mihte of meiðhad, widewen ant iweddede; ant tah is betere a milde wif oðer a meoke widewe þen a prud meiden.[46]

---

[44] One will also remember the Wife of Bath's Tale, the knight appearing before the following court: 'Ful many a noble wyf, and many a mayde, / And many a wydwe, for that they been wise, / The queene hirself sittynge as a justise, / Assembled been, his answere for to here.' (1026–1029)

[45] 'Support widows that you may mingle them as a kind of violets with the virgins' lilies and the martyrs' roses. Such are the garlands you must weave for Christ in place of that crown of thorns in which he bore the sins of the world.' New Advent Encyclopedia http://www.newadvent.org/fathers/3001054.htm
F.A. Wright, ed., *Select Letters of St Jerome*, Cambridge (Mass.): Harvard University Press, Loeb Classical Library, 1963.

[46] B. Millett & J. Wogan-Browne, *Medieval English Prose for Women, Selections from the Katherine Group and Ancrene Wisse*, p.38. 'Though you may be a virgin, do not undervalue widows and married women. For just as a ruby is better than a jacinth in its natural quality, and nevertheless a bright jacinth is better than a dull ruby, so a maiden by the virtue of virginity surpasses widows

177

In passus XVI (B-text) of *Piers Plowman*, William Langland (c. 1330–c. 1386) chose the image of the fruits of the beautiful tree of Charity, a tree cultivated and defended by Piers, while the Devil steals the fruits. Piers explains in details the various grades of purity of life:

> 'Heer now bynethe,' quod he tho, 'if I nede hadde,
> Matrimoyne I may nyme, a moiste fruyt withalle.
> Thanne Continence is neer the crop as kaylewey bastard.
> Thanne bereth the crop kynde fruyt and clennest of alle
> Maidenhode, aungeles peeris, and arest wole be ripe,
> And swete withouten swellyng sour worth it nevere'
>
> I preide Piers to pulle adoun an appul, and he wolde,
> And suffre me to assaien what savour it hadde.
> And Piers caste to the crop, and thanne comsed it to crye;
> And waggede widwehode, and it wepte after;
> And whan he meved matrimoyne, it made a foul noise,
> That I hadde ruthe whan Piers rogged, it gradde so rufulliche.
> For evere as thei dropped adoun the devel was redy,
> And gadrede hem alle togideres, bothe grete and smale. (67–80)[47]

A few lines later, the poet awakes then falls asleep again. In his seventh vision, he meets a man – it is Abraham who stands for Faith. Abraham expands on a lengthy metaphor about the Trinity. God, indeed, revealed himself in three persons. The human condition shows that this can be true for:

> Wedlok and widwehode with virginite ynempned,
> In tokenynge of the Trinite was taken out of o man
> Adam, oure alle fader; (…)
> (…)

and married women; and nevertheless a modest wife or a meek widow is better than a proud virgin.'

47 *The Vision of Piers Plowman*, Electronic Text Center, University of Virginia Library. http://etext.lib.virginia.edu/etcbin/toccer-ew2?id=LanPier.sgm&images= images/modeng&data=/lv1/Archive/mideng-arsed&tag=public&part=17&division= div1. A.V.C. Schmidt, ed., *Piers Plowman: A parallel-text edition of the A B C and Z versions*, (vol 1. Text), London: Longman, 1995.

> Might is it in matrimoyne, that multiplieth the erthe,
> And bitokneth trewely, telle if I dorste,
> Hym that first formed al, the Fader of hevene.
> The Sone, if I it dorste seye, resembleth wel the widewe:
> '*Deus meus, Deus meus, ut quid dereliquisti me?*'
> That is, creatour weex creature to knowe what was bothe.
> As widewe withouten wedlok was nevere yit yseyghe,
> Na moore myghte God be man but if he moder hadde.
> So widewe withouten wedlok may noght wel stande,
> Ne matrimoyne withouten muliere is noght muche to preise.
> (Passus XVI, 203–205 & 211–219)

As for John Gower (c. 1330–1408), he compares our three estates to three of the five daughters (*Bonnegarde, Virginité, Matrimoine, Continence* and *Aspre Vie*) of Dame Chasteté in his long poem written in French *Mirour de l'Omme*. It is particularly revealing to notice that both Langland and Gower prefer the word *continence* to *widowhood*.[48] As is well known, virginity was used in the Middle Ages as 'the image and practice of perfection, the highest form of life, an imitation of the angels'.[49] Second best in this scale of perfection was widowhood because it meant a second chance to lead a chaste and virtuous life. Moralists, though, were rather distrustful often wondering whether widows were really capable of doing without the pleasures of the flesh: as Barbara Hanawalt puts it,

> Medieval lay and ecclesiastical thinkers imbibed the concerns of Saint Paul and Saint Jerome that women's sexual appetites were voracious, particularly if they had already known sexual intercourse. While men mostly could keep a lid on women's sexuality through the father's control over his daughters, a husband's over his wife, and a bishop's over nuns, the one stage in a woman's life that defied such easy dominance was that of widowhood. (…) Most men's real concern was with any material assets that the widow had available, but the moralistic literature seemed much more obsessed with her sexual resources.

---

48   Aldhelm had used the word *chastity*.
49   A. Bernau, R. Evans, S. Salih, eds., *Medieval Virginities*, Cardiff: University of Wales Press, 2003, p.3.

(...) Preservation of chastity came foremost in the minds of the moral advisors to widows.[50]

Consequently, widows are usually described as stock characters: either totally virtuous or lusty and deceitful, with no middle way.

Moralists' View of Widows

The Fourth Lateran Council (1215) decreed that 'all the faithful of either sex, after they have reached the age of discernment, should individually confess all their sins in a faithful manner to their own priest at least once a year' (canon 21). At the same time, it recognized that 'to guide souls is a supreme art' and therefore 'strictly ordered bishops carefully to prepare those who are to be promoted to the priesthood and to instruct them, either by themselves or through other suitable persons, in the divine services and the sacraments of the church, so that they may be able to celebrate them correctly' (canon 27). In order to instruct the people, to develop their intellectual and moral powers so as to help them prepare their yearly confession, the Church appointed preachers who became the kingpin of this large movement of education:

> Among the various things that are conducive to the salvation of the christian people, the nourishment of God's word is recognized to be especially necessary, since just as the body is fed with material food so the soul is fed with spiritual food, according to the words, man lives not by bread alone but by every word that proceeds from the mouth of God. It often happens that bishops by themselves are not sufficient to minister the word of God to the people, especially in large and scattered dioceses, whether this is because of their many occupations or bodily infirmities or because of incursions of the enemy or for other reasons – let us not say for lack of knowledge, which in bishops is to be altogether condemned and is not to be tolerated in the future. We therefore decree by this general constitution that bishops are to appoint suitable men to carry out with profit this duty of sacred preaching, men who are powerful in word and deed and who will visit with care the peoples entrusted to them in

---

50   B.A. Hanawalt, 'Remarriage as an Option for Urban and Rural Widows in Late Medieval England', S.S. Walker, ed., *Wife and Widow in Medieval England*, pp.142–143.

place of the bishops, since these by themselves are unable to do it, and will build them up by word and example. (Canon 10)[51]

Collections of sermons were conceived and edited for lowly, ignorant or lazy preachers. First written in Latin or French, they rarely reached Britain and the English language before the 14th century. These sermons were preached at mass or in the open air and aimed at explaining passages from the Bible or at expounding moral principles. Many manuals for confessors (explaining the duties of parish priests and giving directions for the administration of the sacraments) and didactic treatises also came into being. None of them was particularly original but rather based on translations and adaptations borrowed from other writers on the ten commandments, the creed, the seven deadly sins, the knowledge of good and evil, the seven petitions of the Paternoster, the seven gifts of the Holy Ghost, the seven cardinal virtues and confession. This is why the same episodes, explanations, and *exempla* are to be found from one text to another. The clerics who put these treatises into English were quite indifferent to literary achievement. They were concerned with people's salvation, 'to guard them against sin' as Dan Michel of Northgate notes at the end of his *Ayenbite of Inwyt*. With this aim in view, they wrote in English for the sake of ordinary people who could not read, or simply understand, Latin or French. These collections of sermons and didactic treatises include chapters about widows, making recommendations to them, giving them rules of behaviour, explaining what is proper and what is not.

In these tracts, widows are constantly advised to be the embodiment of discretion, reserve, moderation. Nothing out of the ordinary suits them. In Chaucer's *Book of the Duchess*, Queen Alcyone dreads her husband might be dead, she is overwhelmed with grief, weeps, faints, almost loses her mind. Sir Orfeo who believes he will never see his wife again wanders ten years in the woods, 'noþing he fint þat him is ays / Bot euer he liueþ in gret malais' (239–240). Similarly, when

---

51   N.P. Tanner, ed., *Decreees of the Ecumenical Councils*, http://www.geocities. com/Heartland/Valley/8920/churchcouncils/Ecum12.htm#On%20appointing%20 preachers

Agea dies in *The Tale of Beryn*, her husband is driven to despair, he wishes he was dead, 'and lyvid as an hermyte, soule & destitute, / Withoute consolacioune, pensyff offt, & mut' (1095–6).[52] These overflowing signs of affection were not to our moralists' taste who condemned anything excessive. Widows were expected to be afflicted and grieve for their dead husband...but not too much! In the early Middle English debate *Vices & Virtues*,[53] Reason explains to the Soul that is confessing its sins that sorrow is one of the cardinal sins: it is called '*tristitia mortem operante*' (sorrow working death) because everything displeases it including what is good and done for God's love. A widow wailing, lamenting herself too much was likely to be accused of being a hypocrite or of overdoing the devoted wife bit; the famous French poet Benoît de St Maure was particularly harsh on women when he wrote (speaking of Briseida):

> Mes, se la danzele est iree,
> Par tens resera apaiee;
> Son duel avra tost oblïé
> E son corage si mué
> Que poi li iert de cels de Troie.
> (...)
> A femme dure duels petit,
> A un oil plore, a l'autre rit.
> Molt muent tost li lor corage,
> Assez est fole la plus sage:
> Quant qu'el a en set anz amé,
> A ele en treis jorz oblïé.
> Onc nule ne sot duel aveir. (13429–13433 & 13441–13447)
> [If the maiden is now extremely afflicted, her grief will soon die down. She will soon have forgotten her sorrow and her feelings will have changed so much that she will very little care for the Trojans. (...) A woman's distress never lasts long: she weeps with one eye and laughs with the other. Very often, she is changeable and even the wisest will be carried away. After seven years of love,

---

52 F.J. Furnivall & W.G. Stone, eds., *The Tale of Beryn*, London: Kegan Paul, Trench, Trübner for the Early English Text Society, 1909, EETS, Extra Series, vol. 105.

53 F. Holthausen, ed., *Vices & Virtues*, London: Trübner & Co., 1888, EETS, vol. 89, p.2.

everything is forgotten within three days. No woman has ever known what distress is.]⁵⁴

Alcuin Blamires's anthology, *Woman Defamed and Woman Defended*, includes other very similar French texts. Gautier le Leu (13th century)⁵⁵ describes a widow giving vent to her despair during her husband's funeral, warning us from the start that she is 'acting her part, in which there is scarcely a word of truth.' Jehan le Fèvre in *The Lamentations of Matheolus* (c. 1371–1372) considers that 'as soon as her husband is in his coffin, a wife's only thought day and night is to catch another husband. She observes convention by weeping, but after three days can't wait to be remarried.'⁵⁶ Chaucer's Wife of Bath knows the proper behaviour, she too 'observes convention' because of the neighbours and friends and therefore is careful enough to shed a few tears, look sad, cover her face with her kerchief 'as wyves mooten, for it is usage' (589). Since at her fourth bereavement, she was already provided with another husband she wept but little! The most hypocritical and the most depraved is Dunbar's widow who discloses her skill in duplicity to two girlfriends of hers. She explains she has become an expert in deception, weeping as though she grieved, dressed as though in mourning while her heart is blithing. When she sees relatives of her husband's, she has a trick: 'I haif a watter spunge fo wa, within my wyde clokis / Than wring I it full wylely and wetis my chekis / With that watteris myn ene and welteris doune teris.'⁵⁷ It comes as no surprise to discover that this widow is said to be, 'wantoun of laitis'.

On the ground of reserve and propriety, moralists advocated widows to stay in the background, acting with moderation and restraint. Propriety of behaviour implied no wandering in the streets, no chattering or loud talk. Several moral treatises remind their readers

---

54 E. Baumgartner, ed., *Le Roman de Troie de Benoît de Sainte-Maure*, Paris: Union Générale d'Editions, 10/18, 1987. The English translation is mine.
55 A. Blamires, ed., *Woman Defamed and Woman Defended. The Widow* (Gautier le Leu), pp.135–144.
56 Ibid., *The Lamentations of Matheolus* (Jehan le Fèvre), pp.177–197.
57 William Dunbar, *The Tretis of the Mariit Wemen and the Wido*, lines 437–439. J. Kinsley, ed., *The Poems of William Dunbar*, Oxford University Press, 1979.

that St Paul himself reproved young widows for being idle and fond of gossiping in the houses of others:

> Huerof saynte pauel wyþ-nimþ þe yonge wyfmen wodewen / þet were ydele / and bysye to guonne / an to comene / ganglinde / and to moche spekinde, ac bisset hy ssollen by ine hare house / and yeue ham guode workes to done / ase saynte paul tekþ.[58]

The stock character of the roaming widow derived from a letter by St Jerome to Oceanus in which he took the defence of a noble Roman lady – Fabiola – against 'most widows [who], having shaken off the yoke of servitude, grow careless and allow themselves more liberty than ever, frequenting the baths, flitting through the streets, shewing their harlot faces everywhere.'[59] The proper place for a widow was clearly at home bringing up her children and managing domestic affairs or at church, devoting herself to religious duties: praying, fasting, giving alms. A secluded, retired life was necessary to avoid any sexual temptation. The Biblical model taken up by all moralists was Judith:

> Þre þinges specialliche longeþ to hem þat beþ in þat estate of wedowhode & disposeþ hem to kepe hit in clennes and chastite. One is þat þei schulde kepe hem in pryuete as moche as þei myghte, out of grete companye and þe sighte of men, & noght busye hem to moche aboute þe world. Herof is ensample in Holy Writt of þe noble womman Iudith þat was a faire womman and a clene wedowe, and sche held hir prieueliche in clos in hir hous wiþ hir wommen and wolde noght goon out, but schoned sight of men and los of þe world.[60]

Criseyde appears as the perfect widow when we first meet her, begging Hector in a piteous voice and weeping tenderly, then taking her leave and going home where she lived quietly: 'And in hire hous she

---

58 R. Morris, ed., *Dan Michel's Ayenbite of Inwyt or Remorse of Conscience in the Kentish Dialect*, London: Trübner & Co., 1866, EETS, vol. 23, p.226.
    The same remark is to be found in *A Myrour to Lewde Men & Wymmen* but is attributed to 'St Austin'.
59 W.H. Fremantle, *The Principal Works of St Jerome*, letter 77. http://www.newadvent.org/fathers/3001077.htm.
60 V. Nelson, ed., *A Myrour to Lewde Men & Wymmen, a prose version of the Speculum Vitae edited from B.L. Harley 45*, Heidelberg: Carl Winter Universitäts Verlag, (*Middle English Texts* n°14) 1981, p.189.

abood with swich meyne / As til hire honour nede was to holde; / And whil she was dwellynge in that cite; / Kepte hir estat, and both of yonge and olde / Ful wel biloved, and wel men of hir tolde' (Chaucer, *Troilus and Criseyde*, Book I, 127–131). Yet the privacy of her apartment enables her to read Troilus's love letter without being disturbed, 'ful pryvely' (Book II, 1176) in her own room, and to write her reply to this letter in a 'closet' (1215) therefore well hidden, without anybody suspecting what may be going on. Moreover, critics usually point out Criseyde's ambivalence by emphasizing the fact that, though she is said to live in isolation within her house, the second time we are introduced to her she is next to the door to see the procession of the Palladium and that 'hire goodly lokyng gladed al the prees' (Book I, 123). Such was, indeed, the danger: to seduce or be seduced. Consequently, when a widow went out she had to take great care not to draw anyone's, or rather any man's, attention. For this purpose, she was advised to be dressed in strict mourning, never to wear bright colours or make up:

> Also hit falleþ to wedowes forto vse symple & comune cloþinge of mene colour, & noght gay ne starynge ne of queynte & sotil schap, and take ensample of þe holy wedowe Iudith of whom Holy Writ makeþ mynde, þat anone whan hir housbonde was deed sche lefte all hir gay attyre and apparaile boþe of hir body & of hir heed and toke mekeliche clothing & attyre þat longed to a wydowe to schewe doel of her herte & to eschewe veynglorie for þe loue of God.[61]

Widows were expected to wear black, or at least sombre, clothing. In Chaucer's *Canterbury Tales* the allusion to this black colour is often the only element given to introduce and portray widows: no further characterisation seems necessary. At the beginning of the Knight's Tale, Theseus approaches the town of Athens and meets a company of ladies, 'ech after oother clad in clothes blake' (I, 899). A few lines after, these women lament themselves: Fortune's fickle wheel has turned, all of them are former queens and have lost their husbands during the siege of the town. When old January becomes blind in the Merchant's Tale, he wishes he and his young wife were dead. He

---

61   V. Nelson, ed., *A Myrour to Lewde Men & Wymmen*, p.189.

cannot bear the idea that she might have a lover or another husband: 'but evere lyve as wydywe in clothes blake / Soul as the turtle that lost hath hire make' (2079–2080). January has probably not realized that black may be very becoming as in the case of Criseyde who in her widow's attire is brighter than a star under a black cloud (*Troilus & Criseyde*, Book I, 175). In 1484, William Caxton published *The Book of the Knight of La Tour*, the highly moralistic book of instruction of a knight to his three daughters. The author presents women as dangerous creatures who must be brought under control, as temptresses always on the look out. He gives the example of a man who had three wives. The first one,

> For her pryde and for the grete quantite of gownes and Iewelles that she hadde was loste and dampned for euer. And yet many one is in this world that wel haue the courage soo prowde that wel they dare bye gownes of thre or foure score crownes. And yet thynkyng hit of lytel prys that yf so were they must gyue to poure folke two or thre shyllynges, they shold holde that ouermoche and as halfe loste. Loke and beholde ye thene how they that haue soo many gownes wherof they coyntyse and araye their bodyes, how ones they shalle straitly answer of them. And euery good woman after she is of estate and degree she ought to hold and behaue her symply and honestly in her clothyng and in the quantite of hit.'[62]

The third wife's lot was no better because of her excessive use of cosmetics:

> She had popped and polysshed her face for to seme more faire and plaisaunt to the world. And that was one of the synnes that was moost displesynge to god. For she dyde hit by pryde by whiche men falle to the synne of lecherye. And finally in to all other. For aboue alle thynge it diplesith to the Creatour, as one wylle haue by crafte more beaute than nature hath gyuen to hym.[63]

The only person widows were supposed to please was God. This is the reason why apart from home, the other proper place for a widow was at church. Medieval moralists quoted as an example the New Testament figure Anna 'þat wolde noght go fro þe temple, but dwelled

---

62 M.Y. Offord, ed., *The Book of the Knight of the Tower*, Oxford University Press, EETS supplementary series n°2, 1971, p.76.
63 Ibid., p.77.

þerynne day and nyghte, prayenge & servyng God devoutliche in grete abstinence'.[64] They went on, explaining that abstinence implied not only continence but also going without meat and wine:

> þe þridde þing þat byfalleþ to wedowes is streyt livynge of mete & drinke & forberynge of delices & delicious metes & drinkes, for seynt Poule seith þat a wydowe þat lyueþ in delices is dede, þat is to seie þorgh synne.[65]

What conclusions can we draw from these moral treatises? Moralists and preachers were men and clerics; their writings betray their great fear and distrust of women. They presupposed that 'woman [was] not merely a sexual snare employed by the devil, but even a voluntary one. (...) A woman preacher, however virtuous, would incite immoral thoughts in her auditors. (...) Given this climate of opinion, no wonder moralists were so preoccupied with restraining women from "seeing and being seen"'.[66] For Medieval moralists, exemplary widows were therefore solitary, grieving women who were models of constancy and chastity. The prestige of virginity was such that it ruled out any other way of conceiving and describing a woman's heroic character: a martyred vigin could not be surpassed. Female perfection was characterized by chastity and passivity, two virtues that widows were lucky enough to be able to recapture. They had, however, a long way to go for they had lost purity and innocence for experience and temptation. It was, as we have seen, through the absolute denial of the body: widows were asked to consider themselves as impregnable fortresses, to master and reduce their sexual instincts to nothing. This path to Virtue leading to the salvation of the soul required self-possession, self-control, constant close watch and restraint. Then only would they wash away the blemish in them and recover some of their former purity: 'she that kepeth wel and clenely

---

[64] V. Nelson, ed., *A Myrour to Lewde Men & Wymmen*, p.189. The prophetess Anna is mentioned in St Luke (2: 36–7): 'She was a very old woman, who had lived seven years with her husband after she was first married, and then alone as a widow to the age of eighty-four. She never left the temple, but worshipped night and day with fasting and prayer.'
[65] Ibid.
[66] A. Blamires, ed., *Woman Defamed and Woman Defended*, pp.4–5.

her wydowhede, (...) these be lykened and compared as sayd our lord to the precious margaryte whiche is euer bryght and clene withoute ony macule or tatche.'[67] Nuns were the best example of women rendered harmless. It comes therefore as no surprise that moralists advised widows to live a retired life and to fast regularly. Widows could become uncontrollable by gaining self-confidence thanks to their new independent state. It was, therefore, very important in the eyes of our preachers to make sure they stuck to their proper and inferior place in society: though widows, they were first and foremost women. No equality with men was conceivable. Consequently, moralists insisted on the prayers widows were to say for their late husbands' souls establishing thus a spiritual continuation of the matrimonial bond. Fasting was also a way of reminding them (as well as weakening them) of their bereavement.

Praying for the dead, having masses celebrated for the salvation of their souls were common practices in all families. Several didactic treatises or collections of *exempla* relate that a deceased can even come back to obtain redress or to testify that the prayers already said are effective. The visitors from the After World usually address close relatives and many of them visit their widows. In his *Dialogue of Miracles* written between 1219 and 1223, Caesarius of Heisterbach gave the example of a widow from Liege:

> A usurer from Liege died at that time. The bishop had him expelled from the graveyard. His wife went to the episcopal see to implore that he be buried in consecrated ground. The pope refused. So she pleaded in favour of her spouse: 'I was told, Lord, that husband and wife are one and that, according to the Apostle, the unbelieving husband can be saved by his believing wife. What my husband forgot to do, I (who am part of his body) will gladly do it. I am ready to become a recluse on his behalf and to atone for his sins.'
>
> Giving in to the cardinals' requests, the pope had the deceased sent back to the graveyard. His wife settled next to the tomb and enclosed herself as a recluse. She endeavoured, night and day, to calm God down for the salvation of his soul through alms, fasting, prayers and vigil-keeping. At the end of seven years, her husband appeared to her, dressed in black. He thanked her: 'May God return it to you for, thanks to your hardships, I have been removed from the depths of Hell and the most dreadful torments. If you go on helping me that

---

[67] M.Y. Offord, ed., *The Book of the Knight of the Tower*, p.157.

way, for seven more years, I shall be completely delivered.' She did so. At the end of seven years, he appeared to her again but dressed in white and blissful: 'Thank you to God and to you for I have been delivered today.'[68]

It is of course difficult to assess precisely the impact moralists and preachers had on their readers or listeners. However, there is no doubt that people living in the medieval period were very much concerned with their fate after death: the numerous testaments that have survived show that testators rarely forgot to give religious instructions for the good of their souls. Everyone at that time had heard sermons or tales warning against condemnation to eternal punishment or, conversely, showing the way to salvation. From the 12th century onwards, it was believed that the soul's passage through purgatory (this place of spiritual purging and purification had just been introduced in the Church dogma) would be eased by the suffrages – prayers, masses, almsgiving – of the living. Pious work for the spiritual benefit of others was therefore recommended and encouraged. Moreover, a major religious revival took place in the 12th century. A new approach became apparent and people were now concerned about imitating Christ through poverty and charity in order to return to the true values of Christian life. The Gospels were read over again as historical documents and rules of life. Peter Abelard (1079–1142), for instance, after enduring severe criticism when putting Heloise and her companions at the Paraclete, wrote his famous letter (*Historia Calamitatum*) to a friend of his stating that:

> Methinks the spite of such men as these my enemies would have accused the very Christ Himself, or those belonging to Him, prophets and apostles, or the other holy fathers, if such spite had existed in their time, seeing that they associated in such familiar intercourse with women, and this though they were whole of body. On this point St Augustine, in his book on the duty of monks, proves that women followed our Lord Jesus Christ and the apostles as inseparable companions, even accompanying them when they preached. 'Faithful women,' he says, 'who were possessed of worldly wealth went with them, and ministered to them out of their wealth, so that they might lack none of those things which belong to the substance of life.' And if any one does not believe

---

68 Caesarius von Heisterbach, *Dialogus miraculorum*, XII, 24, J. Stranger, ed., Köln: J.M. Heberle, 1851, vol. n°2, pp.335–336. The translation is mine.

that the apostles thus permitted saintly women to go about with them wheresoever they preached the Gospel, let him listen to the Gospel itself, and learn therefrom that in so doing they followed the example of the Lord. For in the Gospel it is written thus: 'And it came to pass afterward, that He went throughout every city and village, preaching and showing the glad tidings of the kingdom of God: and the twelve were with Him and certain women which had been healed of evil spirits and infirmities, Mary called Magdalene, and Joanna the wife of Chuza, Herod's steward, and Susanna, and many others, which ministered unto Him of their substance.'[69]

Numerous observers, such as Jacques de Vitry, noticed the increasing number of women who devoted their lives to God: nuns but also anchorites, canonesses, or beguines. Thirteen rules written in England describe and recommend enclosure.[70] The earliest was Goscelin of St Bertin's *Liber Confortatorius* (*Book of Consolation*, 1082) for the anchoress Eva. In 1169 Aelred of Rievaulx guided his own sister, a cloistered nun, with his *De institutione Inclusarum* (*The Condition of recluses*). The anonymous *Ancrene Wisse* (*Guide for Anchoresses*, 1215–1222) was composed in English for three young noble sisters. The last rule was written by Walter Hilton in the 14th century (*Epistola ad quendam solitarium*). Anne Warren documents how women regularly outnumbered men as anchorites, as many as four to one in some centuries. Some of the applicants were nuns but many were lay women; young ladies or widows. Not everyone, however, was capable (or even desirous) of giving oneself to withdrawal from the world for a life of solitude. Widows who did not wish to remarry nor to enter a convent, could take a vow of chastity.

---

69   H.A. Bellows, *Peter Abelard: Historia Calamitatum, The story of my Misfortunes*, 1922, [new ed., New York: Macmillan, 1972], http://www.fordham.edu/halsall/basis/abelard-histcal.html For a more recent translation, see B. Radice, *The Letters of Abelard and Heloise*, rev. ed. by M.T. Clancy, Harmondsworth: Penguin, 2003.

70   A.K. Warren, *Anchorites and their Patrons in Medieval England*, Berkeley: University of California Press, 1985.

Widows as Vowesses

As a matter of fact, there existed a special class in the Early Church: the order of devout or consecrated widows. Women living in the circle of Jesus were numerous; it is likely that they were widows or separated wives because they are presented as being independent, free to do what they please and as having free disposal of their property. They are mentioned in the Gospels and at the beginning of the Acts – the three Marys: Mary of Magdala, Mary (the mother of James and Joseph), Mary Salome (Zebedee's wife and the mother of James and John), Joanna, a person of wealth and status and the only one the Scripture says is married, and Susanna:

> After this Jesus went journeying from town to town and village to village, proclaiming the good news of the kingdom of God. With him were the Twelve and a number of women who had been set free from evil spirits and infirmities: Mary, known as Mary of Magdala, from whom seven demons had come out, Joanna, the wife of Chuza a steward of Herod's, Susanna, and many others. These women provided for them out of their resources. (Luke 8:1–3).

This new class rapidly extended beyond Jerusalem: we are told that there lived in Joppa a woman named Tabitha 'who filled her days with acts of kindness and charity.' When Peter heard of her death, he went off with two men and 'when he arrived he was taken up to the room, and all the widows came and stood round him in tears.' Once Peter has raised her from the dead, 'he called together the members of the church and the widows and showed her to them alive.' (Acts, 9:36, 39 & 41). The first Epistle to Timothy already attests to the existence of a specific order of widows:

> A widow under sixty years of age should not be put on the roll. An enrolled widow must have been the wife of one husband, and must have gained a reputation for good deeds, by taking care of children, by showing hospitality, by washing the feet of God's people, by supporting those in distress – in short, by doing good at every opportunity. (I, Timothy 5:9–10)

Ignatius, the second bishop of Antioch who died a martyr in 107, ended his epistle to the Smyrnaeans by saluting 'the families of my brethren, with their wives and children, and the virgins who are called widows',[71] which shows that the word 'widow' here refers to some ecclesiastical order. From the third century onwards, the order of virgins tended to take a more important place than that of widows. Moreover the deaconesses gradually replaced the widows so this institution waned and, in the end, died out.

Because the Church disapproved of bigamy and because it was suspicious of widows who remained unmarried since they were sexually experienced women, it tried to take them in hand by encouraging them to take vows of chastity. It thus distinguished between *relicta*, women stricken by the death of their spouse, and *vidua*, women who recognized themselves as one of St Paul's true widows and who committed themselves to a practice of continence: 'She that is a widow indeed, and desolate, let her trust in God and continue in supplication and prayers night and day. For she that liveth in pleasures is dead while she is living' (I, Tim 5: 5–6). Widowhood took on the appearance of providential and liberating grace: the widow was to realize that her misfortune (solitude, poverty, desertion, etc.) meant the end of her subservience for she would reach Glory by observing modesty, humility, and submission. She rose to a spiritual dimension through the experience of absence thus taking part in the Hope of the Church waiting with confidence for the return of its own Spouse. Distress could therefore be transcended since what was grievous loss was to be understood as the promise of future eternal bliss: as often with the Church, suffering was consequently considered as redeeming. Margery Kempe (c. 1373–c. 1440) conformed to this tradition as far as her relation to Christ is concerned. Throughout her autobiography, one discovers that she kept up a regular dialogue with Christ who called her 'my derworthy derlyng, my blissyd spowse, and myn holy wife' (Book I, chapter 86);[72] he also explained to her: 'I have drawe the lofe of thin hert fro alle mennys hertys into myn hert' (Book I, chapter 65) and added that she had every reason to love him more than anything/anyone else especially 'for thu hast thi wil of chastité as thu

---

71 M. Staniforth, ed., *Early Christian Writings*, Harmondsworth: Penguin Classics, 1968, revised edition by A. Louth, 1987.
72 S.B. Meech & H.E. Allen, eds., *The Book of Margery Kempe*, Oxford: University Press, EETS n°212, 1940.

wer a wedow, thyn husbond levyng in good hele' (Book I, chapter 65). *The Book of Margery Kempe* characterises life as inverted widowhood: the lamentations of the desolate woman come first, to be replaced by the joy of the mystical nuptials to take place between the husband, Christ himself, and his betrothed. This is why the bride-to-be is a widow and why the vocabulary used by Margery to voice her love, not yet fulfilled, is that of bereavement: she mourns her heavenly lover and fears, since 'whan this creatur was twenty yer of age or sumdele mor, sche was maryed to a worschepful burgeys and was wyth chylde wythin schort tyme' (Book I, chapter 1), she might not be allowed to dance with the virgins after her own death. Christ comforts her assuring her they will be (re)united:

> As thu art a mayden in thi sowle, I schal take the be the on hand in hevyn and my modyr be the other hand, and so schalt thu dawnsyn in hevyn wyth other holy maydens and virgynes, for I may clepyn the dere abowte and myn owyn derworthy derlyng. I schal sey to the, myn owyn blyssed spowse, 'Welcome to me wyth al maner of joye and gladnes, her to dwellyn wyth me and nevyr to departyn fro me wythowtyn ende, but evyr to dwellyn wyth me in joy and blysse.' (Book I, chapter 22)

What weighs heavy on Margery is the fact that she still has fifteen years of widowhood to endure. Her lot is compared to that of Mary Magdalene who also lived on for fifteen years after Christ's death (Book I, chapter 74). After these fifteen years – that will seem many thousand years to her as she confesses – Margery will be welcomed by St Mary (the Virgin), St Katherine and St Margaret (two martyred virgins), St Mary Magdalene (the repentant and pardoned sinner), the apostles, martyrs, confessors, and the holy virgins.[73]

Margery never became a vowess though she did once ask the Bishop of Lincoln to give her the mantle and the ring – which she did not receive since her husband was alive (Book I, chapter 15). In

---

73 This list is very traditional, also to be found in *Hali Meiðhad* or *Sawles Warde*. William Langland gives a slightly different version when writing in passus XII of *Piers Plowman* that St John, St Jude, and St Simon are in Heaven together with the virgins, martyrs, confessors, and widows (lines 203–204). One can gather that *the holie widowes* are the women who first witnessed Christ's resurrection.

chapter 70, she also mentions meeting 'a worschipful woman whech had takyn the mentyl and the ryng'. Vowesses had a semi-religious role. They registered with the bishop and vowed to live a chaste life, never to remarry. The vowing ceremony was open to the public, the bishop blessed the woman as well as the ring and mantle she was now to wear. In his long poem *Mirour de l'Omme*, John Gower introduces his readers to *Continence*, one of the daughters of *Lady Chastity*. Among *Continence*'s followers, one finds friars, monks, nuns who are '*obligez a contenir*' [are obliged to be continent] and '*la dame auci qui voet tenir / Sa chasteté, dont revestir / Se fait d'anel par beneiçoun / D'evesque, apres pour nul desir / Se porra lors descontenir,*' (17827–17831) [the lady who wants to remain chaste. She asks to wear the ring blessed by a bishop. Afterwards, never will she be able to give up continence, whatever her desire.][74] Edmund Lacy, Bishop of Exeter between 1420 and 1455, gave a full description of the ceremony (the *benedictio vidue*) in his *Liber Pontificalis*.[75] On a feast day or at least a Sunday, between the Epistle and the Gospel, the widow, kneeling before the bishop, was asked if she agreed to become the spouse of Christ and to renounce the pleasures of the flesh. The widow then handed over the following Profession (in the vernacular) to the bishop:

> I, N., Wedow, avoue to God perpetuell chastite of my body from henceforward, and in the presence of the honorable fadyr in God, my lord N., by the grace of God, Bishop of N., I promytt stabily to leve in the Church, Wedow. And this to do, of myne own hand, I subscribe this wrytyng.

And the widow marked 'this wrytyng' with a sign of the cross. Henry Harrod transcribed the Profession in French put into the hands of the Bishop of Ely by the Countess of Suffolk in 1382: '*Jeo Isabella, jadys la femme William de Ufford, Count de Suffolk, vowe a Dieu, &c. en presence de tres reverentz piers en Dieu evesques de Ely et de Norwiz,*

---

74   G.C. Macaulay, ed., *The Complete Works of Gower*, Oxford; Clarendon Press, 1899–1902.
75   Ralph Barnes, ed., *Liber Pontificalis of Edmund Lacy, Bishop of Exeter*, Exeter: William Roberts, 1847, pp.122–125.

qe jeo doi estre chaste d'ors en avant ma vie durante.'[76] The bishop would then bless the mantle, sprinkle the ring with holy water and put it on the widow's finger while saying: '*Accipe, famula Christi, anulum, fidei signum, connubii indicium, quem devota deferas, casta custodias, quoad amplexus divini sponsi coronanda pervenias. Per Christum Dominum nostrum. Oremus.*': the widow was now married to Christ. Her vow was binding, there was no backtrack possible unless the widow obtained a papal dispensation. Conor McCarthy[77] mentions the case of Joan Warteneys who, in May 1354, was granted permisssion to remarry though she had taken a vow of chastity after the death of her first husband and that of Margaret, widow of William de Slengesby who, in June 1403, was allowed to commute her vow of chastity into other works of piety.

Several literary, often hagiographical, texts allude to vowesses, insisting on their devotion to religious worship and duties. Jacques de Vitry related the story of the ascetic life of Mary of Oignies[78] who died in 1213. Mary was born into a wealthy family and was married at the age of 14. She succeeded in persuading her husband to consent to chaste marriage and to transform their dwelling into a leper-house. Mary led a very austere and saintly life. Her renown, which attracted many visitors, decided her on withdrawing from society and living in a hermit's cell next to the monastery of Oignies where she died. Jacques de Vitry's text was translated into Middle English in the 14th century. Mary of Oignies, she too wedded to Christ, is presented as seeing many visions. One of them concerns a vowess:

> Anoþere tyme, whan a religyous widowe, þat longe in holy wydowshyp hadde serued god and kept hir doghters in holy maydenhode to þe heuenly husbande, laye on hir deþ-bedde atte Villambroc bysyde Niuelle: she sawe oure lady

---

[76] H. Harrod, 'On the Mantle & the Ring of Widowhood', *Archaeologia*, n°40, 1866, p.308.

[77] C. McCarthy, *Marriage in Medieval England, Law, Literature and Practice*, p.142.

[78] Jacques de Vitry, *Vita Maria Oigniacensis* in *Acta Sanctorum*, 1867, n°25, pp.542–572.

standynge by þe holy wydowe and, as wiþ a wisker waftynge wynde vpon hir, temperd mercyfully þe hete þat dissesed hir.[79]

The Middle-English translator did not include Jacques de Vitry's prologue to Mary's Life because, according to him, it was only suited to those trained in theology and rhetoric and therefore would require 'moor expounynge'. Jacques de Vitry reminded his readers of what St Paul expected of true widows: not only that they should pray, fast, weep, keep vigil, and implore but also wash the feet of God's people, take care of children, offer hospitality, practise charity towards the poor and ill. Criseyde alludes to the first part of the list only when she explains to her uncle who urges her no longer to wear her black clothes and her veil but to rejoice and dance:

> 'I! God forbede!' quod she. 'Be ye mad?
> Is that a widewes lif, so God yow save?
> By God, ye maken me ryght soore adrad!
> Ye ben so wylde, it semeth as ye rave.
> It satte me wel bet ay in a cave
> To bidde and rede on holy seyntes lyves;
> Lat maydens gon to daunce, and yonge wyves.' (Book II, 113–119)

The Life of St Elizabeth of Hungary is to be found in the more recent manuscripts of *The Golden Legend* by Jacobo di Voragine (c. 1230–1298).[80] Elizabeth is depicted as the embodiment of Love and Charity. From a little girl she grew up a very religious child. When older, her inclination to prayer and pious observances increased and her husband encouraged her acts of charity and penance, as well as her vigils. She was very much concerned with the well-being of her contemporaries, distributing alms to the poor, having a hospital built for the sick, visiting the unfortunate. William Caxton's Middle English version of the legend reports that during the lifetime of her husband, Elizabeth had made a vow of continence in case of his death so that when he breathed his last, 'she received with devotion the state of widowhood.'

---

79 C. Horstmann, ed., 'Prosalegenden: Die Legenden des ms. Douce 114', *Anglia*, 1885, no.8, p.155.
80 It was one of the sources used by William Caxton for his Middle English adaptation of the *Golden Legend*.

The rest of the text emphasizes the saint's spirit and deeds of constant self-abnegation. She was the true widow in every sense of the word: chaste, pious, and charitable. One cannot, however, help feeling uneasy when reading about the corporal punishments her confessor[81] imposed on her or the countless sacrifices he asked her to make, including the taking away of her children and devoted servants. It is very difficult today to subscribe to the idea that the road to sanctity must go through self-mortification and that suffering is the shortest way to salvation.

Margery Kempe, Marie d'Oignies, Elizabeth of Hungary: these three women really existed; their personalities and lives were recognized as extraordinary and exemplary hence the relations made by their biographers. Vowesses, however, were not only literary paragons of virtue and piety.[82] Ordinary women, who have left no particular trace in History, also chose to bind themselves by vows of chastity. In 1395, Lady Alice West of Hampshire bequeathed to her son Thomas 'a peyre Matyns bookis, and a peire bedes, and a rynge wit whic y was yspoused to god.'[83] In 1424, Roger Flore spoke of his 'welbeloved wife Cecile' in his testament and will and mentioned that 'if she take þe mantel and þe rynge, and avowe chastite, than wul I þat fort my said ioint feffes make her astate, for terme of hir lif, of þe same too lordshipes, vp condicion þat she lyve sool, withoute husbond.'[84] Joel T. Rosenthal cites a more straightforward husband, the Earl of Pembroke (d. 1461) who left no choice to his wife:

> Wyfe, that ye remembre your promise to me, to take the ordre of wydowhood, as ye may be the better mayster of your owne, to performe my wylle and to helpe my children, as I love and trust you.[85]

---

81 Conrad of Marburg was a particularly austere and unsparing man. He is remembered as a preacher of the crusade and an inquisitor.
82 Which can hardly be said of Margery Kempe in any case!
83 F.J. Furnivall, ed., *Fifty Earliest English Wills in the Court of Probate, London, A.D. 1387–1439, with a priest's of 1454*, London: Kegan Paul, Trench, Trübner, EETS, original series, vol. 78, 1882, p.5. Reprinted by Oxford University Press in 1964.
84 Ibid., p.60.
85 J.T. Rosenthal, 'Fifteenth-Century Widows and Widowhood: Bereavement, Reintegration, and Life Choices', S.S. Walker, ed. *Wife and Widow in Medieval England*, p.46.

In May 1450, John Sydey did not explicitly ask his wife Alice to become a vowess after his death but transferred land on to her 'provided she keep pure and unmarried after my decease' while Robert Strut insisted on his wife doing the same in December 1453: 'to Joan all my movable goods, and my tenement, as long as she remain in her pure widowhood.'[86] The motive for such demands may have been exclusive love and sexual jealousy but it seems more likely that the testators were making sure property remained within the family, that their children were protected from the claims of the stepfather or half-siblings, and that life was not made too difficult for the next generation by the successive endowments of the widow. The number of widows who went through a vowing ceremony was probably never great. On the other hand, it is easy to find references to vowesses in letters, wills or church registers, which proves that these women were a fact of medieval society. In a letter dated March 29th 1482, Richard Cely informed his brother George in Calais about the death of Robert Byfeld and added that 'on the morow herby hys whyfe toke the mantell and the rynge'.[87] The Cely family was not an aristocratic or gentry family but wealthy and successful wool merchants. As a matter of fact, vowesses were always to be found within the upper ranks of society because, for obvious economic reasons, less well-off widows could simply not rule out the possibility of their getting remarried. On the other hand, certain high-born or rich widows became consecrated widows precisely because it enabled them not to remarry and, consequently, protected them from fortune-hunters. One of the best-known examples is that of Elizabeth de Clare (1295–1360) who was first married, at the age of thirteen, to John de Burgh (heir to the Earl of Ulster) who died in 1309. After her own brother's death, Elizabeth became one of the greatest heiresses in England and therefore a highly-coveted prey in the aristocratic marriage market. Her uncle, King Edward II, immediately jumped at such an opportunity, intending to marry her to one of his followers. He was beaten to it by

---

86 P. Northeast, ed., *Wills of the Archdeaconry of Sudbury, 1439–1474*, part I: 1439–1461, p.204 & p.293.
87 A. Hanham, ed., *The Cely Letters, 1472–1488*, London: Oxford University Press, EETS, vol. 273, 1975.

Theobald de Verdon who abducted Elizabeth but died five months later. In 1317, Edward II managed to marry his niece to Roger d'Amory. Elizabeth was a widow for the third time in 1322 (she was only 27). A vow of chastity enabled her afterwards to lead her life as she thought best. She enjoyed a very long widowhood (38 years) founding many religious houses.

Many medieval widows, however, did remarry, second and subsequent marriages being extremely common. They did not conform to the stereotyped figure put forward by the Church either because, as in the case of noble ladies, they were forced into remarriage or because, as in the case of many peasant women, to remain on one's own often led to poverty. Widowhood was then far from the promised redeeming experience. Wills that have survived show that husbands knew life would be hard for their surviving wives and their concern is always very touching. Surviving records do confirm, however, that widows were numerous – though widowhood was often a temporary state – and indicate the arrangements and provisions of welfare at their disposal. Widows were considered as vulnerable, defenceless creatures but common and customary laws gave them rights directed to their assistance as well as that of their possible children. Consequently these (presumed) weak women found themselves taking on many traditionally masculine responsibilities, holding and exercising, for instance, legal rights over property. Overnight, bereaved wives became household heads and found themselves in a new position of public authority. This new role in life made them become more conspicuous in their social community and, as a result, in the archives that have survived to this day. Let us therefore leave the disembodied and idealized widows of the preachers and meet flesh and bone *relicta* and see how they faced their new status in society.

Chapter Five
The Socio-economic Reality of Widowhood

The Cost of Death

Burial and Commemoration

Though the Franco-Italian poet Christine de Pizan probably never set foot on English soil, she was well known in England. Several translations of her works were made during the fifteenth century though, as has been noticed, 'all of the translations of her works were done by men and their interest appears to have been primarily in her military, political and didactic works. (...) All the translators have patronage connections to key figures in the interrelated politics of the War of the Roses and the Hundred Years War with France'.[1] Christine's courtly poetry or more personal, feminist, writings were left aside. Such was the case of *Lavision Christine* (1405) which, though not an autobiography, combines personal reminiscences with political and philosophical commentary. At the age of fifteen she was married to Etienne du Castel who was ten years her senior. His death in 1389 left her devastated with three children, a niece and her own widowed mother to support. Many of her early poems gave utterance to her grief and sense of loss:

> *Seulete m'a laissié en grant martyre,*
> *En ce desert monde plein de tristece,*
> *Mon doulz ami, qui en joye sanz yre*
> *Tenoit mon cuer, et en toute leesce.*

---

[1] L.A. Finke, ed., *Women's Writing in English: Medieval England*, p.201 & p.203.

Or est il mort, dont si grief dueil m'oppresse,
Et tel tristour a mon las cuer s'amord
Qu'a tousjours mais je pleureray sa mort.
[Alone and in great suffering / In this deserted world full of sadness / Has my sweet lover left me. / He possessed my heart, in greatest joy, without grief. / Now he is dead; I'm weighted down by grievous mourning / And such sadness has gripped my heart that I will always weep for his death][2]

And Christine to lament herself against Fortune and a life of hardship: everyone will experience '*Et les meschiefs qu'il fault y endurer, Et comment mort vient qui tout met en biere*' [misfortunes that must be endured and Death that comes to put everyone in his coffin] (Ballad XVI).

The first duty that fell to a widow was indeed her husband's funeral. In the collection of wills of the archdeaconry of Sudbury (1439–1474) edited by Peter Northeast, several testators ask their wives to make sure their funeral is properly done: in 1442, John Wymbych of Kentford bequeathed his wife Margery 'all [his] utensils and bedding belonging to [his] house, and all [his] other goods and chattels, on condition that she pay all [his] debts and see [his] funeral efficiently done' (will no.270). In 1452, John Sorell of Chelsworth left to his wife Juliana the messuage he had in that town, 'with all [his] goods and household stuff, on condition that she see [his] burial-day costs met and all [his] debts paid' (will no.516). Similarly Alan Godferey of Little Whelnetham recommended his wife Isabel to pay all his debts and to 'see [him] honestly buried' (will no.533). John Norman, a mercer in Barrow, asked his wife Margaret 'to pay all [his] debts, see [him] buried and keep [his] anniversary day as long as she is able' (will no.693). Every medieval individual anticipated a stay of some length in Purgatory. Yet, according to the Church the souls in Purgatory could be helped by the intercessory prayers of the faithful. In 1438, at the Council of Ferrara/Florence, Julian, Cardinal Cesarini

---

2 Christine de Pizan, *Cent ballades d'amant et de dame*, J. Cerquiglini, ed., Paris: Union Générale d'Editions, 1982, ballad no.XIV. English translation in R. Blumenfeld-Kosinski, ed., *The Selected Writings of Christine de Pizan*, New York, London: W.W. Norton & Co, 1997.

explained the Roman Catholic doctrine of Purgatory to the Eastern Orthodox fathers assembled there:

> The souls of those who after their baptism have sinned, but have afterwards sincerely repented and confessed their sins, though unable to perform the epitimia laid upon them by their spiritual father, or bring forth fruits of repentance sufficient to atone for their sins, these souls are purified by the fire of purgatory, some sooner, others slower, according, to their sins; and then, after their purification, depart for the land of eternal bliss.

The cardinal added 'the prayers of the priest, liturgies, and deeds of charity conduce much to their purification'.[3] The living were thus expected to pray for the dead, give alms, have masses sung on anniversaries all the more so as these deeds were supposed to shorten a loved one's stay in Purgatory as well as one's own. The relationship between the quick and dead was therefore one of mutual reliance. Burials enabled large numbers of people to gather: relatives, friends, fellow members of a craft or gild, and poor parishioners. The greater the congregation was, the more numerous the prayers would be. John Solas of Southwark had a particularly moving wish when he made his will in 1418 stating: 'Also y wole that my wyfe and al my chyldren be atte my berynge, yn case they leue'.[4] In order to make sure the progress of the soul of the dead person was helped, various attractions and rewards were offered to swell the numbers: money was distributed to the poor, food and drinks were provided. Still among the wills of the archdeaconry of Sudbury, Stephen Dele of Oakley stipulated in 1458 in his testament: 'all who are willing to come on the day of my burial, and pray for my soul, to have bread and cheese, and ale enough' (will no.1005). John Wareyn of Bildeston gave more details:

> Dated the vigil of the apostles Simon and Jude, 1446; sick of body; to be buried in the parish churchyard of Bildeston, in the Christian manner; to the high altar of the same church and its rector 6s 8d, he to pray most devoutly in the pulpit

---

3   H. Denziger, *The Sources of Catholic Dogma*, St Louis & London: B. Herder Book Co., [translated from the thirtieth edition by R.J. Deferrari] 1957.
4   F.J. Furnivall, *The Fifty Earliest English Wills in the Court of Probate, London: 1387–1439; with a priest's of 1454*, p.29. http://www.hti.umich.edu/cgi/t/text/text-idx?c=cme;cc=cme;view=toc;idno=EEWills

for my soul; to be distributed among the poor of Bildeston at the time of my obsequies 6s. 8d.; to be distributed among the poor of Bury St Edmunds, in money, 12s.; to be spent in honest expenses about my funeral and burial, as to priests, clerks, ringers of bells, wax, bread, ale, chesse and other necessaries, according to my degree, as seems to my execs most expedient for the health of my soul. (Will no.415)[5]

Immediately after the husband's death, the widow, helped by her family or neighbours, had to wash and wrap the body in a shroud. John Deye of Long Melford (will no.517) mentioned that he left his son and daughter coverlets, his brass and pewter, and bedding 'except a sheet that I shall be buried in'. The body was then watched over by mourners for two or three days. The evening before the funeral, *placebo* (the name given to Vespers in the Office for the Dead because it began with the versicle *Placebo Domino in regione vivorum* [I will please the Lord in the land of the living] from Psalm 114:9 in the Vulgate)[6] was said in the deceased's house or a proper evensong service was held at church. The long 15th-century sermon series in English known as *Jacob's Well* mentions the Office for the Dead saying: 'His body lay on the bere in the cherche, & clerkys seydin Placebo & Dirige for his soule' [His body lay on the bier in the church, and the clerks said placebo and dirge for his soul][7]. One of the points the members of London's gild of Garlekhith had sworn 'on þe bok' to abide by was that '3if any brother oþer suster of þe bretherhede dye, al þe oþer schul comen to þe placebo and dirige, and in morun atte messe'[8] If the body had not yet been removed from the house, it was carried into the church on the day of burial on a bier made of boards. Richard Aniys of Wetheringsett remembered to leave eight pence to

5   Margery Muryell, a widow living in Hawstead, left a large sum of money for food and refreshments on her burial day in her will dated December 13th 1451: 'to be spent on her burail day in giving food and drink to poor people and her neighbours 40 s.' (Will no.640).
6   Psalm 116:9 today.
7   A. Brandeis, ed., *An English Treatise on the Cleansing of Man's Conscience*, London: Kegan Paul, Trench, Trübner, 1900. Early English Text Society, no. 115.
8   T. Smith, ed., *English Gilds*, London, New York, Toronto: Oxford University Press, Early English Text Society, 1870, p.4.

'the four men who carry my body to the church on the day of my burial' (will no.345) while John Broun, a carpenter in Sudbury left four pence 'to each of the four persons carrying my body to burial' (will no.1132). The whole community often took part in the procession of the body to the church. If the dead man had belonged to a confraternity, the members were expected to participate in the procession and required to be present at the divine service. The constitution of Lynn's gild of St Leonard stated that 'þe aldirman shal comand þe oficere to warnyn alle þe bretheryn and sisterynn to bryng þe cors to þe chirche, wit wax brenned'.[9] Inside the church, the body was laid before the high altar, while the bier was covered by a hearse – a framework of wood adapted to carry lighted tapers – which, in its own turn, was covered by a pall. Other candles were lit surrounding the bier. Almeric Molows of Wattisfield mentions in his testament 'the four poor men standing around my hearse, holding four torches in their hands' rewarding each of them with a penny (will no.1409). Similarly, the 1384 statutes of the Gild of St Christopher in Norwich specify:

> Also it is ordeyned, yat on ye day of ye sepulture of eny brother or syster of yis gilde, yt cueryche offre a ferthyng, and yeuen an halpeny to allemesse, and aboute ye dede ij. candels of viij. pounde of wax; and two pouere men shul bene hirede of ye almesse siluer, to holden ye torches aboute ye dede.[10]

The service went on early in the morning with Matins and Lauds celebrated together and known as *Dirige* from the words of the opening antiphon *Dirige in conspectu meo viam tuam* [Direct my way in they sight] (Psalm 5:9 in the Vulgate). The brethren and sisters of Norwich's gild of St Katherine attended *Dirige* reciting prayers according to their education:

> At ye Dirige, euery brother and sister yat is letterede shul seyn, for ye soule of ye dede, placebo and dirige, in ye place wher he shul comenn to-geder; ande euery brother and sister yat bene nought letterede, shyl seyn for ye soule of ye dede, xx. sythes, ye pater coster, wit Aue maria; ande of ye catel of ye gilde shal yer bene two candels of wax, of xvj. pounde weight, aboute ye body of ye

9 Ibid., p.50.
10 Ibid., p.24.

dede. (...) Ande what brother or syster be absent at placebo and Dirige, or at messe, he shal payen two pouncle of wax to ye catel of ye gilde, bot he be resonablely excusede.[11]

Dirige was sometimes followed by mass. In the last book of Thomas Malory's *Morte d'Arthur* Lancelot, who has become a priest, reaches Almesbury after Queen Guenever's death. He first sings mass himself before the solemn Requiem Mass is celebrated by a former Archbishop of Canterbury:

> Than syr Launcelot sawe hir vysage, but he wepte not gretelye, but syghed. And so he dyd al the observaunce of the servyse hymself, bothe the dyryge and on the morne he sange masse. And there was ordeyned en hos-bere, and so wyth an hondred torches ever brennyng aboute the cors of the quene and ever syr Launcelot with his eyght felowes wente aboute the hors-bere, syngyng and redyng many an holy oryson, and frankensens upon the corps encensed.
>
> Thus syr Launcelot and his eyght felowes wente on foot from Almysburye unto Glastynburye; and whan they were come to the chapel and the hermytage, there she had a dyryge with grete devocyon. And on the morne the heremyte that sometyme was Bysshop of Canterburye sange the masse of Requyem with grete devocyon, and syr Launcelot was the fyrst that offeryd, and than als his eyght felowes. And than she was wrapped in cered clothe of Raynes, from the toppe to the too, in thirtyfolde; and after she was put in a webbe of leed, and thna in a coffyn of marbyl.[12]

Indeed, there was usually a pause between *Dirige* and the Requiem mass simply for breakfast or for a greater length of time as the statutes of Norwich's gild of carpenters seem to imply requiring all its members to be 'at [the deceased's] dirige, and praye for þe soule. And, on þe day folwande, ben at his messe of requiem from gynnyng to þe ending'.[13] Those attending mass made offerings of money (as Launcelot who 'was the fyrst that offeryd'), the amount collected being known as the mass-pence and being mainly used for further masses for the deceased's soul. None of the money was meant to assist financially the widow or the dead man's children as would proba-

---

11 Ibid., p.20.
12 Malory, *Works*, E. Vinaver, ed., Oxford, New York, Toronto, Melbourne: Oxford University Press, 1971, p.723.
13 T. Smith, ed., *English Gilds*, p.38.

bly be the case today. Among the numerous wills of the archdeaconry of Sudbury, several testators indicate what the collection should be used for. The vast majority of them wished the mass-pence to be given to the friars of the area; William Olyve of Cavendish, for instance, specified:

> To the four orders of friars, that is at Clare, Sudbury, Babwell and Cambridge, all the mass-pence coming from the brethren and sisters of the gild of the Blessed Mary in Cavendish, to be distributed equally between them. (Will no.776)

Richard Munnyng of Badwell Ash wished 'the Friars Preachers of Thetford to have the mass-pence of the gild of St John the Baptist of Langham, to celebrate for my soul' (will no.842). Others entrusted their parish priest with the task of praying for their souls. William at the Mere of Cavensham bequeathed 'to the vicar of Cavenham church the mass-pence of the gild of St Mary' (will no.387), Lawrence Jakys of Depden left 'to the rector of Depden church all the money coming from the gild of St Mary and St Margaret in the town of Depden, called 'messpence', to celebrate for [his] soul (will no.125) while John Lane of Ixworth gave 'to the high altar[14] all the mass-pence coming from the brethren and sisters of the gild of All Saints and the gild of St Peter and St Paul the apostles of that town' (will no.101). Several testators wished the money to be used for lights, such as John Frost of Wickhambrook (will no.302), or for buildings under repair: his own parish church in the case of John Freman of Ixworth granting 'all the pence coming, on [his] burial day, from the brethren of the gild of Corpus Christi, in the town of Ixworth, to be to the repairing and emending of the same church' (will no.335) and a hall in that of John Wellam giving 'the mass-pence of the other gild to the repairing of the community hall of Hitcham' (will no.772). Matilda Norwold of Icklingham meant the friars of Babwell to have half of the mass-pence while 'the other half [was] to be divided equally among the poor of

---

14 That is to say 'the chief altar of a church, but used in wills before the Reformation to mean the incumbent or priest serving the cure, to whom were due offerings and tithes' (P. Northeast, ed., *Wills of the Archdeaconry of Sudbury*, p.xxiv).

the town' (will no.940). There are only two examples of testators intending the money to be spent for the repayment of debts (consequently a relief for the executors and heir), William Gambon of Pakenham remembering he owed shillings to the gild of St Peter of his town (will no.343) and John Caly of Great Ashfield wishing part of the mass-pence to be given to the parish priest 'for tithes forgotten' (will no.1249). The excerpt from *Le Morte d'Arthur* quoted above proves that offerings did not only concern gild members; another extract from Malory's work shows it even more explicitly – all the more so as the word *mass-penny* itself appears:

> And so many knyghtes yode thyder to beholde that fayre dede mayden,[15] and so uppon the morn she was entered rychely. And sir Launcelot offird her massepeny; and all tho knyghtes of the Table Rounde that were there at that tyme offerde with sir Launcelot.[16]

The fact remains that all the mass-pence mentioned in the collection of wills under our survey refer to the offerings given by fellow gild-members. Not all gilds had a mainly businesslike purpose (which was the case of merchant and craft gilds): some had a more prominent religious element and their statutes exhibit then much solicitude for the salvation of the brethren's souls with, as we have seen, prayers for the dead, attendance at funerals and offerings made by the gildsmen. The donations made varied from a farthing (the quarter of a penny) to a penny. The gild of the Holy Cross in Bishop's Lynn held that 'eueryl broyer and sister schal offre an halpenny at ye chirche'[17], that of St Edmund in West Lynn claimed one farthing for the deceased's soul and another one for alms, that of St John Baptist in West Lynn half a penny for the dead member's soul and another one for alms. The gild of Holy Trinity in Norwich claimed a little more:

> Ande also it is ordeynede, by comoun assente of yis fraternite, yat, at ye day of ye sepulture of ye bretheren and sisteren, euery brother and sister forsayde shul offeren an halpeny, and yeuen an halpeny to almesse; and eueriche brother and

---

15 The fair maid of Astolat.
16 Malory, *Works*, E. Vinaver, ed., p.642.
17 T. Smith, ed., *English Gilds*, p.83

sister shal payen a peny to a messe; and euery brother and sister shal payen, of ye commoun catel, a peny to a sauter for ye dedes soule.[18]

Then arrived the time of the burial in the churchyard or, for the better-off, inside the church. Many more services in commemoration of the deceased took place adding yet another strain on the dead person's property and, consequently, on the heirs' inheritance. A re-enactment of the funeral took place seven and thirty days after death as well as a whole year later on the anniversary day (an obit): the *Placebo* and *Dirige* were then said, Requiem Eucharists celebrated, food and refreshments shared out. Charles Phyntian-Adams, in his study of late Medieval Coventry, notices that 'it is not often appreciated that obits took place with the pall-covered funeral 'hearse' (a frame for candles which stood *over* the bier) standing before the congregation as a last physical symbol of contact with the person being commemorated'.[19] Robert Taylouur of Lavenham was particularly concerned with his salvation leaving much money to priests for masses and mentioning that 40 pence should be 'distributed among the poor on [his] burial day (...) and as much on [his] seven-day and thirty-day' (will no.416). Margery Koo, a widow living in Woolpit, asked her executors to spend '8d. a year for the keeping of the anniversary of the said Margery Koo and Richard her husband, that is, in the singing of masses, bell-ringing and alms to the poor in the same town' (will no.619). William Mannok of Stoke by Nayland urged his relatives

> As soon as one can be got of the money from the sale of my tenement, a suitable priest to celebrate for my soul, and the souls of my parents, my benefactors and all the faithful departed, in the parish church of Stoke by Nayland, for a year, he taking a competent stipend, as it can be managed; my anniversary to be kept once a year for 7 years after my death, with *dirige* and obsequies and mass once a year for that time. (Will no.546)

---

18   Ibid., p.26. A *sauter* = a psalter that is to say 'a selection from the Psalms, said or sung at a particular service' (*OED*); here, of course, the psalms recited in the Office of the Dead.
19   C. Phythian-Adams, *Desolation of a City. Coventry and the Urban Crisis of the Late Middle Ages*, Cambridge University Press, 1979, p.94.

Many testators, finally, left great amounts of money for masses to be celebrated in their memories…any time of the year. Richard Suttone of Oxborough may have had an uneasy conscience for he ordered 'a thousand pennies to be disposed in a thousand masses for my soul, immediately after my death, as soon as it can be done' (will no.489). Roger Ropkyn of Thrandeston wanted 'a priest to celebrate for 2 years in Thrandeston church; a certain[20] to be celebrated for 10 years in the said church for the health of my soul and the souls of my benefactors' (will no.492) while John Jenewes of Eye bequeathed his wife Agnes his 'messuage in the town of Eye, on condition that she, with her coexecs and the advice of Robert Anyell, dispose for my soul, during 30 years after my death, 80 marks[21] in the celebration of masses' (will no.624). More commonly, people asked for trentals[22] to be celebrated, as in the case of John Cryketot of Buxhall who wished 'three trentals to be done, for [him], [his] mother, [his] wife and all [his] benefactors' (will no.1393) or Simon Wryght of Cotton who devised 10 shillings 'to the Friars Minor of Babwell, for a trental' (will no.409). Clearly all of them wished, above all, to avoid the torments in store for those wandering in Purgatory and of which Chaucer's Summoner gives a glimpse at the beginning of his tale through the words of a friar:

> 'Trentals,' seyde he, 'deliveren fro penaunce
> Hir freendes soules, as wel olde as yonge –
> Ye, whan that they been hastily ysonge,
> Nat for to holde a preest joly and gay –
> He syngeth nat but o masse in a day.
> Delivereth out,' quod he, 'anon the soules!
> Ful hard it is with flesshhook or with oules
> To been yclawed, or to brenne or bake.
> Now spede yow hastily, for Cristes sake!' (III, 1724–1732)

A funeral and the commemorative masses that followed were a costly business that reduced accordingly the share of the widow and her children. Many testators provided for the priest's salary in their will. John Goore of Bardwell thought of all those who would take part in

20   A certain was a weekly celebration of mass (for a year).
21   A mark = 160 pence (13s. 4d. or 2/3 of a pound).
22   'A set of 30 requiem masses said on the same day or on different days.' (*OED*)

his requiem mass distributing 'to the vicar 40d; to the high altar 20d; (...) To the parish clerk of Bardwell 6d; to the sacrist 6d; to each chaplain coming to my obsequies 4d; to each clerk 2d and to each boy 1d' (will no.55). So did John Stevynesson of Woolpit granting 'to the parish priest 6d; to the [*holy*] water-carrier 6d; to each priest present at [his] obsequies 4d' (will no.469) or Thomas Crowe of Soham asking for many services:

> To the high altar 3s 4d; to the high altar, for my mother, 12d; to the priests present at my obsequies, that is, on the first day of my death, the seventh, the thirtieth and the anniversary, each of them, 6d; to the parish chaplain 8d; to each adult clerk 4d; to the rest of the boys, according to the disposition of my execs. (Will no.903)

Concerning the commemorative masses, John Archer of Lavenham asked his executors to give 9 marks to a 'suitable chaplain to celebrate divine service for a year' (will no.446), John Cook of Lavenham recommended a 'reasonable stipend' for the chaplain who would 'celebrate divine service in the same church, for 3 years' (will no.454). John Gruggeman of Barnham devised 10 shillings 'to a priest to celebrate a trental of St Gregory' (will no.1078) while Richard Meryell of Long Melford left the sizeable amount of £12 'to a priest, to read and sing for [his] soul in the church of Melford'. This same Richard was probably a very musical man because he bequeathed £5 to his parish church 'for the choir copes' and 'to every priest being at my *dirige* 4d; to every great clerk being at the said *dirige* 2d; to every child that can sing and read 1d.' (Will no.1091)

Many other religious instructions given by medieval testators meant depriving relations of more possessions or properties. Alms came first: alms to prisoners, lepers, the blind, the paralyzed, the crippled, 'the most needy in the town' (will no.471), 'the poor living in the hospital of St Mary Magdalene' (will no.1293). Other charitable deeds included giving money for the repairing of a church, the fabric of the tower of a church (Alice Foster was asked to 'provide the wages and food of the 'hewerys and leggers' of the tower for as long as they are building it' [will no.109]), the maintenance of bridges and highways, for 'a window to be put on Gazeley church and glazed' (will no.303) not to mention pilgrimages to be undertaken by the surviving relatives:

> Joan his wife to pay all his debts, and receive all the debts due to him; the same Joan to perform, personally or through others, all his pilgrimages which he had promised, that is, to Norwich, Ely, Lowestoft, Walsingham, Bury and 'Peterthorp', immediately after his decease. (Will no.1207 of Thomas Pekerell of Rickinghall Superior)

Several testators were in fact well aware of the high cost of funerals and of the various testamentary directions aimed at perpetuating their memory. Christopher Dyer has estimated that most medieval funerals amounted one year's income.[23] People were often obliged to sell or devise real estate to cover such expenses. In 1319, for instance, the testament of John Costyn of Hyntlesham was proved in the town of Ipswich and 'it appears that John bequeathed all his tenement in the parish of St Matthew, Ipswich, to be sold to pay for an annual mass which John assigned in his testament to Walter le Vyneter, chaplain, to celebrate for his soul in the church of Great Belstede'.[24] In 1316, Gilbert le Cartere of Wicham had done the same, bequeathing 'a house, with a curtilage, situate in the parish of St Mary Elms, to sell and to provide for his soul'.[25] Similarly, Nicholas le Clerk of Ipswich had 'bequeathed his house situate against the lane in the parish of St Mary Quay, between the tenement of Henry le Rotoun and the tenement of Margery Godescalke, to be sold by his executors to perform his exequies and fulfill his testament'.[26] In 1323, William Stoyl only attributed one third of a messuage to his son wishing the two remaining thirds to be spent on prayers and masses:

> William made the testament in his last will, namely on Wednesday next after St Calixtus [19 Oct.] 1323, and bequeathed a messuage with its appurtenances in the parish of St Augustine, Ipswich, which Rose Stoyl, William's mother, gave

23 C. Dyer, *Standards of Living in the Later Middle Ages*, Cambridge University Press, 1989, p.85.
24 G.H. Martin, ed., *The Ipswich Recognizance Rolls. 1294–1327. A Calendar*, p.88.
25 Ibid., p.75.
26 Ibid., p.33.

him, and which lies between the messuage of Gilbert Robert and the messuage of a certain Peter le Fullere, to be sold, and the proceeds to be distributed in shares, namely one for the soul of William's mother, the second for William's soul, and the third part to Geoffrey his son.[27]

It must be added, however, that wills disposed only of property acquired during his lifetime by the testator for the property he had inherited was expected to be devised to his own heirs. Inherited patrimony, consequently, was usually not mentioned. Besides (fortunately enough) many husbands specified that their tenements were to be sold to provide for their souls only after the death of their wives. Such was the case in 1311 of Walter le Taverner of Ipswich who 'bequeathed to Clare his wife for her whole life, all that messuage, with all its appurtenances, which he bought of John de Whatefeld in the parish of St Margaret, Ipswich, and after Clare's death he bequeathed the whole to his executors to sell, and to provide for his soul'.[28] Richard Swalw bequeathed in 1322

> To Juliana his wife the messuage in which they lived, with its appurtenances, in the parish of St Margaret, Ipswich, for the term of her life (...) and after her death the messuage to be sold and the money therefrom to be spent for the souls of the said Richard and Juliana. (...) Item he bequeathed to Juliana a barn (...) to have and to hold for the term of her life and after her death to be sold and the money distributed in annuals for their souls.[29]

Visibly the couple had no children for Richard's other bequests concern nieces and nephews. Robert de Elmessete left to his wife Beatrix a messuage but on one condition – that she provided 'from her goods and chattels for three annuals for Robert's soul and for the souls of Thomas Crudde and Rose his wife'.[30] The prize of kindness and trust goes to John Pek in Stowmarket who bequeathed 'to Margaret [his] wife all [his] goods and chattels, of whatever kind, towards the payment of all [his] debts and her well-being while she lives, she praying and doing for [him] in deeds of charity for [his] soul and hers, and for

---

27   Ibid., p.117.
28   Ibid., p.46.
29   Ibid., p.100.
30   Ibid., p.71.

the souls of [their] friends, as she sees best by her discretion to please God and profit [their] souls'.[31]

The Heavy Price of Inheritance Taxes

In *The Treasure of the City of Ladies,* Christine de Pizan tells her readers that a widowed princess:

> *Se tendra closement meismement un temps aprés le service et obseques, a petite clarté de jour, a piteux et adoulé habit et attour. Neantmoins (...) si pourroit bien pachier et courroucier Nostre Seigneur de tant estre adoulee, et par si long espace. Si convient que elle prengne autre maniere de vie, ou grever pourroit son ame et sa santé, si n'en seroit pas de mieulx a ses nobles enfans, qui encores ont tout mestier d'elle.*
>
> *Cette dame, ainsi amonnestee de raison et de bon conseil, pour aucunement mieulx passer ceste grant tribulacion, se prendra a donner de garde de ses besoignes. Tout premierement vouldra avoir cognoiscence du testament de son signeur. Si mettra toute peine que au plus tost que faire se porra.*
>
> [Will keep herself secluded for a time after the funeral and obseques, with only a little daylight and in sad and mournful weeds. (...) Nevertheless (...) she might easily sin and anger our Lord by being so grief-stricken for too long a time. She should take up a new way of living, or she could harm her soul and her health, and that would not be good for her noble children, who still need her.
>
> This lady, thus admonished by reason and Good Advice in order to pass through this great tribulation somewhat better, will begin to give some thought to her own needs. First of all she will want to understand thoroughly the last will and testament of her husband, and she will devote all her efforts to fulfilling his wishes as soon as possible.][32]

If the husband had died leaving a will the latter had to be proved in an ecclesiastical court. Probate was necessary to ensure that the written document was genuinely that embodying the testator's wishes. Indeed, a will could be forged and proven to be false:

---

31 P. Northeast, ed., *Wills of the Archdeaconry of Sudbury*, will no.19, p.9.
32 Christine de Pizan, *Le Livre des Trois Vertus*, C.C. Willard & E. Hicks, eds., Paris: Honoré Champion, 1989, p.83. Translation by S. Lawson, *Christine de Pizan. The Treasure of the City of Ladies or The Book of the Three Virtues*, London: Penguin Books, 1985 [revised edition 2003], pp.58–59.

> Nicholas, son of Roger Tinctor of Huntingdon, appeared in full court and sought seisin of the land and tenement in which the above Roger his father died seised and vested in the manor of Godmanchester. However, Mariota, widow of that Roger le Tinctor of Huntingdon, appeared with a certain will containing the following: I, Roger Tinctor of Huntingdon, bequeath to Mariota my wife and the children begotten of our body all the lands that I have in the fields of Godmanchester and in the meadow of the same place. Nevertheless, since several people said that the above will was false, being neither faithful nor true, therefore, by judgment of the court the bailiffs conferred upon the above Nicholas the son of Roger seisin of the above lands and tenements. And he gave as entry fine 12d.[33]

A complicated network of probate courts existed to deal with the distribution of property following a person's death. The majority of business took place in the courts of archdeacons. Diocesan (or consistory) courts dealt with the wills of people of high status such as knights. There were in addition two higher levels of jurisdiction above each diocesan bishop: the wills of testators having property in more than one diocese were to be proved in the courts of the archbishop of York or Canterbury. The right to grant probate could, however, be attached to peculiar jurisdictions[34] including manorial (presided over by ecclesiastical or lay lords) or borough courts. The custumal of the town of Ipswich mentions this privilege:

> The last will of the testator in right of the tenement divised by testament wrytten or nuncupatyf be preven aforn the baillives of the seyd toun with ynne the ferst fortie dayes after the deth of the seyd testator, and be the preeff resceyved by two men sworn at least and severally examined upon the last will of the dede, and 3if the preeff be founden acording and good, be it enrolled in the rolle of the toun, and be administracion grauntyd and executors of the deth after the foorme of the forseyd preeff, and the sesyn of the tenement divised

---

33 J.A. Raftis, *A Small Town in Late Medieval England. Godmanchester 1278–1400*, Toronto: Pontifical Institute of Mediaeval Studies, 1982, pp.46–47.
34 'A peculiar is an area exempt from the direct jurisdiction of an archdeacon or bishop, in which the judicial role is exercised either by the Crown, another diocesan bishop, a prebend, Chapters of a cathedral or collegiate, individual Chapter members, the incumbent of a parish, a corporate body such as a university, or the lord of a manor.' (York Diocesan Archive http://www.archiveshub.ac.uk/news/05081302.html)

delivered to hym to whom it was divised by the same executours and be syghte of wittenesse of the ballyves of the forseyd toun wit oute eny withsitting.[35]

It is worth noticing that the words 'last will' are being used here. Under feudal law the Church could not deal with real estate; its competence was limited to the testament proper that is to say the bequests of chattels and the giving of religious instructions. In *The Ipswich Recognizance Rolls. 1294–1327* edited by G.H. Martin, the wills proved before the bailiff only concern land and dwelling houses. The standard introductory sentence, however, is slightly confusing: 'On [date given], the testament of X. Z. of Ipswich was proved by N. and N. (or before the bailiffs) in which testament X. in his last will bequeathed…' The proving of wills was not free and testators sometimes mention the fees to be paid by their executor(s). Robert Hamond of Ixworth, for example, stated:

> My tenement called 'Barboures' and 'Sumptones' to be sold to pay my funeral expenses and the costs and fees of my testament and last will, if it will stretch to it, or to be supplemented from my goods by my executors. (Will no.1033)[36]

Roger Tyllot's will was proved at Fornham St Martin July 16th 1459. In the margin, one finds the following addition: 'Paid to the official for the archdeacon 40s; the official granted acquittance to the execs, for which they paid 6s 8d; and whatever more is due for the archdeacon remains to be paid, notwithstanding the acquittance; to be completed with an inventory' (will no.1240). As Peter Northeast commented in a note, 'the obtaining of probate could be an expensive business'.[37]

Other taxes awaited the heir(s) of a dead man. It goes without saying that they had an impact on the share that could go to the widow

---

35 T. Twiss, ed., *The Black Book of the Admiralty or Monumenta Juridica, vol. II: 'Le Domesday de Gippewyz. The Domus Day of Gippeswiche'*, London: Longman, Macmillan, A. & C. Black, *Rerum britannicarum medii aevi scriptores*, no.55, 1873, p.71. This extract is taken from the fifteenth-century English translation of an early fourteenth-century French version (also provided by T. Twiss). http://www.trytel.com/~tristan/towns/ipswich4.html#cap16 for a modern English version of the custumal.

36 P. Northeast, ed., *Wills of the Archdeaconry of Sudbury*, p.358.

37 Ibid., p.425.

and, above all, reduced in proportion the chattels of the family when the heir was under age and in custody of the mother. When the head of the family died, the church had the right to claim a beast or a garment in acknowledgement of spiritual subjection. In the case of villeins, the duty, known as mortuary, was usually the second best animal. The court rolls of Walsham le Willows edited by Ray Lock include the inventory of a villein's goods after an accidental fire. William Lene, the villein, died in the blaze, and his widow and heirs (two boys aged 10 and 6) had to give 'one cow for the church, pr. 6s.8d'.[38] The inventory enables us to see that William Lene had two oxen, eight cows, one bullock, three calves, two stots, one mare, one filly and several pigs and sheep. The collection of wills edited by Peter Northeast shows that by the late Middle Ages, mortuary was gradually disappearing in East Anglia and only upheld in a few parishes. Adam Onge of Barningham selected 'a dun-coloured cow to go before [him] on [his] burial day as a mortuary' (will no.59), John Payntour of Burwell a sheep (will no.150), John Agas of Barningham his best ewe (will no.159), Richard Hovyle of Cowlinge his best cow (will no.549), Andrew Rayner of Soham his best horse (will no.1041) while John Bonde of Fornham St Martin gave his best garment (will no.359).

Lay taxes were even heavier: relief was the inheritance tax (usually a year's rent) levied by the manorial lord upon the death of a vassal. If the vassal was a villein, this was called heriot, and payment was the best beast of the holding. The court rolls of Walsham le Willows often refer to both taxes according to the status of the dead man. William Thurbern 'freeman held from the lord 1 acre of freehold land for fealty and service 1d. per year. His son Thomas aged two years is his nearest heir, and the lord will have relief of 1d' (p.89). In 1336, Walsham Court General 'ordered to retain in the lord's hands a pightle, which Richard Shepherd of Westhorpe, when he died, held from the lord, for services 3½d. per year, until the heir satisfies for relief'. Yet the widow asserted her rights: 'afterwards came Alice, Richard's widow, and showed that she has title in the pightle for her lifetime; she swore fealty' (p.197). In 1376, John Lester died holding both villein and free land. The villein land was held jointly with his

---

38   R. Lock, ed., *The Court Rolls of Walsham le Willows. 1303–1350*, p.135.

wife Rose who went on holding the tenements for the term of her life. 'The same John was also seised of 14 acres of free land of the tenement Gores, paying therefor 22½d. for services, and 1 bushel of oats annually; John Lester, his son, is his nearest heir and he is of full age. He is admitted on payment of 22½d. as relief, and he swore fealty.'[39]

Most of the time cows were given as heriots but one also finds references to oxen, bullocks, calves, mares, stots, or ewes. When the heir was under age, it meant one beast less for the widow to try and provide for her family. Such was the case, for instance, of Amice, the widow of

> John Chapman villein, who held from the lord in villeinage a messuage with 2 acres of land, [and who] recently died; the heriot is an ewe. Agnes, John's daughter, aged three years, is his nearest heir; custody of the heir and of the land is granted to Amice John's wife, until the heir's full age, to hold by customs and services. Amice swore fealty, and paid 6d. fine for having custody. (p.319)

The clerks often noted down the worth of the beast. After Adam Goche's death 'the lord had as a heriot a cow, worth 13s.4d.' (p.51), with Robert Spileman 'a mare worth 8s. 6d.' (p.128), with Gilbert Helpe 'a colt worth 2s. 6d.' (p.223), and with Ricard of Wortham 'an ewe, worth 16d.' (p.255). Certain villeins had no beasts; in that case a fine was paid:

> (17 January 1336). The jurors say that Roger Brook held from the lord, when he died, 6 acres of land, 2 roods of meadow and half a messuage by services and works and that the lord had no heriot because Roger had no beast. Roger's son John aged three is his nearest heir, and he pays no entry fine. Ordered to take the tenements into the lord's hands, and to report the profits. Upon this came Alice Roger's widow and paid a fine for holding the tenements until John's full age. (p.194)

A similar case had concerned William Goche's two under-age sons in 1318. 'Alice William's widow came and paid 40d. for John and Peter to have entry' (p.63). At the peak of the Black Death (June 1349), over a hundred deaths are recorded in the court rolls of the two

---

39   R. Lock, ed., *The Court Rolls of Walsham le Willows. 1351–1399*, p.124.

manors of Walsham le Willows. The lords probably found themselves at the head of herds of cows and horses as well as flocks of ewes since all the surviving heirs of deceased villeins had to give a beast as heriot. On top of that, the heirs had to pay their own entry fines. In the case of John Helpe, who 'when he died, held a portion of a messuage 3 acres of land by the rod; heriot a cow in calf', no heir came. Consequently, Alice John's widow came and paid 6d. fine 'to have the tenement until the heir comes' (p.326). The poor woman found herself alone, with fewer goods and diminished revenues. It comes as no surprise, therefore, that we hear of her remarriage less than a year later: 'Alice Helpe freewoman, who holds customary land, married John Packard without leave, both in mercy' (p.332). Peter J.P. Goldberg, in his anthology *Women in England*, gives the example of a remarried widow who tried to cheat her lord by not surrendering her best beast on the death of her first husband:

> [1276] William de la Penne is distrained to bring Joan his wife to answer the charge that she unjustly and against the liberty holds back and concealed half a sow which ought to be the lord's portion and did not present her best beast, which she ought to have given for her late husband's heriot, but that she concealed to the abbot's loss, viz 20s.[40]

It is unfortunate that we are not told whether Joan did not present her beast out of poverty, by an oversight, or deliberate cheating. Whatever her reason actually was and whatever her situation, she was supposed to pay. Christine de Pizan deplores the fact that widows had little help and no sympathy:

> *Si est livré meschief aux povres ou a celles qui ne sont mie riches, parce que en leurs affaires ne treuvent pitié si comme en nullui. (...) vous trouvez communement durté, pou de pris et de pitié en toute personne, et tieulx vous souloient honnourer ou temps de voz mariz qui officiers ou de granz estat estoient, qui ores en font pou de compte, ou pou les trouvez amis.*
>
> [Trouble comes to the poor or to those who are not rich, because in their affairs they do not find pity from anyone. (...) You commonly find hard-heart-

---

40   P.P.J. Goldberg, ed., *Woman is a Worthy Wight: Women in England c. 1275–1525. Documentary sources*, Manchester University Press, 1995, p.147. Passage translated from Wilson, ed., *Court Rolls of the Manor of Hales*.

edness and little esteem or pity in anyone. Such people as were in the habit of honouring you while your husbands were alive (who were officials or of some high position) are no longer very friendly and have little regard for you.][41]

Christine's father had died impoverished and her husband's estate was involved in numerous lawsuits. It took her fourteen years of legal battle to get her property back. She therefore knew by experience that people often wish *'faire tort de ce qui lui doit apertenir, si comme souventes fois on fait aux dames vesves – soient grandes ou petites'* [to cheat [widows] out of what belongs to [them] (as often happens to widowed ladies, be they great or little.)][42] According to Christine the various suits and requests had to do with *'debtes ou chalanges de terres ou de rentes'* [debts or disputes over land or pensions.][43] Debts are mentioned everywhere in medieval wills. It was one of the duties of the executor(s) to pay off any of the testator's debts. When writing or dictating their wills, dying people named their testators. In the majority of cases husbands designated their wives as one of them. It has been well established since the works of the Cambridge Group for the History of Population and Social Structure under the direction of Peter Laslett that medieval families were already nuclear units and that 'the great family of Western nostalgia' – the three-generation household – had actually preceded industrialization.[44] Most medieval households included parents with their dependent children. Out of the 1041 families on the manor of Halesowen studied by Zvi Razi over the years 1270–1400, only 16% were extended and not conjugal families.[45] Before the very late Middle Ages, wills were made by very limited social groups and they did not become common among the peasantry, including manorial tenants, until the fifteenth century. Even then only those who had some property to dispose of found it neces-

41 Christine de Pizan, *Le Livre des Trois Vertus*, translation by S. Lawson, *Christine de Pizan. The Treasure of the City of Ladies or The Book of the Three Virtues*, pp.140–141.
42 Ibid., p.84, trans. Ibid., p.59.
43 Ibid., p.189, trans. Ibid., p.140.
44 P. Laslett, *Household and Family in Past Time*, Cambridge University Press, 1972.
45 Z. Razi, *Life, Marriage and Death in a Medieval Parish. Economy, Society and Demography in Halesowen (1270–1400)*, Cambridge University Press, 1980.

sary to have a will made and do not, therefore, give a totally faithful image of medieval Britain. On the other hand, they are often the most personal documents many people have left behind and the only ones giving such a wealth of details about family relationships. They show, in particular, that matrimony was not only a community of life but also one of goods and interests, that wives – though considered as subordinate partners – were associated to their husbands in all major deeds as far as the economic life of the household was concerned. Spouses usually ran, sold or disposed of what they owned together. It comes as no surprise, consequently, that most husbands designed wills for the benefice of their wives and found it obvious that their surviving partners should supervise the division and dispersion of the conjugal assets. Robert Aueray, a shoemaker from London specified in his will dated 1410:

> Also y bequeþe al þe resydue of my godys to Ione my wyff, for to beyn myn executorice cheff, and Ion Robert of London for to ben executour wyt her.[46]

In 1415, Thomas Walwayn, esquire in Herefordshire, appointed as his chief executor his wife Isabelle, the other executors including a nephew and two chaplains.[47] In 1417, Thomas Broke, a landowner from Devon mentioned: 'to do good and trewe execucion of þis my testament, yc ordeyne and mak myne executours Iohane my wyfe, William Brerdon, sir Ion Dey, parsone of Bageworthe, Raufe Perceuale, sir Edward Osbourne, vicary of Thornecombe'.[48] Roger Salwayn, a knight from York, chose his wife as well as three other persons to be the 'surveiors' of his testament in 1420.[49] As for Richard Whyteman, a waxchandler from London, he stated that his wife Alice was to be his principal executor assisted by two other executors and the parson of his parish church as 'ouerseer'.[50] The wills contained in *The Ipswich Recognizance Rolls* or those of the archdeaconry of

---

46 F.J. Furnivall, ed., *The Fifty Earliest English Wills in the Court of Probate, London: 1387–1439; with a priest's of 1454*, p.17.
47 Ibid., p.24.
48 Ibid., p.28.
49 Ibid., p.54.
50 Ibid., p.82.

Sudbury lead to the same conclusion, confirming the fact that it was very often for the widow to carry out her late husband's last wishes. On June 10th 1316, the testament of Thomas le Mareschal of Ipswich was proved. He bequeathed to his wife Felicia:

> A messuage with its appurtenances. (...) for the term of her life and after her death the messuage to revert to his daughter Alice and the heirs of her body. And if Alice should chance to die without such heirs the messuage to remain to Felicia and her assigns to sell or bequeath for the souls of Thomas, Felicia, and Alice, as shall seem best to her. And therefore administration and seisin of the said tenement was granted to Felicia as executrix to dispose according to the testament.[51]

Similarly, in December 1321:

> Matilda widow of John de Westirfeld, tailor of Ipswich and executrix of his testament, came and showed his testament which was proved by the oath by John Brodheved and Robert de Colisdone, according to the custom of the town, in which it appears that John bequeathed to Matilda all his messuage, with houses and buildings, curtilages and all its appurtenances, in the parish of St Nicholas, Ipswich, for the term of her life, and to remain after her death to John's heirs. The which testament proved for the said free tenement, seisin is granted to Matilda according to the tenor of the testament, saving the right of any. And she gives by the ancient custom 2s.[52]

An executrix could sometimes be tempted not to carry out all the wishes of her late husband, most of the time in order to keep more for herself. This is what happened with 'Alice the widow of Peter of Angerhale and executrix of his testament [who] unlawfully withheld from Agnes Helpe 2s., which Peter had received as a loan from Agnes; [it was] adjudged that Agnes shall recoup the said 2s. and 3d. damages. Alice amerced 3d.'.[53] Yet entries of that sort are surprisingly rare.

Once the funeral expenses and the various taxes had been paid, the executors' next duty was the settlement of the deceased's debts, if any. Yet, as already mentioned, debts were extremely common. Many

---

51 G.H. Martin, ed., *The Ipswich Recognizance Rolls 1294–1327*, p.71.
52 Ibid., p.98.
53 R. Lock, ed., *The Court Rolls of Walsham le Willows. 1303–1350*, p.87.

of them consisted in tithes unpaid or forgotten. Now to die in debt was considered a great sin and punishable by a long stay in Purgatory. This is why testators always stressed that their debts should be paid in the first place: Thomas Grene of Creeting St Peter urged his executors to give ten shillings to his parish priest 'as restitution of tithes and offerings underpaid and forgotten' (will no.20).[54] Though Robert Sygoo of Mildenhall named both his wife Matilda and a certain Robert Sygo as his executors he clearly considered his inheritance was his wife's concern: 'To Matilda my wife all my utensils and bedding belonging to my house, and all my corn, she to pay my debts and see to my funeral' (will no.65). Robert Sygoo was a fairly poor man since his gift for tithes amounted only 12d. Roger Wygenale of Boxford gave 3s. 4d. 'to the high altar for tithes not well paid' (will no.118). Peter Foster held land in the two parishes of Sudbury for he made gifts 'for tithes forgotten' both to St Gregory's and St Peter's (will no.157). Thomas Pye of Assington felt rather worried and left 20d. 'to the high altar for tithes and other offerings negligently forgotten by [him] in [his] lifetime' (will no.215). Geoffrey Herry of Fornham All Saints was particularly cautious and gave 6s. 8d. 'to the high altar to amend and compensate to God for any payment not made' (will no.271). John Young of Santon Downham, visibly a shepherd, paid in kind offering 'to the high altar, in satisfaction of tithes and offerings owed and forgotten, three ewes' (will no.419).

Executors were also under obligation to pay all the testator's creditors.[55] This could mean a serious drop in living standards for the widow: the executors may have to draw on the meagre savings of the couple, seize goods and chattels or even deprive the family of some of their real estate. In 1280, Albrida Godware of Godmanchester had to pay off the debts of her husband. The debt was £10 and the widow had to part with one and a half acres of arable land and some grass-land that were her own:

---

54 P. Northeast, ed., *Wills of the Archdeaconry of Sudbury*.
55 See P.R. Schofield & N.J. Mayhew, *Credit and Debt in Medieval England c. 1180–c. 1350*, Oxford: Oxbow Books, 2002.

> Albrida Godware, widow of Alexander the reeve, delivered into the hands of the bailiffs to the use of Godfrey Quenyne three one half acres of land and one swath of meadow, defending as one acre, from the land that the above Alexander gave to the said Albrida while he was alive. And the court adjudged it proper for her to sell that land to acquit herself and her son and heir of ten pounds of silver before the itinerant justices at Huntingdon. Her son and heir agreed to this sale to quit his father's debt.[56]

In the archdeaconry of Sudbury, Matilda Wryght of Cotton had to pay back a certain Thomas Heythe which, in her case too, meant selling land and tenements:

> [1445] To the same Matilda all my lands and tenements in Cotton, she paying for the lands and tenements all that is owed to Thomas Heythe by way of arrears, as appears in a deed indented made between the said Simon Wryth and Thomas Hethe; but she to have of those lands and tenements, as dower and my legacy, £10 in money, when they are sold, to keep our sons with. (Will no.409)

In the same year, Robert Lamberd seems to have been heavily in debt, leaving only a basin together with a water-jug to his son while asking all the following to be sold in order to pay out what he owed: two oxen, two horses, four ewes with lambs, two cows and two other beasts of one year old, two pigs, all his utensils as well as two acres of arable land. He then added 'from the sale of these all my debts to be fully paid, and if anything remain, then to the high altar of the parish church of Whepstead 20d.; my daughters to have something from my goods if they will stretch to it, according to the advice of my execs' (will no.417). The widow of John Boxsted of Sudbury found herself deprived of her husband's – hopefully not sole – means of work (and consequently source of income) for though he devised her a stall in Sudbury he also decided that four stalls in the town of Clare and two in Lavenham were to be sold to pay his debts (will no.62). Several husbands laid down strict conditions for their wives to come into their properties: the settlement of their debts came first. In 1452, for instance, Thomas Hervy bequeathed his wife Alice all his possessions in the towns of Wortham and Bressingham 'on condition that she pay

---

56   J.A. Raftis, *A Small Town in Late Medieval England, Godmanchester 1278–1400*, p.183.

Nicholas Hervy my father £30 in money. (...) If Alice do not wish to have the lands on the above condition, they to be sold immediately after my death' (will no.595). John Hokyr of Edwardstone left his wife Lettice all his goods 'on condition she pay all his debts' (will no.931) and Robert Tye of Lavenham having obviously little faith in his wife Joan bequeathed her jewels, his household goods and a tenement 'on condition that she well and truly pay all my debts' (will no.1243). Robert Reydon died in 1334 in Walsham le Willows. His executrix was his widow who died four years later after two long disputes with Michael Nichole and William Hawys about debts of Robert: in November 1336 she eventually agreed to pay Michael at the feast of the Nativity of St John the Baptist [June 24th]. Yet 'on this day she did not pay, but withheld and still withholds, to Michael's loss of ½ mark, and on this he produces suit. Matilda says that she owes him no money, and offers to wage law'. In February 1337, 'a day [was] given to William Hawys and Matilda of Reydon, executrix of Robert of Reydon, in a plea of debt'. When Matilda died, between February and May 1337, both parties stuck to their lines, the dispute remained unsettled.

The last task remaining now to the executors was to distribute the assets to the beneficiaries and to ensure that the heir inherited land according to conditions specified in the will. What was left to the bereaved wife and her under-age children was often a dramatically reduced estate. The goods of William Lene, the villein who died in a blaze in Walsham le Willows in 1329, were estimated at the global sum of £26 9s. 11d. while the accompanying list of funeral expenses reached the total of £13 12s. 4d. therefore half of the value of all his possessions! No wonder that in literary texts, widows were often depicted as the embodiment of poverty. It was recommended in *A Myrour to Lewde Men and Wymmen* to give alms to the poor, to the fatherless 'an to wyfmen wodewen, and to oþre nieduolle'.[57] In Chaucer's *Canterbury Tales*, widows living in the countryside always seem particularly needy. The adjective *poor* is used as an epithet, destitution being characteristic of these widows. The summoner's prey in the Friar's Tale is 'an old wydwe, a ribibe' (1377) who explains she

---

57   V. Nelson, ed., *A Myrour to Lewde Men & Wymmen*, p.193.

cannot pay twelve pence because she is 'povre and oold' (1608). Chauntecleer's owner is 'a povre wydwe, somdel stape in age' (2821). The Friar is presented in the *General Prologue* as a particularly good beggar who can even get a coin from a poverty-stricken widow: 'For thogh a wydwe hadde noght a sho, / So plesaunt was his "*In principio*,"/ Yet wolde he have a ferthyng, er he wente' (I, 253–255). Widowhood was often linked to poverty and old age but in many cases it was not: it goes without saying that there existed widows of all social backgrounds, that some of them were particularly well-off while others 'hadden noght a sho'. It is, therefore, difficult and even meaningless to generalize when considering the everyday lives of these women as we shall now turn to. Widows had rights over their late husbands'goods and properties and most husbands when establishing their wills were concerned with the well-being of their wives. Yet disparities, inequalities were numerous and huge between women of different social groups. This is why when coming to their daily life we shall have to study them separately. Let us first consider another point many of them had in common: the – sometimes difficult – provision of a portion of their deceased husband's estate enabling the happy few to live well, the vast majority to make both ends meet, and for the least fortunate simply to avoid beggary.

Widows and Property

Widows' Material Resources: Dower and the Law

Common Law

King Henry II introduced many important legal reforms in Britain. During his reign, royal legislation emerged: the *curia regis* was re-established, itinerant judges were sent throughout the kingdom, the most widespread customs and judicial practices were collected and gathered to make a more coherent whole by lawyers such as Ranulf de Glanville (1130–1190), chief justiciar of England. The foundations for the growth of English Common Law and of royal administration were thus laid. Ranulph de Glanville is best known for the *Tractatus de legibus et consuetudinibus regni Angliae* (*Treatise on the Laws and Customs of the realm of England*) written around 1188. It was soon accepted as an authority, giving a precise description of the procedure of the king's courts and providing a collection of royal writs – a new legal form of action at that time. Several chapters of the treatise are concerned with the part of a deceased man's real estate that was alloted by law to his widow for her lifetime, in other words, with her dower.[58] Glanville gave the following definition and details:

> VI, 1. In common English law usage dower means that which a free man gives to his wife at the church door at the time of his marriage. For every man is bound both by ecclesiastical and by secular law to endow his wife at the time of his marriage. When a man endows his wife either he nominates certain property as dower or he does not. If he does not nominate dower, then one third of the whole of his free tenement is deemed to be her dower, and the reasonable dower of any woman is one third of the whole of the free tenement of which her husband was seised in demesne at the time of the marriage. If, however, the husband nominates dower and it amounts to more than one third, it cannot stand at such a level, but will be measured up to one third; for a man can give less but not more than one third of his tenement in dower.[59]

It must be first noted that there could be no dowers for villeins: common law only applied to free landholders and from the reign of Henry II onwards only royal courts could try cases involving the ownership of freehold property. The manorial court rolls of Brithwaltham contain an entry for the year 1293 that first sets the scene as follows before expounding the case proper:

> One Alan Poleyn held a tenement in Conholt upon servile terms and had a wife Cristina by name. The said Alan died when Richard was the farmer. Thereupon came the friends of the said Cristina and procured for her a part of the land by

---

58 A nominated dower could also consist of money, rents, services or livestock.
59 G.D.G. Hall, ed. + trans., *The Treatise on the Laws and Customs of the Realm of England Commonly called Glanvill*, London: Nelson, 1965 [revised edition + guide to further reading by M.T. Clanchy, Oxford: Clarendon Press, 1993].

way of dower making a false suggestion and as though the land were of free condition, and this was to the great prejudice of the lord Abbot.[60]

The second emphasized point is that a husband was obliged to secure property to his wife in case she predeceased him: the dower would maintain the widow and provide for the children who did not inherit. Death and widowhood were therefore contemplated from the start, from the negotiations before marriage that ended with the oral, yet binding, contract recited at the church door.[61] In 1277 Richard de Miseberi, butcher, and Johanna his wife granted to Roger 'the lame horsemonger' and his wife Alice their house in the parish of St Sepulchre in London to hold for a term of ten years. This was the house with which Johanna had been 'legally dowered at the church door'.[62] When Margaret, the widow of Hugh de Badewe, died in 1419 an inquiry was made by the escheator to establish what lands she held and who should succeed to them – as was the usage for all tenants in chief. The Inquisition Post Mortem stated that 'she held a manor called Baddow, formerly of Hugh de Badewe, knight, and a toft and 40 acres called "Mascales" in Great Baddow for life by the grant of Hugh before their marriage'.[63] Husbands were bound to endow their wives with a third of their estates; once a widow the woman held the dower in usufruct: she did not therefore control the property involved, for the estate belonged to the husband's heir to which it would revert after her death. There was slight ambiguity as to what property was to be taken into account for the granting of the dower. *Glanvill* was very clear specifying:

---

60   F.W. Maitland, ed., *Select Pleas in Manorial and Other Seignorial Courts*, vol. 1 (Reigns of Henry III and Edward I), The Abbot of Battle's Court at Brithwaltham, London: Bernard Quaritch, 1889. www.fordham.edu/halsall/seth/court-brightwaltham.html

61   See quotation from the Bury St Edmunds missal in preceding chapter.

62   R.R. Sharpe, ed., *Calendar of Letter-Books of the City of London. 1275–1298*, London: the Corporation, 1899, folio 134, pp.207–230.

63   J.L. Kirby & J.H. Stevenson, eds., *Calendar of Inquisitions Post-Mortem and other Analogous Documents preserved in the Public Record Office XXI: 6–10 Henry V (1418–1422)*, Woodbridge: Boydell Press, 2002, p.64.

> It sometimes happens that a husband who has a little land can increase the dower by adding one third or less of his later acquisitions. However, if nothing was said about acquisitions when the dower was originally assigned, then, even if the husband had little land at the time of the marriage and afterwards acquired much land, no more can be claimed in dower than one third of the land which he had at the time of the marriage. I state the same rule when a man who has no land endows his wife with money or other chattels and afterwards acquires many lands and tenements, for nothing can in future lawfully be claimed as dower from these acquisitions. For it is generally true that however much dower and of whatever kind is assigned to a woman, if she consents to this assignment of dower at the church door, she cannot in future lawfully claim any more as dower. (VI, 2)

It was Magna Carta that sowed confusion. Chapter 7 of the 1215 charter secured to widows their dower rights indicating that '[a widow] shall not give anything for her marriage portion, dower, or inheritance which she and her husband held on the day of his death'.[64] The reissues of Magna Carta introduced changes, the 1225 version stating in a rather convoluted way that 'let there be assigned to [the widow] for her dower a third part of all the land of her husband which was his in his life, unless she was endowed of less at the church door'.[65] The great 13th-century jurist, Henry of Bratton (usually referred to as Bracton) wrote his long treatise *De Legibus et Consuetudinibus Angliæ* (*On the Laws and Customs of England*) around 1259. He unambiguously supported Glanvill's position:

> Dower is that which a free man gives his spouse at the church door because of the burden of matrimony and the future marriage, for the maintenance of the wife and the nurture of the children when they are born, should the husband predecease her.
> The rightful dower of every woman is the third part of all the lands and tenements her husband held in his demesne and so in fee that he could endow her on the day he married her.
> (...)

---

[64] A.E. Dick Howard, *Magna Carta. Text and Commentary*, Charlottesville, London: University Press or Virginia, 1964 [revised edition 1998], p.38.

[65] W.S. McKechnie, ed., *Magna Carta*, Glasgow: Maclehose, 1914 (reprinted New York: Burt Franklin, 1958). The book contains both the Latin and English versions of the Charter.

> When? Before the marriage, at the beginning of the marriage. Where? In the face of the church and at the church door. A constitution of dower made on the death bed or in a private chamber is invalid and it therefore must be made publicly and with a ceremony at the church door. Where there is no marriage at all there is no dower, and thus it appears conversely that wherever there is a marriage there is dower, which is true if the marriage is contracted in the face of the church.[66]

As Janet Senderowitz Loengard has proved

> Whatever the intent of the drafters of Magna Carta, on one hand, whatever the theoreticians – or heirs or purchasers or judges or sometimes even widows – might have preferred, on the other, there was no decisive change in dower either in 1217 or 1225. As Maitland concluded (...), the Charter did not in the short run change the rule that, without a specific provision to the contrary, it was the lands held by a husband on the day of his marriage that were subject to dower.[67]

By the end of the thirtenth century, however, things had changed and a widow's dower, unless it was nominated dower, gradually became one third of any estate owned by the husband during his life. This is why widows often held thirds of manors as in the case of Margaret Beauchamp (1374–1420), the widow of Giles Daubeney (1370–1403):

> [she] held in dower of the inheritance of Giles Daubeney, knight, son and heir of Giles Daubeney, knight, named in the writ, 1/3 meadow in Burton Joyce, part of the manor of South Ingleby in Lincolnshire (...) 1/3 pasture next 'Southdyke', part of the manor (...) 1/3 underwood called 'Southwode', part of the same manor. (...) She held in dower 1/3 manor of South Ingleby in Broxholme and Saxilby, with the advowson of the church of Broxholme. (...) 1/3

---

66   G.E. Woodbine, ed., S.E. Thorne, trans., *De Legibus et Consuetudinibus Angliæ. Bracton on the Laws and Customs of England*, Cambridge, Mass.: Belknap Press of Harvard University Press, 1968, vol. 2, pp.265–266. http://hlsl.law.harvard.edu/bracton/

67   See J. Senderowitz Loengard, '*Rationabilis Dos*: Magna Carta and the Widow's 'Fair Share' in the Earlier Thirteenth Century', S.S. Walker, ed., *Wife and Widow in Medieval England,* pp.59–80.

manors of South Petherton and Barrington with the hamlets of Southhorp and Chillington. (…) 1/3 manor of Kempston.[68]

As usual in Inquisitions Post Mortem, the escheator gave all the necessary details as to what these thirds consisted of, starting with the manor house, going on with the various lands then with the rents to be obtained from free or customary tenants, the value of each item being carefully listed. The third of the manor of Kempston, for instance, meant:

> An upper chamber above the doorway there with 2 chambers annexed, a stable, 1/2 bakehouse and chapel, a building called 'le heybern' with the sheepfold annexed, 1/3 building called 'le gest stabill', annual value of all nil, 1/3 dovecot with 1/3 garden, annual value 2s., 83 a. arable worth 3d. an acre yearly, 25 a. pasture worth 4d. an acre yearly, 7 a. meadow worth 18d. an acre yearly; 5s. 1d. rent with 1 lb. Pepper paid yearly at Michaelmas by certain free tenants, 6 virgates, annual value 10s. each, paid by certain customars at Christmas, Easter, the Nativity of St John the Baptist and Michaelmas in equal portions, 8 cottages of certain customars there, annual value 7s. 9¼d., 40s. and called 'le yelt' paid at the above terms, 1/3 several water there, annual value 3s. 4d. at the above terms, 8 a. 2 roods mature wood, annual value nil, 5 a. and 1 rood underwood, annual value nil except every seventh year when the wood is felled, and then 5s. an acre.[69]

In certain cases, the thirds allotted to the widow probably made things rather awkward for everyone. The entries dealing with Joan, the widow of Sir Robert Corbet, make you want to smile for she was only granted a third of the kitchen in all three manor houses she received in dower at the death of her husband![70] It was probably easy to miscalculate what exactly came to Katherine Pabenham, the widow of Thomas Aylesbury, considering that she was to receive from the manor of Milton Keynes '3 bays of the large grange at the east end, (…) 1/3 of the profits of gardens with free ingress and egress, (…) 1/3 of the profits of 2 dovecots within the manor, 1/3 of the profits of a common

---

68   J.L. Kirby & J. Stevenson, eds., *Calendar of Inquisitions Post-Mortem and other Analogous Documents preserved in the Public Record Office XXI*, pp. 163–165.
69   Ibid., p.164.
70   Ibid., pp.68–69.

bakehouse, 1/3 of the profits of view of frankpledge there and of lesser courts, 1/3 of the profits of a water-mill called 'Foxesmilne', 1/3 of the warren and all the conies, 1/3 of a fishery in the river there, 1/3 of the fishery of all ponds in the township or in the fields outside the manor...'[71] One can easily imagine the complicated calculations and the inevitable quarrels in the family!

As a matter of fact, the widow held her dower from her husband's heir which could lead to conflicts because they had diametrically opposed interests. Having a doweress in the family (and sometimes several) could mean that lands remained outside the family control for decades: 'dower, after all, always meant less for the warrantor, whatever his relationship to the widow. Against that loss there were generally no compensating benefits'.[72] Janet Senderowitz Loengard mentions the example of Maud de Bidun who having been married and having become a widow at the age of ten held her dower for seventy years![73] When John de Kirkeby died in 1290, the manor of Great Munden (or Munden Furnivall) in Hertfordshire passed to his brother William till his death in 1302. A third of the manor was then in the hands of Mathiana, the second wife of John de Cobham. The manor eventually came to a certain Margaret, the wife of Walter de Osevill, but diminished by two dowers: Mathiania's third together with the third held by Christine de Kirkeby, William's widow.[74]

The law tried to see to the defence of the rights of both parties. *Glanvill* lists excluded property: the chief messuage could not be given as dower, in case of two or more manors the chief manor was to 'go intact together with the chief messuage to the heir' (VI, 17). If the heir considered the widow had more as dower than really came to her, the sheriff might be asked by the following writ to have it measured:

---

71 Ibid., p.44.
72 J. Senderowitz Loengard, 'Of the gift of her husband: English dower and its consequences in the year 1200', J. Kirshner & S.F. Wemple, eds., *Women of the Medieval World: Essays in Honor of John H. Mundy*, Oxford, New York: Basil Blackwell, 1985, p.237.
73 Ibid., p.238.
74 W. Page, ed., *The Victoria History of the County of Hertford*, vol. 3 (1912), pp.124–129. http://www.british-history.ac.uk/report.asp?compid=43590

The king to the sheriff, greeting. B. has complained to me that M. his mother has more of his inheritance as dower than she ought to have and belongs to her as reasonable dower. Therefore I command you justly and without delay to have it measured, and justly and without delay to cause the said B. to have what he ought to have as his right and inheritance, and justly and without delay to cause the said M. to have what she ought to have and belongs to her as her reasonable dower, that he need no longer complain for default of justice in this matter.[75]

The widow was entitled to use and enjoy her dower but was prohibited from selling it or allowing it to degenerate and therefore see its value decrease. Indeed, as Bracton put it:

> After dower has been constituted and assigned, nothing of the *proprietas* belongs to the woman, nothing but seisin and the free tenement for her life, so that she can do nothing by which anyone may have a perpetuity, only for as long as she can warrant it, because the right of property remains with the heir, or with another to whom the right has come, as in the name of escheat[76] or by reason of alienation and sale, who is the warrantor of her dower. Hence she can claim nothing except to use and enjoy the dotal property, without waste, destruction or exile.[77] She may take reasonable estovers[78] in the woods for building, burning and fencing within her dower, not outside it, and if she commits waste, destruction, or exile in excess of rightful estovers, the heir or other owner may stop her without acting contrary to law.[79]

The 1278 Statute of Gloucester legislated against these dishonest widows, those committing waste were to lose what they had wasted and 'compensate with three times the amount the waste [was] assessed at' (chapter 5) while those selling or giving their dowers in fee dowers were to be deprived of the estates (chapter 7).[80]

---

75 *Glanvill*, VI, 18.
76 An 'incident' of feudal law, whereby a fief reverted to the lord when the tenant died without having a successor qualified to inherit under the original grant. (*OED*)
77 Devastation of property. (*OED*)
78 Gathering of wood.
79 S.E. Thorne, trans., *Bracton on the Laws and Customs of England*, vol. 3, p. 405.
80 H. Rothwell, ed., *English Historical Documents 1189–1327*, London: Eyre & Spottiswoode, 1975, p.417.

Widows complaining that they were barred from entering into their dowers were a common case in the Middle Ages. The author of the anonymous homiletic Middle English poem *Purity* (also called *Cleanness*) intends to show everyone the path to moral perfection. He lists human sins basing himself on the Epistle to the Galatians (5:19–21) and mentions next to theft, envy, intemperance, or betrayal 'dsyheriete & depryue dowrie of wydoez' (185).[81] One should not forget, however, all those who easily and peacefully received their part of property; yet, though outnumbering by far their less fortunate fellow sisters, they have left no trace in history. Consequently, only the voices of widow plaintiffs still resound today. The heir (or his guardian) who refused to grant a widow what she considered her rightful dower could put forward several arguments: that the woman's marriage was not valid (on the basis of consanguinity for instance or, if several women were fighting over the one and same property), that the wife had been 'separated from [her husband] because of some shameful act' (*Glanvill* VI, 17) as in the case of William and Margaret Paynel who sued in 1302 for the latter's dower, by an earlier marriage to John de Camoys. Margaret having left her husband for William, their case was dismissed. Indeed, the 34th chapter of the Statute of Westminster II (1285) had it plain that 'if a wife willingly leaves her husband and goes away and stays with her adulterer she shall be barred forever of action to claim her dower which she ought to have of her husband's tenements'.[82] The two most frequent objections were that the widow had renounced her right to the dower or that the late husband was not enfeoffed with the property. Widows who made donations to religious houses or married women whose husbands transferred or surrendered a tenement were usually asked to make a formal renunciation of their titles in the tenements as a bar to any subsequent action of dower. Among the countless possible examples let us cite a few taken from the cartularies of Bury St Edmunds' hospitals. Sometime between 1258 and 1272, Lecia, widow of William Le Juvene 'in her free widowhood and full power conceded, relaxed

---

81   M. Andrew, R. Waldron, C. Peterson, eds., *The Complete Works of the Pearl Poet*, Berkeley, Oxford: University of California Press, 1993.
82   Ibid., p.448. The story of William and Margaret Paynel is related pp.579–580.

and utterly quitclaimed in perpetuity to the prior and brethren of the hospital of St Peter in the suburb of St Edmunds and to their successors all right and claim which she had or might have had by right of her dower or in any other way in an acre of arable land in the field of St Edmunds, abutting at one headland on the king's highway before the gate of the said hospital.'[83] Quitclaim was made in 1331 by Margaret Amerous, widow of Philip of Whelnetham, 'in her free widowhood for herself and her heirs, to the abbot and convent of St Edmunds of all right which she had or might have had in the name of dower in the tenements, lands, meadows, pastures and woods which her husband Philip once held in the vill of Whepstead. (...) For this quitclaim the abbot and convent gave her a certain sum of money' (p.51). In 1333 Abbot Richard took a lot of precautions with the following couple of donors:

> Quitclaim by Henry of Brightwell and Matilda his wife, widow of Robert of Linholt, to Abbot Richard and the convent of St Edmunds and their successors of all manner of actions, pleas and claims which they have against the abbot and convent by reason of Matilda's dower, from the free tenement of Robert her late husband, of 5 acres of land in Whepstead, or by reason of any other action or real or personal claims, from the beginning of the world to the day of the writing of these presents, so that neither Henry nor Matilda nor anyone in their name may henceforth make any claim against the abbot and convent in any court, ecclesiastical or secular. For greater security Henry and Matilda took a corporal oath to observe herein contained. (p.51)

One could also mention Albreda, widow of Richard the carpenter (p.38), Margery, widow of Robert of Calfhaye (p.38), Margery, widow of Henry le Sauser (p.41), Matilda, widow of William of the Guesthall (p.42), Letitia, widow of Thomas son of Robert (p.61), Muriel, widow of John son of Robert de Daton (p.80), Margaret, widow of Alexander the spicer (p.103), Mabel, widow of Baldwin of Shimpling (p.106), etc. who all granted lands, messuages or rents to the hospitals quitclaiming at the same time all their rights in these estates or incomes. Concerning the other common pretext put forward by heirs, examples are as countless. Peter J.P. Goldberg quotes that of

---

[83] C. Harper-Bill, ed., *Charters of the medieval Hospitals of Bury St Edmunds*, Series Suffolk Charters, Woodbridge: Boydell Press, 1994, p.103.

Claremunda, the widow of Henry Whirll who 'claim[ed] against Thomas Feteplace a third of a messuage with appurtenances in North Osney by Oxford as dower of the endowment of the aforesaid Henry, formerly her husband. And Thomas comes and says that the aforesaid Claremunda ought not thus to have her dower because he says that the aforesaid Henry, formerly the husband of that Claremunda, was never in possession of the aforesaid tenement as of fee so that he was thereby able to endow her'.[84] Paula Dobrowolski mentions an example from the Assize Roll of 1274–1275 in Staffordshire which featured Agnes, the widow of Hugh Bonel who sued her husband's heir, John Bonel (her own son?), who refused to let her have a third of a messuage and eight acres of land – arguing that Hugh was not seised of the land as of fee. Agnes won her case.[85] Another interesting instance concerns Codusa Ground who together with her second husband accused Richard Le Tevene of 'withholding from them a one-third share in a tenement with appurtenances in Chester (...) the which Richard Ground endowed Codusa with at the church door when he married her. (...) Richard comes and says that Richard Ground had no rights in the tenement in question other than for a term of years'.[86] Among the well-known Norfolk Paston family, Agnes was the wife of William – the first of a long and prosperous line. William died in 1444 and Agnes held the advowson of Oxnead as part of her dower.[87] In 1478

---

[84] P.J.P. Goldberg, ed., *Woman is a Worthy Wight: Women in England. c. 1275–1525*, p.146; Translated from J.E. Thorold Rogers, ed., *Oxford City Documents*, Oxford Historical Society, XVIII, 1891.

[85] P. Dobrowolski, 'Women and their Dower in the Long Thirteenth Century 1265–1329', M. Prestwich, R.H. Britnell & R. Frame, eds., *Thirteenth-Century England VI. Proceedings of the Durham Conference*, Woodbridge: The Boydell Press, 1995, p.157.

[86] A.W. Hopkins, ed., *Selected Rolls of the Chester City Courts, Late Thirteenth and Early Fourteenth Centuries*, Manchester: Chetham Society, 3rd series, vol. 2, 1950. Translated by S. Alsford, http://www.trytel.com/~tristan/towns/florilegium/government/gvjust26.html

[87] In a draft will (1466) Agnes uses the word 'jointure' recalling what her husband had left her: 'And in owre presens all he began to reede hijs wyll and spak fy[r]st of me and assynyd to me the maneris of Paston, Latymer, and Schypden and Ropers in Crowmer fore term of my lyffe, and the manerys of Merlyngforthe, Stonsted, and Horwelbury, wyche wasse myn own enheritans, and

her rights were threatened by the John de la Pole, 2nd Duke of Suffolk. Her grandson, Sir John Paston intervened on her behalf writing here to his brother also called John:

> To John Paston, esquyere, be thys lettre delyueryd, ore to my mestresse hys wyffe at Norwych to delyuer to hym.
> (...) and myn oncle William comythe wyth hym. And he tellyth me þat ther is like to be troble in the maner off Oxenhed, wherffore i praye yow take hede lesse þat the Duke off Suffolk councell pley therwyth now at the vacacion off the beneffyse as they ded wyth the beneffice off Drayton, whyche by the helpe off Master John Salett and Donne hys man ther was a qweste made by the seyde Donne þat fownde þat the Duke off Suffolk was verrye patrone, whyche was false yitt they ded it fore an euydence. But nowe iff any suche pratte scholde be laboryd it is, i hope, in bettre case, for suche a thynge most needys be fownde byffore Master John Smyth, whyche is owre olde freende; wherffor i praye yow labore hym þat iff neede bee he maye doo vsse a freendys torne ther-in. Item, bothe ye ande i most nedys take thys matere as owre owne, and it weere for noon other cawse butt for owre goode grawntdames sake. Neuerthe lesse ye woote well thatt ther is an other entresse longyng to vsse afftre here dysceasse. Iffe ther be any suche thynge begune ther by suche a fryere or prest, as it is seyde, i mervayle þat ye sente me no worde ther-off; butt ye haue nowe wyffe and chylder, and so moche to kare fore thatt ye forgete me. (Letter 312)

A year later (1479) Agnes's son William wrote a letter to her servant Richard Lee for the quarrel was still going on. The Bishop of Norwich had been presented with two priests for the one church of Oxned so that, in his eyes, an inquiry and legal action were necessary:

> My moder deliuered Sir William Holle his presentacion the xiij day of August anno xviijo, which was nere a monethe or the day of the vj monethes went out and past; wherfore the Bisshoppe ought to present my moders clarke. Neuerthelesse the Bisshoppys officeres aunsware this sayng þat if ij sondry persones deliuer ij sondrye presentacions for to diuerse clarkes to the Bisshoppes

Oxned, wyche wasse my jontore.' One of the letters (dated 1478) describes in charming terms the then vacant parsonage of Oxned mentioning the little but pleasant church, the house, its hall, chambers, barn, and dovecot, its large gardens and orchard. N. Davis, ed., *Paston Letters and Papers of the Fifteenth Century: Parts I and II*, Oxford University Press, Early English Text Society, 2005 [First edition 1971 (Part I), 1976 (Part II)]. http://etext.lib.virginia.edu/etcbin/browse-mixed-new?id=PasLett&images=images/modeng&data=/lv1/Archive/mideng-parsed& tag=public officeres for one benefice, þat than the seid partyes shuld sue to the Bisshop at ther cost to haue out an jnquerré to inquere *de vero patrono,* sayng forther-more þat if they sue nat out this jnquerré with affect and þat the lapse fall, þan it is lefull for the Bisshop to present. And it is told me þat the lawe is this, that the Bisshop, be his office without any sute of the parties, shall call an jnquerré afore hym to inquere *de vero patrono,* and he shall assign them a day to bryng in a verdett. And he shall warne bothe partyes to be ther-at, and he shall amytte his clarke þat is founde patron. 3et the Bisshopp vseth nat to do this but there as bothe partyes that present are myghty to sue þe Bisshoppe if he did them any wrong, and where as ther is a doubtable mater; but in this case the prest þat... my moder is but a simple felowe and he is *appostata,* fore he was somtyme a White Frere, and of simple repetacion and of litill substans, as my moder can tell; wherfore bisshoppys vse nat in suche litill casys to take so streyte an jnquerré, and specyally where as one hath contynued patron with-out interupcion so long as my moder hath don, for she hath contynued more than 1 wyntere. (Letter 103)

As for the widow, her rights received a high level of protection. Magna Carta stated that her dower was to be assigned to her within forty days after her husband's death (chapter 7). Bracton took up the same figure: 'if the whole of her dower is vacant, then, within forty days, let her lawful dower be assigned her.'[88] Yet the dower might not be vacant. Husbands were allowed to rent out or sell their wives' dowers for, according to *Glanvill* (VI, 3), 'a woman is completely in the power of her husband, it is not surprising that her dower and all her other property are clearly deemed to be at his disposal. Therefore any married man may give or sell or alienate in whatever way he pleases his wife's dower during her life, and his wife is bound to consent to this as to all other acts of his which do not offend against God'. The land might easily be held by a tenant. A widow's claim, however, took precedence over a man's rights as purchaser or heir and alienated land was therefore recoverable. If the widow failed to receive part of her dower, she could take legal proceedings against her husband's heir (who was her warrantor) through 'the writ of right for land belonging to dower' in which the king asked the doweress' lord to have the case considered in his manorial court:

---

[88] S.E. Thorne, trans., *Bracton on the Laws and Customs of England,* vol. 2, p.276.

The king to W., greeting. I command you to hold full right without delay to M. the widow of Robert, in respect of one hide of land in such-and-such a vill, which she claims as belonging to the reasonable dower which she holds of you in that vill by the free service of ten shillings a year for all service, and which N. is withholding from her. If you do not do it, the sheriff will, that she need no longer complain for default of right in this matter. Witness etc. (*Glanvill*, VI, 5)

If the widow's warrantor admitted the woman was right he then had to give her another land (the equivalent worth of the property) in exchange or recover the land from the tenant and so the plea became one between the heir and the tenant (*Glanvill*, VI, 11). If the heir contested the widow's claim then legal battle between the two was instigated. The plea in the writ of right of dower could go to the county court or even to the King's court in Westminster. *Glanvill* specifies that 'the case may be settled by battle' (VI, 17) but resorting to a duel was extremely rare. The usual way to resolve the quarrel was rather through the hearing of witnesses or, less frequently, the bringing forward of charters.

In the case that the widow had received none of her dower, the writ *unde nihil habet* was available to her for its recovery:

> When no part of a woman's dower is vacant, so that she has none of it, then the plea is dealt with from the beginning in the lord king's court, and he who is holding the dower shall be summoned by the following writ:
> The king to the sheriff, greeting. Command N. justly and without delay to cause M. who was the wife of R. to have her reasonable dower in such-and-such a vill, which she claims to have as the gift of the said R. her husband and of which she has none, as she says, and which she alleges he is unjustly withholding from her. If he will not do this, summon him by good summoners to be before me or my justices on a certain day, to show why he has not done it. And have there the summoners and this writ. Witness etc. (*Glanvill*, VI, 14–15)

The Statute of Westminster I (1275) extended the usage of this writ of dower by stating that it was not 'henceforth to be abated by the exception of the tenant that she [had] received her dower from another man before her writ [had been] purchased, unless he [could] show that she had received part of the dower from himself and in the same vill before her writ [had been] purchased'.[89] Twenty years later the Statute

---

89 H. Rothwell, ed., *English Historical Documents 1189–1327*, p.409.

of Westminster II (chapter 4) protected widows against collusive suits designed to cheat them of their dowers.

In 1176 King Henry II divided England into six circuits and appointed justices to each district for the purpose of trying causes. The usual interval between visitations of the justices in circuit eyres was about seven years. The practice continued with great irregularity until the judges of assize were appointed under Edward I. The London eyre of 1276 took place twenty-five years after the preceding one in 1251 and was essentially a crown plea session. Only a few civil pleas *extra coronam* were heard by the justices, for the citizens considered they were not obliged to answer concerning any tenement in the city unless the tenant had vouched a foreigner to warranty. This is why Clarice, the widow of John de Lynde, claiming against 'the master of the house of St Thomas of Acon her reasonable dower due to her from the free tenement which belonged to her husband in London, from which she has nothing' was asked to 'go to the husting and sue there'.[90] If one excludes this particular custom, the pleas of dower heard by the justices follow what has been expounded above and emphasize the pivotal role played by sheriffs:

> Joan widow of John son of Saer sued Henry le Waleys in the husting for the third part of a messuage with appurtenances in London as her dower. Henry appeared in the husting and vouched to warranty Thomas de Warpenbur' who is not of the liberty of the City, but lives outside in Warwickshire. So the plea was respited according to the custom of the City. Henry comes now and vouches Thomas to warranty. They are to have him here on Monday in the third week of Lent [9 Mar. 1276] with the aid of the court. Let him be summoned in Warwickshire.
> (...)
> Henry le Waleys presented himself on the fourth day against Thomas de Wapenbir' on a plea that he warrant him a third part of one messuage with appurtenances in London which Joan widow of John son of Saer claims as dower against him, whereof Henry vouched Thomas to warranty against her. He does not come. The sheriff of Warwickshire was ordered to summon him but did nothing and did not send a writ. So he, William Hamelyn, is in mercy. So as previously the sheriff is ordered to summon him to appear in fifteen days from

90 M. Weinbaum, ed., *The London Eyre of 1276*, London Record Society, 1976. Civil Pleas extra coronam, entry no.484. http://www.british-history.ac.uk/report.asp?compid=36002.

Easter at Westminster in the Bench. The same day has been given to Joan to appear in the Bench. (Entries no.482 & 515)

The suit was put off but it is interesting to note that it was to resume at the Court of King's Bench[91] in Westminster and not at the Husting. During the same eyre session the judges heard Alice, the widow of Gilbert de Preston, who 'sued the prior of Holy Trinity in the husting for the third part of one messuage and one curtilage with appurtenances in London as her dower' (entry no.477) as well as Gilbert de Oxford and his wife Alice who 'sued Stephen le Saltere and his wife Felice in the husting for one messuage with appurtenances in London as Alice's dower' (entry no.478).

Christine de Pizan has related in great details how legal actions could prove real ordeals for a widowed woman who firstly *'ne s'i cognoist et est simple en telz choses'* [does not know all the ins and outs and is naive in such matters], who secondly will soon realize that *'gens sont communement mal diligens des besoingnes aux femmes'* [people are commonly careless about women's affairs], and besides *'n'y puet a toutes heures aler comme feroit un home'* [cannot go to court at all hours as a man would].[92] Christine herself had to endure *'quantes parolles enuieuses, quans regars nyces, que de rigolades de aucuns remplis de vins et graisse d'aise souvent y ouoie, lesquelz choses de paour de empirer mon fait, comme celle qui besoing avoit, je dissimuloie sas riens respondre'* [many annoying remarks. How many stupid looks, how many jokes from some fat drunkard did I suffer; and because I was afraid of putting my case at risk and was so dependent on its outcome, I hid my thoughts][93] Christine went on, explaining that should a widow be obliged to go to law, *'que elle prengne cuer d'omme, c'est assavoir constant, fort et sage'* [she had

---

91 Later Court of Common Pleas.
92 Christine de Pizan, *Le Livre des trois vertus*, p.190. Translation by S. Lawson, *Christine de Pizan. The Treasure of the Cities of Ladies or the Book of the Three Virtues*, pp.141–142.
93 Christine de Pizan, *Le Livre de l'advision Christine*, C. Reno & L. Dulac, eds., Paris: Honoré Champion, 2001, p.105. Translated by G. McLeod, New York, London: Garland, 1993, p.190.

to adopt a man's heart (in other words, constant, strong and wise)],[94] have enough money and be ably assisted by experienced and wise lawyers. English women did not require an attorney or a male relative (as in the case of Agnes Paston who was helped both by her son and grandson) to bring a suit in the royal court. However it gradually became the rule. Codusa Ground and her second husband Richard Le Tevene whom we have already mentioned had to appear twenty-two times in court over a period of one year (April 11th 1295–April 2nd 1296)! They were several times represented by their lawyers. Their defendant delayed proceedings by requesting a view of the property, by not appearing in court at the appointed time (essoins were the most common reason for putting off cases) and by questioning the wording of the writ of right. They eventually gave up perhaps convinced they would never get a judgment and in the end were 'amerced for failing to pursue the prosecution'. This example shows that legal action was a particularly slow and strenuous process. Yet it did not seem to dishearten women: according to Derek Hall '20% of the pleas on the royal court roll for Michaelmas term 9–10 Henry III (1225) were for dower'.[95] Such a high figure also emphasizes the fact that widows were very often cheated upon.

Apart from not being allowed to sell the property, a widow was granted full rights over her dower which she could alienate for her lifetime by lease or by pledge. English law even permitted widows to take their dowers into another marriage. Yet, as these widows now became wives again, they no longer exercised any control over the lands they previously held, their new husbands having full responsibility for them. If it should happen that these wives lost their husbands again, they found themselves endowered twice. Because in the nobility girls were married at a very young age, and often to men by many years their seniors, they found themselves widows several times in

---

94 Christine de Pizan, *Le Livre des trois vertus*, p.190. Translation by S. Lawson, *Christine de Pizan. The Treasure of the Cities of Ladies or the Book of the Three Virtues,* pp 142–143.

95 S.S. Walker, *Wife and Widow in Medieval England*, p.6 referring to G.D.G. Hall, review of *Curia Regis Rolls of 9 to 10 Henry III*, London 1957, *English Historical Review*, 74, 1959, pp.107–110.

their lives – consequently accumulating dowers. In this respect Inquisitions Post Mortem are invaluable documents even though they only applied to tenants in chief leaving aside all the others. Let us take two particularly striking examples. Elizabeth de la Plaunche was born about 1347. She was first married in 1356, at the age of nine, to John of Bermingham who died before 1385 without heir by Elizabeth. At the time of her own death in 1423 (thirty-eight years later) 'she held 1/2 manor of Kingston Bagpuize [Berkshire] in dower by endowment of John Birmyngham, chevalier, her former husband'. Meanwhile she had remarried three time: first to Robert Grey, 4th Lord of Rotherfield, who died in January 1387 leaving her Oxfordshire manors as dower: that of Cogges and Hardwick, half of the manors of Somerton, Fringford (together with the advowson of their churches), a quarter of the manor of Standlake (with the advowson of its church) and the advowson of Arley church in Warwickshire. She was then Lord John Clinton's third wife (before October 24th 1388, date of pardon for marrying without a license) who died September 6th 1398. The Inquisition mentions that he gave her as dower 1/3 of the manor of Pirton (Hertfordshire) together with 40s. assize rents belonging to the manor and the manor of Temple Guiting in Gloucestershire. She eventually married Sir John Russell (before February 14th 1399) and, though the latter died in 1405, no land held in dower of his inheritance is mentioned. On the other hand she held many estates and manors in fee tail 'to herself and the heirs of herself and John Russell, knight, her former husband now deceased'.[96] Though married four times, Elizabeth died without issue her only daughter, Joan de Grey, having died a widow and the mother of three young children at the age of twenty-two. Elizabeth FitzAlan (1366?– July 8th 1425) was first married to William de Montacute, Earl of Salisbury and Lord of Man (1356–1382) when she was eleven or twelve. In 1384 she married Thomas Mowbray, first Duke of Norfolk with whom she had five children. The Duke died in Venice in September 1399 leaving her a colossal number of manors all over England in dower.[97] She got married again,

---

96   K. Parkin, ed., *Calendar of Inquisitions Post Mortem 1–5, Henry VI. 1422–1427*, vol. XXII, Woodbridge: Boydell Press, 2003, pp.306–316.
97   Ibid., pp.365–385.

September 1st 1401, to Sir Robert Goushill (Lord Hoveringham) of whom she was the fourth wife and with whom she had three more children. Robert Goushill was killed at the battle of Shrewsbury in July 1403 and Elizabeth remarried for a last time wedding Gerard Usflete in 1414. In both cases their huge wealth (they also possessed many estates as heiresses, through grants and purchases or as co-feoffees) was the reason why they often remained widows for less than a year. They were still coveted when they got older and far beyond the age of begetting children (Elizabeth de la Plaunche married for the last time when she was fifty-two and Elizabeth FitzAlan forty-eight).

Lastly, another advantage of a dower was that it could not be seized to pay the late husband's debts. Bracton had it clear that 'dower, once assigned, ought to be free. The wife should contribute nothing of her dower toward paying the debts of her husband, for if the *peculium* of the husband does not suffice to meet his debts, whatever is still to be paid will be a burden on the heir and the inheritance'.[98] As already mentioned, the dower was directed to the assistance of the widow and her possible children and dower common law was generous with women.

Customary Law

Customary law was often even more generous. One has to distinguish between town custom and customary law applying to manors. The liberties and free customs granted to cities gave their townsmen a highly coveted superior status which they guarded jealously; borough custom only concerned the citizens of the town. Marrying a widow was not a way of becoming a burgess. The customs of the town of Maldon underlined the fact that 'no alien that marries the widow of a freeman is to be received into the franchise on those grounds'. On the other hand foreign wives of freemen continued enjoying the franchise when they became widows: 'the widow may retain the rights of a

---

98   G.E. Woodbine, ed., S.E. Thorne, trans., *De Legibus et Consuetudinibus Angliæ. Bracton on the Laws and Customs of England*, p.281.

freeman while she remains single'.[99] The town of Ipswich had the same rule: '3if a burgeys of the forseid toun of Gippeswiche wedde a foreyn womman and that womman overlyve her husbond, thanne reiosse that womman the fraunchise of the toun the mene tyme that shee kepyth her wydewe'.[100]

Customs varied from one place to another but it was a widespread rule that under such settlements dowers amounted to half of the husbands' real estates. *Capitulum* 52 of the customs of the borough of Ipswich, for instance, stipulated that:

> Also in right of wommen that after the deth of his husbond owyn not for to have fre banch, duelle they in the cheif mees fortye dayes after her husbondes deth with outyn doyng of wast, withynne the which dayes be hem assigned resonabele dowarye be the heyre of her forseid housbond after the usage of the toun, that is to wyttin the halvyndel of all the tenementz enheryng to the forseid toun when of her husbond deyed sesyd in her owen demene as of fee, that is to wittyn, 3if the heir wil of his good wil with ynne the ferst xl dayes assignen dowarye.[101]

In London, wives left alone with children received one third of the husband's estate but if there was no child the share rose to one-half.[102] Alice Bokerel had therefore had children, one may even imagine that Juliana le Akatur was her daughter:

> Tuesday after the Translation of St Thomas, Martyr [7 July], the same year, came Alice, relict of William Bokerel, and quitclaimed to Josep le Akatur and Juliana his wife her third part of a certain house, claimed as dower; for which quitclaim the said Josep and Juliana owe the said Alice 8 marks and a gown of the value of 20s.; of which they have paid her 26s. 8d. and 20s. for the gown.

---

99 S. Alsford's modern version of the 1468 edition of the custumal. http://www.trytel.com/~tristan/towns/maldon6.html
100 T. Twiss, ed., *The Black Book of the Admiralty or Monumenta Juridica, vol. II: 'Le Domesday de Gippewyz. The Domus Day of Gippeswiche'*, p.139.
101 Ibid., p.139.
102 B.A. Hanawalt, 'The Widow's Mite; Provisions for Medieval London Widows', L. Mirrer, ed., *Upon My Husband's Death: Widows in the Literature and Histories of Medieval Europe*, pp.21–45.

Of the residue they will pay her 2 marks at the next Court and 4 marks at Michaelmas following.[103]

Customary law usually followed common law in giving widows their dowers for the duration of their lives, even if they remarried. The custumal of the town of Maldon stated that 'the widow has dower right in her late husband's property, even if she remarries – although the children are not to lose their inheritance as a result of her remarriage'.[104] It also followed common law in permitting husbands to sell their wives' dowers. The 1324 custumal of the small Huntingdonshire town Godmanchester states unambiguously:

> If a man and his wife should acquire lands or tenements, the said man can sell and alienate the said lands and tenements without his wife's leave and against her will, during his lifetime; and if after his death his wife comes to the court of Godmanchester to claim her dower of the lands and tenements which her husband sold, by the custom of the manor of Godmanchester she shall not have her dower of the said lands and tenements.[105]

In order to avoid such dower claims, titles of transfers of property were often witnessed in borough courts. A married woman was asked to renounce publicly her right in the tenement that she and her husband had just made over. She was then examined privately before the magistrates in order to ensure she willingly agreed to the transfer of land in which she had an interest. There was no way of going back on such a formal relinquishment. In 1303, in the full court of Ipswich, Philip de Laghtone and his wife Mabel surrendered a messuage to a certain Henry Cobbe. 'And Mabel examined alone before the bailiffs and coroners, as to whether it was done of her own spontaneous will or under duress and coercion, or from fear of her husband, says that with her good will and no coercion of her husband's, etc., and there-

---

103 R.R. Sharpe, ed., *Calendar of Letter-Books of the City of London: I 1400–1422*, folio 24b (pp.42–65).
104 S. Alsford's modern version of the 1468 edition of the custumal. http://www.trytel.com/~tristan/towns/maldon6.html
105 J.A. Raftis, *A Small Town in Late Medieval England. Godmanchester, 1278–1400*, p.433.

fore it was well granted'.[106] Two years later Thomas Faber of Kerseye and his wife Matilda granted Henry and Agnes le Rotuin a curtilage in the suburbs of Ipswich. 'And Matilda examined alone before the bailiffs confessed herself well content with the said charter and recognizance, relinquishing for herself and her heirs all right and claim in the curtilage and its appurtenances that could henceforth ever be claimed'.[107]

Many borough customs granted the deceased's chief messuage to the widow in the name of 'free bench'. The widow, provided she did not remarry, was therefore allowed to remain in the house in which she had lived with her husband and family. Ipswich custumal gives a definition of this usage:

> [if] the wiff overlyve the husbond, thanne have the womman after the husbondes deth all the cheif mees of her husbond, wher of he deyed dedyd in the same toun in his owen demene as of fee, to holden in the name of fre banche the same tyme that she kepeth her wydwe with oute wast or alienacioun of disheritacioun of the heir of hyr husband.[108]

Moreover free bench did not exclude the widow's dower rights in half of the husband's other property. Barbara Hanawalt quotes the London custumal that gives practical everyday details:

> Wives, on the death of their husbands, by the custom of the city shall have their free bench. That is to say, that after the death of her husband the wife shall have of the tenement in the said city, whereof her husband died seised in fee, and in which tenement the said husband and wife dwelt together at the time of the husband's death, the hall, the principal private chamber, and the cellar wholly, and her use of the kitchen, stable, privy and curtilage in common with the other necessaries appurtenant thereto, for the term of her life. And when she marries again, she shall lose the free bench and her dower therein, saving to her her dower of the other tenements as the law requires.[109]

---

106 G.H. Martin, ed., *The Ipswich Recognizance Rolls 1294–1327*, p.28.
107 Ibid., p.30.
108 T. Twiss, ed., *The Black Book of the Admiralty or Monumenta Juridica, vol. II: 'Le Domesday de Gippewyz. The Domus Day of Gippeswiche'*, p.139.
109 B.A. Hanawalt, 'The Widow's Mite: Provision for Medieval London Widows', p.23.

Traces of this custom are to be found in the *Calendar of Letter-Books of the City of London* edited by Reginald Sharpe. In 1384, for instance,

> It was considered by Sir Nicholas Brembre, the Mayor, and the Aldermen that Cristina, late wife of Thomas Clenche, should have her free-bench, viz., the principal tenement of which her husband was seised at his death, according to the ancient custom of the City. Precept was accordingly issued the same day to Philip Walworth, Serjeant of the Chamber, to deliver to the said Cristina her free-bench of a certain tenement in the parish of St Clement near Candilwykstret of the yearly value of £4; and further, to deliver to her, by view of the sworn City Masons and Carpenters, one third of the other tenements and rents within the liberty of the City of which her said husband died seised, to hold the same by way of dower.[110]

The borough of Oxford had similar rules but Alice, the widow of William Attemontes, did not abide by them in 1285 when she claimed against

> Walter de Witteney and John Attemontes the third part of a messuage with appurtenances in Oxford as dower. Walter and John come and say that the aforesaid Alice after the death of the aforesaid William, formerly her husband, held the aforesaid messuage in the name of free bench and was thereby in possession for forty days and more, and they say that the custom of the town of Oxford is such that when a woman after the death of her husband resides in a tenement in the name of free bench for forty days or more and afterwards she married someone, that she is ever after prevented from claiming an action for her dower in respect of that tenement.[111]

The jury decided in the favour of the two men and 'Alice [was] in mercy'. In spite of such customs husbands often specified in their wills that their dwelling place was to come to their wives – perhaps as a supplementary precaution, to make sure the issue was beyond dispute. In 1417, Stephen Thomas of Lee (Essex) insisted upon his wife had 'þe place þat sche dwelythe in, terme of her lyff'.[112] In 1431

---

110 R.R. Sharpe, ed., *Calendar of Letter-Books of the City of London: I 1400–1422*, folio clxxxv. http://www.british-history.ac.uk/report.asp?compid=33473&str query =free%20bench#s20
111 P.J.P. Goldberg, ed., *Women in England c. 1275–1525*, p.146.
112 F.J. Furnivall, ed., *Fifty Earliest English Wills*, p.38.

William FitzHarry of Cosin Lane in London wished his wife to have his house in London 'with all the rentes that y haue in Cosynlane' (p 88). In 1434, Rauf Heth of Hackney mentioned 'y will that, aftur my decese, Anys my wyf haue & reioyse duryng her lyf all my mesuage, with the curtylage and all the appurtenance, set & lyeng in the paress of Hakeney aboue seyde' (p.100).

As far as manorial custom was concerned 'free-bench' was the title a widow had in the copyhold lands of her husband.[113] It differed from a dower insofar as it was not property taken from the late husband's possessions since villeins did not own any tenement: in legal theory the villein's holding was granted at the will of the lord though, in practice, the right to hold came to be hereditary. This is why Matilda, the widow of Thomas Koke, who lived at Hemingford Abbots (a manor that belonged to Ramsey Abbey) was able to obtain 'two acres of meadow previously held by Richard Ive, for life, for services and customs' with the formal assurance that 'after her death, the property will revert to their sons, John and Nicholas, naïfs of the lords, in bondage for the same services, for life'.[114] The same *Liber Gersumarum of Ramsey Abbey* shows that at the death of his father, John Lytholf of Chatteris entered into several plots and tenements including 'a half-acre in Hersladefeld reserved for life to Margaret, mother of John Newman' (p.56). Customs varied from village to village: Kentish custom granted the whole of the late husband's property to the widowed wife. Many customs accorded half of it: the 1328–9 manor court rolls of Great Cressingham (Norfolk), for instance, mention such a free-bench/dower of a half. Vincent of Lakinhatn was seised of several tenements, 'in villenage at the will of the lord doing thence the services and customs due. All rights being saved. And he gives to the lord for his entry. And saving to Alice who was the wife of Hugh the son of Lawrence half of the said tenements to hold in

---

113 Though the word *dower* is often (incorrectly) used in the translation of primary sources.
114 E.B. DeWindt, ed., *The Liber Gersumarum of Ramsey Abbey: a Calendar & Index of B.L. Harley Ms 445*, Toronto: Pontifical Institute of Mediaeval Studies, 1976, p.33.

dower for the term of her life'.[115] Both manors of Walsham le Willows (Suffolk) also reserved half of the late husband's tenement for the lifetime of the widow. In July 1328 two widows claimed what they were due: Matilda 'the widow of William Coppelowe received from the lord a messuage 7 acres of land, of which her husband died seised, and half of which she has in dower following the custom of the manor' and Isabella, 'the widow of Walter Osbern received from the lord 4 acres of land and half of a messuage, of which her husband died seised, and half of which she has in dower following the custom of the manor'.[116] In 1362, John at the Meadow was 'amerced 2s. because, without the lord's leave, he cut down and sold to Robert Rampolye 1 acre of underwood of the lord's bondage, from the tenement Wither, worth 4s., of which the same John [was] to be charged for half, because the other half of the same underwood belong[ed] to his wife Eleanor in the name of dower'.[117] Let us also cite the case of Margaret Syre who 'claimed from Adam Syre half of 3 acres of villein land as her dower, because William her husband was seised of the said tenement. Adam had illegally deprived her of it, to her loss of ½ mark. Adam was unable to deny that she is entitled to the said tenement in dower'.[118] Widows of the manor of Bedlow (Buckinghamshire) depending on the abbey of Bec[119] had a third part of their late husbands' properties:

> [1249] Peter Coterel gives two marks to have seisin of the land which was his father's, saving to Roise his mother a third part of the same land.[120]

---

115 E.P. Cheney, *English Manorial Documents*, Philadelphia: University of Pennsylvania, 1896. Series, Translations and Reprints from the original Sources of European History, vol. 3, no.5. http://www.shsu.edu/~his_ncp/Manor.html
116 R. Lock, ed., *The Court Rolls of Walsham le Willows 1303–1350*, p.113.
117 R. Lock, ed., *The Court Rolls of Walsham le Willows 1351–1399*, p.62.
118 Ibid., p.77.
119 In fact, King John sequestrated the properties of the abbey in 1211. From the end of the 13th century and particularly after the beginning of the Hundred Years' War in 1337, the English properties of French abbeys were often confiscated by the Crown. The Prior of Ogbourne was allowed to retain properties of the abbey of Bec in exchange for a heavy annual farm.
120 F.W Maitland, ed., *Select Pleas in Manorial and Other Seignorial Courts*, p.21.

The manor of Atherstone in Warwickshire (also held by the abbey of Bec) had the same rule. This is why in 1291 Agnes 'formerly the wife of Walter Muck demands against Reginald Miller a third part of a burgage as her reasonable dower, whereof (as she says) the said Reginald unjustly deforces her; and this she puts upon the court'.[121] In spite of its name, free-bench was not always free – depending here too on the customs of the manor. Widows living on manors belonging to the abbey of Ramsey seem to have been expected to pay a fine to the abbot on entering upon their late husbands' holdings. Yet the abbot could be moved to pity as in the case of Katerina Chicheley of Elsworth who was granted 'one *camera* within a certain cote previously held by her late husband Simon, and now held by Robert Braughyg, freely, without any burdens, for life, with free access to that *camera* by the King's road'. Katerina did not have to pay any *gersum* 'because she is a pauper'.[122] In Walsham le Willows, mentions of entry fines for widows' dowers are very rare. Alice Robhood, whom we have already met, paid 6d. fine for entry when her dower was restored to her in 1317. A year later Matilda, the widow of Geoffroy Kembald was to pay 6d. 'so that her dower be granted to her' but the fine was waived by the lord. No entry fines for dowers are mentioned afterwards.

Very often the villein and his wife took up their holding in both their names. If the husband died the widowed wife went on enjoying the whole, half or third of the tenement without being admitted again – in other words without paying anything to the lord. In 1316 in Walsham le Willows:

> Walter le Machunn surrendered into the lord's hands a messuage with two buildings and all appurtenances, to the use of Robert of Rydon and Matilda,[123]

---

121 Ibid., p.40.
122 E.B. DeWindt, ed., *The Liber Gersumarum of Ramsey Abbey: a Calendar & Index of B.L. Harley Ms 445*, p.57.
123 We have already come across this couple when dealing with the question of debts.

his wife, and their heirs, and seisin is delivered to them to hold in villeinage, at the lord's will.[124]

In the same court rolls, one finds mention of John Stronde 'who lately died, holding jointly with his wife Emma, for the term of their lives a messuage 16 acres of land, by the lord's demise, and they held 3 acres of customary land purchased in court by the rod' (vol. 1, p.57), of William Springfold 'villein [who] when he died, held from the lord a messuage, 30 acres of land and ½ acre of meadow; (...) Isabella William's wife will hold, for her lifetime, 5 acres of land, ½ acre of meadow and half of the messuage, which she and William purchased jointly' (vol. 1, p.198) or of John Lester the elder who 'when he died, held from the lord a messuage of villein land, and 16 acres of free land, jointly with Rose Lester, his wife, who will hold the tenements for the term of her life' (vol. 2, p.124). On certain manors, men sometimes surrendered their tenement to the lord in order to be seised again jointly with their wives in order to give them full possession of the land at the moment of their death so that they would not have to pay a heriot.

Villein widows often complained of being cheated upon and sued for their free bench/dower at the manor court. The often quoted court rolls of the manor of Wakefield mention for the year 1274 'Alice, mother of the said Emma who unjustly claimed dower in the said land after the death of Thomas, her husband, and is in mercy because she has no right' and also 'Avice, widow of Thomas de Staynland [who] offers to put herself on an inquisition as to one-third of half a bovate of land, which John son of Thomas unjustly holds and keeps from her'.[125] Similar examples can be quoted from the court rolls of Walsham le Willows with Cristina, the widow of Walter Kembald, who on May 2nd 1317 'complained against Simon Kembald in a plea of dower'. Simon was amerced 6d. and 'Cristina granted and released to Simon all her right in dower in ½ acre of villein land'.[126] On the same day, Alice, the widow of William Fenner [Robhood] 'complained

---

124 R. Lock, ed., *The Court Rolls of Walsham le Willows 1303–1350*, p.39.
125 W.P. Baildon, ed., *Court Rolls of the Manor of Wakefield, vol. 1, 1274–1297*, Leeds: the Yorkshire Archaeological Society, Records Series vol. 29, 1901.
126 R. Lock, ed., *The Court Rolls of Walsham le Willows, 1303–1350*, p.54.

against Matthew Hereward and Robert his brother in a plea of dower, and they have a day until the next court' (p.56). At the next court (October 11th), Robert was 'amerced 6d. because he unlawfully deprived Alice the widow of William Robhood of her rightful dower of the tenement, formerly held by William in bondage, half a messuage 1 ½ acres of land; ordered the reeve and hayward to have her rightful dower delivered to Alice, following the verdict of the homage and the custom of the manor' (p.59). In 1318, it was Robert Godefrey's turn to be fined 6d. 'because he deprived Alice the widow of Hereward Gunter of her rightful dower, as he acknowledged in court. (...) The bailiff was ordered that she should have that which was hers by right' (p.66). These examples show that cases were usually promptly dealt with in manor courts. Who was entitled to what was common knowledge and, in case it was not, the court rolls were there for the steward to check what arrangements had been recorded. Although peasants who could read and write were extremely uncommon and although oral witnessing was the rule villeins also lived in a world of written evidence. In 1294, for instance, 'the wife of Ralph Butler came before the lord of Ramsey after Michaelmas and showed a certain charter in which was contained that she was enfeoffed of the whole tenement which was that of her late husband Ralph Butler in Cranfield'.[127] In the same year, Cecilia Moyllard 'was distrained and has respite until Michaelmas to show the charter whereby she says that she is enfeoffed of the tenement in Barford, whereof her infant daughter Isabella became heir upon the death of her father'.[128] On September 26th 1386 Walter and Matilda Tailor's claim rested entirely on written documents:

> Now to this court came Walter tailor and Matilda Tailor his wife, and they say that before the purchase by the said Willima Springold, the said tenements were held of the manor of Wyverstone in villeinage, and were villein tenements of the said manor. And thereupon they showed the court roll of Wyverstone, dated the day of St Martin the bishop in the year of the reign of Edward II and they also produced the indented charter of Robert Hovell, lord of the manor of

---

[127] F.W. Maitland, ed., *Select Pleas in Manorial and Other Seignorial Courts*, p.74.
[128] Ibid., p.75.

Wyverstone, dated the 31st year of Edward III granting to Robert Manchild and Matilda his wife, and the heirs issuing from their bodies, the reversion of the tenements, belonging to the lord.[129]

Similar rules to those observed with borough customs were put into practice to prevent land disputes. When a couple surrendered a tenement in Walsham le Willows, wives were examined in private so that there should be no doubt about their assent. Such were the cases of Massilia Hawys in 1335 ('she being examined in court', vol. 1, p.191), Isabella of Mileham in 1341 ('she being examined by the lord', vol. 1, p.250) or Alice King in 1390 ('she being duly examined', vol. 2, p.169). Widows who parted with a tenement were asked to publicly quitclaim all their rights:

> Presented that outside the court John Cook and Matilda Crask, who has dower in the tenement of the said John, of the lord's bondage, agreed between themselves that Matilda would relinquish all her right and claim to dower in the said tenement; and for this release the said John granted to Matilda and her heirs 1 acre of villein land (...). Thereupon they came to this court and Matilda surrendered and released all her aforesaid right to the said John. (Vol. 2, p.169)

Juries or charters were there to protect people's rights. As Ray Lock writes in his introduction to the court rolls of Walsham le Willow:

> The interests of a wife who held land jointly with her husband, and of the widow of a tenant, or his under-age heirs were all protected. The wife was examined in private to ensure that she willingly agreed to the transfer of land in which she had an interest; in Walsham the widow was entitled to hold in dower a half-share of her late husband's tenement for life; and the land inherited by minors was taken into the lord's hands until the court approved custody of them and their inheritance during their minority.[130]

In spite of differences due to the great number of customs, several common principles clearly emerge. The first and most important one is that all women were entitled to dower or free bench when they became widows. Their economic role in the family unit was undisputed and it stood to reason that they should have a share of the

---

129 R. Lock, ed., *The Court Rolls of Walsham le Willows, 1351–1399*, p.156.
130 R. Lock, ed., *The Court Rolls of Walsham le Willows, 1303–1350*, p.15.

inheritance since what their husbands left was also the result of their own work. Moreover, as with feudal law, primogeniture gradually became the rule; dowers were also meant to enable widows provide for their younger children. The combination of these two elements explains why, though widows were not full owners of their dowers, they were fully responsible for their management and whatever profit they might yield was theirs. The second guiding principle, however, was that the property should remain within the family. As we have seen, widows were not supposed to sell or alienate the settlements and the holding reverted to the heir at the woman's death. These common lines did not conceal huge differences in terms of wealth and living conditions. Many widows were impoverished but, if the husband had been sufficiently well off, the dower could allow women to live independent lives. It must be added that for many widows, dowers were not their sole source of income: in actual fact the death of their husbands meant they regained control over their own independently acquired land.

Widows' Material Resources: Land in Full Ownership

Wives had no control over property during their marriage and widows who did not remarry were, in fact, the only women who could call their land their own. *Glanvill* (VI, 1) states that 'the word *dos* has two meanings': first 'dower' and second (VII, 1) 'that which is given with a woman to her husband, which is commonly called *maritagium*; a marriage-portion'. Both *Glanvill* and *Bracton* indicate that *maritagium* was always given by the bride's family and that it could be given to the husband alone and his heirs, to the wife alone and her heirs or to both and their heirs. Homage was not performed until the third heir entered into the inheritance to protect the donor's (or his heirs') rights. Even when the dowry had been granted to the wife alone it passed under the control of the husband immediately upon marriage. Only after her husband's death could she come into what was left (she could not prevent its alienation while the husband lived). This is why between 1183 and 1197, Hawise countesss of Gloucester was able to grant 'God and the church of St Mary, Nuneaton, and the nuns of the order of Fontevrault serving God there (...) lands and rents freely and quietly, peacefully and honourably, in pure and perpetual alms, as [her] lord William earl of Gloucester held them or [her] father who gave that manor to [her] in free marriage'.[131] In his study of Godmanchester J.A. Raftis gives several examples of dowries – most of the time land settled by the father on his daughter:

> [1313–1314] Nicholas the son of Roger le Barbour de Huntingdon is seised of a half acre in gift from Joan his mother, which land John de Hamerton her father gave to that Joan in marriage.
> [1331] Isabella, daughter of Margaret daughter of William de Warmington, clerk, is seised of an entire messuage that lies in Longelane next the curtilage of the Prior of Merton, coming to the above Isabella after the death of Margaret her mother by right of inheritance. This same messuage William Clerk formerly gave to Margaret his daughter and mother of this Isabella in free marriage.[132]

The letter-books of London allude to similar habits:

> [1284] Adam le Potter and Sabine his wife, daughter of William de Durem', conveyed to Aubrey called 'Pechoheros', merchant of Dinaunt, certain houses in the parish of All Hallows de Bredstrete (received on their marriage from William de Durem' aforesaid and Sabine his wife, which Sabine inherited the same from John Vigel her brother), in return for the sum of 46 marks lent to them by the said Aubrey. To hold the same for a term of twelve years from Midsummer next.
> [1284] Roger de Combe, feliper, and Isabella his wife demised to Adam de Blakeneye 1 mark annual quitrent which the said Isabella had by bequest of Agnes her mother, the same being reserved on a house which Robert le Sayer gave to Richard de Dunstaple in free marriage with Johanna his daughter, situate in the parish of St Andrew Huberd. To hold the said quitrent for a term of thirteen years from Christmas, anno 1285, or until the executors of Henry de Farnham are satisfied of a debt due from Stephen, son of Robert le Sayer aforesaid.[133]

---

131 J. Ward, ed., *English Noblewomen in the Later Middle Ages*, London: Longman, 1992, pp.95–96.
132 J.A. Raftis, *A Small Town in Late Medieval England. Godmanchester 1278–1400*, pp.21–22.
133 R. Sharpe, ed., *Calendar of Letter-Books of the City of London A: 1275–1298*, folios 72 & 74, http://www.british-history.ac.uk/report.asp?compid=33027

By the early fourteenth century, however, *maritagium* had become rare – especially among the aristocracy. It was replaced by a sum of money paid by the bride's family, while the groom's family often gave land (to be held by the husband and wife together) to the newly married couple.[134] As B. Hanawalt has explained 'the usual arrangement was for the husband to contribute property and perhaps a trade or business, while the wife contributed money, goods, and perhaps livestock. The wife's contribution, the dowry, was to provide capital for establishing the family, and it would usually go to the children of the marriage'.[135] Wills show that fathers were usually very much concerned with the setting up of their daughters. Their sole inheritance, indeed, was often their marriage portion. In certain wills uncles provide such marriage portions for their nieces and godfathers for their goddaughters, while other men leave money for the marriage of unknown poor maidens as alms.

Widows also recovered full rights over property they had inherited, been granted as gifts or had purchased. Certain widows of the aristocracy were great heiresses. We have already mentioned the case of Elizabeth de Clare[136] who, after the death of her brother Gilbert at the Battle of Bannockburn in 1314, became one of the three heiresses of the huge Clare estates with her two sisters, Eleanor and Margaret. Elizabeth was granted her share of the inheritance in 1317 when she agreed to marry Roger Damory – one of King Edward II's supporters. Five years later she was widowed for the third and final time, free to enjoy her vast lands. Her household account rolls show that she travelled from one residence to another, mainly Clare in Suffolk, Anglesey (Cambridgeshire), Usk (Gwent), and Great Bardfield (Essex). The well-known household account books of Alice de Bryene kept by her

---

134 See documents 11–13 in J. Ward, ed. *Women of the English Nobility and Gentry*, Manchester University Press, 1995, pp.27–30.
135 B. Hanawalt, 'Marriage as an Option in late Medieval England', S.S. Walker, ed., *Wife and Widow in Medieval England*, p.144.
136 F.A. Underhill, *For Her Good Estate: The Life of Elizabeth de Burgh*, New York: St Martin's Press, 1999. The study is based on many documents including Elizabeth de Burgh's household accounts, her will, her statutes for Clare College. See also J.C. Ward, *English Noblewomen in the Later Middle Ages*.

steward, John, show that Alice, the daughter of Sir Robert de Bures had returned to Suffolk as a wealthy widow after her husband's death, succeeding to her father in the manors of Acton and Bures (St Mary).[137] Inquisitions Post Mortem have enabled us to list the numerous dowers held by Elizabeth FitzAlan or Elizabeth de la Plaunche. They also provide a particularly interesting insight into inherited and granted property. Elizabeth de la Plaunche, for example, was, with three other kinswomen, the heiress of Sir Roger Hyllary and consequently:

> Elizabeth late Lady de Clynton died seised in her demesne as of fee of a moiety of the 2 parts of the manor [of Darlaston] and a moiety of the 2 parts of the land, and a moiety of the advowson [of Darlaston church], and the reversion of the third part of the land.

Moreover, she held several messuages in Southwark granted to herself by her late husband John de Clynton, had surrendered four years before her death the remainder of the manor of Compton Chamberlayne and of the advowson of Barford St Martin church (Wiltshire), of 'Plankus manere' manor of Haversham and of the advowson of Haversham church, of Claybrooke manor (Leicestershire) which she had held by a fine levied in the court of Henry IV, possessed a messuage with four cottages in London which had been granted to her and her husband John Russell in fee tail, 'Belneys' manor in Haversham (Buckinghamshire) demised to her and John Russell, the manor of Birmingham as well as many 'lands, tenements, fairs, market and advowsons' in Birmingham, Edgbaston and Erdington (Warwickshire), the castle of Maxstoke, the manor of Shustoke, the manors of Bole Hall, Perry Croft and Austrey as well as 'the messuage, land, tenement, meadow, wood and close called Colesleys in Coleshill parish' (Warwickshire) in fee tail granted to her and her husband John

---

137   V.B. Redstone, ed. & M.K. Dale, trans., *The Household Book of Dame Alice de Bryene of Acton Hall, Suffolk: September 1412 to September 1413*, Bungay, Suffolk: Paradigm Press, 1984 [originally published Ipswich: Suffolk Institute of Archaeology & History, 1931].

Clynton. Lands in Berkshire are also mentioned.[138] Inquisitions Post Mortem often recorded demesne lands held by heiresses of lower social status. When Thomas Howse, esquire, died in 1418 it was recalled that he held several tenements belonging to his former wife:

> Joan daughter of John Fylliol of Thorpe le Soken held in her demesne as of fee a tenement called 'Foulton Bernes', 40 acres arable and 40 acres marsh in Ramsey; a tenement and 20 acres called 'Panteries' in Divercourt; and a tenement called 'Badons' and 80 acres arable and 6 acres wood in Tendring. She married Thomas Howse, had a son, Walter, and died. Then Thomas held by the courtesy of England, and died holding. (...) Walter his son and next heir is aged 16 years and more.[139]

These documents also show that manors were usually granted to women by their parents or a relative or, even more frequently, by their husbands. Indeed, while inherited property could only be handed down according to strict rules, the testator could bequeath purchased tenements with complete freedom. Wills lead us to the same conclusion: when possible, fathers often bequeathed tenements to daughters and granddaughters while husbands showed concern for their wives, often leaving them property on top of the obligatory dower.

Daughters were usually – literally speaking – the poor relations of the family since, under common law, land descended to the eldest son. It is quite common to see in wills that fathers left nothing other than a sum of money to their daughters for their marriage. Yet exceptions were also numerous: Agnes Capell of Brockford demised to her daughter Margery 'all the lands and tenements which [she] had of Stephen Gardener [her] father in the town of Cotton to her and her right heirs'.[140] Among the wills proved at Ipswich, Nicholas le Clerk cared for his daughter Alice demising her a stall and adding that he 'willed and granted that Alice his daughter should have her share, namely so much as any of his sons should have, of all his houses at the

---

138 K. Parkin, ed., *Calendar of Inquisitions Post Mortem 1–5, Henry VI. 1422–1427*, pp.306–316.
139 J.L. Kirby & J. Stevenson, eds., *Calendar of Inquisitions Post-Mortem and other Analogous Documents preserved in the Public Record Office XXI: 6–10 Henry V (1418–1422)*, p.1.
140 P. Northeast, ed., *Wills of the Archdeaconry of Sudbury*, p.276.

tavern against the Quay, to herself and her heirs'.[141] In 1316 Roger dil Wode 'bequeathed in his last will in the said testament to Christiana his daughter all that messuage with appurtenances that he once bought of Robert son of Christiana de Boketon' (p.74). In 1320 John le Cuteler 'bequeathed to Matilda, his daughter, and her heirs of the body of John de la Lane, her husband, all the whole messuage, with buildings and all its other appurtenances, which lies in the parish of St Mary Tower'. In the same testament he gave to his servant Thomas a tavern and a shop against a rent to be paid to Matilda and went on determined to favour his younger daughter: after Thomas's death the tavern and shop were to revert to Matilda 'without any contradictions. And if Matilda die during Thomas's lifetime, then Thomas shall pay the said fifth penny each year throughout his life to Christine and Alice, Matilda's elder sisters' (p.93).

A minority of husbands demised tenements for their wives to become the sole owners. One finds in the collection of wills of the archdeaconry of Sudbury (1439–1474) that Richard Mowe of Bradfield St Clare passed on to his wife '[his] messuage and [his] garden, with a piece of land, to her and her heirs for ever, to sell if she so wish',[142] that William Atherne of Bardwell bequeathed his wife Isabel '3½ acres of land in the field of Bardwell, by the footpath-boundary called "Hundrydmere" to give and to sell to whom she pleases' (p.307). John Chyldriston of Mildenhall did the same with a messuage passed on to Margaret his wife, 'she being free to dispose or sell it as she pleases and sees best' (p.311) and so did Thomas Wyskyn of Hundon who left to his wife Margery 'all [his] messuage in "le Cherche Strete", to give or to sell, and to do with what she will; [his] feoffees in the said messuage to transfer full possession and legal estate in it to the said Margery, when so required by her' (p.333). A few wills proved at the city court of Ipswich are very similar. Hugh Scoot gave his wife Emma and her heirs 'all that messuage, with buildings and all its appurtenances, which Geoffrey le Colt of Ipswich once bequeathed to him, after the death of Belicencia, Geoffrey's wife, in his testament, (...) to have and to hold to the said Emma and

141 G.H. Martin, ed. *The Ipswich Recognizance Rolls 1294–1327*, p.33.
142 P. Northeast, ed., *Wills of the Archdeaconry of Sudbury*, p.305.

her heirs and assigns heritably for ever' (p.48). John de Bogham left in sole ownership to his wife Alice a messuage which was 'once of Agnes le Cartere, his mother' (p.124) and Henry le Tannour 'bequeathed to Petronilla his daughter and to Isabel her daughter all his messuage with buildings, curtilages, and all its appurtenances, lying in the parish of St George, Ipswich, to have and to hold to them and their heirs and assigns of the capital lords heritably for ever' (p.47). The grant made by Robert Brabon is particularly interesting because the entry explains in details what the owner of a tenement was entitled to do – though in this particular case the aim and use of whatever transaction might be considered later on was imposed by the testator:

> [1325] Robert in sound mind and good memory in his last will bequeathed to Alice, his wife, a messuage, with curtilage and with a stall and all its appurtenances, lying in the parish of St Matthew (...) to hold for the whole of her life, so that nevertheless she may sell, assign, and bequeath it whensoever and to whomsoever she will, and the said messuage may be sold without contradiction of heirs or others, and the money distributed in alms for Robert's soul as shall seem best to Alice. (p.125)

Many husbands, however, laid down conditions to their bequests. The great majority of them let their wives have one or several tenements for their lifetime only. Such was the case of Ralph le Skynnere who handed down a messuage in the suburbs of Ipswich to Lenota his wife in 1314 'to support Lenota and her children' (p.58), of William Tulet who, in 1312, transferred to his wife Katherine two messuages, 5d. annual rent, a piece of land with appurtenances 'for the term of her life' (p.52) or Richard Coulot who demised his wife a messuage he had bought 'and after Margaret's death Richard granted the messuage to remain to his nephew Reginald and the heirs of his body, if Reginald should survice' (p.77). In 1415, Thomas Walwayn passed onto his wife Isabelle lands in Marcle, Ledbury and Eastnor (Herefordshire) 'to holde hit to terme of here lyue',[143] Stephen Thomas mentioned 'it is my wyll þat my wyff schele haue þe place þat sche dwelythe in, terme of her lyff' (p.38), while Rauf Heth in 1434 wished that after his decease his wife Anys 'haue & reioyse

---

143 F.J. Furnivall, ed., *Fifty Earliest English Wills*, p.24.

duryng her lyf all [his] mesuage, with the curtylage and all the appurtenance st & lyeng in the paress of Hakeney' (p.99). Very often the widow was to enjoy the bequeathed property till her children came of age. The husband was providing the mother with a home and incomes to support those of her offspring still financially dependent. In 1411 Sir William Langeford specified:

> Y wille, tochaunde þe londes þe weche y haue asynyd to William my sone, þat Lucie my wyf have gouernauns þer-of, and þe profete, vn-to þe forseyd William ge of age xviij. And also of þe londes þat ben assyngnyd to Henre, þat my wyfe have þe governauns and þe profyte of, vn-to þe forseyd Henre be of age xviij. (p.20)

One finds several similar examples in the collection of wills of the archdeaconry of Sudbury edited by Peter Northeast. Robert Dyster of Boxford first required his feoffees 'to enfeoff Margaret [his] wife of and in a messuage on the south side of the tenement in which [he] lived, with a garden, in Groton and Boxford, to her and her heirs for ever' while limiting the use of a second messuage by his wife 'until [his] son be of the age of 24, allowing Margaret [his] wife to have all the income and benefit from it, and then to enfeoof him of it' (p.109). Roger Nicole of Chevington insisted upon his feoffees allowing his wife Joan to hold his lands and tenements in Chevington and elsewhere in Suffolk for term of her life 'so long as she remains unmarried, she to meet the charges, keep up due repairs and maintain John the younger, [his] son, and Henry his brother with the necessaries of life out of the lands, until they come to the age of 24' (p.221). John Caly let his wife Marion have several lands and tenements, both free and bond, in the towns and fields of Norton and Tostock until their son came to the age of twenty (p.507) and Robert Wareyn saw to it that his wife Agnes took the profits of 'lands and tenements, woods, meadows and pastures' until his son John was twenty-three and his son Robert eighteen (p.508). John Bullok's testamentary dispositions seem to summarize the various points that have just been set forth: the widow is provided with material means to raise her children; once a grown-up the eldest son is to recover the property and become an independent head of household; children who did not inherit would get a rather raw deal from life, girls only getting money to take into marriage:

> 2 Feb. 1453; to Margery my wife all my lands and tenements in the town of Woolpit, except 3 pieces of arable land, containing altogether an acre, (...) to hold for 14 years from now, on condition she remain unmarried and that she keep up the dues and repairs of the property in that time, at her own cost; after the end of the 14 years the premises to remain to Adam Bullok my son, to him and his heirs for ever, on condition that he pay Margery 6s. 8d. a year during her lifetime, if she remain unmarried; if Adam die during the 14 years, the lands to remain to the child that Margery is now with, if it be male, to him and his heirs for ever; if it be female, the lands to be sold, she having 20s. out of the money at her marriage. (p.273)

Only a small minority of men (even fewer women) made wills in the Middle Ages. One must constantly keep in mind that the documents that have reached us are not representative of medieval society as a whole and exclude the poor and very poor (therefore a very large proportion of the population). Yet they are the most personal documents that have survived and give us an illuminating insight into what family life was – at least for the social group of these people who had lands and goods to bequeath. Most wills show that husbands wanted the best for their wives; they felt much concern for their well-being. Men whose wives were already aged, with grown-up or married children, usually saw to it that they were not thrown out into the street. The widows being too old to till the land, the children needing the lands to survive and pay the rents and services to the lord, these women were not bequeathed whole tenements but part of a dwelling to end their days peacefully. Walter Bekysby of Thorpe Morieux had arranged it with his son Robert (not the eldest son consequently not the heir) that he would get his land after his death but in exchange Robert would have to give his mother two quarters of malt every year. Moreover,

> Margery also to be allowed to dwell in two downstairs chambers, with the solars over them, in the west part of my dwelling house, together with the courtyard annexed to the said chambers, and a small chamber in the courtyard, with free entrance and exit to the chambers and courtyard for the term of her

life, she to carry out repairs to the chambers at her own cost during that time. (p.426)

William Waschepoke of Haverhill demised his married daughter Eleanor several roods of land and the capital tenement in which he lived 'provided that Eleanor [his] wife shall have her dwelling in the tenement, with the bakehouse, with free entrance and exit, and easement most convenient for her, for term of her life' (p.189). John Reve of Wickham Skeith shared out his tenements among his four children. His wife Isabel was to have her dwelling in the tenement bequeathed to his son John 'the upper chamber in the said tenement, with free ingress and egress and access to the fire when she wishes, she having firewood wherever she wants in the tenement, and easement in the bakehouse and kitchen when she pleases' (p.431). Certain details contained in these wills are touching revealing the thoughtfulness and kindness of the testator: John Fuller of Sudbury wished his wife Joan to have 'three chambers with the solar over, in the upper part of [his] capital messuage' and to have free access 'to the well for drawing necessary water, and into the yard or garden there to walk in and collect herbs and have other reasonable easement when and as frequently as suits her' (p.310).

Other wills are less pleasant with husbands spelling things out, warning their wives they were not to contest their final settlements. These disputes usually concerned dowers: Katherine Dunkon of Mendlesham was to be pleased with 'a messuage next to the road called "Dunkonys" for term of her life. She to be content with it as dower and not demand her "le moryeve"' (p.124), Agnes Muryell was to have, after her husband's decease, the messuage in which he lived 'with two acres of arable land at "Fowlaker", for term of her life, on condition that she claim no dower of [his] other messuages and lands' (p.131). Thomas Bere of Norton specified that if his wife Isabel claimed 'any dower in the tenement in Stowe, or in any part of it, or refuse[d] to give acquittance of that dower when so requested, she to be given nothing of the legacies assigned to her above, but be content with her dower as by the law' (p.169). John Mannyng of Norton was not any kinder with his wife Christine to whom he left 'all the goods and belongings which were hers when we married, or their true estimated value, and, in addition, 40s. on condition that she release, when required, any claim that she has as a wife on any of the tenements and lands that he, John, has had or will have in the future; otherwise his will, where it concerns Christine, to be null and void' (p.244) and to make sure Christine had well understood, he designed her as one of his two executors. Christine, however, renounced probate. Among the fifty wills published by F.F. Furnivall that of Sir Ralph Rochefort is cast in the same mould:

> First, he will that Margarete his wyf haue hir laufull dower of all his maners londes and tenementes, rentes and seruices, of his enheritaunce in the countes for-saide, for terme of hir lif. All-so he will that the saide Margarete haue xx markes of laufull money yerly out of the maners of Fenne and Skreynge, with their appurtenaunces, yn the counte of Lincoln, ouer hir dower forsaid, for terme of hir lyf. Vnder this condicion, that she kepe hir in honeste and worshupfull gouernaunce, or elles that she be maried to hir worshipe and to hir estate, by assent and counsaill of all or of the most partye of his executours and surveyours of his testament. And all-so that she clayme no dower nor ioyntfef-fement, nor no thyng do, ne wirke (that might greue his heires or his executours) in no maner degree contrarie his will, nor that she claims no iointestate in none other of his londes ne rente of his purchace, nor in no londes, tenementes nor annuities wic he hat graunted to eny of his seruaunte for terme of lyf or othir wyse. And if she doo the contrarie to eny thyng of this his last will, or make eny clayme yn the contrarie ther-of, than that she hauer oonly but hir dowere of all his maners landes and tenementes of his enheritaunce forsaid. (p.122)

These examples of discord, rather entertaining for us today, are not numerous compared to the great number of wills that convey the obvious anxiety of the husbands at the idea of leaving behind their wives and families. Widows who were lucky enough to have had wealthy husbands (and parents) managed to lead an independent life free of material and financial needs thanks to their dowers and other inherited properties.

Women of the nobility went on, as in the pre-Conquest period, making donations to religious houses or founding nunneries. Susan Johns argues that 'given the Church's claim to afford widows special protection, the cultivation of Church support by a powerful widow would not only make sense spiritually, but would also ensure support if ever the widow required help in the future'.[144] Elizabeth J. Gardener mentions that 'noble women as well as royal ladies sought refuge in convents. This may explain why a large number of nunneries were founded by wealthy widows of aristocratic rank'.[145] She goes on giving the examples of Lucy, dowager Countess of Chester who founded Stixwould nunnery in Lincolnshire in 1140 and that of Ela Countess of Salisbury, the founder of Lacock priory (then abbey) in Wiltshire in 1232. Both women settled and died in the nunneries they had established. The manor of Lacock belonged to the Countess of Salisbury, Ela being the only child of William, second Earl of Salisbury from whom she inherited large estates in Wiltshire. In 1229 she planned to set up an abbey there and with this aim in view gave the whole of the manor (as well as the manors of Hatherop, Bishopstrow and half of the manor of Heddington) 'to God and blessed Mary and St Bernard'.[146] She became a nun in 1237 and the first abbess three years later till 1257 when Beatrix of Kent succeeded her. Though by then seventy years old she remained much involved in the administration of the abbey and obtained the rights of markets and fairs from the Crown.[147] The community of Amesbury was recruited from the highest ranks of society and became the retreat of several royal ladies. This Benedictine nunnery had been founded in 980 by Queen Aelfthryth and then attached by King Henry II to the abbey of Fontevrault in Anjou. It was the refuge of Eleanor of Provence when King Henry III died in 1272, taking the veil in 1286 and dying there in 1291. Before entering the priory she had been a patron procuring royal gifts, persuading her son, King Edward I, to issue letters of protection and to allow his six-year-old daughter Mary to enter the convent there. Another of her granddaughters was already there, Eleanor of Brittany (the daughter of her own daughter Beatrice married to John II, Duke

---

144   S. Johns, 'The Wives and Widows of the Earls of Chester, 1100–1252: the Charter Evidence', *Haskins Society Journal*, 1995, vol. 7, p.130.
145   E.J. Gardner, 'English Nobility and Monastic Education, c. 1100–1500', J. Blair & B. Golding, eds., *The Cloister and the World, Essays in Medieval History in Honour of Barbara Harvey*, Oxford University Press, 1996, p.81.
146   J. Ward, ed., *English Noblewomen in the Later Middle Ages*, p.201.
147   S. Thompson, *Women Religious: The Founding of English Nunneries after the Norman Conquest*, Oxford: Clarendon Press, 1991.

of Brittany). It was for the latter's benefice that she bought Chaddleworth manor and the advowson of Poughley Priory (Berkshire) which were eventually given to the priory.[148] Another great lady was Matilda de Clare (born Maud [Matilda] de Lacy) who made several grants 'in her pure and liege widowhood' to the priory of Augustinian friars founded by her late husband Richard de Clare, 6th Earl of Hertford, for the salvation of her soul, that of her husband, and those of their ancestors and successors.[149] She was the mother of Gilbert de Clare who married Joan of Acre, another daughter of King Edward I and Queen Eleanor of Castile, and therefore the grandmother of Elizabeth de Clare – whom we have already come across several times – under her name of Elizabeth de Burgh. Elizabeth offered much support to Clare priory, patronized many other religious houses such as the Prior and Convent of Ely or Walsingham Austin Priory. In 1347 she obtained licence from King Edward III to found a house to accommodate twelve friars in Little Walsingham to the great annoyance of the Augustinian canons. She also supported the friary of the minoresses without Aldgate granting in 1355 '£20, ornaments, and furniture to the house, £20 to the abbess Katherine de Ingham, and 13s. 4d. to each of the sisters'[150] and being allowed, thanks to a papal indult, to enter the precincts of the priory with three ladies.

Widows of (far) more modest means were also great conveyors of land very often using the land market to provide for their children. J. Raftis noticed the important role played by endowed women 'as much from the donors as recipients of gifts' in his study of the records of the small town of Godmanchester: 'well over one half of the gifts were granted by mothers. Most of these gifts by mothers were to daughters. (...) The use of gift by mothers, and especially in relation to unmarried daughters, parallels similar practice in last wills in England

---

148 R.B. Pugh & E. Crittal, *A History of Wiltshire* (vol. 3), Oxford University Press, series Victoria History of the Counties of England, 1957.
http://www.british-history.ac.uk/report.asp?compid=36534
149 C. Harper-Bill, ed., *Clare Priory Cartulary*, Woodbridge: Boydell & Brewer, Suffolk Charters Series, 1991.
150 W. Page, *The Victoria History of London. Vol I: London within the Bars, Westminster and Southwark*, London: J. Street, 1906. [Reprinted by Boydell & Brewer, 1974]. http://www.british-history.ac.uk/report.asp?compid=35371

at this time'.[151] This is why 'Isolda wife of Robert Alryth took seisin of one acre of land and one rod of meadow and 12 beddis of curtilage in West crofts by the gift of Dyonisis her mother' (p.21) or why 'Henry, the son of John Pellage took seisin of a certain bakeshop that came to him in gift from his mother, which shop he is to defend as for one half acre. And it was testified before the court at that time that Philippa, the mother of the above Henry, lawfully during her life gave the said shop to Henry her son' (p.193). In the borough of Ipswich many widows are mentioned selling properties: 'Emma, widow of John de Langeston, in her pure and legitimate widowhood has granted to Thomas, Juliana and Matilda, a curtilage with appurtenances'.[152] In 1322 Joan 'in her pure and legitimate widowhood has granted to Thomas dil Stonhous a messuage with buildings and its appurtenances (...) a house and a brewhouse with a curtilage adjacent (...) a messuage, with buildings, curtilages, and all its appurtenances. (...) Joan present in court. And Thomas gives 2s.' (p.98). Wills of widows proved in the same city show that a certain number of them died owning all sorts of tenements and landed estates. Alice, the widow of Philip Harneys, was one of these capitalists who bequeathed her chief messuage, a house 'with two shops, two solars, and the windows belonging to the said house', the annual rents for a tavern, a shop and eight messuages (p.50). Alice, the widow of William le Mayden bequeathed to her daughter a tavern, a plot of land and a barn, to Clement le Spicer and his wife a messuage with buildings, to Baldewyn de Balliol and his wife a shop, to Thomas del Weston and his wife a shop with basement and asked her executors to sell a tenement, with buildings and appurtenances 'that her debts might be discharged' (p.54). In literary texts widows are often compared to greedy spiders coveting men's goods as in this lyric:

> Wedowis be wol fals, iwys,
> For they cun bothe halse and kys

---

151 J.A. Raftis, *A Small Town in Late Medieval England. Godmanchester 1278–1400*, p.25.

152 G.H. Martin, ed., *The Ipswich Recognizance Rolls 1294–1327*, p.83.

Til onys purs pikyd is,
And they seyn, 'Go, boy, goo!'[153]

The Wife of Bath and William Dunbar's *wedo* underline the importance they attach to economic matters for they are uncompromising business women. The Wife of Bath explains that:

> (...) tho housbondes that I hadde,
> As thre of hem were goode, and two were badde.
> The thre were goode men, and riche, and olde.
> (...)
> They had me yeven hir lond and hir tresoor;
> Me neded nat do lenger diligence
> To wynne hir love, or doon gem reverence. (III, [D] 195–197 & 204–206)

The widow of Dunbar's *Tretis of the Tua Mariit Wemen and the Wedo* (*Treatise of the Two Married Women and the Widow*) is careful enough to obtain notarial deeds when she deprives her husband of his property:

> And yit hatrent I hid within my hert all;
> Bot quihilis it hepit so huge, quhill it behud out:
> Yit tuk I nevir the wosp clene out of my wyde throte,
> Quhill I oucht wantit of my will or quhat I wald desir.
> Bot quhen I severit had that syre of substance in erd,
> And gottin his biggingis to my barne, and hie burrow landis,
> Than with a stew stert out the stoppell of my hals,
> That he all stunyst throu the stound, as of a stele wappin.
> Than wald I, efter lang, first sa fane haif bene wrokin,
> That I to flyte wes als fers as a fell dragoun.
> I had for flattering of that fule fenyeit so lang,
> Mi evidentis of heritagis or thai wer all selit (333–344)[154]

---

153 E. Salisbury, ed., *The Trials and Joys of Marriage*. http://www.lib.rochester.edu/camelot/ Teams/sltxt.htm

154 J. Kinsley, ed., *The Poems of William Dunbar*. The poem is provided with a translation into modern English [And yet I hid all my hatred in my heart, though at times it heaped up so much that it was hard to restrain. Yet I never quite took the stopper out of my throat as long as I lacked anything I had set my mind to or anything I desired. But when I had separated that man from his wordly goods and got his buildings and his tall city tenements for my child, the

Needless to say, the aim of both texts was to entertain and make the readers laugh with the familiar topic of the poor henpecked husband held up to ridicule. Everyone would probably have agreed at the time that what the two women were describing was nothing but the world turned on its head!

Widows' Material Resources: Legitim

Widows were also entitled to a third of their late husbands' movable property which was called their *legitim*. *Bracton* gives the general rules:

> If after deducting his debts and the necessary expenses mentioned above something then remains, let that be divided into three parts, the first to be left to his children, if he has children, the second to his wife, if she survives him, and let the testator be free to dispose of the third as he wills. If he has no children, then let one half be reserved for the deceased and the other for the wife. If he dies without a wife but with children, then let one half be assigned to the deceased and the other to the children. If he dies without wife or children, then the whole will remain at the deceased's disposal.[155]

In William Langland's *Piers Plowman*, Piers decides to have his will drawn up before going on life's last pilgrimage. Piers first leaves one third to his wife 'Work-in-time' and one third to his children: 'My wif shal have of that I wan with truthe, and namoore, / And dele among my doughtres and my deere children; / For though I deye today, my dettes are quyte; / I bar hom that I borwed er I to bedde yede.' (Passus VI, 96–99). As to the third, he was free to dispose of that as he wished:

> stopper flew out of my throat with a vengeance so that he was quite stunned with the impact as if with a weapon of steel. Then, after so long, I was so eager to be avenged that I was as fierce in quarrel as a terrible dragon. I had been pretending so long in order to flatter the fool, until my documents of ownership were all sealed].

155 E.S. Thorne, trans., *Bracton on the Laws and Customs of England*, vol. 2, p.180.

> And with the residue and the remenaunt, by the Rode of Lukes!
> I wol worshipe therwith Truthe by my lyve,
> And ben His pilgrym atte plow for povere mennes sake. (VI, 100–102)

Wives were not allowed to make wills since all they had brought into marriage passed on to their husbands. Yet *Bracton* specified that it was proper an exception should be made for personal goods:

> If she is under her husband's authority she will not be able to make a will without his consent. Nevertheless, because it is only proper, she is sometimes permitted to dispose by will of that reasonable part she would have had if she had survived her husband, especially things given and granted her for personal adornment, as robes and jewels, which may be said to be her own.[156]

Such was the theory. In practice these thirds or halves were not strictly respected. Many testators bequeathed all their movable goods to their wives without making any precise inventory or detailed account. The most common phrases to be found in wills were then 'To N. my wife all the ostilments[157] and utensils of my house', 'To N. all the goods and chattels in my dwelling' or 'To N. my wife all the utensils and other necessaries in my house'. Widowers, on the other hand, always clearly indicated who was to have each of the objects, making the final sharing out their wives would have done had they outlived them. Though we have emphasized the fact that husband and wife were fully aware of being partners and of making a financial and work unit and though a woman's personal property passed under the control of her husband, wills show that, as far as movables are concerned, husbands and wives made a clear distinction between what belonged to the one and the other. The collection of about nine hundred mid-fifteenth-century wills edited by Peter Northeast for the archdeaconry of Sudbury underlines this fact. Thomas Sawer of Thelnetham, for example, gave back to Matilda his wife 'all the chattels and utensils which she brought to me when we first married, according to what is seen to be hers, and what mine' as well as six sheep (will no.969), John Prynchet restituted Agnes 'all her own goods and chattels' (no.204), John Mannyng of Norton demised to 'Christine his wife all the goods and

---

156 Ibid., vol. 2, p.179.
157 That is to say 'utensils, equipment, furnishings, household goods' (*MED*).

belongings which were hers when we married, or their true estimated value' adding 40s. (no.671), Richard Salysbery returned to Isabel, who had been his wife less than a year, 'all the goods which were hers before she was my wife' (no.871), John Waryn gave his wife Amflote '£20 in money and all the bedding that belongeth to [him], with all the stuff that she brought to [him]' (no.474), John Copenger of Buxhall left Alice 'four beds of her choice and 8 silver spoons and a half dozen pewter vessels with all her own vessels' (no.90). Robert Wareyn drew up a list of what had in fact belonged to his wife and what were his proper gifts to her:

> To Joan my wife 10 marks; also to Joan all the firewood at 'Goryslond', the best cooking-pot, a brass pot, 2 brass pans, a peel and a spit, which were hers previously, all the bedding not before bequeathed, such as donges, covers and sheets, 2 cows, 2 quarters of wheat and 4 quarters of barley, to be delivered by my execs at the feast of St Michael next. (no.1258)

Several husbands gave their wives movable possessions insisting they were their own – one may imagine simply to avoid any confusion and subsequent disputes. Such were the cases of Thomas Rokell of Lavenham who wished his spouse to have 10 marks 'together with all the ostilments and bedding of [his] house and chamber belonging to [him]' (no.376) or of John Waryn again giving more to his wife:

> Also to Amflote my mazers and my best piece of silver, with 6 silver spoons of the best, and all the bankers and cushions, with the 'hallyng' that is belonging to me, and all the brass and pewter, and all other ostilments belonging to me'. (no.474)

In fact almost all husbands speak of 'the chattels of *my* house' reflecting once again the fact that married women did not own any property. Only three wills made by men in the collection mention *the* house, John Turnour leaving 'to Alice [his] wife all [his] goods and chattels, and the utensils and ostilments belonging to the house' (no.60), John Gardener bequeathing 'to Agnes [his] wife all the utensils and other necessaries in the house' (no.190) and William Atherne of Bardwell giving 'to the said Agnes all [his] live cattle and all the utensils of the house' (no.858). William Kyng of Thorney is the only one to use the possessive *our* (here the bequest concerns real property):

> Agnes my wife to have our messuage and lands which we hold and in which we live, in Thorney, for term of her life, she to keep herself in the necessities of life. (no.600)

All the others make repeated use of the adjective *my;* Robert Sygoo of Mildenhall, for instance, wrote: 'To Matilda my wife all my utensils and bedding, belonging to my house, and all my corn' (no.65), Alan Roberd's will mentions 'To Alice my wife all the ostilment of my house and all my goods and chatels' (no.128), that of Edmund Clerk 'To Joan my wife all my ostilments and bedding of my house' (no.130). Many of them made cash donations to churches, religious houses or gilds or a few bequests of clothing or household articles to relatives or servants and simply added: 'residue of all my movable goods to the disposition of my wife'. John Browster did not bother making a list: 'residue of my goods, the utensils and bedding, as well as all the other things wherever they may be, to Margery my wife, executrix' (no.216). Others did – to the delight of historians! The most frequent bequest was bedding (pairs of sheets, coverlets, donges [mattresses]), then came other domestic utensils such as brass pots and pans, silver spoons or mazers (drinking-bowls). Jewels and money in cash were also often handed down. Robert Kerve explained what he meant by 'all the necessaries and utensils of [his] house': 'that is, beds, napery, pewter, silver spoons, mazers and other things, except the ornaments and jewels relating to [his] body' (no.1115). John Watlock of Clare also made a sort of catalogue: 'To Joan all my utensils, such as linen, cups, spoons, pots, pans and all other necessaries' (no.112) and so did John Derby of Sudbury:

> To the said Joan all the utensils, ostilments and bedding of my house, except the jewels and silver cups, mazers, spoons, belts, basilards, brooches and rings, half of which I bequeath to Joan my wife and the other half to be reserved for disposal for my soul. (no.803)

Several men distinguished between goods 'in and out the house' bequeathing domestic items on the one hand and farm implements, animals or crops on the other. Very few widows received horses, Isabel Jakys was given 'a horse called "Brok"' (no.125) and Joan Deynes her late husband's 'best horse' (no.740), a greater number of them inherited cows or pigs and a few of them whole herds of sheep. Crops are very frequently referred to mainly wheat, barley (malt), rye and wheat (maslin). Ploughs, carts and harrows are mentioned when, clearly, the widow was expected to go on with her husband's farming activity: William Paxman left to his wife Matilda 'all [his] chattels, such as draught animals, carts, ploughs and everything related to cultivation' (no.682), John Staloun specified his wife Joan was 'to have half of all [his] grain (...), also a hundred sheep, that is 60 wethers and 60 ewes, and all [his] horses, with plough, cart and harness, and everything belonging to them' (no.708) and John Wrygh left many chatels to his wife Alice:

> All the ostilments and utensils belonging to my house; to the same Alice 3 horses (...), 7 cows, a cart, a tumbrel and 2 ploughs, with all the traces, shares and coulters, and other necessaries belonging to them; also to Alice 2 quarters of wheat, 4 bushels of barley, 2 pigs and all the corn and grain now growing on my land. (no.1200)

Several women were lucky enough to receive all (or nearly all) their late husbands' movables, to be told explicitly they could do what they wished with them and to be designed one of the executors of their husbands' testaments. Ralph Farewell, for instance, stated: 'Alice my wife to have all my lands and tenements, goods and chattels, live and dead, and the utensils of my house, wherever they may be, to her and her heirs, to do with as she will, for ever' (no.381). John Newman of Sudbury left his wife 'all the utensils and bedding, jewels and ostilments of [his] house, to do with freely as she wishes' (no.818), John Wymere decided his wife should have 'all [his] utensils and necessaries in [his] house' even adding 'without any bickering by anyone' (no.1272). Some wills reveal the kindness or once again the preoccupation of the testators who felt concerned about their wives' well-being. William Baron of Newmarket pointed out that his goods and chattels were for his spouse's 'maintenance and that of [his] three daughters until they marry' (no.28), William Ottley of Little Saxham also left his movables 'to Agnes [his] wife for upkeep of her and [his] children' (no.34), John Pek of Stowmarket explained his goods were for his wife's 'well-being while she lives' (no.19) while John Frost of Wickhambrook bequeathed 'to Agnes [his] wife all the ostilments of [his] dwelling and two cows and everything necessary for her support' (no.302).

Qualifications must however be brought because the situation was not always that rosy. The vast majority of testators left to their wives what in fact remained of their goods and chattels once their legacies had been fulfilled, their funerals and debts paid for. The quantity of goods may then have been dramatically reduced depending on the wealth of the husband and the amount of his debts. In his testament John Norman gave all his movables to his wife Margaret 'for her maintenance, she to pay all [his] debts, see [him] buried and keep [his] anniversary day as long as she is able' (no.693), John Wykham left 'residue of all [his] goods and chattels to Margery [his] wife, she to bury [him] and pay [his] debts' (no.722), Richard Mowe named his wife Margery his executrix and bequeathed her the remainder of his goods and chattels but she was 'first and before all else to pay the debts for which [he] was beholden' (no.848). John Muschat of Drinkstone was as clear:

> To Agnes my wife all my sheep, of whatever kind, a cow, and after my debts have been paid and my will performed, all the other movable goods. (no.1079)

Similarly John Wagge of Haverhill mentioned in his testament that he handed down his movable possessions to his wife Alice 'to carry out [his] funeral, pay [his] debts, and do with as she pleases' (no.1092) and John Hyll of Elmswell expressed the same conditions:

> To my wife all my movables, apart from my bequests, on condition that she pay all my debts and fulfil my will. (no.1337)

John's bequests included offerings to his parish church and priest, bequests of money to friaries, to a certain Katherine Pundyr and to his godchildren a ewe and a lamb plus 12d. to his serving-maids. John Derby of Sudbury left all the house equipment to his wife Joan 'except the jewels and silver cups, mazers, spoons, belts, basilards, brooches and rings, half of which I bequeath to Joan my wife and the other half to be reserved for disposal for my soul' (no.803). Endless examples could be quoted. The conclusion to be drawn from this brief survey is that most widows left alone, or with young children, got all the remaining domestic utensils... after everybody else had been served. Widows with grown-up children usually got less, for fathers often left money in cash and objects to their married children, though very rarely in the proportion of the third of their movables. This corroborates Richard Helmholz's point that 'a man's rights to bequeath his personal property were quite circumscribed if he were married' in the thirteenth century, but by the fifteenth century 'this restriction had largely disappeared from English practice. (...) The husband's power of testation over his chattels became absolute'.[158] A close study of the fifty wills edited by F.J. Furnivall emphasizes the same general trends, the main difference being that the lists of movables are far more impressive because of the higher social condition of the testators.

All these arrangements and legal rights over property were meant to enable widows to go on living decently. They also assured them a control over their own lives unknown to other women. In 1895 F.W. Maitland described single women's rights, insisting on the facts that they 'can hold land, even by military tenure, can own chattels, make a will, make a contract, can sue and be sued'.[159] Legally recognized as *femme sole*, a widow could theoretically be – to use Criseyde's words – her 'owene womman' (II, 750). Yet what was reality like?

The Degree of Independence of Widows

In the Towneley plays, Noah's wife longs for the well-being that would come if she were to become a widow:

> Lord, I were at ese and hertely full hoylle,
> Might I onys haue a measse of wedows coyll;
> ffor thi saull, without lese shuld I dele penny doyll,

[158] R.H. Helmholz, 'Married Women's Wills in Later Medieval England', S.S. Walker, ed., *Wife and Widow in Medieval England*, p.167.
[159] F. Pollock & F.W. Maitland, *The History of English Law before the Time of Edward I*, Cambridge University Press, 1895. [2nd edition, 1968, p.482].

> so wold mo, no frese that I se on this sole
> of wifis that ar here,
> ffor the life that thay leyd,
> Wold thare husbandis were dede
> ffor, as euer ete I brede,
> So wold I oure syre were. (388–396)

Criseyde is reluctant to marry Troilus wavering betwen love and the freedom she enjoys as a widow: '(...) Allas! Syn I am free, / Sholde I now love, and put in jupartie / My sikernesse, and thrallen libertee?' (II, 771–773). Rather more unexpectedly, the marquis in the Clerk's Tale sees matrimony in a very similar way: 'I me rejoysed of my liberte, / That seelde tyme is founde in mariage; / Ther I was free, I moot been in servage' (IV, 145–147).

Gentlewomen

Contrary to what one may first believe, aristocratic widows were not those who enjoyed the greatest freedom – far from it. Even after her husband's death, a noble widow still had another lord to serve: her feudal overlord who often happened to be the king himself. Anglo-Norman and Angevin kings could require widows of their vassals to remarry men of their choice – a convenient way to reward valuable supporters and to collect money since a hefty sum was to be paid by the selected candidates. As a matter of fact, Norman and Angevin kings, William the Conqueror to begin with, had granted English lands to their barons in return for their military and political services. The subsequent kings needed to feel secure about the loyalty of the heirs of these barons. This is why all the wealthy orphan boys became the sovereigns' wards or those of faithful tutors while the rich orphan girls were married to trustworthy vassals. Widows of tenants-in-chief, whatever their age, also became wards of court. In the 12th century kings had an army of mercenaries rather than knights less and less inclined to make war. The consequence was that they literally sold the hands of rich heiresses and wealthy widows. The thirteenth-century English chronicler Matthew Paris condemned the marriage of Margaret de Redvers and Faukes de Breauté in particularly harsh terms:

The same year (1252), on October 2nd, Dame Margaret, Countess of Lisle, died. She was of noble lineage, known under the name of de Redvers,[160] the widow of late Faukes, an extremely bloodthirsty traitor. The consequence was that a noble lady was married to a detestable being, devoutness was joined to impiety, and beauty to ugliness. She had been given to him, under duress, by John the Tyrant who had no qualms about committing such crimes.[161]

In 1185 King Henry II Plantagenêt had an enquiry made into the assets of widows, heiresses and minor heirs under his direct feudal control. The information was gathered into an Anglo-Latin document known as *Rotuli de dominabus et pueris et puellis* minutely recording the ladies' and orphans' ancestry and family ties, their ages, the names, ages and status of the widows' children, describing their lands and assessing their value, counting their beasts and indicating the additional quantity necessary to complete the stock. The names of the widows and maidens are followed by the words *in donatione Domini Regis* (in the king's gift): they were his to give in marriage. When several suitors were in the running, the lady was married to the highest bidder. The woman could even take part in the auction and pay to choose her husband or to remain single – though that was particularly expensive.[162] Susan Johns in her study of the wives and widows of the

---

160   Margaret (or Margery) was the daughter of Warin Fitzgerold (Chamberlain of the King) and Alice de Courcy. She first married Baldwin de Redvers Earl of Devon who died on September 1st 1216. Their son was born in 1217. Margaret was immediately remarried by King John (who died October 19th 1216) to one of his captains against the rebellious barons – Faukes de Breauté, a notorious cruel and lowborn mercenary soldier.

161   Matthew Paris, *Chronica Majora*, H.R. Luard, ed., London: Longman / Trübner, 1880, vol. V, p.323. (*Rerum britannicarum medii aevi scriptores*, 57). The translation is mine.

162   To be fair it must be added that certain entries concern men (probably underage therefore still wards of court) and not women: '[Yorkshire] Walter de Chauncey renders account of £15 that he may marry a wife of his own choosing.' J. Hunter, ed., *Magnum rotulum scaccarii, vel magnum rotulum pipae, de anno tricesimo-primo regni Henrici primi*, London, Record Commission, 1833.
Also in C. Stephenson & F.G. Marcham, eds., *Sources of English Constitutional History. A Selection of Documents from A.D. 600 to the Present*, New York, Evanston, London: Harper & Row, 1937, p.52. http://www.constitution.org/sech/sech_025.htm

Earls of Chester (1100–1252) mentions the case of Lucy Countess of Chester (1070–1136): 'a considerable heiress to lands in Lincolnshire [and consequently] an attractive marriage partner'. Lucy married three times and 'it was as a widow that she was most independent of family control but to get this she had to pay. The 1130 Pipe Roll shows that she fined with the king not to be forced to remarry. She paid 500 marks for the privilege of not marrying within five years':[163]

> Lucy, countess of Chester, renders account of £266. 13s. 4d. for the land of her father. In the treasury £166. 13s. 6d. And she owes £100; also 500 marks of silver that she need not take a husband inside five years. And the same countess renders account of 45 marks of silver for the same agreement, to be given to whom the king pleases. To the queen 20 marks of silver. And she owes 25 marks of silver. And the same lady owes 100 marks of silver that she may hold justice in her court among her own men.[164]

The same 1130 pipe roll (dating from the 31st year of the reign of Henry I) also reveals that Wiverona, the wife of Euerwacrus de Ipswich paid £4 and 1 mark not to remarry:[165] the king made money by selling dispensations. Janet Loengard has pointed out that 'widows' dower and remarriage were built into the economic and political policy of Henry II and his sons'.[166] The 1175–6 pipe roll (dating from the 22nd year of the reign of Henry II) gives proofs of the king's political and financial interests in the remarriage of widows. One can read that the sheriff of Oxfordshire 'renders account of £6 12s. 9d. from the farm of the land of the countess of Clare in his bailiwick before the king gave her to William d'Aubigny'.[167] In 1194, under

---

163 S. Johns, 'The Wives and Widows of the Earls of Chester, 1100–1252: the Charter Evidence', p.122.
164 C. Stephenson & F.G. Marcham, eds., *Sources of English Constitutional History. A Selection of Documents from A.D. 600 to the Present*, p.53. http: //www.constitution.org/sech/sech_025.htm
165 J. Hunter, ed., *Magnum rotulum scaccarii, vel magnum rotulum pipae, de anno tricesimo-primo regni Henrici primi*, p.96. Quoted by J. Loengard, 'English dower in the year 1200', p.233.
166 J. Loengard, Ibid., p.234.
167 *The Great Roll of the Pipe for the Twenty-second year of the Reign of King Henry the Second, A.D. 1175–1176*, London: Pipe Roll Society, 1904, p.30. Quoted by J. Ward, *English Noblewomen in the Later Middle Ages*, p.42.

King Richard's reign, twelve elected knights of the county of Kent were asked to gather for the general eyre in order to 'make response concerning all the [following] articles for the entire hundred or wapentake' including article five 'concerning the wardships over children to which the king is entitled' and article six 'concerning the marriages of girls or widows to which the lord king is entitled'.[168] Loengard gives the example of an entry in the pipe roll for the sixth year of King Richard's reign stating that 'the sheriff had rendered account of £115 16d. of the stock of the Countess of Aumale, sold in the first year of King Richard because she was unwilling to marry William de Forz'.[169] One can also mention the often quoted case of Nichola of Hermingford who was fined £100 in 1199 not to be forced to marry again. In that last year of Richard's reign, thirty-nine entries in the pipe roll concern women who paid fines in order not to be married or to be allowed to choose their husbands. Under King John's reign things went for the worse. As John struggled with financial difficulties he blatantly exploited his feudal rights. He went on demanding money for his consent for a widow or heiress to marry. In 1199, for example:

> The widow of Ralph de Cornhill gives the lord king 200 marks and three palfreys and two goshawks in order that she should not be married to Godfrey de Louvain, and that she can marry whom she wishes, and for having her lands.[170]

As one can notice, the fines were particularly hefty and not many women could afford to pay them; they would have had to part with their dower and so lose their means of subsistence. The 1130 pipe roll gives us an idea of the huge sums of money men paid to secure marriages with these women 'in the king's gift' – first and foremost in order to obtain their lands:

---

168 C. Stephenson & F.G. Marcham, eds., *Sources of English Constitutional History. A Selection of Documents from A.D. 600 to the Present*, p.104. http://www.constitution.org/sech/sech_040.htm
169 Ibid., p.234.
170 T. D. Hardy, ed., *Rotuli de Oblatis et Finibus in Turri Londinensis asservati tempore Regis Johannis*, London: Record Commission, 1835, p.37. Quoted by J. Ward, *English Noblewomen in the Later Middle Ages*, p.42.

[Nottinghamshire & Derbyshire] Robert de Lusors renders account of £8. 6s. 8d. that he may marry the sister of Ilbert de Lacy.

[Kent] Turgis, [bishop of] Avranches, renders account of 300 marks of silver and 1 mark of gold and a war-horse for the land and the widow of Hugh d'Auberville and to have wardship over his son until the latter is twenty years old.

William de Hocton paid £200 for his son and 10 marks gold for himself, Geoffrey de Trailli 300 marks silver, 2 marks gold and four horses, William FitzRichard £52 11s. 8d.[171] The women themselves did not count as individuals, the rolls do not even give their names but only mention whose former wives they were. For instance William FitzRichard bought 'the wife of Fulbert de Dover with her dower and *maritagium*' and it is nowhere to be found that the lady was called Athelize. The rolls mention 'the widow of Ralph de Cornhill', 'the widow of Geoffrey de Fauarc' or 'the sister of Ilbert de Lacy': only their lands – usually their dowers, so consequently their late husbands' lands – really mattered.

Most widows had no choice but to comply. The practice, however, was very unpopular with the barons and baronesses themselves. When Henry I managed to seize the throne for himself in 1100, he immediately issued his *Coronation Charter*. As he needed the nobles' support against his brother Robert, the rightful successor to the throne, he granted them liberties and declared in particular that widows were no longer to be married against their wishes:

> 3. And if any one of my barons or other men wishes to give in marriage his daughter, sister, niece, or female relative, let him talk with me about this matter; but I will neither take anything from him for this permission nor prohibit him from giving her, unless he wishes to wed her to any enemy of mine. And if, on the death of a baron or other man of mine, a daughter remains as heiress, I will give her, together with her land, by the counsel of my barons. And if, on the death of a husband, his wife survives and is without children, she shall have her dower and marriage portion, and I will not give her to a husband unless it is in accord with her own wish.
>
> 4. If, moreover, the wife survives with children, she shall yet have her dower and marriage portion so long as she keeps her body legitimately, and I will not give her except in accord with her wish. And the guardian of the land

---

171 Ibid., pp.233–234.

and the children shall be either the widow or another one of the relatives who more justly ought to be guardian. And I command that my barons shall conduct themselves in the same way toward the sons or daughters or wives of their men.[172]

We have seen in what way Henry kept his word! So the practice went on for 115 more years until the nobles forced King John to sign Magna Carta (1215) to make sure he did not go beyond his rights as feudal lord. Article eight concerns widows of baronial rank:

> No widow shall be compelled to marry so long as she has a mind to live without a husband, provided, however, that she give security that she will not marry without Our assent, if she holds of Us, or that of the lord of whom she holds, if she holds of another.[173]

Magna Carta was written the year of the Fourth Lateran Council that synthesized medieval views on marriage, underlining once again the importance of mutual consent: both texts brought about visible changes. It became more difficult to compel widows to remarry.

The *Rotuli de dominabus et pueris et puellis* also shows that noble widows did not always have custody of all their children. Feudal law allowed the lord to take control and receive the income of the fief of a minor heir or heiress until he or she came of age. It was not unusual that the custody of the heir and of the lands were in different hands. In theory, this right of wardship had been established to protect defenceless children and their mothers from greedy relatives. The result was that young children might be separated from their family and home:

> Alicia, who was the wife of Thomas de Bellofago and the daughter of Waleran d'Oiri, is in the gift of the Lord King, and is 20 yeard old. (...) She has one son who is three years old and is in the custody of Nigel FitzAlexander.
>
> Beatrice, who was the wife of Robert Mantel, the Lord King's servant in the Honor of Nottingham, is in the gift of the Lord King, and she is 30 years old. (...) She has three sons and one daughter; the eldest son is 10 years old and is in

---

172   A.B. White and W. Notestein, eds., *Source Problems in English History*, New York: Harper and Brothers, 1915. http://www.fordham.edu/halsall/source/hcoronation.html

173   A. E. Dick Howard, ed., *Magna Carta. Text and Commentary*, p.38.

the custody of Robert de Salcey, it is said, on the king's orders. The other children are with their mother.[174]

Should we be reminded of the fact that customs change with the times and should not, consequently, be judged from our twenty-first century mentality? Some medieval mothers visibly disapproved the practice: when John Drayton died in 1417, the sheriff of Bedford was asked to inquire about concealments and deceptions. Indeed 'Joan and Elizabeth, [John Drayton's] daughters and next heirs, are aged 8 years and more and 5 years and more. They were taken away, hidden, abducted and detained by his widow Isabel to the king's deception'.[175] As texts are always more complex than what they seem to imply at first reading, it must be added that abduction by mothers did not always derive from some overflowing maternal instinct but sometimes concealed financial motives, forceful entry into property and the desire, on the part of the mothers, to arrange or sell themselves the marriage of their offspring. Once a child was in the custody of a lord, the latter was entitled to control the marriage of his *protégé*. In a will edited by F.J. Furnivall one discovers that Roger Flore had planned that:

> As touching þe warde and mariage of Thomas Dale, my will is, but if he and my daughter Anneys mowe acorde by þe asseynt of hire moder Cecile, elles I wul þat þe warde and mariage of him be sold to my profit þer hit may be to his worshipe. And I wul þat þe profit, þat comeþ þer-of, helpe to fulfylle my testament and wille.[176]

174　J.H. Round, ed., *Rotuli de Dominabus et Pueris et Puellis de XII Comitatibus*, London: The Pipe Roll Society, 1913. Quoted by E. Amt, ed., *Women's Lives in Medieval Europe. A Sourcebook*, New York, London: Routledge, 1993, p.156. J. Walmsley, ed., *Widows, heirs, and Heiresses in the Late Twelfth Century: the Rotuli de Dominabus et pueris et Puellis*, Tempe: Arizona State University, series Medieval and Renaissance Texts and Studies, vol. 308, 2006. See also S.M. Johns, *Noblewoman, Aristocracy and Power in the Twelfth-century Anglo-Norman Realm*, Manchester University Press, 2003.
175　J.L. Kirby & J.H. Stevenson, eds., *Calendar of Inquisitions Post-Mortem and other Analogous Documents preserved in the Public Record Office XXI: 6–10 Henry V (1418–1422)*, p.4. John Drayton was Isabel Russell's third husband.
176　F.J. Furnivall, ed., *Fifty Earliest English Wills*, p.63.

As we have already noted many times noble heiresses were married at a very early age. The *Rotuli de dominabus et pueris et puellis* mentions several cases of very young girls 'in the gift of the Lord King'. One of them was already a widow – even though she was only ten years old:

> She who was the wife of John de Bidun the younger, Matilda by name, is in the gift of the Lord King, and she is 10 years old and was the daughter of Thomas FitzBernard. Her land in Kirkby is worth £6, with stock of one plow-team, and it cannot be worth more.[177]

Such a practice was widespread among the aristocracy. Between 1288 and 1500 five of the marital unions that were sealed in the great Berkeley family concerned spouses who were both under eleven. It is a well-known fact that royal children were particularly ill treated. Most of Alienor of Aquitaine and King Henry II's children were married very young as was then the custom: Henry the young king was wedded to Marguerite of France when he was five (she was only two). His sister Matilda became Henry the Lion's wife at the age of twelve. Richard was betrothed to Alice of France when he was only ten, Leonora became Queen of Castile as wife of Alfonso VIII when she was eight, Joan was betrothed to the king of Sicily at the age of eleven. Leonora is the best possible example to prove that even such marriages can become love matches for, when her husband died, she was so devastated with grief that she passed away twenty-eight days later. Among the aristocracy girls were often married to older men, their very young age accounting for why they were widowed several times in their lives, wars and disturbed political times being other main reasons. Isabel Russell, whom we have just mentioned, was first married to William le Scrope, a close supporter of King Richard II. William was beheaded in Bristol in 1399 when Henry Bolingbroke returned to England and managed to seize Richard's throne. Isabel then married Thomas de la Riviere of Westrop who died in 1405 or 1406. Her third husband was Sir John Drayton, the father of the two little girls. She eventually got married a fourth time to Stephen Hatfield and died in 1437. The fact that she was co-heiress with her

---

177 E. Amt, ed., *Women's Lives in Medieval Europe, a Sourcebook*, p. 157.

sister Margaret of the tenements of her father (Sir Maurice Russell) explains once again her appeal and high value on the marriage market. The well-known correspondence of the Norfolk Paston family (*The Paston Letters*) written between 1420 and 1504 spans three generations. It shows, once again, how common remarriage was. Yet, because the Pastons belonged to the gentry and not to the nobility, they got married at a far more advanced age. Elizabeth (born in 1429) got married when she was twenty-nine, she lost her husband three years later and remarried when she was forty-two. Edmond wedded two widows successively: Catherine in 1480 and Margaret, already twice a widow, in 1491. The story of the Pastons begins with William and Agnes. The latter was a widow for thirty-five years and died of the plague in 1479. Her husband had died in 1444 at the age of sixty-six therefore not in his prime – especially for the time. William was forty-two when he married Agnes and they had five children born between 1421 and 1442. Since in 1442 William was sixty-four it is quite obvious that his wife must have been, at least, twenty years his junior. The letters reveal that men got married rather late – around the age of thirty-three/thirty-four. John III, for instance, first married Margery Brews when he was thirty-three and wedded Agnes Morley, already twice a widow, when he was fifty-one. One can also mention *The Householder of Paris* (*Le Mesnagier de Paris*) in which the anonymous author addresses his young wife:

> *Chiere seur, pour ce que vous estans en l'eage de quinze ans et la sepmaine que vous et moy feusmes espousez, me priastes que je espargnasse a vostre jeunesse et a vostre petit et ygnorant service jusques a ce que vous eussiez plus veu et apris.*
> [Dear sister. At the age of fifteen years, in the week that you and I were wed, you asked me to be indulgent to your youth and to your small and ignorant service, until you had seen and learned more.][178]

Works of fiction also allude to the age discrepancy between husbands and wives. Old January in the Merchant's Tale '(...) sixty yeer a

---

178 G.E. Brereton & J.M. Ferrier, ed., *Le Mesnagier de Paris*, Paris: Librairie Générale Française (Le Livre de Poche), 1994, p.22. English translation by E. Power, *The Goodman of Paris*, London: Routledge & Sons, 1928. Quoted by E. Amt, ed., *Women's Lives in Medieval Europe. A Sourcebook*, p.317.

wyflees man was bee. (...) And certeinly, as sooth as God is kyng, / To take a wyf it is a glorious thyng, / And namely whan a man is oold and hoor; / Thanne is a wyf the fruyt of his tresor. / Thanne sholde he take a yong wyf and a feir, / On which he myghte engendren hym an heir' (IV, 1247, 1267–1272). January addresses his friends and explains:

> 'But o thyng warne I yow, my freendes deere,
> I wol noon oold wyf han in no manere
> She shal nat passe twenty yeer, certayn;
> Oold fissh and yong flessh wolde I have fayn.
> Bet is,' quod he, 'a pyk than a pykerel,
> And bet tna old boef is the tendre veel.
> I wol no womman thritty yeer of age;
> It is but bene-straw and greet forage.
> And eek thise olde wydwes, God it woot,
> They konne so muchel craft on Wades boot,
> So muchel broken harm, whan that hem leste,
> That with hem sholde I nevere lyve in reste. (IV, 1415–1426)

In William Dunbar's *Tretis of the Mariit Wemen and the Wido* the three ladies discuss matrimony. The first one would like to have a new partner every year for she is married to '(...) ane wallidrag, ane worme, ane auld wobat carle' (line 89) [a slack sloven, a worm, an old crawly], the second one, conversely, would rather have an old man than her faded away reveller (line 170). The widow's first husband was an elderly man (line 286) so the pretty lady had a lover. Her second husband 'was a man of myd eld' (line 297) [a middle-aged man] whom she ruled with a rod of iron, deprived of all goods for her benefit and that of her son and to whom she was unfaithful. William Langland gives his moral point of view in *Piers Plowman* condemning both those who marry young girls and those who choose middle-aged but wealthy widows. Wit exclaims:

> It is an uncomly couple by Crist! as me thynketh –
> To yeven a yong wenche to an [y]olde feble,
> Or wedden any wodewe for welthe of hir goodes
> That nevere shal barn bere but if it be in armes! (Passus IX, 162–165)

Later on the narrator tells his confessor: 'By my feith, frere!' quod I, 'ye faren lik thise woweris / That wedde none widwes but for to welden hir goodes. / Right so, by the roode, roughte ye nevere / Where my body were buryed, by so ye hadde my silver!' (Passus XI, 71–74). It is obvious that wealthy widows were under family pressure to remarry as Claudia Opitz explained:

> Widows of the late medieval aristocracy had far more say in the matter than young girls, yet even this often amounted merely to a choice between two or three candidates proposed by the family. Remaining unmarried was extremely difficult for a widow of marriageable age, especially if she possessed land or a fortune.[179]

The only solution for a widow wishing to remain 'her own woman' was to find support with the Church by taking a vow of chastity or by finding refuge in a nunnery, either by taking the veil or by purchasing a corrody. We have already mentioned that noble ladies were used to making sizeable donations to religious houses and we have also seen that some of them withdrew from society and became nuns. Katherine Ingham was the abbess of the friary of the minoresses without Aldgate after widowhood (mid 14th century). After the death of her second husband during the battle of St Albans on May 22nd 1455 (the first battle of the Wars of the Roses), Lady Eleanor Neville – the Nevilles being one of the most powerful families in England – was another of the abbesses of the same friary. It was also possible to find a retreat from the world without taking the veil. Well-to-do women could indeed purchase corrodies. A corrody was a sort of pension granted by a religious house to a person – often to its servants on account of old age or poverty – as in the case of John Cobbold and Mabel his wife who were granted 'for both of their lifetimes a minor corrody given to needy and aged servants of the abbey'[180] of Bury St Edmunds in 1429. The cartulary of St Saviour's Hospital in Bury St Edmunds also records the 'grant to Margaret, widow of Hugh of Babington, because

---

179 C. Klapisch-Zuber, ed., *A History of Women in the West, II. Silences of the Middle Ages*, C. Opitz, chapter 9, 'Life in the Late Middle Ages', p.308.
180 C. Harper-Bill, ed., *Charters of the Medieval Hospitals of Bury St Edmunds*, no.238 p.149.

of his good service, out of special favour for her son, Br. William of Babington, monk of Bury, and because of her old age and many infirmities, of a minor corrody for the duration of her life. Hugh until his death had held such a corrody, granted to faithful servants in their old age and infirmity, by the grace of the abbot's predecessor'.[181] The grant of corrodies, however, could concern people who were not servants of the house. In 1432 the sister and brother-in-law of the abbot of Bury St Edmunds obtained such a pension:

> Grant to William Monke of Burt and Joan his wife a corrody of 1s. 4d. per week for their lifetimes. If William outlives his wife he may choose whether to take this 1s. 4d. per week or a corrody of a loaf of white bread, a gallon of best beer, with potage, meat and fish each day, just like one of the chaplains, with a decent chamber with free entry and exit at any reasonable hour. If Mabel outlives her husband, she shall have 1s. 4d. per week for life.[182]

Religious houses also granted corrodies to wealthy people for a certain sum of money and, most of the time, in exchange for the transfer of real estate and the assurance of sizeable bequests. A.G. Little mentions the agreement made in 1377 between the Carmelite friary of South Lynn and Hugh and Cecilia de Ellingham who obtained for their lifetimes 'a hall with a double chamber – that is, one below and one above – and with two fireplaces and two latrines at the end of their main hall next to the friars' refectory. Also at the other end of the hall, a lower chamber for storage and another lower chamber for their food and other supplies; with a chamber above the two lower chambers, containing a small kitchen with fireplace'. Husband and wife were also conceded a large space for their garden and their servants were allowed to go and 'fetch from the friars' fresh-water supply whenever and as often as they have need'. The allowance in food consisted of '18 conventual loaves of white bread and 6 loaves of bran bread weighing 50 shillings and 16 gallons of the convent's best ale'.[183] In 1374 Agnes, the wife of John Grace of Beechamwell, came

---

181   Ibid., no.247, p.150.
182   Ibid., no.241, p.149.
183   A.G. Little, 'Corrodies at the Carmelite Friary of Lynn', *Journal of Ecclesiastical History*, vol. 9, no.1, 1958, pp.18–20. Translated by S. Alsford http://www.trytel.com/~tristan/towns/florilegium/lifecycle/lcret04.html

to an agreement with the same friars before her husband had actually died. She was to have:

> Lodgings within the friary grounds consisting of a chamber with upper and lower rooms, chimney and latrine; twelve white loaves and two bran loaves and eight gallons of beer weekly, with pittance for herself as the prior had, and pittance for her maid like one of the friars.[184]

According to William Page in his *Victoria History of London* Margaret Ferrers, the daughter of the third Lord of Groby and the wife of Thomas de Beauchamp Earl of Warwick, had an indult from the pope after the death of her husband to reside in the friary of the minoresses without Aldgate with three matrons as long as she pleased. Helen Bradley mentions the case of Lucia Visconti, Countess of Kent who was a widow for sixteen years: 'during her widowhod, Lucia stayed for many years at the Minories. (...) She was most certainly living there by July 1421. Lucia probably lived in the town house which Elizabeth de Burgh had built in the precinct in 1352. (...) The house in the precinct acquired a reputation as the home of well-born wives and widows of men who had suffered a temporary or permanent political reversal'.[185] In Norwich the widows of prominent local landowners and citizens found a place of retreat in the priory of Carrow. This Benedictine nunnery was the only royal medieval foundation in East-Anglia and is mostly remembered for having supported the famous recluse Dame Julian of Norwich. It also welcomed vowesses and attracted a great many pious female patrons. Christopher Harper-Bill and Carole Rawcliffe list '[Thomas Wetherby's] widow, Margaret, [who] ended her days there, while another daughter, who married the influential lawyer John Jenney, boarded at Carrow for long periods as a paying guest' as well as Agnes and Anne Appleyard (1456 and 1520 respectively), Amy Aslak (1456) and Lady Eleanor Wymondham (1503) 'perhaps intending to devote their sunset years to contempla-

---

184 Ibid., p.11.
185 H. Bradley, 'Lucia Visconti, Countess of Kent', C.M. Barron & A. Sutton, eds., *Medieval London Widows 1300–1500*, pp.81–82.

tive seclusion'.[186] Heirs did not always look on these dispositions favourably fearing they might be dispossessed. Everything converged for the widow to feel particularly pressurised by her family to remarry.

Urban Widows

The status of widows in English medieval towns depended on the customs of each city. It was the practice in many boroughs that the widow of a freeman should go on enjoying the franchise – that is to say the set of rights and privileges that townsmen had acquired from their lords. Very poor widows were not concerned for, the poorest townspeople not being burgesses, these rights did not apply to them. *Capitulum* 53 of Ipswich custumal goes as follows:

> Also 3if a burgeys of the forseid toun of Gippeswiche wedde a foreyn womman, and that womman overlyve her husbond, thanne reioysse that womman the fraunchise of the toun the mene tyme that shee kepyth her wydewe.[187]

The custumal of the town of Maldon had a similar entry, its twelfth *capitulum* stating that 'no alien that marries the widow of a freeman is to be received into the franchise on those grounds. However, the widow may retain the rights of a freeman while she remains single'.[188]

Being thus entitled to take up the freedom of the city, these widows were allowed to carry on their husbands' trades and to maintain apprentices. It is now well established that, apart from the very rich, medieval women all worked and played a major part in the economic development of towns. The statutes of the vast majority of socio-religious guilds reflect this situation aiming at 'all sisters and brothers' (Norwich Tailors' Gild), 'alle ye bretheren and ye sisteren' (Norwich, Guild of St Botulph), 'þe brethryn and sisteryn' (Lynn,

---

186 C. Harper-Bill & C. Rawcliffe, 'The Religious Houses', C. Rawcliffe & R. Wilson, eds., *Medieval Norwich*, London: The Hambledon Press, 2004, p.94.
187 T. Smith, ed., *English Gilds*, p.139.
188 Paraphrase of the 1468 edition of the custumal provided by S. Alsford. http://www.trytel.com/~tristan/towns/maldon6.html

Guild of St Leonard), 'eueriche broyer and syster' (Lynn, Guild of St Peter), etc. Most of the work undertaken by women, however, was the result of skills transmitted from mother or father to daughter not that of years of apprenticeship. Female apprenticeship, indeed, was not common except for silkwomen[189] and the statutes of most craft guilds speak of 'masters' and male journeymen or apprentices. Yet most guilds permitted widows to continue in the trade of their late husbands; the workshop then being managed by a 'mistress'.[190] However enterprising women may have been S.H. Rigby notes that, in London, 'they do not seem to have entered the freedom by right of patrimony or by purchase, since of 2000 people who purchased the freedom of the city between 1437 and 1497, only three were women. In practice, women enjoyed such privileges through marriage to freemen.'[191] Women were not to be found in all crafts and trades. They often ran businesses associated with the textile industry: they worked as carders, spinners, shearers, weavers, fullers, seamstresses, tailors, hosiers and dressmakers. The manufacturing of linen and silk fabric in particular was an almost exclusively female activity. Traditionally, brewing was another. Margery Kempe was one of the greatest brewers in King's Lynn for three or four years before running a horse-mill.[192] Many women were butchers, cooks, cheesemongers, poulterers, hostelers, chandlers and retailers of all sorts:

> At Norwich, as in other medieval towns, many women both married and unmarried were involved in the sale of food and drink. Cheese, oats, fish, flour,

---

189 See E. Amt, ed., *Women's Lives in Medieval Europe. A Sourcebook*, 'Parisian Guild Regulations', pp.194–196.
190 E. Amt gives the example of the statutes of the fullers in Paris which specified that: 5. If a master dies, his wife may practice the craft and keep the apprentices, freely, in the manner described above; and with the two apprentices she may teach the children of her husband and her brothers born of a legal marriage. 6. If a widowed woman practising the aforesaid craft of fullers marries a man who is not a member of the aforesaid craft, she may not practice the craft. And if she marries a man who is a member of the craft, even if he is an apprentice or a worker, she may practice it freely.' p.196.
191 S.H. Rigby, *English Society in the Later Middle Ages, Class, Status and Gender*, Basingstoke: Macmillan, 1995, p.271.
192 S.B Meech & H.E. Allen, eds., *The Book of Margery Kempe*, Book I, chapter 2.

malt and ale could all be bought from women, with some specialities, such as the retailing of oats and cheese and the brewing of ale, being almost exclusively in their hands.[193]

If their husbands died they found themselves in charge of their late spouses' workshops and the range of crafts widened considerably: the various contributors to the volume *Medieval London Widows* edited by Caroline Barron and Anne Sutton focus on the widows of tanners, bell-founders, mercers, skinners, or fishmongers. Robert A. Wood's study of the wills of forty-nine poor widows show that these women's late husbands were not only wool bearers, clothiers, haberdashers, girdlers, glovers but also wiredrawers, goldsmiths or lockyers (locksmiths). S.H. Rigby explains that 'the wills of carpenters, shipwrights, plasterers and plumbers assume that their widows will complete the training of their apprentices.'[194] Yet, as alluded to before, these wives were obviously capable of carrying on their husbands' trades and, that women were real partners in their husbands' jobs, is suggested by the fact that most master craftsmen did not set up their own businesses until they were married. Several guild regulations show that women were considered as their husbands' co-workers: the founders' guild in York 'ordained and agreed that none of the said masters instruct anyone in their said craft only their wives and their apprentices.'[195] In Coventry the cappers' guild ordained the same. Other guilds, however, considered that widows had a merely transitional role: the rule for the dyers in York was that 'no woman of the said craft shall occupy the said craft after her husband's death longer than a whole year unless her servant who shall occupy the said craft is put by her of the franchise of the city'.[196] The weavers in Shrewsbury warned that 'no woman shall occupy the craft of weaving after the death of her husband except for one quarter of the year, within which time it shall be lawful to her to work out her stuff that remains with her un-

---

193 E. Rutledge, 'Economic Life', C. Rawcliffe & R. Wilson, ed., *Medieval Norwich*, p.181.
194 S.H. Rigby, *English Society in the Later Middle Ages, Class, Status and Gender*, p.275.
195 J.P. Goldberg, ed., *Women in England c. 1275–1525*, p.203.
196 Ibid., p.203.

worked.'[197] Examples of successful entrepreneurs among widows are easy to find but the general rule was that, in fact, they played a temporary managing and guardianship role. It is obvious that the trade was in reality to be passed on to the children (or rather the sons) of the deceased.

The husbands of the Ipswich wills of the recognizance rolls of 1294–1327 all bequeathed real property to their wives. They usually left their chief messuage but also shops, stalls, taverns, barns, lands. One shall of course never know the percentage of husbands in that town who had no real estate, or even no goods whatsoever, to transfer. Barbara Hanawalt explained that

> The London wills recorded in the Court of Husting wills show that 86% of testators left their wives with real property. (...) Another court, that of the Archdeaconry of London permits us to investigate the estates of the less prosperous. Only 18% of the men leaving wills mention real property while 65% simply refer to the residue of their estate.[198]

Hanawalt went on explaining that, though many London widows 'were left with the equipment and apprentices from their former husband's craft or business [and though] London did not prohibit women from carrying on businesses of their own and trading *feme sole* in the city, few women did.'[199] Caroline Barron and Anne Sutton's study on medieval London widows led them to the same conclusion: some bereaved women kept up their husbands' trades but many preferred to remarry lest the business should collapse.[200] Diane Hutton has shown that in Shrewsbury several butchers' widows took over their husbands' trade but only until their sons were old enough to run the enterprise. The wills of the inhabitants of smaller towns (or even villages) contained in the collection edited by Peter Northeast for the archdeaconry of Sudbury reflect the same situation. Apart from looms, all husbands bequeathed the tool of their crafts to male relatives or

---

197 Ibid., p.204.
198 B.A. Hanawalt, 'Widows', Carolyn Dishaw & David Wallace, ed., *Medieval Women's Writing*, Cambridge University Press, 2003, p.62.
199 Ibid., p.63.
200 C.M. Barron & A.F. Sutton, eds., *Medieval London Widows 1300–1500*.

descendants. William Curteys of Mildenhall excluded from his bequests to his wife 'what pertains to [his] craft of carpentry, such as tools' (will no.219), John Bownde of Lavenham demised 'to Edmund [his] son all the things in [his] workshop pertaining to the craft of weaver' (no.511). So did John Boteld of Sudbury who bequeathed to his son Robert his business, 'that is the craft of weaver and all that relates to it' (no.667). John Wareyn of Long Melfors specified that he gave his wife Alice all his utensils, in both his chamber and his house 'except the woad and ashes belonging to [his] craft of dyer' (no.790). Thomas Baron of Hitcham requested his executrix, his wife Joan, to sell 'everything belonging to [his] craft or mystery and all [his] timber and [his] boards' (no.820). John Watlok of Rede left all his iron to his brother and to his nephew 'all the equipment relating to [his] craft' (no.960). John Rogyn of Rattlesden gave all the tools and all the timber of his craft to his son Robert (no.1031). John Crymbyll of Worlington demised to his brother John 'an iron hammer called "Monday", a handhammer, a hammer called "schoying hamyr" and a beetle' (no.1119) while Nicholas Smyth of Walsham le Willows left to his son John 'all [his] smithy' (no.1370). Thomas Brounewyn of Wetheringsett, eventually, made the following bequest:

> To William my son my stall in Eye market, and my stall at the gates of Wethreringsett churchyard, if he wish to follow my craft, but otherwise the stalls to be sold by my execs. (no.1023)

Thomas's wife was to have a tenement, for term of her life, as well as two cows and a brass pot. It was not expected that she should carry on her husband's business since the executors were to sell the stalls if the eldest son did not follow his father's craft.

Many widows chose to remarry, often to someone in the same trade as that of their late husband. It was likely that suitors were numerous since the new husband was to obtain the woman's dower for life use (one third or even half of the previous husband's real estates). The well-known *Cely Papers* contain a few delightful letters in which one discovers Richard and his brother George combing various places for wives. In 1484 George eventually married Margery Rygon, the wealthy and childless widow of a London draper. She was the perfect match for a wool trader of the Staple. The *Letter Books of the City of London* also show that widows very naturally married fellow guild brothers of their former husbands. Such was the case of the widow of Stephen Maplisdene whose name is not given:

> [1402] The guardianship of John and William, sons of Stephen Maplisdene, late goldsmith, [was] committed to Reymund Standelf, goldsmith, who married their mother. Sureties, viz., John Standelf and Gregory Cressy, goldsmiths.[201]

In the same year 'the guardianship of Geoffrey and Johanna, children of John Cowlyngge, late grocer, together with their property, [was] committed to Robert Downe, grocer, who married Catherine, widow of the said John'. In 1404 'the guardianship of Simon, son of John Pays, late brewer, together with his patrimony, [was] committed by William Askham, the Mayor, and Stephen Speleman, the Chamberlain, to Robert Marchall, brewer, who married the mother of the said Simon.' John Yonge, a fishmonger, married the widow of Edmund Olyver, 'stokfisshmonger,' in 1404. He received in 1405 the sum of twenty marks 'in trust for the said orphan'. Simon having died under age, 'the money was delivered to the above John Yonge and Johanna his wife to dispose of according to the will of the orphan's grandfather.' In 1406 John atte Lee, a chandler, married Matilda, the widow of Thomas Reygate, who had also been a chandler, and obtained the guardianship of his new wife's son William 'together with his patrimony.' Or again in 1409:

> The guardianship of Alice, daughter of William, son of William Coventre, late mercer, committed by Drew Barantyn, the Mayor, and John Proffyt, the Chamberlain, to Richard Harpour, mercer, and Johanna his wife, mother of the said orphan. In the event of the orphan dying before coming of age one half of her money is to go to John Coventre, mercer, her uncle. Sureties, viz., Walter Cottone and John Lane, mercers.

Widows were not always appointed guardians of their children. The custumal of Maldon unambiguously states that underage children will be in the custody of their mothers or stepmothers. That of Ipswich

---

201 R.R. Sharpe, ed., *Calendar of Letter-Books of the City of London: I 1400–1422*, http://www.british-history.ac.uk/source.asp?pubid=172

distinguishes between the heir and the other children. Underage heirs were to be in the care of 'the next freend on the fader syde or on the moder syde, yo whom that heritage may not descendyn, the norture til that the heir be of ful age after vsage of the toun, that is to wetyn of xiiij 3er with outen doyng of wast or distruccioun in the heritage.'[202] The city of London had the same rule till the early years of the fourteenth century. This is why on July 5th 1300:

> William May was summoned to answer Walter Diri and Alice his wife concerning Jakemina, daughter of Michael de Pountif, then in the defendant's wardship. The plaintiffs alleged that, though the wardship of minors ought not to be in the hands of a kinsman to whom her inheritance could descend, the defendant was the heir of Jakemina; and accordingly they demanded that the wardship be transferred to themselves, in accordance with the will of the above Michael which they produced in Court. The defendant answered that Jakemina was in the wardship of her aunt, the Prioress of Kelingburne, and that the plaintiff Alice ought not to have the wardship, because the girl's inheritance was derived from her mother, and that her father left her nothing, and could not devise her wardship, since her inheritance lay within the Liberty of the City. As it was found that the above Michael by his will left the girl nothing, judgment was given that the wardship remain with the Prioress.[203]

Afterwards the rule was that the choice of the guardian was the entire responsibility of the Mayor and the Aldermen. According to B. Hanawalt 'the widow was appointed guardian of her children in 55 per cent of the cases coming into the mayor's court of orphans' (in London). Studying feudal law and romances Noël James Menuge has shown that 'though a mother did not automatically assume guardianship of her children after the death of their father', she might be the child's *de facto* guardian if the legal guardian agreed. 'This period in the child's life was for the benefit of nurture and usually lasted until

---

202   T. Twiss, ed., *The Black Book of the Admiralty or Monumenta Juridica, vol. II: 'Le Domesday de Gippewyz. The Domus Day of Gippeswiche'*, p.89.
203   A.H. Thomas, ed., *Calendar of Early Mayor's Court Rolls Preserved Among the Archives of the Corporation of the City of London at the Guildhall, A. D. 1298–1307*, http://www.british-history.ac.uk/report.asp?compid=31969&strquery=Wardship.

the child was about seven.'[204] As we have already seen the feudal right of wardship placed both the ward and his/her estates under the lord's control until he or she came of age. Borough custom did not prohibit the mother from administrating her children's inheritance though records show that a child's assets were very often entrusted to a man's care: in the excerpts from the *Letter Books of the City of London* quoted above the guardianship of the children was committed to their mothers' new husbands. The latter, therefore, were awarded the use of the children's portions in addition to their new wives' dowers. The children, consequently, were not a burden on them but a source of income and an extra incentive to marry their mothers! In Ipswich, children reached the age of majority when they were fourteen (they knew then 'how to measure cloth and reckon money')[205] while in London minors came of age as late as twenty-one years of age which meant bigger profits for the guardian. The following extract from the London *Letter Books* concerns a female guardian but it gives a detailed description of the respective rights and duties of both guardians and wards:

> Tuesday of St Hillary [January 13th], the year aforesaid, by the assent of Gregory de Rokesle, Mayor, and other reputable men of the City of London, the wardship of John, William, and Matilda, children of Alan Godard, was committed to a certain Sarah, daughter of Alexander Haberdas, together with the houses, buildings, possessions, rents, chattels, and all goods belonging to the said children, until they should come to lawful age. On this condition, that the said Sarah shall find the said children in food, linen and woollen clothing, shoes, and all other necessaries, until they come to full age, and when the said children arrive at lawful age the aforesaid houses, &c., shall revert to the said children in as good or better condition than the said Sarah received them, without any opposition of the said Sarah or her heirs; which premises the said Sarah will faithfully maintain throughout the term aforesaid. Pledges for the said Sarah, Alexander Haberdas her father, Henry le Coffrer, Geoffrey de Parys, saddler, William de Parys, cordwainer, and William de Parys, mercer.

---

204 N.J. Menuge, 'A Few Home Truths: The Medieval Mother as Guardian in Romance and Law', N.J. Menuge, ed., *Medieval Women and the Law*, Woodbridge: the Boydell Press, 2000, pp.79–80.
205 G.H. Martin, ed., *The Ipswich Recognizance Rolls 1294–1327*, p.62.

Similarly in 1282, 'the wardship of Thomas and Matilda, children of Walter de Kyngestone, was in full Husting entrusted to Thomas Clerk, 'poleter,' together with their houses, rents, &c., until they come to lawful age, on condition that the said Thomas provide the said children with food, clothing, and all other necessaries, and restore to them their property in good condition upon their coming of age.' One can also mention the case of Walter Haweteyn who in 1278 had the wardship of the five children of William le Gode 'together with the sum of £37, so that he will maintain the said children until they come to lawful age.' Five years later Walter had to give back £7. 8s. to Johanna, the eldest daughter. In 1287, Thomas received the same amount of money as his share of the sum of £37. Then came Margery in 1288 and Nicholas in 1293. The fifth child is not mentioned. Walter Haweteyn profited from William le Gode's property for, at least, fifteen years. William de Laufare also did his accounts when his ward came of age. It is interesting to note that this time the child's mother is mentioned; she visibly had her word to say in the matter:

> [1290] William de Laufare, cotiler, who had the guardianship of Robert, son of Robert Deumars, granted to him by the Mayor and Aldermen, anno 6 Edward I., came before Sirs John de Banquell, Alderman, and William de Bettoyne, Chamberlain and Alderman, and others, and rendered an account of the sum of £9 6s. 8d. received in money and of 13s. annual rent issuing from a certain house in the City of London. And after all costs and expenses he answered for the sum of £20 clear to the use of the aforesaid Robert, which sum remains in the charge of the said William with the consent of the auditors aforesaid, of Cristiana, the mother of the said Robert, and other friends, to be disposed of for the benefit of the said Robert wheresoever and whensoever required.

Widows who, for whatever reason, did not remarry and could not work were probably amongst the poorest members of urban society. P.J. Goldberg has a moving list of short extracts from wills showing that testators often linked widowhood and poverty: Roger de Burton, a mercer in York, for instance, left forty shillings 'to be divided and distributed among the poor and widows continuously lying in their beds in York who are unable to go out to seek for themselves the necessities of life.' William Skynner, also from York, left 3s. 4d. 'to the poor women in the maisondieu on Ouse Bridge' while Richard

Wartere left 'to each poor woman or widow having a child or children within the aforesaid parish of St Saviour 12d.'.[206]

Socio-religious guilds provided for sick or aged members. The other sisters and brothers gave money, or sometimes food, drink or clothing to those who had become destitute. The Carpenters' Guild of Norwich, for example, required a farthing (the quarter of a penny) every week from its members, these farthings being given to the poor man or woman at the end of each month. The Tailors' Guild stipulated that whoever fell into poverty was to have seven pence a week while the Peltyers' Guild mentioned fourteen pence and the Poor Men's Guild only three. Certain guilds also helped their old and impoverished members find a place in a religious house where they might stay.

Hospitals were places of refuge for homeless widows. A papal letter from Rome granted 'relaxation of five years and five quadragene[207] of enjoined penance' to penitents who visited and gave alms on certain feast days for 'the sustentation and conservation of (...) the Augustinian monastery of St Mary de Altopassu, without the walls, London, the chapels and altars situate therein and those in the solemn hospital of the Blessed Virgin, in which hospital very many poor widows, wards, and orphans are continually sustained.'[208] Medieval hospitals were often founded as lazar houses (that is to say, leperhouses). However they were not only establishments for the sake of the sick but also institutions for the accommodation of pilgrims and travellers, and asylums for the destitute, infirm or aged. The word *hospital* was therefore used both for a hospital in its current sense, a hostel / hospice, and a poorhouse. Hospitality was offered to those merely passing through the town but also to boarders needing accommodation for a longer time. Assistance to the poor, the aged and the sick was a free service, 'the incurably sick and the aged being received as permanent members of an associated community, living together

---

206 P.J.P. Goldberg, ed., *Women in England c. 1275–1525*, pp.162–163.
207 An indulgence for forty days. (*OED*)
208 W.H. Bliss & J.A. Tremlow, eds., *Calendar of Entries in the Papal Registers relating to Great-Britain and Ireland: Papal letters. Vol. IV. AD 1362–1404*, p.393.

under the discipline of a rule of life designed to prepare the pilgrim soul for the stronger air of its heavenly country.'[209] Widows were often admitted as lay sisters who provided nursing care and other services to those who lived in the hospital.

Gradually however, as time went by, most houses had to struggle with financial difficulties and impose charges. The most common way of raising money was the sale of corrodies (not granting the benefits and luxurious life conditions that well-to-do widows might enjoy but guaranteeing applicants bed and board). In such a case the applicants made over whatever property they had to the hospital for the brethren to take care of them. Carole Rawcliffe mentions the example of 'the widowed Alice de Chalvedon who made over all her lands in Chaldon to St Thomas's Hospital, Southwark, on the condition that she would have a 'suitable bed' there for life with all reasonable necessities for herself and a maid, plus 5s. 6d. a year for clothing and food.'[210] In London St Bartholomew's Hospital welcomed both needy, deeply indebted widows in order to prevent them from becoming destitute or homeless and women who simply looked for retirement contracts and thus procured funds for the house.[211] In 1316 the Bishop of London condemned the latter practice which dramatically reduced the part of charitable relief to the poor.

The six hospitals of Bury St Edmunds were all dependent on the abbey. The biggest one was dedicated to St Saviour and was originally founded in about 1184 for a warden, twelve chaplain priests, six clerks, twelve poor men and twelve poor women. Pope Urban III mentioned that he took under his protection the hospital 'built for the sustenance of the sick and poor.'[212] On March 12th 1294 John, the

---

209 J. Rowe, 'The Medieval Hospitals of Bury St Edmunds', *Medical History*, 1958, 2(4), p.256.
210 C. Rawcliffe, 'The Hospitals of Later Medieval London', *Medical History*, 1984, no.28, p.3.
211 S.M.B. Steuer, 'Family Strategies in Medieval London: Financial Planning and the Urban Widow, 1123–1473', *Essays in Medieval Studies*, Illinois Medieval Association, vol. 12, 1995, (N. Clifton, ed., *Children and the Family in the Middle Ages*).
212 C. Harper-Bill, ed., *Charters of the Medieval Hospitals of Bury St Edmunds*, p.120.

abbot of St Edmunds, explained that 'some of the measures instituted by his predecessors [had] with the passing of time fallen into disuse' (p.133). He severely condemned certain wardens who had 'converted charity into profit' and who had not hesitated 'to admit many persons of both sexes, who were not sick, for a sum of money.' The abbot took measures: the poor flocking to the hospital for alms were to receive the said alms and 'since the cohabitation of the two sexes is regarded as suspect, the abbot decrees and ordains that as the sisters now dwelling there shall die, no other woman shall be admitted to live there, but as each woman dies in her place the number of aged and sick priests should be increased' (pp.133–134). Widows could no longer be admitted as sisters. The cartulary of the hospital shows that only the widows of the abbey's servants were henceforth helped when necessary. Such was the case in 1444 of Agnes after the death of her husband Simon Gillot:

> The majority of their children are still in their infancy, she is seriously ill, she cannot support the children from the goods left to her by her husband and she would have no means of sustaining them save by begging. She is therefore granted the corrody recently held by her late husband in St Saviour's, to be held for her lifetime. (p.150)

Elizabeth Rutledge mentions that in Norwich 'St Giles's hospital used older women to care for the sick poor'.[213] Yet the same general evolution is to be noticed in this town: the nursing sisters in the various hospitals were first paupers but, due to depressing economic circumstances and to a decrease in the donations of the burgesses, these poor women were gradually replaced by corrodians. Carole Rawcliffe in her study of *The Hospitals of Medieval Norwich* gives the example of the widowed Mary de Attleborough who, as early as 1309, 'settled her late husband's estates in Seething upon the house [St Giles's hospital], being promised a refuge there for life as one of the sisters.'[214] Wondering whether women found freedom in widowhood, Claudia Opitz notes that:

---

213 E. Rutledge, 'Economic Life', C. Rawcliffe & R. Wilson, eds., *Medieval Norwich*, p.181.
214 C. Rawcliffe, *The Hospitals of Medieval Norwich*, p.125.

The 'freedom of maiden and widow to serve their king' could be found only behind convent walls for the most part, and was accessible only to those with the means to buy entry into the rather exclusive communities of Benedictine, Cistercian, and later Dominican nuns. Poor women could hope to enter them only as lay sisters, that is to say, as servants. Such a step brought them no increase in personal freedom, for they lived at the beck and call of the religious sisters, noblewomen accustomed to giving orders.[215]

Peasant Widows

Utter poverty could easily be the lot of peasant widows. Court rolls and other documents evoke the state of dire poverty of certain women. The much-studied court rolls of the manor of Wakefield (Yorkshire) mention that Wymark, the widow of Robert Blodhehe, was sent to prison in 1275 for taking a hare found in her yard and 'she lay in prison for three weeks and has no goods. Let her go quit.'[216] *The Liber Gersumarum of Ramsey Abbey* set down that the lord granted to Katherina Chicheley 'one *camera* within a certain cote previously held by her late husband Simon (...) freely, without any burdens, for life, with free access to that *camera* by the King's road'. Katherina did not pay any fine 'because she [was] a pauper.'[217] In his anthology *Women in England c. 1275–1525*, P.J.P. Goldberg quotes several coroners' rolls that relate the fate of women reduced to vagrancy and beggary. As we have already mentioned in Chaucer's *Canterbury Tales* widows living in the countryside all seem poverty-stricken. Chantecleer's owner lives very poorly:

> A povre wydwe, somdeel stape in age
> Was whilom dwellyng in a narwe cotage,
> Biside a grove, stonfynge in a dale.
> This wydwe, of which I telle yow my tale,
> Syn thilke day that she was last a wyf
> In pacience ladde a ful symple lyf,

215 In C. Klapisch-Zuber, ed., *A History of Women*, p.309.
216 W. Paley Baildon, ed., *Court Rolls of the Manor of Wakefield. Vol.I 1274–1297*. http://www.fordham.edu/halsall/source/1274wakefield-courtrolls.html
217 E.B. DeWindt, ed., *The Liber Gersumarum of Ramsey Abbey: a Calendar & Index of B.L. Harley Ms 445*, p.57.

> For litel was hir catel and hir rente.
> By housbondrie of swich as God hire sente
> She foond hirself and eek hir doghtren two.
> Thre large sowes hadde she, and namo,
> Three keen, and eek a sheep that highte Malle.
> Ful sooty was hire bour and eek hir halle,
> In which she eet ful many a sklendre meel.
> Of poynaunt sauce hir neded never a deel.
> No deyntee morsel passed thurgh hir throte; (VII, 2821–2835)

Documents, however, very rarely concern landless and destitute people though these made up a not insignificant social group. Charters, registers, court rolls deal first and foremost with land transfers and taxes to be levied. The very poor, consequently, go unnoticed unless they were involved in some theft or murder. Records at our disposal show peasant widows who seemed to deal with the situation, who assumed their new responsibilities with courage and energy. They probably had no other choice. At the death of their husbands the question of carrying on or of giving up the latters' occupations did not crop up. Wives tilled the land: once widows they simply went on. It comes as no surprise therefore, that husbands unhesitatingly bequeathed their farming tools, grain and crops to their wives. Moreover, customary law shows that lords were not reluctant to seize widows in land since, as we have already detailed, rural law usually granted to widows from one-half to all of their husbands' tenures as their free-benches. Many widows purchased additional land while some of them recovered tenements they had inherited or that they may have brought as *maritagium*. In 1295 Isolda, the widow of John Quenyng, living in Godmanchester was seised for several plots of land and meadow and 'in addition she was seised of one messuage which formerly belonged to her father (...) along with 12 acres of land in the fields of Godmanchester from which the same Isolda holds four acres of land by title of free marriage and eight acres as heir and for these she pays the due services.'[218] Alice Smith, the widow of William Smith of Ashfield, was assigned her dower in 1393 in Walsham le

---

218   J.A. Raftis, *A Small Town in Late Medieval England. Godmanchester 1278–1400*, p.23.

Willows. As no heir came for the other half of the messuage and pieces of land, the lord granted it to her. In exchange:

> Alice will pay to the lord 4d. per year at the usual terms, and render, for the lord, to the capital lords of the fee the services and customs due therefrom; she will also pay to the lord of this manor the ancient rent of one hen per year.[219]

The other side of the coin was that, as can be noticed from these quotations, these women had to go on paying the various rents and perform the particular duties... on their own. *The Liber Gersumarum of Ramsey Abbey* indicates what was expected of villeins. Indeed, in October 1402 Nicholas atte Hyll of Burwell was seized in a tenement of twenty acres for twenty years: he was to 'render annually 15s. at the customary times, 4d. as common fine, and reaping, binding, and tribute of two acres of grain of the demesne land' while Nicholas Martyn of Little Raveley obtained 'one plot with building and one virgate of servile land (...) rendering annually 16s. At the customary times, as well as performing boon ploughing and autumn boon works, sheep-shearing, and mowing of the lord's meadow in Thornbriggemede.'[220] When Matilis, the widow of Thomas Koke, was seised of two acres of meadow previously held by a certain Richard Ive she was to render the same services and customs as the former male tenant. Unfortunately no further details are given. One can also mention Johanna, the widow of William Wassyngle, who was seized of 'one toft with a half-virgate of servile land recently held by William, for life, rendering annually 13s. 6d., *capitagium*[221] of 2d., and all other services and customs owed therein. In addition she will not dig *gabulum*, but she will cut timber within the vill to rebuild the toft and pay 10s. Heriot when it occurs.' (p.169). In 1279, on the manor of Altwalton (also in Huntingdonshire) held by the abbot of Peterborough Hugh Miller, a villein, had to pay 3s. 1d. for one virgate of land. Moreover

> The same Hugh works through the whole year except 1 week at Christmas, 1 week at Easter, and 1 at Whitsuntide, that is in each week 3 days, each with 1

---

219 R. Lock, ed., *The Court Rolls of Walsham le Willows. 1351–1399*, p.186.
220 E.B. Dewindt, ed., *The Liber Gersumarum of Ramsey Abbey*, p.51 & p.21.
221 Poll-tax, capitation (to be paid by the unfree tenants of a manor).

man, and in autumn each day with 2 men, performing the said works at the will of the said abbot as in plowing and other work. Like wise he gives 1 bushel of wheat for benseed and 18 sheaves of oats for foddercorn. Likewise he gives 3 hens and 1 cock yearly and 5 eggs at Easter. Likewise he does carrying to Peterborough and to Jakele and nowhere else, at the will of the said abbot. Likewise if he sells a brood mare in his court yard for 10s. or more, he shall give to the said abbot 4d., and if for less he shall give nothing to the aforesaid. He gives also merchet and heriot, and is tallaged at the feast of St Michael, at the will of the said abbot.

As this detailed description was established for the 1279 Hundred Rolls – a national census often considered as a second *Domesday Book* – the complete list of tenants is provided. There were seventeen other villeins and among them two women Emma ate Pertre and Emma widow of Ralph. All of them held one virgate of land in villeinage 'paying and doing in all things, each for himself, to the said abbot yearly just as the said Hugh Miller.' The survey went on with the thirty-four cotters of the manor. All of them, out of whom nine women (seven of whom were widows), had to pay a yearly rent and had to 'work for three days in carrying hay and in other works at the will of the said abbot, each day with 1 man and in autumn 1 day in cutting grain with 1 man.' The cotters, except the widows, also had 'to give yearly after Christmas a penny which is called head-penny.' The income of the widows was consequently considered as lower than that of the others.

'Villein tenants owed fealty and suit at all courts; their tenure was always at the lord's will and carried the burden of labour services at the lord's summons. In Walsham [le Willows] there is no evidence that the call to work was anything other than when needed. (...) Labour services were unavoidable and deeply unpopular.'[222] Here too female tenants were asked the same services as male villeins. It was the size of the tenure that determined the amount of agricultural services due to the lord – not the person who held it. For instance 'Olivia of Cranmer, when she died, held from the lord a quarter of a messuage 3 acres of land by services, as by others of the same tenure'

---

222 R. Lock, ed., *The Court Rolls of Walsham le Willows. 1303–1350*, introduction, p.15.

(p.103). Even more explicitly: John Hawys was amerced 20s. in 1391 for withholding labour work at harvest and at hay-making as well as not giving one hen, all of which 'he owes because he resides on a villein tenement' (vol. 2, p.172). The precise kinds of labour owed to the lord are rarely specified, the scribe usually simply mentioning that the new tenant is to render the same services and customs as the preceding one. Only a few entries give more details. In 1327, William Kembald entered one acre of land previously held by his father 'for services 2d. at Michaelmas, and at Christmas one hen, and one boon-work in autumn with food provided by the lord.' Boonwork was agricultural service due to the lord at peak periods, especially at ploughtime and harvest. In 1355 (vol. 2, p.44) John Packard held a third part of a messuage in six acres of land: the rent amounted 12d. 'and he will reap in autumn six days, and one hen; and he will plough per year two days', John Wodebite holding a much larger plot (twenty-four acres) and a whole messuage was charged 3s. 7¾d. and asked 'to reap in autumn 23 days; and will perform works after Michaelmas ten days; and he will pay in the first year six hens, and in the second year five hens; and he will be reeve or hayward, and he will plough two days per year, and 10 eggs.' Agnes Wodebite holding a messuage as well as ten acres of land was logically asked more than John Packard and less than John Wodebite:

> [She] pays per year 2s. 1¾d; and will reap 20 days; and will perform after Michaelmas 10 days and two hens in this year. And in the second three hens and 10 eggs; and will plough two days per year.

Once again the fact that she was a *femme sole* did not make any difference; she had to render the same services as the male tenants. This is why Agnes Chapman who held a messuage and three roods of land paid 6d. per year 'and will reap in autumn five days, and two hens' (vol. 2, p.45) and why Agnes Qualm was fined 2d. in 1390 'because she withheld from the lord 1¼ days work in autumn' (vol. 2, p.170). In 1353, John Spileman was fined 6d. 'because he withheld Cristina Springfold from reaping service in the autumn against the order of the bailiff.' At the same court Cristiana Lene and Isabella Spileman were punished and had to pay 3d. each 'because they were summoned to winnow the lord's corn for money at ¼d. per tass, and did not come' (vol. 2, p.41). In 1384 John Hawys was amerced 3d. 'because he withheld one hen, and other services at hay-making, and one day in autumn, which he ought to have performed for having the right of common, and which other free and villein tenants perform for the same right' (vol. 2, p.143). In this case the services were not performed in exchange of land but in order to be allowed to graze his sheep on the common of Walsham. Hoeing, gleaning or carting services are also sometimes mentioned.

Agricultural services often included the providing of supplementary workers. We have seen that Hugh Miller on the manor of Altwalton was to bring two men in autumn. John Jay was amerced 2s. 6d. in 1389 'because he did not come at the reeve's summons to perform three ploughing services with half a plough-team' (vol. 2, p.163). Widows would have had to provide the same workforce, which may have been yet another source of worry and difficulty. Moreover, ploughing and sowing were essentially masculine activities and most female householders probably hired day labourers for these tasks. A small number of widows preferred to make arrangements with relatives or neighbours and concluded contracts granting their real property in return for maintenance – accommodation, food and clothing – for the remainder of their lives. The maintainer was then the sole responsible for the various duties and services to the lord. Such was the case of William Hawys who obtained all of Olivia de Cranmer's lands and one tenement in Walsham, two horses, three cows and four quarters of corn. William 'allowed easement of the buildings in the messuage of the said tenement for the said Olivia, her servants, beasts and poultry', was to pay annually for Olivia's lifetime '2 quarters 4 bushels of wheat and 1 quarters 4 bushels of barley at Christmas and Easter' promised to maintain the tenement and buildings in good state and committed himself to rendering 'on Olivia's behalf, to the capital lords of the fee all the services and customs and all other obligations whatsoever, arising or occurring upon the said tenements' (vol. 2, p.133). Olivia had never married and was about sixty years old. The few widows choosing such an option were obviously old and/or with no dependent children. In 1380 Margaret Gilbert surrendered to her grown-up daughter 'all her portion of the messuage formerly of Matthew Gilbert [her late husband], and 1 acre 3 roods of land in a croft, granted to her by the rod, to hold by services and customs' (vol. 2, p.137). In 1388 John Patel died. In 1392 Catherine his ageing widow, clearly deep in debt, concluded an agreement with John Vincent, her son-in-law. She turned him over a messuage and twenty acres of villein land and pasture that had been held by her late husband together with all her chattels and utensils. The transfer was made under such condition that:

> John shall find for Catherine sufficient food and drink as her status demands, for her lifetime; and also to pay, or cause to be paid to her 6s. 6d., in place of clothing and footwear, at Christmas and Midsummer Days in equal portions. And also to pay, or cause to be paid, to the same Catherine 4 bushels of barley annually always at Michaelmas, during her lifetime, and also to pay, or cause to be paid, to her 2s. annually on 1 August, for hay produced from ½ acre of meadow. And Catherine shall have from the said John, on the day of her burial, a cow to go before the bier.[223] And she shall have for her lifetime easement of a chamber next to the door, for her own use, with free ingress and egress of the same. (...) Catherine shall perform well and properly the services of the said John at the appropriate times, whine she is able to work adequately, saving nevertheless to the said Catherine, the right to sell annually 12 ells of woollen cloth from her own wool, while she is able to work. (Vol. 2, p.181)

Ray Lock underlines the fact that there are only six instances of such provisional transactions in the rolls – therefore a tiny minority. Apart from Catherine the widow and Olivia the spinster, the other cases concerned one widower and three elderly couples. They all had in common to have been advanced in age. In her study of the widows of medieval Brigstock (Northamptonshire), Judith M. Bennett also noted the very small proportion of these bereaved women who were 'unwilling to meet their responsibilities as householder. Of the 101 unremarried widows in the community whose careers have been reconstructed (...) [only] three made arrangements for retirement.'[224] Most widows assumed their new responsibilities often helped, or sometimes

---

223 This means the son-in-law will pay a mortuary to the Church.
224 J.M. Bennett, *Women in the Medieval Countryside. Gender and Household in Brigstock before the Plague*, New York, Oxford: Oxford University Press, 1987, chapter VI 'Widows', p.151.

clearly maintained, by their children. In many wills husbands insist on their children supporting their mothers. Among the *Wills of the Archdeaconry of Sudbury* the most personal note comes from John Baldre of Thorney (Stowmarket) who stated:

> Richard my son to have all my lands and tenements, meadows, pastures and feedings, he to be good to Margaret his mother, to guide and support her for the whole of her lifetime, and to provide and dispose for our souls as a son should for his parents. (Will no.444)

The other instances are more down-to-earth but lead to the same conclusion: established children were expected to provide for their mothers when the need arose. Certain fathers bequeathed property to their sons or daughters on the strict condition they supported them. In 1445, for example, Peter Tilbrook left houses and lands to his son Thomas who was 'to keep his mother in food and clothing' (no.337), Richard Chapman demised his daughter Agnes all his customary lands and tenements 'on condition that she provide Margaret [his] wife with food, drink and all other necessities of life, as befits such a lady, and support her in sickness as in health for the whole term of her life' (no.393); Richard Adgor inherited his father's tenement and lands, both free and bond, 'on condition that he keep and support Isabel his mother' while his brother John was to pay his mother 'for term of her life 6s. 8d. at the usual terms of Easter and St Michael, by equal portions, for her own use' (no.609). Thomas Paxman transferred his tenement, a croft and several lands to his son 'on condition that he provide his mother Alice with sufficient food and drink and all her other necessaries for her lifetime' (no.911). John Meller demanded his son showed respect to his wife and provided everything for her 'as a woman of her degree ought to be provided for, and [paid] her 40d. annually, for term of her life' (no.1248). *The Liber Gersumarum of Ramsey Abbey* records similar dispositions, similar conditional land transfers. In 1407 John Biller was seised of his father's messuage and land 'with the condition that his mother, Agnes Biller, naif of the lord, will have one *camera* in the above messuage and be supported in all things for life by him' (p.77). In 1452 the same requirements were imposed on John Yvet for his father's messuage. He was also 'obligated to repair [his mother's] *camera* during the period' (p.350). The same year Isabella Marchall 'surrendered one messuage and a half-virgate of land recently held by her husband to the use of John Pope, his wife, Johanna, and their son, Thomas.' Isabella had more than a mere chamber: she kept a house and a parcel of the garden 'together with another parcel next to the house for supplying fuel, and fruits and yields of apple trees and one pear tree, with easement for one rooster and two hens' (p.349). John Pope, his wife and son were bound to repair and maintain the house during Isabella's lifetime. Obviously enough, the husbands knew that their wives would not be able to provide for themselves and would not be capable of doing hard farm work or seeing to the upkeep of the various buildings.

At a time when old age pensions did not exist it is not surprising that children should have been a prop to their elderly parents. Moreover, such agreements were to the advantage of both parties. They emphasize, once again, the importance of land which was the only real wealth. One must not forget, however, that many people were non-tenants on medieval manors. For Walsham le Willows Ray Lock estimates that before the outbreak of the Black Death (1349) there was 'an adult population of 940, of whom 176 were tenants and 764 were non-tenants (317 male and 447 female). (...) Among adults tenants were greatly outnumbered by non-tenants, particularly among women: two out of three men, and 19 out of every 20 women, were landless.'[225] These people go almost unnoticed in the rolls. 'Many of them were members of a tenant's family and worked on the family tenement. Some worked for other tenants, and some for the lord.'[226] In order to give a general idea of the various activities of these non-tenants one can mention that one finds references to labourers, servants, dairymaids, the lords' shepherds, cowherds, gooseherds, or swineherds; the gooseherd of the prior of Ixworth, the servants and shepherd of Sir Edmund de Pakenham are mentioned vol. 1, p.94, a certain Agnes is called 'the house servant of the lord' (vol. 1, p.166), Nicholas was Robert of Walpole's shepherd in 1344 (vol. 1, p.274). Margery Broun, a maidservant of the manor, was fined twelve pence

---

225   R. Lock, ed., *The Court Rolls of Walsham le Willows. 1303–1350*, p.17.
226   Ibid., p.18.

'because she unlawfully took apples and other things', three pence 'because she knocked over a vat containing three gallons of ale, to the lord's loss', and twelve pence 'because she took away flour from the bakehouse, to the lord's loss' (vol. 1, p.274). In 1317, Alice Lefe was amerced three pence 'for damage in the lord's beans by her servant' (vol. 1, p.55), in 1319 it was Eda Rede's turn 'because her servant took away the lord's straw without leave' (vol. 1, p.80). In 1327 Marsilia Hawys had to pay ½ mark because Oliver her servant 'unlawfully took corn from the lord in the autumn' (vol. 1, p.103). In 1339 Olivia Isabel was fined twelve pence for trespass against the lord 'because she did not make a linen cloth for the lady, as she was ordered' (vol. 1, p.238). Tenants in Walsham held relatively small tenements (9½ acres in average for those holding a messuage and land before the Black Death and only 3½ acres for those holding just land). It was probably very difficult for them to make both ends meet. One can easily imagine that life was even harder for the non-tenants and that elderly widows (or widowers) had next to nothing to offer to their children or relatives when they could no longer work.

It goes without saying that widows with young children had no choice but to go on working. In Walsham children reached full age when they were sixteen years old.[227] Before that age they were in the custody of their mothers 'by right and custom of the manor' (vol. 1, p.51). There were two manors in Walsham: Walsham manor (sometimes called Walsham Hall) and High Hall which was much smaller. Walsham Churchhouse was the name given to the holding of the Prior of Ixworth (from 1409 onwards). The oldest written custumal that has survived for Walsham le Willows dates back to 1577. It confirms that inheritance law in Walsham was gravelkind, that is to say the division of the lands and goods of a deceased between all his sons, not just the eldest inheriting all. The 1577 *Field Book of Walsham le Willows* states that:

---

[227] This too varied greatly from on place to another. In Godmanchester girls came of age at 16 and boys at 20.

> It is our custom of this manor that if any tenant die seised of his copy lands and tenements, the same to be equally divided and parted amongst all his sons, according to the law of gravelkind.[228]

This is why at the death of Robert Kembald his heirs were his three sons John, Thomas and John. Yet as they were all under age, 'the tenement was granted to Catherine Kembald their mother, to hold until their full age, by services and customs' (vol. 2, p.117). As the lord got a horse worth 13s. 4d. as heriot no entry fine was paid. Richard Reve's two heirs, his sons John and William, were entrusted to their mother's care (vol. 1, p.205) and so were ten-year-old William and six-year-old Robert, the two sons of Hilary Lene. Her late husband had died holding a messuage, a cottage, thirty-seven acres of arable land, one acre and two roods of meadow, one acre and two roods of wood. Hilary obtained half of all these goods as her dower and the custody of the other half:

> She being answerable to the lord and to the heirs, when they come of age, for the income from the land and chattels over and above the maintenance and repair of the buildings and land; and she pays 40s. Fine for entry and custody.' (Vol. 1, p.132)

The rolls show that when a beast had been given to the lord as a heriot, the widow was often not asked to pay any entry fine. In the case of William Lene an ox, worth 13s. 4d., had been given. The size of the tenement probably explains why Hilary Lene had to pay both. As a matter of fact the entry fine was not fixed but proportional to the number of acres of the holding. Cecilia Wyndilgard, who was granted custody of a quarter of a messuage and three roods of land until her five-year-old son came of age, was only asked six pence because of the small size of the holding and 'because John had no beast' (vol. 1, p.52). Amice Chapman also gave six pence for a messuage with two

---

[228] K. Melton Dodd, ed., *Field Book of Walsham le Willows, 1577*, Suffolk Records Society, vol. XVII, 1974, p.50. Walsham Churchhouse had a different system since 'if any tenant of this manor die seised then the custom of this manor is that his eldest son is his heire to his copyhold lands and tenements holden of this manor, if he have daughters and noe sons, then the same is to be equally deivided between them.'

acres of land but added an ewe as a heriot when she was granted custody of her three-year-old daughter and of the latter's land (vol. 1, p.319). Matilda Lene did not pay anything: her late husband only held half a rood of meadow and a sheep, worth twenty pence had been given to the lord. 'Therefore seisin is granted to Matilda Lene, Nicholas' mother, so that the heir may have entry by the heriot, following the custom of the manor' (vol. 2, p.82). William Coppelowe died seised of a bigger (though small) tenement, a messuage seven acres of land, half of which his widow had as dower. She was granted the custody of the other half until the full age of her two-year-old son 'by services and customs, on condition that she maintains the house and messuage in as good a state as she received it. Fine for custody 40d.' (vol. 1, p.113). On that subject, Matilda Wodebite was amerced twelve pence in February 1334 for she 'allowed [her son's] house to decay' and was ordered to have it rebuilt by Michaelmas (September 29th) (vol. 1, p.172). Matilda had been given custody of her son's holding five years earlier, paying then the high sum of 6s. 8d. because there were '2½ messuages and 23 acres of land' (vol. 1, p.126). The tenement may have proved too big for the poor woman. It comes then as no surprise to see five entries below that Matilda remarried that same year (1334), her new husband paying ½ mark 'for entry to the tenement of Matilda his wife which she holds from the lord in villeinage.'

Remarriage was a common option for young widows with small children. Most studies concerning English rural society conclude that about twelve/fourteen per cent of villagers were widows.[229] Men seem to have remarried rapidly and to have died, as is still the case today, younger than women. Out of the 1497 wills and probates edited by Peter Northeast, 214 were made by women and 1283 by men; 83 of the 213 women were explicitly widows and only 46 of the men were unmistakably widowers. Local and general economic conditions also played a major role in remarriage: availability of land was a key factor. Before the Black Death, widows were highly coveted for their lands but as after the plague there was more land available for every-

---

[229] There were, of course, variations: in Halesowen, studied by Zvi Razi, where land was scarce, six widows out of ten remarried.

one and they were then less in demand. Judith Bennett's examination of the marriage licence fines in Ramsey's *Liber Gersumarum* shows that between 1398 and 1458 only 47 out of the 426 *merchet*[230] payments mentioned were from widows.[231] The court rolls of Walsham le Willows edited by Ray Lock begin in 1303 and end in 1399: this almost complete series spans a whole century enabling us to assess the situation before and after the Black Death. The peak of the plague epidemics reached Walsham in June 1349. At the next court general in November 1349 there had clearly been a frenzy of matrimonial activity in the previous months or weeks. In particular many women, having lost their husbands because of the plague, were amerced for having remarried without leave. The roll records that Margaret, the widow of Richard Patel († June 1349), was amerced 3s. 4d. 'because she married Adam Fitzpiers without leave' (vol. 1, p.328), that Alice Fraunceys who had married John Deeth in 1342 only paid 2s. when remarrying Nicholas Deneys for her late husband only had a cotland and no beast, or that Alice (sometimes called Agnes), the widow of John Rampolye was fined 4s. for marrying Edmund Lene without leave. Eleanor, the widow of William Wither (who also died in June 1349) surrendered her tenement to the lady in order to be seised again jointly with her new husband, John at the Meadow. John obtained thus full possession of the land: 'if they die without heirs, the tenement shall revert to John's rightful heirs. (...) They pay a fine for entry. Eleanor pays a fine for leave to marry John' (vol. 1, p.329). Both fines amounted to 26s. 8d. Alice Terwald married Robert of Cranmer in October 1348 paying 20s. fine for leave. Robert died eight months later in June 1349. Alice did remarry but not before 1359 when, by the lady's leave, she wedded Roger Prede of Gislingham. Unfortunately we are only told that 'she paid a fine' (vol. 2, p.54). One hundred and three victims of the plague are recorded in the roll. Nothing is said of

---

230 A fine paid by a tenant or bondsman to his overlord for liberty to give his daughter in marriage (*OED*). A widow who happened to be a villein by blood (the daughter of a villein) was liable for the fine.
231 J. Bennett, 'Medieval Peasant Marriage: an Examination of Marriage License Fines in the *Liber Gersumarum*, J.A. Raftis, ed., *Pathways to Medieval Peasants*, Toronto: Pontifical Institute of Mediaeval Studies, 1981.

the widows who did not remarry and of all those whose husbands had no land and therefore were not listed among the deceased.

Let us now meet a few of the widows who lived in fourteenth-century Walsham le Willows and see what solutions they opted for after their husbands' deaths. Wives play almost no role in the rolls, their husbands acting on their behalf in all domains. Widows, on the other hand, come to the front, swearing fealty to the lords, purchasing and surrendering land, entering into contracts, suing for debt, answering for their own crimes and offences... and disappear again when they remarry. Eleanor was William Wither's wife for at least twenty-two years and though her husband is mentioned many times, we only hear of her twice: once in 1327 when she was Olivia of Cranmer's nearest heir for 'a quarter of a messuage 3 acres of land' (vol. 1, p.103) and in 1349 when she remarried John at the Meadow after only a few months of widowhood. She is mentioned one last time in 1362 because her husband sold, without the lord's leave, an acre of underwood from the tenement Wither that was part of her dower. As for her husband, John at the Meadow, he is mentioned many other times till 1376. Similarly the name of Margaret Patel/Fitzpiers only occurs when a land transfer concerns the tenement she obtained after the death of her late husband: in November 1350 she and her second husband were amerced six pence 'because they demised the tenement of Richard Patel the younger to Robert Tanne for a term of years, without leave' (vol. 1, p.335). She had not even been mentioned when Adam Fitzpiers had been ordered to 'make good waste in the bondage on the tenement formerly of Rochard Patel the younger' (vol. 1, p.334).

Because Cristina Machon was a widow she conducted her own land transactions and, as most peasant widows, was primarily concerned with the sharing out of the lands she held to her children. She was actively engaged in purchasing and selling (very small) pieces of land, surrendering first one and a half rood of land to Robert Lene in 1317, then half an acre to William Lene and one acre to William of Cranmer in the same year, one rood to William Lene in 1318, and eventually 'a messuage and 2 acres of land in two pieces' to her daughter Catherine in 1319. In 1319, Agnes Machon sold her one and a half acre of land. We also learn that her son Walter, who is often reported in the rolls as a fugitive, surrendered to William of Cranmer the right he had by inheritance in one and half acre of land which she held in dower and which should have reverted to her son after her death.

The court rolls of Walsham le Willows shed light on three generations of widows in the Kembald family. The Kembalds seem to have been a troublesome family. We first meet Matilda, Simon Kembald's wife, in 1317 when she was amerced six pence 'for the regrating of ale' (vol. 1, p.37). Two years later she was caught unawares 'taking away the lord's crop from villein land into a free tenement' (p.87) and fined five pence, her husband pledging for her. Her husband had been fined six pence in 1316 for taking 'goods and chattels from the lord's bondage into the free tenement where he lives' (p.35). In 1324, she was 'amerced because she took away straw and firewood from the lord's yard' (p.93). She was engaged in plea of trespass with William Kembald about the sowing of their land and the quarrel lasted several months. At the same time 'William [was] amerced 3d. because he intervened against Matilda in a plea of covenant, and Matilda [was] amerced 3d. for a false claim against William in a plea of debt' (p.95). During these same years Simon, Matilda's husband, was several times called to order while their two daughters, Catherine and Alice, 'gave birth outside wedlock. Simon is free. His daughters are not with him, and were not with him for five years before the time of the births' (p.88). This same Catherine, together with Hilary Kembald, 'took away handfuls of the lord's oats' in 1321 (p.91). On March 18th 1325, Matilda, together with her daughter Alice and her son William, were present at the court presided by Nicholas de Walsham: Simon being dead, his widow and heirs owed fealty and suit at all courts as all villein tenants. Things went from bad to worse. In March 1326 the jurors said that

> The tenement Kembald is wasted and damaged by William Kembald chaplain and Nicholas Kembald, amerced 12d; ordered to warn them to rebuild by the next court, under penalty. Also that Matilda Kembald has made waste in her tenement, amerced 6d; ordered that she repairs it by the next court.
> (...)
> The whole homage elected William Kembald the younger to the office of reeve for the whole tenement Kembald which contains 12 acres of land.

(...) William declined to hold office as elected.
(...) William Kembald chaplain amerced 3d. for default; ordered to distrain him to reply to the lord concerning apple and other wood, taken by him from the manor house. (p.98)

One can wonder whether the size of the tenement is not the clue to so many petty thefts, twelve acres being small for so many adults. Unless they all held other lands, either on the manor itself or from another lord (Simon had lived on a free tenement), so that nobody really felt responsible for the tenement. At the next court, in April 1327, the Kembalds were given a deadline 'to repair and make good the aforesaid tenement, under penalty of forfeiting all the crops of their tenements. Matilda Kembald also has a day until Michaelmas to rebuild, repair, and make good her tenement' (p.99). In 1330 Nicholas, another of Matilda and Simon's sons, paid three pence 'because he did not rebuild on the tenement Kembald' (p.139). Meanwhile Matilda, clearly unable to cope with the situation, had remarried in 1327: 'Matilda the widow of Simon Kembald holds in dower 6 acres of land of villeinage, and she pays 12d. fine for leave to marry' (p.101). She imediately quarrelled with two of her sons and was asked to pay six pence 'for a false claim against Nicholas and William Kembald, in two complaints' (p.99). Life went on as hectic as before for Matilda. She and her new husband, Oliver the Shepherd, were often in trouble for lack of money and all sorts of dishonest deeds. Matilda was accused of detention of chattels (p.130), the couple was amerced three pence for a false claim in a plea of dower (p.137), Oliver was twice fined for not giving back bushels of wheat or of barley borrowed from other villeins. Oliver died in 1335 leaving a cotland that was retained in the lord's hands. Matilda's death is nowhere recorded. Her son William died between 1362 and 1366. Her other son, Nicholas, died in 1335 leaving three sons under the age of twelve. He only held from the lord three roods of land. His wife obtained custody of the children. When she died of the plague in 1349, only two sons were mentioned. Thomas became a chaplain and surrendered his goods to his brother Robert '12 acres of land, 1 acre of meadow and half of a villein messuage'. Obviously he had either bought land or rather his father's three roods were his customary land, his other real estates not being mentioned. One must not forget that their grandfather lived on a free tenement and that they were listed in 1361 as 'freemen holding villein land' (vol. 2, p.59). In 1367 Robert demised to his brother Thomas a solar, a store-room and a garderobe within his messuage (p.90). Robert died in 1373 leaving a messuage, 18 acres of land, 3 acres of meadow and three underage sons. 'Because they are under age, the tenement was granted to Catherine Kembald their mother, to hold until their full age, by services and customs' (p.117). In September 1375 Alice swore fealty to the lords. Her eldest son died in 1376, 'seised of a messuage and 25 acres of land, and 3 acres of customary land. Thomas Kembald, John's uncle, is his nearest heir and of full age' (p.124). Thomas who had got rid of all his lands in 1360 by giving them to his brother was now at the head of a tenement twice larger. After the Black Death the average holding of tenants who had a messuage was 12½ acres and for those holding land only, 6½ acres. Thomas was on his own with twenty-eight acres of land while so many people of the Kembald tenement had visibly struggled along at the beginning of the century. What happened to Alice and the two other sons is not clear, none of them being ever mentioned afterwards. Thomas the chaplain eventually surrendered 'to John Hereward and his heirs, a messuage and 26 acres of land and 3 acres of meadow, together with the reversion of 1 rood of meadow, which Agnes Warde holds for her lifetime. (...) Easement of the bakery in the same tenement was granted to the same Thomas for his lifetime' (p.135). Thomas is last mentioned in 1385. That was the end of the line.

 One can easily imagine the problems, both affective and material, the numerous family quarrels that these repeated marriages were likely to entail: literary works, especially folk tales, give evidence of the strained relationships that the existence of step-mothers, step-fathers and step-children brought about. Widows often had to cope with these tense situations. The widow of William Dunbar's *Tretis* glorifies herself for having favoured her own children to the detriment of those of her husband of a previous marriage:

> I buskit up my barnis like baronis sonnis,
> And maid bot fulis of the fry of his first wif.
> I banyst fra my boundis his brethir ilkane;

His frendis as my fais I held at feid evir. (402–405)
[I brought up my children like noblemen's sons and made the fry of his first wife creatures of no account; I banished from my bounds all his brothers and his relations I always held in hatred as my enemies.]

In *The Tale of Beryn* dying Agea begs her husband Fawnus to take care of their son:

Let hym have no Stepmodir; for Children have to-fore,
Comenlich they lovith nat. Wherfor, with hert I prey,
Have cher on-to yeur sone, aftir my endyng day. (984–986)[232]

Later on when Fawnus is remarried, his son Beryn explains that stepmothers are all shrews (1282). Some of these tensions are reflected in Walsham's court rolls. Peter Angerhale died childless in 1315. His widow, Alice, remarried John Packard, a free plough-holder, in 1320. We are not told when Alice died but John remarried in 1350: 'Alice Helpe, freewoman, who holds customary land, married John Packard without leave.' Alice was the widow of John Helpe who had died in 1349. Alice had then paid six pence to have her late husband's tenement, 'a portion of a messuage 3 acres of land by the rod (...) until the heir comes.' The rest of the story shows that Alice was pregnant. The relationship between John Packard and John Helpe junior were very bad. John came of age in 1366 and asked admittance to '12 acres 3 roods of land, with a messuage and a third part of 1 acre of wood, as the nearest heir of John Helpe his father. ' (vol. 2, p.86). His stepfather was unwilling to surrender to John what belonged to him. A long list of John's goods is given: 'the jurors say that John Packard is in unlawful possession of 2 mares, 2 calves, a cart with all its equipment, a tumbril without a rack, a pair of shafts for the same, a coulter, a ploughshare, a bucket, 2 trivets, a spade, a mattock, 1 bushel of straw, a worn winnowing fan, etc.' (p.87). Moreover John Packard had not maintained his step-son's tenement:

---

232 F.J. Furnivall & G. W. Stone, eds., *The Tale of Beryn, with a Prologue of the Merry Adventures of the Pardoner with a Tapster at Canterbury*, Chaucer Society (Supplementary Canterbury Tales, 1), London: Trübner, 1887.

> John Packard amerced 3d. for waste made in the tenement of John Helpe, two barns being demolished and other buildings fallen into ruins. (p.87)

It must be noted that the manor court was essential in the protection of the interests and rights of the weakest, the widows but also the under-age heirs.

Another step-father who quarrelled with his step-son was John Man. In 1334 John, a widower, married Matilda, the widow of John Wodebite († 1329) paying ½ mark for entry to the tenement of Matilda. Matilda had three children, all of age. She had badly maintained her late husband's holding 'allowing the house to decay' (vol. 1, p.172). In 1336 after an enquiry of the whole homage it was decided that Matilda should be deprived of the tenement she held in dower the upkeep of which she and her husband had not seen to. Rather alarmed, John Man immediately paid the fine for the waste. In the summer of the same year John Wodebite junior complained that his step-father had not given him the money for a quarter of wheat worth 6s. 8d. 'which John Man cannot deny' (p.201). He also explained that John Man was supposed to find for him 'his reasonable upkeep in food, clothing and all necessities from Michaelmas for three years. But John Man refused to keep the agreement and still does, to the loss of John Wodebite of 40s.' (p.201). John Man was obliged to pay the 40s. claimed by his wife's son. A third quarrel, a plea of waste, brought the two men into conflict. Unfortunately we never hear the mother's voice: as a wife she had no say in the matter. Her husband only was expected to settle the affair and, consequently, only his version of the facts is given. In 1338 John Wodebite died, his two sisters were his nearest heirs; they shared '11 acres of land, meadow and wood, with two built messuages and half a messuage' (p.223). The eldest was Agnes (Alice) who first married John Rampolye in 1346 and Edmund Leve in 1350 after her first husband's death in 1349.

The story of the Coppelowe family is the saddest. William died in 1328 holding a messuage 7 acres of land. His son, William, was only two years old and the mother obtained custody in 1328. The following year there appeared a quarrel between Matilda and Hilary Coppelowe, her step-daughter. The jurors 'ordered to attach Matilda the widow of William Coppelowe, to satisfy Hilary William's daughter concerning goods and chattels bequeathed to Hilary by William, which are in Matilda's keeping' (p.125). At the next court, only a month later in July 1329, the list of the goods and chattels was given. The unlawful detention included:

> A cow, worth 5s., 2 piglets, worth 8d., 4 bushels of wheat, worth 5s., 4 bushels of oats, worth 2s., 1 tub, worth 3d., 1 brass bowl containing 1½ gallons, worth 7d., and 2 hens. (...) Memorandum that the goods together with Hilary were delivered to Walter Osbern for custody, because he is her blood relation. (p.128)

Matilda Coppelowe remarried in 1332, wedding Geoffrey Rath. They chose not to keep Matilda's now five-year-old son with them:

> Geoffrey Rath and Matilda Coppelowe his wife come into open court and surrender into the lord's hands the custody and care of William Matilda's son, aged five years, together with all her dower, until his full age. (p.152)

Here too only the bare facts are recorded. The reason(s) why the couple decided not to keep the child is not explained. One is not told whether it was a joint decision or if Matilda was forced to do so by her new husband. Because the mother rejected her son she was asked to relinquish her dower. Geoffrey Rath may have considered that the boy would cost him more than the yield of the 7 acres of land. To whom the boy was entrusted is not specified. And nothing is said about the feelings of the various protagonists. Hilary died in June 1348 holding only 1½ rood of customary land. Her heir was her brother William 'who [did] not come' (p.311). The next mention of William Coppelowe occurs in 1353 (vol. 2, p.40). William died in 1358 at the age of thirty-one. In 1365 'the lord granted to John Terwald all those lands and tenements which William Coppelowe formerly held, which have remained in the lord's hands for the past seven years, because nobody was willing to receive them' (p.80). The Black Death had not killed William but had totally devalued his probably not very fertile land.

Wills also testify to possible disharmony between mothers and children. Testators sometimes insisted on their children behaving well towards their mothers. Widows brought up their children on their own; they had to deal with all the various difficulties: sickness, teen-age years, inheritance quarrels and money matters with the senior ones. Adam Onge bequeathed all his property to his son after the death of his wife. But 'if he do not behave well towards his mother, he is to have nothing.'[233] John Fen asked his son John 'to be obedient to his mother' and had the same recommendation for his daughter Agnes (will no.235). John Lenge demanded that 'none of his children to trouble Katherine their mother on account of anything assigned to them above' (no.287). Thomas Godard took into account the fact that his wife and his son might not agree in his tenement in the town of Bradfield, 'she then to have all my tenement and pay William half the farm of the tenement yearly' (no.412). John Pyke threatened his daughter: '(...) provided that Isabel be obedient to her mother in all things, but if she act contrarily the two tenements to be sold' (no.634). Conversely wills show that many step-fathers or step-mothers got on well with their step-children. Robert Blak demised 'to [his] wife's son [his] furred gown' (no.45), John Swayn made no difference betwen his daughter and his step-daughter: 'to Agnes Barker my daughter 6s. 8d.; to Agnes Mellere my wife's daughter 6s. 8d.' (no.164), Nicholas Baret left 'to Eleanor, the daughter of Agnes my wife, 6s. 8d. out of [his] goods (no.222), Anne Catour forgot neither her servant nor her stepchildren (no.321), John Schomer left 'to Alice, [his] wife's daughter, 26s. 8d.' (no.334) John Waryn bequeathed 'to Joan, the daughter of Amflote [his third] wife, [his] best chest and a little piece of silver and 5 marks in money' (no.474). Though John Borle had a son and a daughter he was particularly generous with his step-sons. He left 'to Thomas Pellycan, [his] wife's son a tenement with the adjacent garden, next to the tenement assigned to Joan [his] daughter, to him and his heirs. (...) to James Pellycan, [his] wife's son a tenement with the adjacent garden, next to the tenement assigned to the said Thomas, to him and his heirs' (no.800).

Other wills, on the other hand, prove that many husbands considered their wives possible remarriage with a critical eye. One can imagine that some of them may have felt sad or, even, jealous. John

---

233 P. Northeast, ed., *Wills of the Archdeaconry of Sudbury. 1439–1474*, will no. 124, p.48.

Olney says that his wife is 'his most trusty friend' while Roger Flore speaks of his 'welbeloved wife'.[234] Most of them, however, were more practical and well aware of the difficulties that a second marriage could bring about as far as inheritance was concerned. Their reluctance was therefore the result of their concern about protecting the interests of their family in general and of their children in particular. Thomas Struth demised all his tenement called 'Hervyis' to his wife Alice 'that is, provided she remain unmarried' (no.456), Robert Schucford left to his wife Agnes his tenement and the utensils belonging to the house 'as long as she remains a widow' (no.506), John Derby left the residue of all his goods and chattels to his executors, including his wife 'provided that Joan keep herself a widow for the whole term of her life' (no.803), John Bullok bequeathed to his wife Margery all his lands and tenements in the town of Woolpit:

> To hold for 14 years from now, on condition she remain unmarried and that she keep up the dues and repairs of the property in that time, at her own cost; after the end of the 14 years the premises to remain to Adam Bullok my son, to him and his heirs for ever, on condition that he pay Margery 6s. 8d. a year during her lifetime, if she remain unmarried. (no.757)

Regnold Facon insisted he did not want his wife to remarry: 'Alice also to have my tenement in Groton, to her and her heirs, on condition she remain unmarried after my death; if she do remarry, contrary to my wish, the tenement to remain to Alice for term of her life only' (no.843). Roger Pekerell was less generous deciding that if his wife remarried the tenement he had bequeathed to her was to pass to his son Thomas (no.1451). And John Markys was straightforward:

> If Marion marry again before my children come to legal age, she to have nothing of, nor take any profit from, the said lands and tenements, but they to remain in the hands of my feoffees, or of the feoffees of the said John Markys and Richard Markys or their attorneys, to dispose as above, according to their discretion, and Marion to be removed from the tenements and lands, and the profits from them, after she has remarried. (no.1296)

---

234 F.J. Furnivall, ed., *Fifty Earliest English Wills*, p.48 & p.56.

Whatever the reason, many peasant women did not remarry, all the more so after the Black Death. Like Judith Bennett's Alice in Brigstock, Alice Pye in Walsham le Willows 'assumed many of the functions of her dead husband' and was 'left in a new position of public authority.'[235] Actually Alice did remarry: when we first meet her in the rolls in 1316 she is referred to as 'Alice, the widow of Stephen Spileman'. As she died in 1377 she was probably very young at the time. In January 1317 'Walter Pye [paid] for leave to marry Alice Spileman' and 'Alice Spileman paid 2s. fine for leave to marry Walter Pye' (vol. 1, p.46). Alice released to the lord a tenement ('2 acres 1 rood of land lying in two pieces') she had just bought, she and Walter paid a new entry fine and held the tenement in joint tenancy: 'the lord granted the tenement to Walter Pye and Alice, and the heirs born to them' (p.47). Walter was a brewer and till his death in 1341 was very often fined because 'he brewed and sold ale in breach of the assize'. In 1340 a new tenement (a messuage 14ft wide and 6 perches long as well as another messuage) was seized to the couple 'to hold for the lifetime of them both. After their death, the tenement shall revert to Amice and Robert, the children of Walter and Alice' (p.249). A year later Walter was dead:

> Walter Pye, who died since the last court, held from the lord 2 acres ½ rood of customary land, by services and works. (...) William and Robert Walter's sons are his nearest heirs, and they have entry by the heriot. He also held 1 acre of free land of the fee of Robert Sare, for fealty and services 1d per year. (p.255)

The various messuages that Alice and Walter held jointly were naturally not mentioned. They were now held by Alice alone for the remainder of her life. Alice and Walter had been married twenty-four years and Alice was to be a widow for the following thirty-six years. Though she had probably brewed ale with her husband, especially as brewing was a very common female activity in the Middle Ages, her name never appears next to that her husband who was amerced nineteen times between 1327 and 1341 for being in breach of the ale

---

[235] J.M. Bennett, *Women in the Medieval Countryside. Gender and Household in Brigstock before the Plague*, p.143.

assize.[236] The husband was solely responsible for the couple's deeds. Once a widow, Alice had no choice but to take full responsibility, she was now the new head of the household. Immediately after Walter's death Alice was 'amerced 9d. because she brewed and sold ale in breach of the assize' (vol. 1, p.258). She was fined eleven times between 1342 and 1360. Her two sons succeeded her as both of them are referred to as brewers in the 1380s. Alice ran her tenement for many years. Apart from brewing ale, she also tended beasts. In 1349 she had to pay nine pence 'for having a fold of 30 sheep' (vol. 1, p.328) while in 1367 it was ordered 'to retain a cow taken upon Alice Pye, and to take more, until she justifies herself in reply to Robert Kembald in a plea of debt' (vol. 2, p.93). Nothing more is said about this matter. Alice and Robert Kembald did not get on very well because she had to respond to other complaints lodged by this villager: as widow, and therefore as householder, she came to court many times. In March 1368, Robert tried an action against her but in July of the same year was amerced three pence 'for an unjust complaint against Alice pye in a plea of trespass' (p.96). In January 1369 Robert started again for the jurors ordered 'to attach Alice Pye to reply to Robert Kembald in a plea of trespass' while he was fined a penny 'for trespass against Willam Pye [Alice's son] in his peas, to the loss assessed by the enquiry at 2d.' (p.101). Alice came to court in March 1370 to reply to Robert and was eventually 'amerced 2d. for leave to agree with Robert Kembald in a plea of trespass' in July 1370. Alice's public assertion also took the form of her swearing fealty on two occasions to

---

236 This 13th-century statute concerning bread and ale was enforced by manorial courts. It stated that 'When a quarter of wheat is sold for 3s. or 3s. 4d. and a quarter of barley for 20d. or 2s., and a quarter of oats for 16d., then brewers in cities ought and may well afford to sell two gallons of beer or ale for a penny, and out of cities to sell 3 gallons for a penny. And when in a town 3 gallons are sold for a penny, out of a town they ought and may sell four; and this Assize ought to be holden throughout all England.' A. Luders, ed., *The Statutes of the Realm: Printed by Command of His Majesty King George the Third, in Pursuance of an Address of the House of Commons of Great Britain, From Original Records and Authentic Manuscripts*, 11 vols., (London: Record Commission, 1810–1828), vol. 1, p. 200. http://www.fordham.edu/halsall/source/breadbeer.html

Walsham's new lords: in 1369 she was one of the four women among fifty-seven men who attended the first court of William de Ufford, Earl of Suffolk and one of the eleven women (against seventy-two men) who swore fealty to Robert de Swillington and Sir Roger de Boys in 1375. She did not pledge for William her servant when he was wrongfully accused of cutting 'a hedgerow badly to the lord's loss' in 1364 (p.74) for in Walsham, contrary to other manors, widows did not seem to pledge for their dependents.[237] And she did not serve as one of the officers (juror, affeerer, reeve, hayward, aletaster) because these were masculine functions only. Alice died in 1377:

> [She was] seised of a pightle and 5 acres of villein land. The lord has a cow as heriot; William Pye, her son, who is her nearest heir, came and the lord granted seisin to him. (p.132)

Alice is a good example of an 'independent' widow having full power over her affairs and managing her property within the strict bounds of the manorial law and customs (but the latter applied to men just the same). Most of us would tend to believe that she certainly enjoyed the privileges conveyed by her status. This may, however, be a twenty-first-century view and one will never know whether Alice may have liked to have been a wife for longer years.

Widows' Last Wishes

Another right that widows enjoyed was that they could make a will and testament – which was not the case of wives (unless authorized by their husbands to do so). Many widows required to be buried beside their husbands and almost always remembered to provide for the souls of their late spouses. Apart from gentlewomen, widows did not usually have much land to bequeath, their dower and tenements held in jointure automatically reverting to the heir. Unsurprisingly those who did possess landed property demised it to their relatives: children came first but they also left land to brothers and sisters or nephews and nieces and, exceptionally, to cousins. Wills made by women are,

[237] I have found only one reference to a woman pledging for her daughter: vol. 1, p.285.

on the whole, much shorter than those written or dictated by men. They prove again, if need be, that widows were less involved than men in acquiring and managing property and that they simply had fewer goods to transmit. They, above all, made their wills once all the family property had been shared out, therefore what they could hand over was reduced to their own personal belongings. This is probably why wills made by widows are usually less formal and give fascinating details of medieval everyday life. As the testatrixes could do what they wanted with their (sometimes few) belongings, one gets a glimpse of their network of friends and of the people they valued. Very often their bequests focused on female members of the family, but not always. Lady Alice West, for instance, made bequests to her son, daughter-in-law, daughter and sister but also to her servants and poor tenants:

> I bequethe xl.yi. to be departed among my pouere tenauntes oueral where I haue lordschipe.
> (...)
> Also I bequethe to Elizabeth Rogers wif Newe whic that was my seruaunt somtyme c.s. Also I bequethe to Iuliane Arny, and to Ion Arny her hosebonde, of dudlynton c.s. Also I bequethe to Richard Forstrer, whic is a blynd man dwellynge in Hanefeld, that was somtyme seruant with my forsed lord Sir Thomas West, xx marcs. Also I bequethe to Roger, my parkere, of Ewhurst, c.s. Also I bequethe to Iohn Smart that was somtyme my forseyd lordes bailiff, Sir Thomas West, atte Hempston c.s. Also I bequethe to Iohn Smyth, my reue of Trestwode, c.s.[238]

Widows rarely forgot to leave something to their godsons or goddaughters and to their servants. They usually demised their clothes to their daughters or daughters-in-law as Margaret Payn[239] who wished his son's wife to have a tabard (p.78) or Margaret Smyth who left her daughter-in-law '[her] clothing, with [her] beads, and other necessities' (p.114). Marion Smyth of Stowmarket thought of her 'husband's mother and Helen her daughter' (p.59). Isabel Turnour of Sudbury gave Joan her servant '[her] violet hood' and her granddaughter her

---

238 F.J. Furnivall, ed., *Fifty Earliest English Wills*, p.8.
239 All following references to P. Northeast, ed., *Wills of the Archdeaconry of Sudbury*.

'green gown lined with blue card, and a pair of amber beads' (p.65). Anne Catour of Ixworth left a long list of household items to her servant to the value of forty shillings, another to the value of twenty shillings to her daughter and also left money for her stepchildren (p.120). Katherine Hynton mentioned her mother, sister, nephews, brother, daughter, goddaughter, and husband for she was a remarried widow (p.140).

The bequests made by these widows consisted mainly in household articles similar to those found in testaments made by men: chests, pots and pans, table wares, bedding, clothing, and jewels. Women tend to give more details: Isabel Lane left 'to John Meller [her] oldest cloak, to [her] daughter [her] best furred gown, [her] best cloak and the best furred tunic and a pair of jet beads' (p.23). Joan Boleman was very precise:

> To Joan a blue gown lined with blue card; to Joan Godad my goddaughter my russet cloak lined with'blewcard'; a green coat furred with rabbit skin, a red kirtle, a kerchief and a smock; to Alice Peyton my blue tabard lined with red cloth; to Avice Dey my red bed-cover with a blanket and a sheet, a kerchief, my green hood, a russet coat and my red kirtle. (p.57)

Rose Walter Place's list was short but as concrete: 'To Christian Boun a chest and a pair of sheets; to John Broun a black chest; to Agnes Broun a brass pan holding 7 gallons, to Matilda Kemp, my daughter, a cow' (p.46). The rest of her bequests were alms 'to the fabric of the tower' and a sum of money for the gild of St Mary. All the wills made by women in the collection are full of these details. Close to reality and everyday life, they are moving lists of personal belongings. Widows showed interest in distributing material goods, possessions they had used and valued, to their relatives and friends: both things and people counted. Disposing as they wished of their personal property was a right most widows used. Making a will may have been the moment in a widow's life when she reached maximum female autonomy; it was probably one of the rare official occasions when she spoke entirely in her own name, saying *I* or *It is my wish* and when she had the possibility – for family pressure should not be totally excluded – to act according to her own will.

Conclusion

There remains the main question: did women gain freedom in widowhood? As already stated several times in this volume, this is probably a question that was not medieval women's main preoccupation. Chaucer's Criseyde does appreciate the fact that as a widow she is 'her own woman' and Dunbar's widow explains that when her husband died, all her grief and depression died at the same time: 'now done is my dolly nyght, my day is upsprungin / Adew dolour, adew! My daynte now begynis / Now am I a wedow, I wise and weill am at ese' (412–414) [My dismal nights are ended, my dayspring is at hand. Farewell, sorrow, farewell! Now my voluptuous joy begins. Now I am a widow, I am aware of it and am well at ease][1] but personal freedom was not one of the main claims of medieval people. In the Middle Ages, the word *liberty* was rarely used in the singular. Liberties or franchises referred to the rights and privileges enjoyed by townsmen (known as freemen) that had been acquired through charters of freedom from their lords as well as to the long established customs of the locality. Entering the freedom, through heredity or through an admission fine, meant enjoying a privileged status. It required, however, the observance of strict rules. These rules, though a brake on individual initiative, protected interests, guaranteed everyone's rights. At that time, security, safety, social unity and order were far more sought after than individual freedom. Regulations brought safe, clear and, above all, unchanging social ties. Life was only conceived of in terms of communities, of unified groups and unifying relationships. It is not surprising that there should have been no well-defined conception of the individual as a worthwhile object of concern. It is consequently very unlikely that many widows considered their new state as a liberating and enviable experience. Writers and moralists rather insist on the isolation, poverty and increasing dependence that was the lot of many widows.

---

[1] *The Tretis of the Mariit Wemen and the Wido*, J. Kinsley, ed., *The Poems of William Dunbar*, p.293.

What is unquestionable is that widows had many more rights than wives and that they exercised them. Though all Anglo-Saxon women were dependent on a male relative, widows were landholders in their own rights who could buy, sell and bequeath property. Many of the wealthy Anglo-Saxon widows we have met demised large estates to religious communities – though one can also wonder whether they were not sometimes 'implementing arrangements made by husbands and fathers'.[2] After the Conquest, especially from the 13th century on, widows were gradually freed from guardianship, though family pressure here too should not be minimized. Great landowners, be they male or female, were powerful figures in medieval society. An unmarried or widowed woman of property had an equal right to that of men. The lordship of Walsham Manor was several times in the hands of women: those of Rose de Valognes alone or jointly with her two successive husbands between 1307 and 1353 or those of Mary de Pakenham (the widow of the rightful heir) between 1358 and 1360. Widows of all social backgrounds had to manage their own affairs, pay off the couple's debts, run their estates, small farm, or the family craft, keep accounts, etc. They went on being great conveyors of land mainly bequeathing what they possessed to their children or to the Church. Wives, on the other hand, were prohibited from making a will unless their husbands allowed them to do so. This is why Christine Rote's will begins as follows: 'made with the agreement and at the bidding of the same John, my husband'.[3] Widows could also sue and defend themselves at court, which was not the case of married women. In 1202, for instance, in the area of Manley (Lincolnshire):

> Hawise, Thurstan's daughter, appeals Walter of Croxby and William Miller of the death of her father and a wound given to herself. And she has a husband, Robert Franchenay, who will not stir in the matter. Therefore it is considered that the appeal is null, for a woman has no appeal against anyone save for the

---

2   P. Stafford, *Unification and Conquest*, p.175.
3   P. Northeast, ed., *Wills of the Archdeaconry of Sudbury*, p.149.

death of her husband or for rape. And let Robert be in mercy on his wife's account, for a half-mark, and let the appellees be quit.[4]

A not insignificant proportion of widows entered convents and nunneries. For widows of high social standing it was a way of evading remarriage. Some of them became abbesses taking on responsibilities denied to them in the outside world. Others simply found refuge by purchasing corrodies. Relatives often disapproved the vast sums of money widows paid these convents for that meant a huge drain on their own inheritance. It was far more difficult for poor women to enter a religious community: they were only offered to work as lay sisters. A small number of wealthy widows chose to have a semi-religious role by becoming vowesses: their binding vow of chastity enabled them not to remarry. Remarriage was an option less wealthy widows could simply not rule out and, for the poorer of them, it was often a necessary survival strategy. The widow of a miserable tenant, who held one third of her late husband's lands in dower, could not make both ends meet. What awaited her was 'frequent hunger and thirst, cold, poor shelter, a friendless old age, sickness without comfort'.[5] Moreover medieval husbands have too often been considered as insensitive masters oppressing their wives. What strikes immediately when reading medieval wills is the benevolence (devoid of paternalism) most husbands show towards their wives. These documents, though following a standardized pattern, betray the anxiety they often felt for the companion they were leaving behind, how deeply aware they were of what the future might be holding for her: poverty, sickness, solitude. What mainly stands out, probably unexpectedly to many of the twenty-first-century readers of such documents, is this strong attachment to the spouse, this bond uniting husband and wife. This is why those who had enough property to do so very often bequeathed many more tenements and lands than the required third to their wives. The centre of the household was first and foremost the couple. More than a liberating experience, widowhood was rather a

---

[4] F.W. Maitland, *Select Pleas of the Crown: Volume 1 A.D. 1200–1225*, London: Bernard Quaritch for the Selden Society, 1888. http://www.fordham.edu/halsall/seth/pleas-lincolneyre.html
[5] Christine de Pizan, *The Treasure of the City of Ladies*, part III, chapter 13.

distressing trial especially since as wives, women were so legally and socially dependent on their husbands. As widows they suddenly found themselves on their own having to see to everything. The fate that awaited them was more likely to be one of economic insecurity, loneliness and sickness in the image of the poor cotter in the Nun's Priest's Tale, 'A povre wydwe, somdeel stape in age / (...) In pacience ladde a ful symple lyf / (...) Hir diete was accordant to hir cote / Repleccioun ne made hire nevere sike' (VII 2821 / 2826 / 2836–2837). We have seen that some of them, thanks to their strength of character, hard work and tenacity did cope well in the face of adversity. In actual fact, life for most widows was harder, more precarious and more dismal. Independence, autonomy, freedom were reserved for the (though not too wealthy) happy few.

Bibliography

Primary sources

Patristic sources

AMBROSE
    H. De Romestin, trans., *Some of the Principal Works of St Ambrose*, Oxford: Parker and Co., Select Library of Nicene and Post-Nicene Fathers ser. 2, vol. 10, 1896.

AUGUSTINE
    Saint-Martin, J., ed. + trans., *Oeuvres de saint Augustin (De Continentia, De sancta virginitate, De bono viduitati, De opere monachorum, De nuptiis et concupiscentia)*, Paris: Desclée de Brouwer, 1939.

JEROME
    Fremantle, W.H., ed., *The Principal Works of St Jerome,* Select Library of Nicene and Post-Nicene Fathers, ser. 2, vol. VI, Edinburgh, 1892.
    Wright, F.A., ed., *Select Letters of St Jerome*, Cambridge, Mass.: Harvard University Press, Loeb Classical Library, 1963.

JOHN CHRYSOSTOM
    The Homilies of St John Chrysostom, Archbishop of Constantinople on the Epistles of St Paul the Apostle to Timothy, Titus and Philemon, Library of Fathers of the Catholic Church, Oxford: John H. Parker, 1843.
    Ettlinger, G.H., ed., Grillet, B., trans., *A une jeune veuve. Sur le mariage unique (Lógos 'eis neōtéran chīreúsasan. Perí monandrías)*, Paris: Le Cerf, 1968.

STANIFORTH, M., ed., *Early Christian Writings*, Harmondsworth: Penguin Classics, 1968. [Revised ed. by Andrew Louth, 1987].

TERTULLIAN
>Le Saint, W.P., trans., *Treatises on Marriage and Remarriage. (To his Wife. An exhortation to Chastity. Monogamy)*, London: Longmans, Green & Co., Westminster: Newman Press, 1951.
Corpus Christianorum Series Latina, vol. 1 & 2, E. Dekkers, ed., *Tertulliani Opera,* Turnhout: Brepols, 1953.
Moreschini, C., ed., Fredouille, J.-C., trans., *De exhortatione Castitatis,* Paris: Le Cerf, 1985.
Turcan, M., ed. + trans., *De cultu Feminarum,* Paris: Le Cerf, 1971.

Anglo-Saxon records

ANGLO-SAXON CHRONICLE
>Bately, J.M., ed., *The Anglo-Saxon Chronicle, Ms A,* Cambridge : D.S. Brewer, 1986.
Garmonsway, G.N., trans., *The Anglo-Saxon Chronicle,* London & Melbourne : Dent (Everyman's Library), 1953–1972.
Thorpe, B., ed., *The Anglo-Saxon Chronicle* (*Rerum Britannicarum Medii Aevi Scriptores* 23), London : Longman, 1861, 2 volumes, vol. 1 : ' Original Texts '.

ATTENBOROUGH, F., ed., *The Laws of the Earliest English Kings,* Cambridge University Press, 1922.
HARMER, F.E., ed., *Anglo-Saxon Writs,* Manchester University Press, 1952.
—— *Select English Documents of the 9th and 10th centuries,* Cambridge University Press, 1914.
KEYNES, S. & LAPIDGE, M., eds., *Alfred the Great, Asser's Life of King Alfred and other Contemporary Sources,* Harmondsworth: Penguin Books, 1983.
ROBERTSON, A.J., ed., *Anglo-Saxon Charters,* Cambridge University Press, 1939.
—— *The Laws of the Kings of England from Edmund to Henry I,* Cambridge, 1925.
SAWYER, P.H., *Anglo-Saxon Charters: An Annotated List & Bibliography,* London: Royal Historical Society, 1968.

THORPE, B., ed., *Diplomatarium Anglicum aevi Saxonici. A collection of English Charters, from the reign of King Æthelberht of Kent A.D. DCV. to that of William the Conqueror. Containing I. Miscellaneous Charters. II. Wills. III. Guilds. IV. Manumissions and Acquittances. With a translation of the Anglo-Saxon*, London, 1865.
WHITELOCK, D., ed., *Anglo-Saxon Wills*, Cambridge University Press, 1930.
—— *English Historical Documents c. 500–1042*, London: Eyre & Spottiswoode, 1955.

Medieval Records

BLISS, W.H., ed., *Calendar of Entries in the Papal Registers relating to Great Britain and Ireland: Papal Letters*, Vol. 1, 1198–1304, London: HMSO, 1893.
HENRY OF BRATTON/BRACTON
   Woodbine, G.E., ed., Thorne, S.E., trans., *De Legibus et Consuetudinibus Angliæ. Bracton on the Laws and Customs of England*, Cambridge, Mass.: Belknap Press of Harvard University Press, 1968, 2 vols.
CHENEY, E.P., ed., *English Manorial Documents*, Philadelphia: University of Pennsylvania, 1896.
DeWINDT, E.B., ed., *The Liber Gersumarum of Ramsey Abbey: a Calendar & Index of B.L. Harley Ms 445*, Toronto: Pontifical Institute of Mediaeval Studies, 1976.
DOMESDAY BOOK
   Williams, A., & Martin, G.H., trans., *Domesday Book. A Complete Translation*, London: Alecto Historical Editions, 1992. London: Penguin Books, 2000.
DOUGLAS, D.C. & GREENAWAY, G.W., eds., *English Historical Documents 1042–1189*, London: Eyre & Spottiswoode, 1953.
FURNIVALL, F. J., ed., *Fifty Earliest English Wills in the Court of Probate, London, A.D. 1387–1439, with a priest's of 1454*, London: Kegan Paul, Trench, Trübner, Early English Text Society,

original series, vol. 78, 1882. [Reprinted Oxford University Press, 1964].
GLANVILL
Hall, G.D.G., ed + trans., *The Treatise on the Laws and Customs of the Realm of England Commonly called Glanvill*, London: Nelson, 1965. [Revised ed., Clanchy, M.T., Oxford: Clarendon Press, 1993].
GREGORY IX (*Decretales*)
Richter, E.L. & Friedberg, E., eds., *Corpus Juris Canonici, Pars secunda: Decretalium Collectiones*, Leipzig: B. Tauchnitz, 1879–1881 [new ed. Union (N.J.): The Lawbook Exchange, 2000].
GRATIAN (*Decretum*)
Richter, E.L. & Friedberg, E., eds., *Corpus Juris Canonici, Pars prior: Decretum Magistri Gratiani*, Leipzig: B. Tauchnitz, 1879–1881 [new ed. Union (N.J.): The Lawbook Exchange, 2000].
Thompson, A., & Gorley, J., trans., *The treatise on Laws (Decretum DD. 1–20) with the Ordinary Gloss*, Washington D.C.: Catholic University of America Press, 1993.
HARPER-BILL, C., ed., *Charters of the medieval Hospitals of Bury St Edmunds*, Series Suffolk Charters, Woodbridge: Boydell Press, 1994.
KIRBY, J.L. STEVENSON, J.H., eds., *Calendar of Inquisitions Post-Mortem and other Analogous Documents preserved in the Public Record Office* XXI: 6–10 Henry V (1418–1422), Woodbridge: Boydell Press, 2002.
LOCK, R., ed., *The Court Rolls of Walsham le Willows*, Woodbridge: The Boydell Press, Suffolk Records Society, vol. 1 (1303–1350), 1998, vol. 2 (1351–1399), 2002.
MAGNA CARTA
A.E. Dick Howard, A.E., *Magna Carta. Text and Commentary*, Charlottesville, London: University Press or Virginia, 1964 [revised edition 1998].
McKechnie, W.S., ed., *Magna Carta*, Glasgow: Maclehose, 1914 (reprinted NewYork: Burt Franklin, 1958).

MAITLAND, F. W., ed., *Select Pleas of the Crown: Volume 1–A.D. 1200–1225*, London: Bernard Quaritch for the Selden Society, 1888.

—— *Select Pleas in Manorial and Other Seignorial Courts*, vol. 1 (Reigns of Henry III and Edward I), London: Bernard Quaritch, 1889.

MARTIN, G.H., ed., *The Ipswich Recognizance Rolls 1294–1327*, Suffolk Records Society, 1973.

MYERS, A.R., ed., *English Historical Documents 1327–1485*, London: Eyre & Spottiswoode, 1969.

NORTHEAST, P., ed., *Wills of the Archdeaconry of Sudbury 1439–1474*, Wodbridge: The Boydell Press, Suffolk Records Society, 2001.

PARKIN, K., ed., *Calendar of Inquisitions Post Mortem 1–5, Henry VI. 1422–1427*, vol. XXII, Woodbridge: Boydell Press, 2003.

ROTHWELL, H., ed., *English Historical Documents 1189–1327*, London: Eyre & Spottiswoode, 1975.

ROTULI DE DOMINABUS ET PUERIS ET PUELLIS
Round, H., ed., *Rotuli de Dominabus et Pueris et Puellis de XII Comitatibus*, London: The Pipe Roll Society, 1913.
Walmsley, J., ed., *Widows, heirs, and Heiresses in the Late Twelfth Century: the Rotuli de Dominabus et pueris et Puellis*, Tempe: Arizona State University, series Medieval and Renaissance Texts and Studies, vol. 308, 2006.

SHARPE, R. R., ed., *Calendar of Letter–Books of the City of London. 1275–1298*, London: the Corporation, 1899.

SMITH, T., ed., *English Gilds*, London, New York, Toronto: Oxford University Press, Early English Text Society, 1970.

TWISS, T., ed., *The Black Book of the Admiralty or Monumenta Juridica, vol. II: 'Le Domesday de Gippewyz. The Domus Day of Gippeswiche'*, London: Longman, Macmillan, A. & C. Black, *Rerum britannicarum medii aevi scriptores*, no.55, 1873.

Old English Literary Texts

AELFRIC
 Thorpe, B., ed., *The Homilies of the Anglo-Saxon Church. The first part containing the Sermones Catholici or Homilies of Aelfric*, London: Aelfric Society, 1844–1846.
 Skeat, W.W., ed., *Aelfric's Lives of Saints*, London: Trübner, 1881–1900, Early English Text Society o.s. 76, 82, 94, 114.
 Wilcox, J., ed., *Aelfric's Prefaces*, Durham Medieval Texts, no.9, 1994.
BRADLEY, S.A.J., trans., *Anglo-Saxon Poetry*, London & Melbourne: Dent (Everyman's Library), 1982.
HAMER, R., ed., *A Choice of Anglo-Saxon Verse*, London, Boston: Faber & Faber, 1970.
SWANTON, M. trans., *Anglo-Saxon Prose*, London: Dent, 1975.
TREHARNE, E., ed. + trans., *Old and Middle English, an Anthology*, Oxford: Blackwell Publishers, 2000.
VERCELLI HOMILIES
 Scragg, D.G., ed., *The Vercelli Homilies and Related Texts*, London: Oxford University Press, Early English Text Society, o.s. 300, 1992.
WULFSTAN
 Bethurum, D., ed. *The Homilies of Wulfstan*, Oxford: University Press, 1957.

Middle English Literary Texts

THE BOOK OF THE KNIGHT OF THE TOWER
 Offord, M.Y., ed., *The Book of the Knight of the Tower*, Oxford University Press, Early English Text Society supplementary series no.2, 1971.
CELY (*letters*)
 Hanham, A., ed., *The Cely Letters, 1472–1488*, London: Oxford University Press, Early English Text Society, vol. 273, 1975.

CHAUCER, G.
> Benson, L.D., ed., *The Riverside Chaucer*, Oxford University Press, 1988.

DUNBAR, W.
> Kinsley, J., ed., *The Poems of William Dunbar*, Oxford University Press, 1979.

FELLOWS, J., ed., *Of Love and Chivalry, An Anthology of Middle English Romance*, London: J.M. Dent & Sons, 1993.

GOWER, J.,
> G.C. Macaulay, ed., *The English Works of John Gower*, Vol. II., 1901.

HAVELOK
> Smithers, G.V., ed., *Havelok*, Oxford: Clarendon Press, 1987.

JACOB'S WELL
> Brandeis, A., ed., *An English Treatise on the Cleansing of Man's Conscience*, London: Kegan Paul, Trench, Trübner, 1900. Early English Text Society, no.115.

KEMPE, M.
> Meech, S.B. Allen, H.E., eds., *The Book of Margery Kempe*, Oxford University Press, Early English Text Society no.212, 1940.

LANGLAND, W.
> Schmidt, A.V.C., ed., *Piers Plowman: A parallel-text edition of the A B C and Z versions*, London: Longman, 1995.

McNEILL, J.T. & GAMER, H.M., eds., *Medieval Handbooks of Penance: a Translation of the Principal 'libri poenitentiales' and Selections from Related Documents*, New York: Columbia University Press, 1938.

MALORY, Sir T.
> Vinaver, E., ed., *Malory. Works*, Oxford University Press, 1971.

MANNYNG OF BRUNNE, R.
> *Handlyng Synne*, Sullens, I., ed., Binghamton (N.Y.): Center for Medieval and Early Renaissance Studies, State University of New York, 1983.

MICHEL OF NORTHGATE
> Morris, R., ed., *Dan Michel's Ayenbite of Inwyt or Remorse of Conscience in the Kentish Dialect*, London: Trübner & Co., 1866, EETS, vol. 23.

MILLETT, B. & WOGAN-BROWNE, J., ed. + trans., *Medieval English Prose for Women from the Katherine Group and Ancrene Wisse*, Oxford: Clarendon Press, 1990.

MILLS, M., ed., *Six Middle English Romances*, London: J.M. Dent & Sons, Everyman's Library, 1973.

A MYROUR TO LEWDE MEN & WYMMEN
Nelson, V., ed., *A Myrour to Lewde Men & Wymmen, a prose version of the Speculum Vitae edited from B.L. Harley 45*, Heidelberg: Carl Winter Universitäts Verlag, (Middle English Texts no.14) 1981.

PASTON (*Letters*)
Davis, N., ed., *Paston Letters and Papers of the Fifteenth Century: Parts I and II*, Oxford University Press, Early English Text Society, 2005 [First edition 1971 (Part I), 1976 (Part II)].

PURITY
Andrew, M., Peterson, C. & Waldron, R.A., eds., Finch, C., trans., *The Complete Works of the Pearl Poet*, Berkeley, Oxford: University of California Press, 1993.

TALE OF BERYN
Furnivall, F.J. & Stone, W.G., eds., *The Tale of Beryn*, London: Kegan Paul, Trench, Trübner, Early English Text Society extra series, vol. 105, 1909.

VICE AND VIRTUES
Holthausen, F., ed., *Vices & Virtues*, London: Trübner & Co., 1888, EETS, vol. 89, p. 2.

Medieval Literary Latin texts

ALDHELM (*De Virginitate*)
Ehwald, R., ed., *Aldhelmi Opera,* series *Monumenta Germaniae Historica Auctores antiquissimi*, vol. 15, Berlin, 1919.
Lapidge, M. & Herren, M., trans., *Aldhelm, The Prose Works*, Ipswich, Cambridge: D.S. Brewer, Totowa: Rowman & Littlefield, 1979.

BEDE
>Sherley-Price, L., trans., *A History of the English Church and People*, Harmondsworth: Penguin Books, 1955–1968.
Life of St Cuthbert. Lives of the Abbots of Wearmouth and Jarrow in *The Age of Bede* Webb, J.F. & Farmer, D.H., trans., Harmondsworth: Penguin Books, 1965–1988.
McClure, J. & Collins, R., trans., *The Ecclesiastical History of the English People. The Greater Chronicle. Bede's Letter to Egbert*, Oxford University Press, 1994.

BONIFACE
>Emerton, E., trans., *The Letters of St Boniface*, New York: Columbia University Press, 1940.
Talbot, C.H., ed. + trans., *The Anglo-Saxon Missionaries in Germany. Being the Lives of SS. Willibrord, Boniface, Sturm, Leoba and Lebuim, together with the Hodoeporicon of St Willibald and a Selection from the Correspondence of St Boniface*, London & New York: Sheed, & Ward, 1954.

ENCOMIUM EMMAE REGINAE
>Campbell, A., ed. + trans., London: Offices of the Royal Historical Society, Camden 3rd series, vol. 72, 1949.

LIBER ELIENSIS
>Fairweather, J., trans., Woodbridge: Boydell & Brewer, 2005.

THE LIFE OF LEOBA
>Talbot, C., trans., *The Anglo-Saxon Missionaries in Germany*, London: Sheed & Ward, 1954.

VITA AEDWARDI
>Barlow, F., ed. + trans., *Vita Aedwardi Regis/The Life of King Edward*, London: T. Nelson & Sons, 1962.

Women's Studies. Sourcebooks

AMT, E., ed., *Women's Lives in Medieval Europe*, New York, London: Routledge, 1993.
BLAMIRES, A., ed., *Woman Defamed and Woman Defended*, Oxford University Press, 1992.

GOLDBERG, P.J.P., ed., *Woman is a Worthy Wight: Women in England. c. 1275–1525*, Manchester University Press, 1995.
LARRINGTON, C., ed., *Women and Writing in Medieval Europe*, New York, London: Routledge, 1995.

Secondary sources

Death, burials, mourning

JUPP, Peter C. & GITTINGS, C., *Death in England. An illustrated History*, Manchester University Press, 1999.
PELLING, M. & SMITH, R.M., *Life, Death and the Elderly: Historical Perspectives*, London: Routledge, 1991.

Law

BIANCALANA, J., 'Widows at Common Law: the Development of Common Law Dower', *Irish Jurist*, new series, xxiii, (1988), 255–329.
BRUNDAGE, J.A., 'Widows and Remarriage: Moral Conflicts and their Resolution in Classical Canon Law', S.S. Walker, ed., *Wife & Widow in Medieval England*, Ann Arbor: University of Michigan Press, (1993), 17–31.
FLEMING, R., *Domesday Book and the Law: Society and Legal Custom in Early Medieval England*, Cambridge University Press, 1998.
KLINCK, A.L., 'Anglo-Saxon Women and the Law', *Journal of Medieval History*, 8, (1982), 107–121.
LOENGARD, Senderowitz J., 'Legal History and the Medieval Englishwoman: A Fragmented View', *Law and History Review*, vol. 4, no.1 (1986), 161–178.

—— '"Legal history and the medieval Englishwoman" revisited: some new directions', Rosenthal, J.T. ed., *Medieval Women and the Sources of Medieval History*, Athens, University of Georgia Press, (1990), 210–36.

LOWE, K.A., 'The Nature and Effect of the Anglo-Saxon Vernacular Will', *Legal History*, 19, (1988), 23–61.

MENUGE, N.J., ed., *Medieval Women and the Law*, Woodbridge: the Boydell Press, 2000.

POLLOCK, F. & MAITLAND, F.W., *The History of English Law before the Time of Edward I*, Cambridge University Press, 1895. [2nd edition, 1968].

RIVERS, T.J., 'Widows' Rights in Anglo-Saxon Law', *American Journal of Legal History*, 19, (1975), 208–215.

SHEEHAN, M.M., *The Will in Medieval England. From the Conversion of the Anglo-Saxons to the end of the Thirteenth century*, Toronto: Pontifical Institute of Medieval Studies, 1963.

—— *Marriage, Family, and Law in Medieval Europe*, University of Toronto Press, 1995.

SIMPSON, A.W.B., *An Introduction to the History of the Land Law*, Oxford University Press, 1961.

YOUNG, E., 'The Anglo-Saxon Family-law', Adams, H., ed., *Essays in Anglo-Saxon Law*, Boston: Little, Brown & Company, (1876), 121–183.

Marriage

BARTLETT, R., *England under the Norman and Angevin Kings 1075–1225*, Oxford: Clarendon Press, 2000, pp. 547–558.

BENNETT, J., 'Medieval Peasant Marriage: an Examination of Marriage License Fines in the *Liber Gersumarum*', J. Ambrose Raftis, ed., *Pathways to Medieval Peasants*, Toronto: Pontifical Institute of Mediaeval Studies, (1981), 193–246.

BROOKE, C.N.L., *The Medieval Idea of Marriage*, Oxford University Press, 1989.

BRUNDAGE, J.A., *Sex, Law and Marriage in the Middle Ages*, Aldershot: Variorum, 1993.

DUBY, G., *The Knight, the Lady and the Priest: the Making of Modern Marriage in Medieval France*, New York: Pantheon Books, 1983.
GIES, F. & GIES, J., *Marriage and Family in the Middle Ages*, New York, London: Harper and Row, 1987.
McCARTHY, C., *Marriage in Medieval England, Law, Literature and Practice*, Woodbridge: the Boydell Press, 2004.
MURRAY, J., *Love, Marriage, Family in the Middle Ages*, Peterborough (Ont.): Broadview, Ormskirk: Thomas Lyster, 2001.
SEARLE, M. & STEVENSON, K.W., eds., *Documents of the Marriage Ceremony*, Collegeville (Minn.): Liturgical Press., 1992.
STEVENSON, K.W., *Nuptial Blessing: a Study of Christian Marriage Rites*, Oxford University Press, 1983.
VAN HOECKE, W. & WELKENHUYSEN, A., *Love and Marriage in the Twelfth Century*, Mediaevalia Lovaniensia, ser. 1, studia 8. Leuven University Press, 1981.

Religion

ANDRE, J.L., 'Widows and Vowesses', *Archaeological Journal*, 49, (1892), 69–82.
BURTON, J., *Monastic and Religious Orders in Britain 1000–1300*, Cambridge University Press, 1994.
ECKENSTEIN, L., *Women under Monasticism: Chapters on Saint-Lore and Convent Life between A.D. 500 and A.D. 1500*, New York: Russell & Russell, 1963.
HARROD, H., 'On the Mantle & the Ring of Widowhood', *Archaeologia*, no.40, (1866).
HOLLIS, S., *Anglo-Saxon Women and the Church – Sharing a Common Fate*, Woodbridge: The Boydell Press, 1992.
OWST, G.R., *Literature and Pulpit in Medieval England: A Neglected Chapter in the History of English Letters and of the English People*, Cambridge University Press, 1933.
RIDYARD, S.J., *The Royal Saints of Anglo-Saxon England: A study of West Saxon and East Anglian Cults*, Cambridge: University Press, 1988.

THOMPSON, S., *Women Religious: the Founding of English Nunneries after the Norman Conquest*, Oxford: Clarendon Press, 1991.

THURSTON, B.B., *The Widows: A Women's Ministry in the Early Church*, Minneapolis: Fortress Press, 1989.

Social Conditions

ARCHER, R.E., 'Rich Old Ladies: the Problem of Late Medieval Dowagers', Pollard, T., ed., *Property and Politics: Essays in Later Medieval English History*, Gloucester: Sutton, (1984), 15–35.

BENNET, J.M., *Women in the Medieval English Countryside: Gender and Household in Brigstock before the Plague*, New York, Oxford: Oxford University Press, 1987.

CLARK, E., 'Some Aspects of Social Security in Medieval England', *Journal of Family History*, 7 (1982, no.4), 307–320.

FLEMING, P. *Family and Household in Medieval England*, Basingstoke: Palgrave, 2001.

GOLDBERG, P., *Medieval England: A Social History 1250–1550*, London: Hodder Arnold, 2004.

—— *Women in Medieval English Society*, Stroud: Sutton, 1997.

LACEY, K., 'Women and Work in 14th and 15th century London', Charles, L. & Duffin, L., eds., *Women and Work in pre-Industrial England*, London: Croom Helm, 1985.

LASLETT, P., *Household and Family in Past Time*, Cambridge University Press, 1972.

HANAWALT, B.A., *The Ties that Bound: Peasant Families in Medieval England*, New York, Oxford: Oxford University Press, 1986.

HOLDERNESS, B.A., 'Widows in pre-Industrial Society: an Essay upon their Economic Functions', Smith, R.M., ed., *Land, Kinship and Life-Cycle*, Cambridge University Press, (1984), 423–442.

RAFTIS, J.A., *A Small Town in Late Medieval England. Godmanchester 1278–1400*, Toronto: Pontifical Institute of Mediaeval Studies, 1982.

RAZI, Z., *Life, Marriage and Death in a Medieval Parish. Economy, Society and Demography in Halesowen (1270–1400)*, Cambridge University Press, 1980.
RIGBY, S.H., *English Society in the Later Middle Ages, Class, Status and Gender*, Basingstoke: Macmillan, 1995.
STAFFORD, P., *Unification and Conquest: A Political and Social History of England in the Tenth and Eleventh Centuries*, London: Edward Arnold, 1989.

Gender & Women's studies

BARRON, C.M. & SUTTON, A., eds., *Medieval London Widows 1300–1500*, London: The Hambledon Press, 1994.
CAMPBELL, M.W., 'Queen Emma and Aelfgifu of Northampton: Canute the Great's Women', *Medieval Scandinavia*, 4, (1971), 66–79.
CARSON, C. & WEISL, A., eds., *Constructions of Widowhood and Virginity in the Middle Ages*, Basingstoke: Macmillan, 1998.
CAVALLO, S., & WARNER, L., ed., *Widowhood in Medieval and Early Modern Europe*, Harlow: Longman, 1999.
COSS, P., *The Lady in Medieval England, 1000–1500*, Stroud: Sutton, 1998.
CRICK, J., 'Men, Women and Widows: Widowhood in pre-Conquest England', S. Cavallo & L. Warner, ed., *Widowhood in Medieval and Early Modern Europe*, Harlow: Longman, (1999), 24–36.
—— 'Women, Wills and Moveable Wealth in pre-Conquest England', Donald, M. & Hurcombe, L., eds., *Gender and Material Culture from Prehistory to the Present*, Basingstoke: Macmillan, New York: St Martin's Press, 2000.
DAMICO, H. & OLSEN, A.H., eds., *New Readings on Women in Old English Literature*, Bloomington: Indiana University Press, 1990.
DIETRICH, S.C., 'An Introduction to Women in Anglo-Saxon Society c. 600–1066', KANNER, B., ed., *The Women of England from Anglo-Saxon Times to the Present*, Hamden, Conn., (1979), 32–56.

DINSHAW, C. & WALLACE, D., eds., *Medieval Women's Writing*, Cambridge University Press, 2003.

DOBROWOLSKI, P., 'Women and their Dower in the Long Thirteenth Century 1265–1329', M. Prestwich, R.H. Britnell & R. Frame, eds., *Thirteenth Century England VI. Proceedings of the Durham Conference*, Woodbridge: The Boydell Press, 1995, 157–164.

FELL, C., CLARK, C. & WILLIAMS, E., *Women in Anglo-Saxon England and the Impact of 1066*, Bloomington: Indiana University Press, London: British Museum Publications, 1984.

JEWELL, H., *Women in Medieval England*, Manchester University Press, 1996.

JOHNS, S., 'The Wives and Widows of the Earls of Chester, 1100–1252: the Charter Evidence', *Haskins Society Journal*, 1995, vol. 7.

—— *Noblewoman, Aristocracy and Power in the Twelfth-century Anglo-Norman Realm*, Manchester University Press, 2003.

KLAPISCH-ZUBER, C., ed., *A History of Women. II Silences of the Middle Ages*, Cambridge (Ma.): Belknap Press, 1992.

LEYSER, H., *Medieval Women. A Social History of Women in England 450–1500*, London: Weidenfeld & Nicolson, 1995.

LEWIS, K., MENUGE, N. J., PHILLIPS, K.M., eds., *Young Medieval Women*, Stroud: Sutton, New York: St Martin's Press, 1999.

LOENGARD, Senderowitz, J. 'Of the gift of her husband: English dower and its consequences in the year 1200', Kirshner, J. & Wemple, S.F. eds., *Women of the Medieval World: Essays in Honor of John H. Mundy*, Oxford, New York: Basil Blackwell, (1985), 215–255.

MIRRER, L., ed., *Upon My Husband's Death: Widows in the Literature and Histories of Medieval Europe*, Ann Arbor: University of Michigan Press, 1992.

NELSON, J.L., 'The Wary Widow', DAVIES, W. & FOURACRE, P., eds., *Property and Power in the Early Middle Ages*, Cambridge University Press, 1995, 82–113.

RICHARDS, M.P. & STANFIELD, B.J., 'Concepts of Anglo-Saxon Women in the Laws', DAMICO, H. & OLSEN, A.H., eds., *New*

Readings on Women in Old English Literature, Bloomington: Indiana University Press, (1990), 89–99.
ROSENTHAL, J.T., ed., *Medieval Women and the Sources of Medieval History*, Athens: University of Georgia Press, 1990.
STAFFORD, P., *Queens, Concubines, and Dowagers: the King's Wife in the Early Middle Ages*, Athens: Georgia University Press, 1983.
—— 'Women in *Domesday*', *Reading Medieval Studies*, vol. XV, (1989), 75–94.
—— 'Women and the Norman Conquest', *Transactions of the Royal Historical Society*, series 6, vol. 4, (1994), 221–249.
—— *Queen Emma & Queen Edith: Queenship and Women's Power in Eleventh-century England*, Oxford: Blackwell, 1997.
—— & MULDER-BAKKER, A., eds., *Gendering the Middle Ages*, Oxford: Blackwell, 2001.
STENTON, D.M., *The English Woman in History*, London: Allen & Unwin, 1957.
STEUER, S.M.B., 'Family Strategies in Medieval London: Financial Planning and the Urban Widow, 1123–1473', *Essays in Medieval Studies*, Illinois Medieval Association, vol. 12, 1995.
WALKER, S.S., ed., *Wife and Widow in Medieval England*, Ann Arbor: University of Michigan press, 1993.
WARD, J., ed., *English Noblewomen in the Later Middle Ages*, London: Longman, 1992.
—— *Women of the English Nobility and Gentry*, Manchester University Press, 1995.

Index

Abba, reeve 83, 86, 108, 123
abduction 41, 93, 95–98, 199, 283
Abelard, Peter
   Historia Calamitatum/Story of his Misfortunes 189, 190
Acha, Queen (wife of King Aethelfrith of Northumbria) 44
adultery 26, 96, 163, 164, 166
Aebbe, Abbess of Coldingham 31, 57, 70
Aelfflæd, Abbess of Whitby 59, 70
Aelfflæd, (wife of Brihtnoth, Aelfgar's daughter) 61, 106, 112, 114, 122, 125, 127, 128, 133–140, 145
Aelfgar, Ealdorman 61, 114, 115, 118, 124, 127–129, 132–135, 137, 139, 140
Aelfgifu, Queen (wife of King Aethelred 'the Unready') 51, 53, 113–115
Aelfgifu, Queen (wife of King Eadwig) 50
Aelfheah, Ealdorman 50
Aelfhelm, clerk of Ely 57, 66, 84, 105, 113, 114, 137
Aelfric, 16, 28, 33–36, 58, 65, 73, 77, 105, 173
   Catholic Homilies 31, 34, 35
   Festival of St Agatha 62
   Glossary 105
   The Life of St Aethelwold 33
Aelfstan, Bishop 88
Aelfthryth, (King Alfred's daughter) 42
Aelfthryth, Queen (wife of King Edgar 'the Peaceful') 47, 50, 72, 113
Aelfwynn, (daughter of Aethelflæd, granddaughter of King Alfred) 49
Aelred of Rievaulx
   De institutione Inclusarum 190

Aethelbald, King of Wessex 40, 41, 90, 110
Aethelbald, King of Mercia 76, 98
Aethelberht, King of Kent 37, 38, 40, 45, 75, 79, 81, 84–86, 89, 90, 94, 97, 99, 102, 104, 106, 124
Aethelburh, Queen (wife of King Edwin of Northumbria) 13, 45, 49
Aethelburh, Queen (wife of King Ine of Wessex) 47, 49
Aethelburh, Abbess of Faremoutiers 54, 56
Aethelburh, Abbess of Barking 65
Aethelflæd, Lady of the Mercians 13, 14, 47, 48, 50, 143
Aethelflæd of Damerham, (daughter of Ealdorman Aelfgar, wife of King Edmund) 61, 105, 109, 112, 114, 115, 118, 124, 125, 127–135, 138–140, 143
Aethelfrith, King of Northumbria 46
Aethelred, King of Mercia 47, 48
Aethelred, King of Wessex 13
Aethelred 'the Unready', King 51, 76, 84, 91, 113, 114, 119
Aethelred, Lord of the Mercians 48, 143
Aethelric, Ealdorman of the Hwicce 87, 88, 107, 114, 122, 124
Aethelstan, King 75, 102, 143
Aethelstan the Aetheling (eldest son of King Aethelred II and Queen Aelfgifu) 113, 114
Aethelthryth, St (Queen then Abbess of Ely) 31, 54–59, 62, 63, 65, 66, 72, 110, 124, 125, 143, 144
Aethelwold, Bishop of Winchester 33, 65, 72, 73, 77, 87

349

Regularis Concordia 72
Aethelwulf, King of Wessex 40, 41 49, 90, 143
Aethelwulf, Bishop of Winchester 50
Agatho, Pope 58
age
   difference of age between spouses 242, 284–287
   full age 218, 261, 262, 282, 296–298, 311–313, 318–321, 323
   old age 226
   under-age 95, 102, 144, 149, 217, 218, 225, 254, 295, 296, 312, 318, 320
affinity (*see also* consanguinity) 44, 156, 157, 163
Aldhelm of Malmesbury, 16, 28, 29, 31–33, 66, 67, 173, 179
   De virginitate 28, 32, 62
Alexander III, Pope 161, 167
Alfred, King 14, 40–42, 47, 49, 65, 79, 85, 97, 99, 101, 102, 121, 122, 129, 137
Alienor of Aquitaine 284
Ambrose, St, of Milan, 23, 27, 28, 160
   De viduis 23, 26, 27
Amis & Amiloun 161–162
Ancrene Riwle 190
Anglo-Saxon Chronicle 31, 36, 37, 45–47, 49–51, 59, 69, 72, 98, 114, 119, 141–143
Anglo-Saxon law 16, 17, 46, 48, 49, 75, 78, 79, 103
   Laws of Aethelberht of Kent 75, 81, 89, 90, 94, 97, 99, 102, 104, 106
   Laws of Aethelred II ('the Unready') 76, 78, 79, 83, 86, 92, 124
   Laws of Alfred 75, 79, 82, 85, 95, 97, 99, 101, 102, 121, 137
   Laws of Cnut 76, 78, 83, 86, 90, 92, 96, 97, 114, 124
   Laws of Hlothhere and Eadric of Kent 17, 75, 81, 88, 100
   Laws of Ine of Wessex 75, 79, 100, 104, 106
   Laws of Wihtred of Kent 75, 82, 95
   wergeld 80, 82, 85, 86, 91, 94–96, 99, 100–102, 104
Anna (biblical widow) 92, 186
Anna, King of East-Anglia 54
Anselm, Archbishop of Canterbury 51, 153
apprenticeship 291
Aquinas, St Thomas 168–170
Asser
   De rebus gestis Aelfredi/Life of King Alfred 40, 49, 143
Augustine of Hippo, St 22, 25, 26–28, 35, 66, 160, 164, 189
   De bono viduitatis 25–27
   De nuptiis et concupiscentia/On Marriage and Concupiscence 164
Augustine of Canterbury, St 30, 37–40, 43, 45

Baldwin Iron-Arm (Count of Flanders) 41, 42
Barron, C.M. 292, 293
Battle of Maldon, The 106
Bebbe, Queen (wife of King Aethelfrith of Northumbria) 46
Bede, St 16, 30, 36–39, 45, 46, 53–56, 58, 59, 62, 65–67, 69, 73, 75, 89, 124, 126 143, 146
   Historia Ecclesiastica Gentis Anglorum/The Ecclesiastical History of the English People 36, 38, 39, 45, 53, 54–58, 62, 67, 69, 73, 89, 124, 126 143, 146,
   Vita sancti Cuthberti/Life of St Cuthbert 70, 126
Begu, nun 56
Bennet, J.M. 308, 313, 324

Benoît de St Maure 182
Beornthryth (wife of Earl Oswulf) 61
Bertha, Queen (wife of King Aethelberht of Kent) 45
bigamists 170, 192
Black Death 218, 310, 311, 313, 314, 317, 318, 321, 324
Blamires, A. 183
Bonaventure, St
 Commentaria in Quatuor Libros Sententiarum 168
Boniface, St 30, 31, 42, 44, 59, 62, 69, 70, 76, 80, 98
Book of the Knight of la Tour, The 186–188
bookland 116, 121
Bracton 229, 230, 233, 238, 244, 255, 270, 271
Brihtnoth 106, 125, 133–135, 138
Brundage, J.A. 168, 172
Bryene, Alice de 257–258
Burgh, Elizabeth de *see* Elizabeth de Clare
Burgred, King of Mercia 121
burial 201–204, 209, 326
Bury St Edmunds 171, 204, 228, 234, 235, 287, 288, 300

Caesarius of Heisterbach
 Dialogi miraculorum/Dialogue on Miracles 188
Carruthers, L. 175
Caxton, William 186, 196
Cedd, Bishop of the East Saxons 62
celibacy 9, 20, 149, 159, 174–179, 190, 244, 247, 278, 279, 282, 290, 298, 322–324, 331
Cely Papers 294
Cenwalh, King of Wessex 13, 48
Ceolburh, Abbess of Berkeley (mother of Aethelric) 87

Charles the Bald, (King of the Western Franks) 40–42, 49
charter 103, 111, 113, 121, 150
chastity 15, 22, 23, 25, 26, 28, 29, 31, 32, 36, 39, 49, 56, 65, 120, 149, 180, 187, 190, 192, 194, 195, 197, 199, 287, 331
 three grades of 24, 25, 29, 32, 34, 174–180
Chaucer, Geoffrey
 The Canterbury Tales 23, 154, 172, 173, 177, 183, 185, 210, 225, 226, 277, 285, 286, 302, 332
 The Book of the Duchess 182,
 The Legend of Good Women 176
 Troilus & Criseyde 176–177, 184–185, 186, 196, 276, 277, 329
Chronicle of Aethelweard, The 42, 46
Clare, Elizabeth de (Elizabeth de Burgh) 199, 257, 267
Clare, Matilda de 267
Clement III, Pope 165
Clement V, Pope 158
Christine de Pizan, 8, 149, 201, 202, 214, 219, 220
 Lavision Christine 201
 Trésor de la cité des dames/The Treasure of the City of Ladies 214, 220, 241, 331
Cnut, King 51, 76, 77, 104, 120, 131
confession 180
consanguinity (*see also* affinity) 43, 44, 155, 157–159, 163, 234
corrody 287, 288, 300, 301
councils and synods 27, 33, 39, 43, 58, 72, 73, 76, 153, 154, 156–159, 162, 164, 165, 167
 Fourth Lateran Council (1215) 155, 157, 162, 180, 282
crafts and trades 290–294

Crick, J. 16
Cuniburg, Abbess 62, 69, 80
custody
　of child 9, 88, 89, 145, 217, 282–283, 295–297, 311, 313, 317, 320, 321
　of land 282
Cuthbert, St 64, 70, 126
Cuthburh, Queen (wife of King Ealdfrith of Northumbria, Abbess of Wimborne) 31, 32, 68
Cwenburh, Cuthburh's sister 31
Cyneberht, Bishop 37
Cyneburh, St (wife of Alhfrith, Sub-King of Deira, Abbess of Castor) 47
Cyneswith, St (Abbess of Castor) 47
Cynethryth, Queen (wife of King Offa of Mercia) 46
Cynewulf
　Elene 14
　Juliana 14

Daniel, Bishop of Winchester 37
debts 202, 208, 212, 213, 220, 222–225, 244, 251, 268, 270, 275, 316, 330
Dhuoda, *Liber manualis/Manual of Instruction* 60, 66
Dobrowolski, P. 236
Domesday Book 80, 106, 108, 109, 122, 129–132, 138, 140, 142, 305
dower 106–108, 123, 224, 226–236, 238–255, 258, 259, 264, 265, 279–281, 294, 297, 303, 308, 312, 313, 315–317, 320, 321, 326, 331
　plea of 237, 238, 240
dowry 103, 108, 109, 255–257
Duby, G. 7
Dunbar, William
　Tretis of the Tua Mariit Wemen and the Wedo 183, 269, 286, 318, 329

Dunstan, Archbishop of Canterbury 33, 47, 72, 88

Eadbald, King of Kent 37–39, 89, 143
Eadburh (daughter of King Offa) 46
Eadburh (King Alfred's mother-in-law) 49
Eadgifu, Queen (wife of King Edward the Elder) 13, 51, 109
Eadwig, King 50, 114
Ealdfrith, King of Northumbria 31–33, 58, 69
Ealhswith, Queen (wife of King Alfred) 50
Eanflæd, Queen (wife of King Oswiu of Northumbria), Abbess of Whitby 13, 45, 59, 89
Eangyth, Abbess 59, 69, 70
Ebba *see* Aebbe
Ecgferth 87
Ecgfrith, King of Northumbria 54–58, 143
Eddius Stephanus 124
　Vita Wilfredi/Life of Wilfrid 54, 55, 58
Edgar, King 47, 50, 65, 71, 72, 76, 113, 143
Edith, Queen (wife of King Edward I) 51–53, 71, 119–121, 143, 144
Edmund 'the Elder', King 61, 75, 98, 109, 118, 125
Edward 'the Confessor', King 51–53, 111, 119, 120, 143, 144
Edward I 'Longshanks', King 240, 267
Edward II, King 199, 257
Edward III, King 267
Edward 'the Elder', King 13, 75
Edwin, King of Northumbria 13, 45, 46, 143
Egbert, King of Kent 57
Ela, Countess of Salisbury 266
Eleanor of Brittany 266
Eleanor of Provence, Queen 266

Elizabeth, St, of Hungary 196, 197
Emma, Queen (Aelfgifu) 13, 51, 53, 77, 119, 120
Encomium Emmae Reginae 77, 112, 119
Eorcenberht, King of Kent 13, 54, 58
Eormenhild, Queen (wife of King Wulfhere of Mercia, Abbess of Ely) 59, 62
Eve 24–26, 165

family
    extended 111, 220
    nuclear type 111, 113, 118, 220, 331
Fell, C. 16, 56, 89, 104
Finke, L.A. 7, 104
FitzAlan, Elizabeth 243, 244, 258
folkland 116
free-bench (*see also* dower) 247, 249, 251, 254
freedom 9, 16, 45, 71, 125–146, 149, 150, 276–328, 329, 331, 332
Frithugyth, Queen 49
funeral 202, 205–212
    mass-pence 206–208
    Office for the Dead 205–208

Gautier le Leu
    La Veuve 183
gild 203–208, 273, 290, 292, 299, 328
Glanvill 226–229, 232–234, 238, 239, 255
Godmanchester 215, 223–224, 246, 256, 267, 268, 303, 311
Godwine, Earl 52, 98, 123
Goldberg, P.J.P. 219, 235, 298, 302
Goscelin of St Bertin
    Liber Confortatorius 190
Gower, John
    Confessio Amantis 158
    Mirour de l'Omme 179, 194
Gratian 160, 163, 164, 166, 167
    Decretum 160, 168
Gregory I, Pope 30, 38–40, 43, 64, 66, 157, 163

Gregory II, Pope 31, 42
Gregory III, Pope 42
Gregory IX, Pope
    Decretals 161, 164–168, 172
guardianship 234, 293, 295–298, 330
Guenever 206
Guibert de Nogent
    De Vita Sua 89
Guthlac, St 64, 65, 113

Hadrian, Abbot 32
Hali Meiðhad 35, 174, 177
Hanawalt, B. 7, 179, 247, 257, 293, 296
Harthacnut, King 51, 119
Havelok the Dane 175
Heloise 189
Henry I, King 51, 279, 281, 282
    Coronation Charter 281
Henry II, King 226, 227, 240, 266, 278, 279, 284
Henry III, King 228, 242, 266
Henry IV, King 258
Hereburh, Abbess of Watton 58
heriot 114, 115, 117, 128, 129, 217–219, 252, 304, 305, 312, 313, 324, 326
Hild(a), St (first Abbess of Whitby) 59, 63, 65, 67, 69
Hilton, Walter
    Epistola ad quendam solitarium 190
Hincmar, Archbishop of Rheims
    Annales Bertiniani/Annals of St Bertin 40, 41
Hollis, S. 32, 55, 56
Hospital 211, 234, 235, 287, 299–301
Householder of Paris, The 285
(1279) Hundred Rolls 305
Hyginus, Pope 164

Ignatius, Bishop of Antioch 191
incest (*see* also affinity, consanguinity) 159, 163
Ine, King of Wessex 31, 47, 68

Ingeld, King of Wessex 31
Ingham, Katherine (Abbess) 267, 287
inheritance 90, 102, 106, 114, 116, 209, 214, 217, 223, 229, 233, 243, 244, 246, 254–257, 296, 297, 311, 316, 322, 323, 331
  bequests 213, 216, 261, 273, 275, 288, 294, 327, 328
  heiress 109, 116, 123, 243, 257, 258, 277, 278, 280–282, 284
  legatee 114, 116–118, 137
Innocent, Pope 164, 172
Ipswich 150, 212, 213, 215, 216, 221, 221, 244–247, 259–261, 267, 279, 290, 293, 295, 297
Isidore of Seville 66, 160
Iurminburh, Queen (wife of King Ecgfrith of Northumbria) 58

Jacob's Well 204
Jacobo di Voragine
  The Golden Legend 196
Jacques de Vitry
  The Life of Mary of Oignies 190, 195, 196
Jehan le Fèvre
  Les lamentations de Matheolus/The Lamentations of Matheolus 183
Jerome, St 4, 21, 22, 24–26, 28, 33, 163, 173, 177, 179, 184
  Adversus Jovianianum/*Against Jovinian* 22–26, 173
John, King 250, 277, 278, 280, 282
John, St Chrysostom 21, 160, 163
  Homilies on First Timothy 22
jointure 217, 236, 251–252, 324, 326
Judith, Countess 142
Judith, Queen (wife of King Aethelwulf of Wessex and King Aethelbald of Wessex) 13, 40–42, 49, 71, 90, 110, 143
Judith 14

Julian of Norwich 289

Kempe, Margery 192, 197, 291
  Book of 193
Keynes, S. 121
King Horn 161
Klapisch-Zuber, C. 7

Lacy, Edmund (Bishop of Exeter)
  Liber Pontificalis 194
La3amon
  Brut 155
La(u)ncelot 206, 208
land
  landholding 103, 108–110, 227, 255–265, 303, 326, 330
  services 303–307
  transfer of 123; 124, 246, 265–270, 315, 330
Lanfranc, Archbishop of Canterbury 142, 156
Lapidge, M. 32, 33, 121
law
  Anglo-Saxon *see* Anglo-Saxon law
  canon law 149, 153–173
  common law (*see also* Bracton; Glanvill; Statutes) 226–244
  customary law 244–255, 290, 295, 303, 311
  lawsuit 131, 132, 220, 234, 240–242, 252, 253, 316, 320, 321, 325
legitim 270–275
Leo, Pope 164, 167
Leofgifu 112, 114, 118, 122, 123, 125–127, 139
Letter Books of the City of London, The 228, 245, 247, 248, 256, 295–298
Leyser, H. 7, 68
Liber Eliensis 57
Life of St Gertrude of Nivelles, The 64
Life of St Salaberge of Laon, The 64

Loengard, Senderowitz, J. 230, 232, 279, 280
Lombard, Peter (Bishop of Paris) 160, 168, 169
Lucy, Countess of Chester 266, 279

Maitland, F.W. 230, 276
Magna Carta 229, 230, 238, 282
Malcolm, King of Scotland 150, 244, 245, 290, 295
Malory, Sir Thomas
   Le Morte d'Arthur 206, 208
Maldon 150, 244, 245, 290, 295
Mannyng of Brunne, Robert 162
   Handling Synne 163
Mary of Oignies 195, 197
marriage 15, 20–44, 153–173, 227–230, 234, 242, 246, 255–259, 263, 271, 277–287, 291, 303, 314
   banns 154, 155
   consent 160–162, 164, 169, 171, 282
   indissolubility of 25, 30–32, 39, 57, 149
marriage-portion (*maritagium*) 255, 256, 281, 303
McCarthy, C. 195
Menuge, N.J. 7, 296
Michel, Dan of Northgate
   Ayenbite of Inwyt 181
monasteries (and all religious houses) 53–73, 235, 265–267, 287, 288, 299, 302, 330, 331
   abbesses 31, 33, 36, 52–54, 57–60, 62–64, 66–72, 266, 267; 287; 331
moralists 149, 173, 174, 179, 180, 182–184, 186–190, 329
morgengifu 105, 107, 124, 138
mortuary 217, 308
mourning 93, 119–121, 146, 181, 193, 201, 202
mund (*see also* protection) 83, 84, 86, 87, 97, 144, 149, 330

Myrour to Lewde Men and Wymmen, A 185, 187, 225

Nennius
   Historia Brittonum 46
Neville, Eleanor 287
Nicholas, Pope 30, 160
Norwich 150, 205, 206, 208, 212, 237, 289–291, 299, 301
Nothelm, Archbishop of Canterbury 44

Oethelwald, Sub-King of Deira 62
Offa, King of Mercia 46
Old English Martyrology 58, 65
Opitz, C. 287, 301
Osburh, Queen (wife of King Aethelwulf of Wessex) 41
Osthryth, Queen (wife of King Aethelred of Mercia) 47
Oswald, Archbishop of York 33, 47
Oswald, King of Northumbria, St 45, 61, 89
Oswine, King of Northumbria 45
Oswiu, King of Northumbria 13, 45
Oswulf, Earl 61

Paris, Matthew 277–278
Pascal II, Pope 163
Paston
   family 236, 237, 242, 285
   Paston Letters 285
Paul, St 19, 20–22, 26–32, 38, 93, 163, 173, 174, 179, 184, 192, 196
Pehthelm, Bishop of Whithorn 44
penance 299
Perrot, M. 7
Plaunche, Elizabeth de la 243, 244, 258
Post Mortem Inquisition 150, 228, 231, 243, 258, 259
poverty 76, 77, 219, 225, 226, 287, 298–302, 329, 331
property 76, 78, 86, 88–94, 103–111, 226–327

355

movables 116, 127, 128, 270–276, 326–328
real property 114, 116, 118, 122–127, 129, 130, 133–138, 216, 273, 293, 307
protection 76, 79, 81–88, 103, 115, 149, 238, 240, 245, 265, 266, 276, 320
Purgatory 189, 202, 203, 210, 223
Purity 234

Rædwald, King of East-Anglia 45, 46
Raftis, J.A. 256, 267
Ramsey 251, 253, 259
   Liber Gersumarum of Ramsey Abbey 249, 302, 304, 309, 314
rape 94, 95, 98, 331
Rawcliffe, C. 301
Razi, Zvi 220, 313
relief 217, 218
remarriage 9, 19–28, 36, 39, 71, 78, 91–93, 124, 149, 150, 163, 176, 199, 219, 242, 243, 246, 247, 255, 277, 279, 281, 282, 285, 294, 298, 313, 315, 317–324, 331
Richard I, King 160, 280
Richard II, King 284
Ridyard, S. 63
Robertson, A.J. 50
Rosenthal, J.T. 197
Rotuli de dominabus et pueris et puellis/ Register of Rich Widows and of Orphaned Heirs & Heiresses 278, 282–284
Rudolf of Fulda, 67–69
   Vita Leobae/Life of Leoba 68

sacrament 149, 153–161, 162, 167–170
Saethryth, Abbess 54
sainthood 26, 28, 59, 62–68
Seaxburh, Queen (wife of King Cenwalh of Wessex) 48

Seaxburh, Queen (wife of King Eorcenberht of Kent, Abbess of Ely) 13, 54, 58, 59, 62
Seinte Margarete 175
sermons 78, 175, 181, 189, 204
sexuality 24, 25, 30, 37, 38, 93, 96, 159, 160, 173, 175, 179, 192
Sir Orfeo 181
Sir Isumbras 165
Stafford, P. 16, 56, 89, 108, 132, 143, 144
Statute of Gloucester 233
Statute of Westminster 234, 239
Sutton, A. 292, 293
Swein, Earl Godwine's son 98

Tacitus
   Germania 103
Tale of Beryn, The 182, 319
Tertullian, 22–24, 26
   Ad uxorem/On the apparel of Women 22
   De exhortatione Castitatis/Exhortation to Chastity 22
   De monogamia/On Monogamy 22
testament (*see also* will) 203, 205, 212, 214–216, 221, 222, 260, 262, 265, 274, 275, 283, 326–328
Tette, Abbess 67, 69
Theodore, Archbishop of Canterbury 31, 32, 39, 40, 57, 58, 67, 92
Thompson, P. 56
Thompson, V. 138
Tondberht, Ealdorman of the South Gyrwas 54, 143
Towneley Plays 276, 277

Urban III, Pope 167, 168, 300

Vercelli Homily X 77
Vices & Virtues 182
virginity (*see* also chastity, three grades of) 19, 24–35, 54–56, 63, 73, 97, 98, 170, 173, 174, 179, 187

Vita Aedwardi Regis/Life of King Edward 111, 120
vowess 191–198, 287, 289, 331

Walsham le Willows 150, 217–219, 222, 225, 250–252, 254, 294, 303–305, 310–312, 314–316, 319, 324, 326, 330
   (1577) Field Book of Walsham le Willows 311, 312
wardship 277–282, 296–298
wedding ceremony 153, 170, 228, 229
   nuptial blessing 153, 154, 162, 167–172
Werburh, St 59
wergeld see Anglo-Saxon law
Whitelock, D. 113, 114
Wife's Lament, The 13, 18, 119
Wilfrid, Bishop of York 54–58, 64, 124

Wilfrid, St 113
will (*see* also testament) 103, 113, 117, 118, 127, 202, 207–216, 220–225, 257, 259–265, 272, 293, 309, 313, 321, 322, 326–328, 330
   executor/executrix 220–225
   probate of 214–216, 264, 313
William I, King 52, 142, 143, 277
Wihtburh, Abbess of East Dereham 54
wives *see* chastity, three grades of
Wulfhere, King of Mercia 47, 59
Wulf and Eadwacer 14, 119
Wulfstan, Bishop of Worcester and Archbishop of York 78, 91, 92, 107, 143, 144
   Institutes of Polity 91
   Sermo Lupi ad Anglos 78, 92

Zacharias, Pope 30, 43